Innovation and Modernisation in Contemporary Russia

This book examines how technological modernisation and innovation policies have been implemented in Russia from the Soviet era to the present day. It discusses how since about 2000 the Russian state has attempted to address the country's excessive dependence on natural resources by implementing an ambitious programme of economic modernisation, including giving innovation more policy prominence, boosting state funding for research and development and innovation, and emphasising science towns and technology parks as key instruments for stimulating innovation. Based on extensive original research, taking a multidisciplinary approach, and including detailed case studies, the book explains why, despite these efforts, Russia is performing comparatively poorly in innovation outcomes. It argues that a key factor is the country's political economy model in which science, technology, and innovation policies are mainly controlled and funded by the federal centre of power and led by domestic political and economic elites.

Imogen Sophie Kristin Wade is an Associate Faculty member at the Science Policy Research Unit at the University of Sussex, Brighton, United Kingdom.

Routledge Contemporary Russia and Eastern Europe Series

99 **Tatarstan's Autonomy within Putin's Russia**
Minority Elites, Ethnic Mobilization and Sovereignty
Deniz Dinç

100 **The State and Big Business in Russia**
Understanding Kremlin – Business Relations in the Early Putin Era
Tina Jennings

101 **Queering Russian Media and Culture**
Edited by Galina Miazhevich

102 **Shamanism in Siberia**
Sound and Turbulence in Cursing Practices in Tuva
Mally Stelmaszyk

103 **Stalin and Soviet Early Cold War Policy**
Southern Neighbours in the Shadow of Moscow, 1945–1947
Jamil Hasanli

104 **Disinformation, Narratives and Memory Politics in Russia and Belarus**
Edited by Agnieszka Legucka and Robert Kupiecki

105 **The Nagorno-Karabakh Conflict**
Historical and Political Perspectives
Edited by M. Hakan Yavuz and Michael Gunter

106 **Innovation and Modernisation in Contemporary Russia**
Science Towns, Technology Parks and Very Limited Success
Imogen Sophie Kristin Wade

For more information about this series, please visit: www.routledge.com/Routledge-Contemporary-Russia-and-Eastern-Europe-Series/book-series/SE0766

Innovation and Modernisation in Contemporary Russia

Science Towns, Technology Parks and Very Limited Success

Imogen Sophie Kristin Wade

Routledge
Taylor & Francis Group
LONDON AND NEW YORK

First published 2023
by Routledge
4 Park Square, Milton Park, Abingdon, Oxon OX14 4RN

and by Routledge
605 Third Avenue, New York, NY 10158

Routledge is an imprint of the Taylor & Francis Group, an informa business

British Library Cataloguing-in-Publication Data
A catalogue record for this book is available from the British Library

Library of Congress Cataloging-in-Publication Data
A catalog record for this book has been requested

ISBN: 978-1-032-18779-2 (hbk)
ISBN: 978-1-032-18780-8 (pbk)
ISBN: 978-1-003-25620-5 (ebk)

DOI: 10.4324/9781003256205

Typeset in Times New Roman
by Apex CoVantage, LLC

To Amrita and Ira – my youngest readers

Contents

Figures

Tables

Acknowledgements

First and foremost, I am indebted to my PhD supervisors at UCL, Professor Slavo Radošević and Dr Peter Duncan, for their dedicated and extremely patient guidance, support, and expertise as it is on this research project that the present book is based. I would also like to thank my PhD thesis examiners, Dr Richard Connolly and Professor Alena Ledeneva, for their insightful questions and comments that helped to improve my thesis, upon which this book is based.

I am also most grateful to colleagues in Russia and abroad for fruitful discussions and exchanges: Olga V., Irina D., Ksenia G., Yevgeny K., Ksenia T., Peter S., Andrei Z., Zinaida V., Timur A., Galina O., Alexandra K., Victoria D., and Roman K. I am also grateful to all those who agreed to be interviewed by me.

Colleagues and friends at the Institute for Statistical Studies and Economics of Knowledge (ISSEK) in the Higher School of Economics (HSE) in Moscow provided me with an academic base during trips to Moscow. The editing and research work I did for HSE between 2014 and 2016 helped pay for my fieldwork trips and opened up new questions and avenues for research. My thanks to Professors Leonid Gokhberg, Alexander Sokolov, Dirk Meissner, and Carol Leonard for welcoming me to HSE. I am grateful to Olga for her invaluable help in negotiating the demands of Russian bureaucracy, and to Konstantin, Mikhail, Vitaly, Elena, and Valya for sharing many cups of tea, cakes, and lunches with me.

I must also thank my fellow research students and colleagues at UCL School of Slavonic and East European Studies (SSEES) who kept me motivated and supported me in countless ways while doing my PhD: Philip, Kaneshko, Costanza, Anna B., Anna R., Vesna, Esther, Filipa, Randolph, Michal, Michael, Eva, Paulina, and Anna-Cara. I am also grateful for the comments and suggestions on my research from attendees of SSEES seminars and other members of the SSEES community.

For financial support that enabled me to undertake fieldwork and present my work at conferences and workshops, I am grateful to the Centre for East European Language-Based Area Studies in the United Kingdom (CEELBAS), the Russian Presidential Academy of National Economy and Public Administration (for enabling me to participate in their historical project on Obninsk from 2012 to 2014), UACES, the Ronald Coase Institute, the UCL Graduate School, and UCL SSEES.

And finally, I could not have completed my PhD thesis and this book without the continuing support from my parents and husband.

I alone am responsible for any errors and omissions that may remain in this book.

Definitions and abbreviations

AIRKO	Agency of Innovation Development-Centre of Cluster Development of Kaluga oblast (region)
ABM	agent-based model
AIRKO	Agency of Innovation Development-Centre of Cluster Development of Kaluga regions
ANVAR	French state agency for innovation
BERD	Expenditures by business enterprises on research & development
BERR	UK Government Department for Business Enterprise and Regulatory Reform
BES	business enterprise sector
BESSY	Berlin Electron Storage Ring Society for Synchrotron Radiation), abbreviated BESSY, a research establishment in the Adlershof district of Berlin, Germany
BIC	Boreskov Institute of Catalysis, Akademgorodok, Novosibirsk
BISA	British International Studies Association
BRICS	Brazil, Russia, India, China, and South Africa
CEE	Central and Eastern Europe
CERN	European Organization for Nuclear Research
CIS	Commonwealth of Independent States
EBRD	European Bank for Reconstruction and Development
ECEI	European Cluster Excellence Initiative
EEG	evolutionary economic geography
ESRF	European Synchrotron Radiation Facility (ESRF)
FANO	Federal Agency of Scientific Organisations
FASO	Federal Agency for Scientific Organizations (existed from 2013 until 2018 when it was abolished by President Putin)
FASIE	Fund for Assistance to Small Innovative Enterprises
FDI	foreign direct investment
GDP	gross domestic product
GERD	gross expenditures on research & development
GMP	good manufacturing practice
GNP	gross national product
GOV	Government

IAE	Institute of Automatics and Electrometry
IASP	International Association of Science Parks and Areas of Innovation
IPPE	Institute for Physics and Power Engineering
ILTP	Integrated Long-Term Programme of Cooperation
INTAS	International Association for Cooperation with Scientists from the former Soviet Union
IP	intellectual property
IPRs	intellectual property rights
IT	information technology
ITC	innovation technology centre
MBA	Master of Business Administration
MEPhI	MEPhI National Research Nuclear University (Moscow Engineering Physics Institute National Research Nuclear University)
MIT	Massachusetts Institute of Technology
MNCs	multinational companies
NATO	North Atlantic Treaty Organization
NSI	National system of innovation
NSU	Novosibirsk State University
NTBFs	new technology-based firms
NWO	The Dutch Research Council (NWO Dutch: Nederlandse Organisatie voor Wetenschappelijk Onderzoek)
OCST	Obninsk Centre of Science and Technology
OECD	Organisation for Economic Co-operation and Development
PPP	purchasing power parity
QPQ	quid pro quo
OUS	Open University Skolkovo
R&D	research and development
RAS	Russian Academy of Sciences
RDI	Research, development and innovation
RFBR	Russian Foundation for Basic Research
RFH	Russian Foundation for the Humanities
RFTD	Russian Fund for Technological Development
RPA	Research Production Association
RTTN	Russian Technology Transfer Network
SABIT	The Special American Business Internship Training (SABIT) programme, which builds partnerships and provides technical assistance by training Eurasian business leaders in USA business practices
SBIR	Small Business Innovation Research
SB RAS	Siberian Branch of the Russian Academy of Sciences
SD SAS	Siberian Division of the USSR Academy of Sciences
SEZs	Special Economic Zones
SMEs	small- and medium-sized enterprises
S&T	science & technology
STI	science, technology, and innovation

STPs	Science or Technology Park
TACIS	Technical Assistance to the Commonwealth of Independent States programme
TTOs	Technology Transfer Offices
UKSPA	United Kingdom Science Park Association
USIA	US Information Agency
USSR	Union of Soviet Socialist Republics
VIF	Venture Innovation Fund
WC	Washington Consensus
ZATO	Closed administrative-territorial entities ["zakrytye administrativno-territorialnye obrazovanye"]

1 Introduction

Political economy of technological modernisation in the Russian Federation

Overview of the book's argument and contributions

On 2 July 2021, Putin approved Russia's updated National Security Strategy that was first written in 2015. This strategic, overarching policy document acknowledges that Russia has some serious internal weaknesses threatening its national security, as well as the usual external enemies. The internal weaknesses include weak economic performance, heavy dependence on oil and gas, adverse demography and lagging technologies. As Dmitri Trenin (director of the Carnegie Moscow Center) commented to the FT: *The Russian leadership has every reason now to turn inward to address the glaring weaknesses, imbalances and inequalities of the country's internal situation* (Stephens, FT, July 2021). The national security strategy also outlines plans to promote state-controlled science and technology to make Russia a world leader, including in the spheres of scientific international cooperation, cooperation between civilian science and military-industrial complex, and in innovation in business and research. In fact, the Russian government has been investing heavily in technological development – both military and civilian – for decades. What has happened to these investments? This book attempts to answer this question.

It is about the political economy of technological modernisation in Russia. More specifically, it looks at how Russia – a country with a very state-dominant market economy and authoritarian political system – has been trying to ignite technological innovation since the end of the Second World War. The focus of the book, however, is on Russia's technological modernisation programme that began in the first decade of the 21st century with the aim of diversifying the economy to provide for long-term growth based not solely on natural resources. The first decade of the 21st century marks a qualitatively different approach to policy making in Russia, one that strongly emphasises technological innovation as a source of economic diversification and growth. Innovation support is considered a part of a broader programme of economic modernisation. In this book, the focus, therefore, is particularly on state support for innovation infrastructure (publicly funded organisations devoted to creating and diffusing innovations in Russian industry, science and technology parks, science towns, clusters, special economic zones, etc.)

DOI: 10.4324/9781003256205-1

Innovation matters because it helps firms be more productive, which cumulatively can raise a country's productivity and living standards. Innovation-based growth is a more sustainable path to growth than relying on natural resources (e.g. oil and gas) or volatile commodities such as iron ore and coal (Webster, 2015). Science towns and science and technology parks are two kinds of location-based innovation policies that have been popular across the world since the mid-20th century. Their appeal is rooted in the expectations that they can lead to localised knowledge spillovers and are relatively easy to create and manage. These two approaches are also popular because they are perceived as channels to invest substantial amounts of capital in R&D projects which, in turn, will strengthen national competitiveness (Park, 1999; Zheng et al., 2015; Kocak and Can, 2013; La Rovere and Melo, 2012; Link and Scott, 2003). Governments in many countries, moreover, are motivated to replicate the handful of cases, such as Silicon Valley and Research Triangle in the United States, which have resulted in innovation outcomes.

Almost all transition countries in Eastern and Central Europe, the Baltic states, and Russia have experimented with a wide range of approaches to accelerate innovation-based growth. Many of these approaches constitute location-based innovation policies, such as science and technology parks, science towns, and innovation clusters. Russia has enthusiastically experimented with policies such as this partly because of the legacies from the Soviet Union which pioneered special enclaves for research and development (R&D) (Cooper, 2012), some of which were called *akademgorodki* (academy villages) and *naukograday* (science towns).

The book seeks to answer two principal research questions:

(1) How has the authoritarian state of Russia addressed technology-based growth (as distinct from growth based on increasing inputs – labour, capital, etc.)?
(2) How does Russia's political economy model explain the problems it has faced in pursuing technology-based growth (substantial R&D investment yet comparative poor performance in innovation outcomes)?

The key findings of this book are that Russia has experimented with a wide range of approaches to accelerate innovation-based growth, and the institutional context strongly shapes how these approaches have fared. The empirical analysis (Chapters 4–6) looks specifically at how Russia has fared in implementing science towns and technology parks. The empirical evidence is interpreted by drawing on a model of economic growth that sees the process as occurring in three stages, starting from the micro or most local level where the role of first movers (firms or organisations such as a science or technology park) is critical. The second stage takes places at the meso level and is when critical mass of firms and state agencies is built up, and collective action institutions such as firm associations, public agencies, or design bureaus are formed to assist with inter-organisational cooperation. The third stage is when firms and other organisations form global linkages and become globally competitive.[1]

The focus of this book is limited to the issues involved in accelerating technological modernisation.[2] Initiating sources of growth (growth poles) that are not based on natural resources is a policy challenge that Russia has set for itself since the early 2000s and requires government intervention. Some have argued that this policy challenge to diversify away from oil and gas is hard, even economically unfeasible, because it stands in contrast to Russia's natural resource advantage (Gaddy and Ickes, 2013: 98). Innovation and technology are public goods, hence the need for government intervention. Yet, there is a high likelihood of government failure because of the difficulties in designing and implementing innovation policies effectively (Goldberg et al., 2011). Hence, the focus of this book – how Russia is trying to initiate growth poles based on new technology and innovation – is on one country's state intervention in technological innovation. The Russian state has chosen to invest in innovation infrastructure that creates "enclaves" or growth poles because such an approach was advocated by the linear model in innovation policy research, which predominated until the 1980s when scholars introduced the interactive or systemic model of innovation to better reflect how innovation processes actually happen. The policy recommendations based on the linear model may be more compatible with the governing principles in an authoritarian regime because state officials can more easily control growth using linear innovation model logic. This book sees these policy initiatives as part of the evolutionary path of science, technology, and innovation (STI) policy in the Soviet Union and Russia.

Science towns are physical clusters of scientific institutes, educational establishments, and firms in a concentrated area that were first set up across the Soviet Union in the 1950s. Science and technology parks are a widespread institution adopted by Russia from foreign countries from the year 1990. Aiming to stimulate economic diversification, science and technology parks provide – in a concentrated territorial space – office and/or lab space, access to shared equipment, and facilities for start-ups, older firms, and research organisations.

To examine science towns and science and technology parks, the present book analyses a variety of sources, including secondary (academic literature) and primary sources (gained from semi-structured interviews, site visits, an original questionnaire-based survey, and public documents in Russian and English).

Some of Russia's Soviet-era science towns, two of which are analysed here, successfully reinvented themselves to survive the crisis period of the 1980s and 1990s and show some encouraging signs of building critical mass by forming linkages with their surrounding regional and national economy. They also have some international linkages but the extent of these global relationships remains quite marginal.

Science and technology parks (STPs) were first introduced in Russia in 1990 and, like the Soviet-era science towns mentioned previously, were also new entities funded by the state; federal resources for the parks were earmarked largely for infrastructure building. At the same time, managers of Russian parks emphasise that their roles include supporting resident firms to network and access business services (such as finance and accounting). This book finds evidence from a survey of park managers that some STPs are starting to build critical mass locally and regionally through cooperation with other firms outside the STP. Russian STPs have some global linkages through joining an international network of STPs from 2014, which is a professional body for STP managers and resident firms. However, with few exceptions, Russian STPs have not yet made global linkages through co-production or exporting. Most of the STP resident firms that responded to the author's survey and had products ready for sale were only active on the domestic market. However, national level factors (e.g. customs regimes) are serious obstacles to the further development of access to foreign markets by STP firms. This indicates that Russia is a country behind the global technology frontier. Therefore, we do not expect young firms in such an economy to be exporting internationally.

Skolkovo is the focus of the third empirical chapter of this book (Chapter 6) and is described here as a kind of hybrid between a science town and a science and technology park. Started as a purely "governmental project" (Dezhina, 2011: 97) in 2010, it shows that the Government of Russia favours creating a " 'technological heaven' in a closed territory" (ibid.: 97), while simultaneously wanting it to be globally connected from the outset. This emphasis on global linkages makes Skolkovo a new kind of innovation city for Russia, yet at the same time, path dependency and the institutional context influence how it is developing.

The scope of this book does not extend to all aspects of technological modernisation in Russia. Existing firms' innovation performance and the observed gap between high levels of invention and low levels of innovation, defined as commercialisation, have been well-analysed by the existing literature on economics of innovation (e.g. Gokhberg and Kuznetsova, 2015; Gokhberg, 2015; OECD, 2007; Graham, 2013).

Contributions of the book

A key theoretical contribution of the book is in demonstrating how authoritarian regimes implement science and technology parks and science towns as instruments of modernisation and innovation policy. An authoritarian regime chooses these models as key modes of support (see Chapter 1 for an overview of other instruments implemented in Russia) because they are relatively easy to control on the one hand, and because, on the other hand, they are a popular policy option globally and so seen as a "desirable" tool for catching up with nations that are at the technology frontier.

The book draws on and adds to three strands of literature. First, it **engages with and complements the social science literature on modernisation and the state**. What is meant by modernisation? Is it more realistic to talk about a plurality of modernities and modernisation paths? The literature on modernisation policy in non-Western contexts supports the idea of multiple paths of modernisation and outcomes (democracy, authoritarian regime, etc.). Russia has pursued technological modernisation by borrowing and reproducing certain institutional forms and mechanisms from a Western context and by creating new structures and processes that display strong Soviet legacies because of path dependency and the slow nature of institutional and regime transformation. The case studies of two Russian science towns and Russian science and technology parks analysed in the present book (Chapters 4 and 5) offer novel empirical evidence that sheds light on how an authoritarian country has experimented with diverse policies to accelerate technological modernisation.

Russia's economic modernisation of the early 21st century is also predominantly top-down in terms of control and funding, although local initiatives do exist (e.g. the naukogrady – one kind of science town – pursued a strategy of "survival through development" in the 1990s whereby local scientists and political elites acted collectively to ensure their towns muddled through the crisis years rather than waiting for handouts from Moscow; see Rabkin, 1997 and Chapter 4). Thus, the book contributes to a political economy model of modernisation that considers foreign and domestic aspects of modernisation, as well as the issue of who controls modernisation policies (state, non-state, or other).

Second, the book contributes to **the literature on the political economy of innovation systems and science and technology parks, science towns, and clusters**. This is connected to, and furthers, the growing literature on developmental states, innovation, firm and industry upgrading, and institutional transformation. This book expands the literature on industrial policy and innovation in East Asian countries, many of which have had authoritarian regimes leading successful industrial policies (e.g. South Korea under General Park Chung-hee's repressive authoritarian rule from 1963 to 1979 pursued a policy of export-oriented industrialisation which boosted the country's economy). The present research also offers empirical evidence from an authoritarian country that helps us understand how firms and organisations can transform from being in an isolated enclave to being globally connected, pointing out the obstacles faced along the way which are related to the institutional context. Russia's science towns and science and technology parks have not yet managed to form many global linkages.

Third, the book engages with and contributes to **the literature on governing science and technology in authoritarian regimes**. It explores the tensions between authoritarian control and the networked character of a competitive, innovative economy. The wider significance of the book is that it examines how authoritarian states with weak institutions – as exemplified by the case of Russia – govern STI as tools of modernisation policy.

Structure of the book

The overall structure of the book is as follows. The remainder of this chapter sets out the context and relevance for the book. Chapter 2 presents the conceptual framework that helps understand how processes of growth are accelerated. Chapter 3 shows the structure and performance of science and technology and innovation systems in the USSR and the Russian Federation. It outlines the main actors funding and performing R&D and innovation and the main trends in terms of performance in publications, patenting, and production. It also sets out the inputs to and outputs of R&D and innovation in Russia in a comparative perspective.

The empirical contribution of this book is presented in Chapters 4–6, which analyse case studies of three different strategies pursued by the Russian state to try to accelerate technological modernisation in the 1990s and first two decades of the 21st century. Chapter 4 analyses two cases of science towns in Russia (Obninsk and Akademgorodok in Novosibirsk), interpreting the findings with the help of a three-stage growth model. It asks to what extent these two science towns have been able to move beyond an enclave (Stage 1), build up critical mass (Stage 2), and forge global networks and become globally competitive (Stage 3). Chapter 5 looks at the performance of science and technology parks in post-Soviet Russia. Chapter 6 analyses Skolkovo, the latest unit of innovation infrastructure created by the Russian state as a hybrid form between a science town and a science and technology park that is by design simultaneously a closed territory and globally connected. Finally, Chapter 7 draws conclusions and suggests avenues for future research.

Relevance of the book

The book is relevant to the current international positioning of Russia in terms of economic growth. Russia has a middle-income economy and is one of a group of "emerging economies" labelled as the BRICS group (Brazil, Russia, India, China, and South Africa). In less than three decades since it emerged from the collapse of the Soviet Union, Russia has transitioned to a market economy and by 2012 achieved parity with countries in the Organisation for Economic Co-operation and Development (OECD) on several macroeconomic and social indicators (examples of macroeconomic indicators include Russia's better fiscal sustainability after 1998 and improvement of its sovereign rating to attain investment grade in 2003, see OECD, 2009: 58). Russia also deepened its participation in global chains of production (Gokhberg and Roud, 2012), although it remains relatively unconnected compared to other countries. In 2019, Russia had the highest gross domestic product (GDP) per capita compared to the other BRICS countries in purchasing power parity, current international dollars (Figure 1.1).

However, in terms of economic growth since 1989, Russia's performance has been relatively weak by most measures of economic growth. From 1998 to the global financial crisis in 2008, Russia experienced relatively rapid and stable economic growth largely driven by high global oil prices and also by the effects of the institutional reforms of the 1990s. Russia's GDP grew by an average of 6.9% per year in this decade and GDP per capita (measured in US nominal dollars) increased nearly ninefold (World Bank, 2013). Russia has had stagnant growth since the global financial crisis of 2008 and aspires for more growth. The pace of GDP decline has nonetheless slowed since 2016 (World Bank, 2016), a sign that the country has emerged from the crisis years.

Russia also fares poorly in terms of productivity. Labour productivity was less than half the average of OECD countries in 2011 (World Bank, 2013). In 2013, unemployment was very low (below 7%), and average hours worked per person was very high, meaning the country had almost run out of its existing excess labour capacity.

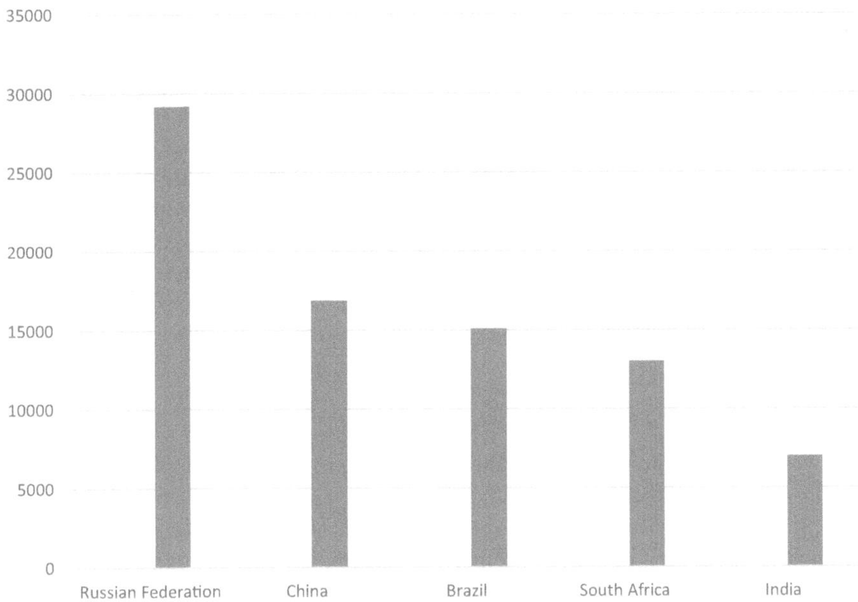

Figure 1.1 GDP per capita, PPP (current international $) for BRICS countries

Source: World Bank, International Comparison Program database, 2019 [last accessed 21 July 2021]. Available at: DataBank, World Development Indicators. https://databank.worldbank.org [last accessed 28 July 2021].

Russia's dependence on natural resources

Russia continues to depend on natural resources, particularly oil and gas (Gaddy and Ickes, 2002: 7; Yakovlev, 2014; Kordonsky, 2016). In 2015, there was limited growth and investment activities in non-oil exports, which points to the continued dominance of natural resources in the country's economy (World Bank, 2016). Over 80% of Russia's total exports came from raw materials in 2011, while just 13% of exports were accounted for by machinery and equipment (Gokhberg and Roud, 2012). However, the COVID-19 global pandemic that started in early 2020 had a big negative impact on demand for oil and gas which badly affected Russia: its oil and gas revenues fell by one-third in 2020 year-on-year; and its exports of non-energy products increased by 11.9% year-on-year primarily composed of gold, metals, and agricultural goods. There are early signs though that demand for oil and gas will pick up again as countries ease COVID-19-related lockdowns and other restrictions in 2021, with the increase of Russia's oil prices in the first quarter of 2021 (World Bank, 2021: 14–23). This growth model (often labelled as development within the "carbon-hydrogen paradigm") is reliant on the export of raw materials and is therefore unsustainable (Gokhberg and Roud, 2012). An alternative, more sustainable growth model is one based on internal sources of growth: productivity gains through innovation and more efficient use of resources.

Since the turn of the 21st century, the government of Russia has attempted to address the country's excessive dependence on natural resources by implementing an ambitious programme of economic modernisation. This includes giving innovation more prominence on the federal policy agenda and boosting state funding for R&D and innovation. As evidence, we note that Russia's share of government spending on R&D (GERD) as a share of GDP slowly rose since 2000 and peaked in 2015–2017 at 1.1% (Figure 1.2). This spending increase in Russia is manifested in the appearance in this period of a plethora of innovation-related strategy documents, the creation of R&D funding institutions, and the provision of state support for various innovation-boosting infrastructure.

Russia's relatively poor innovation outcomes

However, despite investing substantial resources in science and technology since 2000 in a variety of forms and with an impressive legacy of scientific R&D from the Soviet period, Russia is still faring comparatively poorly in innovation outcomes. Innovation is commonly defined as "the implementation of a new or significantly improved product (good or service), or process, a new marketing method,

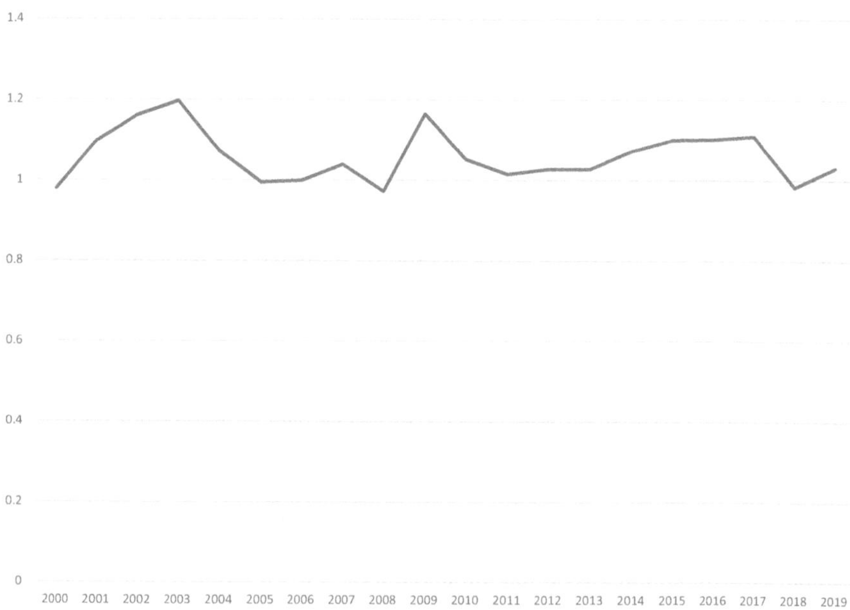

Figure 1.2 Russian Federation: Gross domestic spending on R&D, total, percentage of GDP, 2000–2019

Source: Main Science and Technology Indicators, OECD (2021), Gross domestic spending on R&D (indicator). Available at: https://doi.org/10.1787/d8b068b4-en [last accessed 2 August 2021].

or a new organisational method in business practices, workplace organisation or external relations" (OECD, 2005, paragraph 146: 46). The percentage of innovative enterprises of all industrial enterprises in Russia has not surpassed 11% since 2000, and the share of innovation products of total sales between 1995 and 2009 has remained constant at around 5%–6% (Gokhberg and Roud, 2012). In 2016, just 8% of Russian companies reported engaging in technological, organisational, and marketing innovation (compared to 49% in the EU 28 countries) (European Parliament Research Service, 2018: 13).

Another common indicator for innovation is patents. For patenting, Russia is also faring comparatively poorly, particularly in relation to China. China is ahead of Russia in activity both behind and at the technological frontier and has now reached the level of technological frontier activity in high-income countries. Russia, on the other hand, performs better relatively speaking in international patenting activity as compared to the other BRICS countries of Brazil, India, and South Africa. Russia surpassed these three countries in terms of activities at and behind the technology frontier for the period 1980–2010 (Dominguez Lacasa et al., 2018).

Why is Russia performing comparatively poorly in innovation outcomes (such as patenting) in relation to China? Why has China managed to catch up with high-income countries in terms of technological frontier activity but not with Russia, despite the latter having invested substantial resources into science and technology in the last decade? Following Taylor's (2016) emphasis on the political economy of STI policies, this book suggests that a country's political economy model is an important driver of innovation performance. It takes a multidisciplinary approach to examine why Russia is not doing as well in economic catch up and innovation as, for example, China. Failures in the design of a system of innovation at national, regional, and local levels may help us understand this.

The actors funding science and innovation are also of importance: China has seen a very significant increase in gross spending on R&D since 1994, largely due to a 25-fold rise in business expenditures (BERD) (Balzer and Askonas, 2014: 3), whereas Russia's R&D spending is predominantly from the state.[3] Moreover, China's model of industrial development has been based on a combination of domestic and foreign led modernisation since the 1980s.

China's model for industrial development specifies patterns of interactions with foreign actors. China's authoritarian state welcomes foreign firms and technological borrowing from abroad while retaining control of its domestic economy. Multinational companies (MNCs) are welcome to enter the Chinese market, but the Chinese state has found a way to maintain control over the economy and modernisation processes through following quid pro quo (QPQ) policies. Such policies had been implemented by several developing countries, including China, by the 1970s. Many countries stopped these policies in the 1990s when they started to liberalise their economies. QPQs essentially mandate that MNCs must transfer some of their technology capital (products, know-how, etc.) to the host country in exchange for market access. By analysing micro-evidence from Chinese patents, Holmes et al. (2015) found that quid pro quo policies have had a significant impact on innovation in China. For example, when taking QPQ transfers into account, they found that China owned 50% more technology capital in the country by 2010 than it otherwise would (Holmes et al., 2015).

Russia, in contrast, has been less willing to welcome international influences and investment in its modernisation programmes since 1991, including in modernising the country's science & technology (S&T) system. Another key factor that can help us understand this puzzling situation is the dominance of natural resources in Russia's economy which creates economic rents that discourage innovation (Gaddy and Ickes, 2002, 2005). As will be discussed in Chapter 2 (section "Rents"), the concept of *sistema* (Ledeneva, 2013) helps us understand the nature of Putin's regime that has ruled Russia since 2000, particularly how rents from natural resources are captured by a select few actors in state bodies and agencies.

Technological modernisation and the need for a broad political economy perspective

Russia's technological modernisation programme analysed in this book is happening in a country which, in recent history, has been widely characterised as having an authoritarian regime. Some periods of the Soviet Union's existence have been described as authoritarian with a high degree of centralised power (Graham, 2013). Russia's political regime since 2000 has been labelled by many scholars as centralised and centred on the President, as well as (competitive or electoral) authoritarian (Gel'man, 2012; Schedler, 2006; Graham, 2013). Some other scholars argue that democratic institutions in post-Soviet Russia are undermined by the persistence of informal power networks that underpinned the state in the Soviet Union, so prefer to label Russia post-2000 as a "network state" that is ambiguous and a barrier to modernisation (Kononenko and Moshes, 2011). Part of this notion of informal power networks is the important concept of *sistema* which helps us understand the dynamics of power and influence at a federal level in Russia and thus also helps us understand state support for innovation in Russia. Technological modernisation can also be understood by a neo-Schumpeterian approach to innovation, one stressing the co-evolution of growth and institutions and sees growth as an inherently social and local process where R&D is shaped by institutional context.

Notes

1 Chapter 2 elaborates further on this model.
2 This book has a similar scope to *Igniting Innovation: Rethinking the Role of Government in Emerging Europe and Central Asia* (Goldberg et al., 2011) published by The World Bank. However, this book draws on more theoretical perspectives than the World Bank Report, which is largely policy-oriented in nature.
3 See Chapter 3 on the main trends in Russian R&D and innovation funding and outputs.

References

Balzer, H. and Askonas, J. (2014) *Innovation in Russia and China Compared*, Aris, S., Neumann, M., Orttung, R., Perović, J., Pleines, H., Schröder, H. H. and Snetkov, A.

(eds.) (pp. 2–10). Russian Analytical Digest No. 155, 23 September. Available at: https://css.ethz.ch/content/dam/ethz/special-interest/gess/cis/center-for-securities-studies/pdfs/Russian_Analytical_Digest_155.pdf.

Cooper, J. (2012) 'Science-Technology Policy and Innovation in the USSR', Presentation at workshop Russia's Skolkovo in Comparative and Historical Perspective, UCL SSEES, London, 13 June.

Dezhina, I. (2011) 'Policy Framework to Stimulate Technological Innovations in Russia', *Journal of East-West Business* 17/2–3 (pp. 90–100). Available at: https://doi.org/10.1080/10669868.2011.634770 [last accessed 31 July 2021].

Dominguez Lacasa, I., Jindra, B., Radošević, S. and Shubbak, M. (2018) 'Paths of Technology Upgrading in the BRICS Economies', *Research Policy* 48/1 (pp. 262–280). Available at: https://doi.org/10.1016/j.respol.2018.08.016 [last accessed 31 July 2021].

European Parliament Research Service (2018) *Seven Economic Challenges for Russia: Breaking Out of Stagnation? In-Depth Analysis* (pp. 1–32), July. Available at: www.europarl.europa.eu/RegData/etudes/IDAN/2018/625138/EPRS_IDA(2018)625138_EN.pdf [last accessed 30 November 2019].

Gaddy, C. G. and Ickes, B. W. (2002) *Russia's Virtual Economy*. Washington, DC: Brookings Institution.

Gaddy, C. G. and Ickes, B. W. (2005) 'Resource Rents and the Russian Economy', *Eurasian Geography and Economics*, 46/8 (pp. 559–583). Available at: https://doi.org/10.2747/1538-7216.46.8.559 [last accessed 31 October 2019].

Gaddy, C. G. and Ickes, B. W. (2013) *Bear Traps on Russia's Road to Modernization*. Abingdon, Oxon and New York: Routledge.

Gel'man, V. (2012) 'Subversive Institutions, Informal Governance, and Contemporary Russian Politics', *Communist and Post-Communist Studies* 45 (pp. 295–303).

Gokhberg, L. (ed.) (2015) *Russian Regional Innovation Development Ranking. Issue 3*. Moscow: National Research University Higher School of Economics (HSE).

Gokhberg, L. and Kuznetsova, T. (2015) *Russian Federation*. UNESCO Science Report: Towards 2030. Available at: https://en.unesco.org/unesco_science_report [last accessed 11 January 2019].

Gokhberg, L. and Roud, V. (2012) 'The Russian Federation: A New Innovation Policy for Sustainable Growth', *The Global Innovation Index* (pp. 121–130).

Goldberg, I., Goddard, J. G., Kuriakose, S. and Racine, J. L. (2011) *Igniting Innovation: Rethinking the Role of Government in Emerging Europe and Central Asia*. Washington, DC: World Bank.

Graham, L. (2013) *Lonely Ideas: Can Russia Compete?* Cambridge, MA: The MIT Press.

Holmes, T. J., McGrattan, E. R. and Prescott, E. C. (2015) 'Quid Pro Quo: Technology Capital Transfers for Market Access in China', *Review of Economic Studies* 82 (pp. 1154–1193). Available at: https://doi.org/10.1093/restud/rdv008 [last accessed 31 July 2021].

Kocak, O. and Can, O. (2013) 'Determinants of Inter-Firm Networks Among Tenants of Science Technology Parks', *Industrial and Corporate Change* 23/2 (pp. 467–492). Available at: https://doi.org/10.1093/icc/dtt015 [last accessed 31 July 2021].

Kononenko, V. and Moshes, A. (eds.) (2011) *Russia as a Network State: What Works in Russia When State Institutions Do Not?* Basingstoke: Palgrave Macmillan.

Kordonsky, S. G. (2016) *Socio-Economic Foundations of the Russian Post-Soviet Regime: The Resource-Based Economy and Estate-Based Social Structure of Contemporary Russia*. Stuttgart: Ibidem-Verlag. Summary. Available at: https://publications.hse.ru/books/179279268 [last accessed 31 October 2019].

La Rovere, R. L. and Melo, L. J. (2012) 'Science Parks and Their Role in the Innovation Process: A Literature Review for the Analysis of Science Parks as Catalysts of Organizational Networks', in Farley, S. N., Walker, D. and Harris, R. (eds.) *Technological, Managerial and Organizational Core Competencies: Dynamic Innovation and Sustainable Development*. Hershey, PA: Business Science Reference (An Imprint of IGI Global) (pp. 230–143).

Ledeneva, A. (2013) *Can Russia Modernise? Sistema, Power Networks and Informal Governance*. Cambridge: Cambridge University Press.

Link, A. N. and Scott, J. T. (2003) 'U. S. Science Parks: The Diffusion of an Innovation and Its Effects on the Academic Missions of Universities', *International Journal of Industrial Organization* 21 (pp. 1323–1356).

OECD (2005) 'Organization for Economic Cooperation and Development and Statistical Office of the European Communities (Eurostat)', in *The Measurement of Scientific and Technological Activities: Guidelines for Collecting and Interpreting Innovation Data: Oslo Manual*, 3rd edition. Paris: OECD Publishing. Available at: http://ec.europa.eu/eurostat/ramon/statmanuals/files/9205111E.pdf [last accessed 7 December 2017].

OECD (2007) *Stimulating Innovation in Russia: The Role of Institutions and Policies*, Gianella, C. and Tompson, W. (eds.). Economics Department Working Papers No. 539. Available at: www.oecd.org/eco/working_papers [last accessed 31 December 2018].

OECD (2009) *OECD Economic Surveys: Russian Federation, Chapter 2 'Ensuring Growth-Friendly Fiscal Policy in Both the Short and the Long Term*. Available at: www.oecd-ilibrary.org/economics/oecd-economic-surveys-russian-federation-2009_eco_surveys-rus-2009-en [last accessed 12 December 2019].

Park, S. C. (1999) 'The Comparative Role of High-Tech-Oriented Public Institutions and Private Companies in Tsukuba Science City', *AI & Society* 13 (pp. 301–311).

Rabkin, Y. M. (ed.) (1997) 'Diffusion of New Technologies in the Post-Communist World', Proceedings of the NATO Advanced Research Workshop on Marketing of High-Tech Know How, St Petersburg, Russia, June 1994. NATO Science Partnership Subseries: 4 (Closed), Volume 13, 1st edition, Springer, Dordrecht, Netherlands.

Schedler, A. (ed.) (2006) *Electoral Authoritarianism: The Dynamics of Unfree Competition*. Boulder, CO: Lynne Rienner.

Stephens, P. (2021) 'The Brittle Façade of Vladimir Putin's Russia', *Financial Times (FT)*, 15 July. Available at: www.ft.com/content/52af1d80-f725-453c-84f9-01cdefd3462a [last accessed 27 July 2021].

Taylor, M. Z. (2016) *The Politics of Innovation: Why Some Countries Are Better Than Others at Science and Technology*. Oxford: Oxford University Press.

Webster, B. (2015) 'What Is Innovation Anyway, and Why Should You Care About It?', *The Conversation*, 30 November. Available at: https://theconversation.com/what-is-innovation-anyway-and-why-should-you-care-about-it-50601 [last accessed 1 May 2019].

World Bank (2013) *Developing Skills for Innovative Growth in the Russian Federation (English)*, Vasiliev, K., Lukiyanova, A., Chugunov, D., Maltseva, I., Shulga, I., Rutkowski, J. J., Cahu, P. M., Travkin, P., Roshchin, S. and Nellemann, S. (eds.). Report No. ACS1549. Washington, DC: World Bank, 10 June. Available at: http://documents.worldbank.org/curated/en/460821468107067600/Developing-skills-for-innovative-growth-in-the-Russian-Federation [last accessed 25 July 2016].

World Bank (2016) *Russia Economic Report, the Russian Economy Inches Forward: Will That Suffice to Turn the Tide?*, November. Available at: http://pubdocs.worldbank.org/en/429441478647721427/Russia-RER-36-Eng.pdf.

World Bank Group (2021) *Russia's Economic Recovery Gathers Pace*. Washington, DC: World Bank. Russia Economic Report, No. 45. © World Bank. License: CC BY 3.0

IGO, May. Available at: https://openknowledge.worldbank.org/handle/10986/35653 [last accessed 28 July 2021].

Yakovlev, A. (2014) 'Russian Modernization: Between the Need for New Players and the Fear of Losing Control of Rent Sources', *Journal of Eurasian Studies* 5/1 (pp. 10–20). Available at: https://doi.org/10.1016/j.euras.2013.09.004 [last accessed 31 July 2021].

Zheng, S., Sun, W., Wu, J. and Kahn, M. E. (2015) *The Birth of Edge Cities in China: Measuring the Spillover Effects of Industrial Parks*. NBER Working Paper No. 21378, JEL No. H42, H72, July. Available at: www.nber.org/papers/w21378 [last accessed 29 December 2018].

2 Three-stage model and conceptual background

The issue of technological modernisation is not driven by one discipline because it is a matter of public concern and a problem to be solved by a diverse range of institutions and societal actors. Similarly, technological modernisation is enlightened by several conceptual perspectives. The aim of this chapter is to present the conceptual framework used here to interpret the empirical findings. This framework draws on previous research. First, that about political economy: modernisation theories, the idea of rents or who benefits and who does not from modernisation processes, as well as theories that help us understand the political economy of authoritarian political regimes such as the concept of *sistema* to explain Russia's authoritarian system under Putin. Second, the expansive literature on innovation systems and evolutionary approaches to economic growth.

Conceptual framework of a three-stage model of economic growth: challenges, pitfalls, and outcomes

Theoretical foundations for the conceptual framework used in this book

This chapter introduces the conceptual framework used to interpret the empirical material analysed here. This framework is a highly stylised (i.e. ideal type not found in reality) three-stage model that is rooted in the literature on evolutionary economic geography (EEG), evolutionary theory, and systems of innovation.

EEG emerged as a sub-field within economic geography in the late 1990s, and its key conceptual idea is the notion of how an economy transforms itself from within in a dynamic and irreversible way (Kogle, 2015). EEG posits that change is endogenous, following the Schumpeterian tradition of economics of innovation (for more information on EEG, see e.g. Boschma and Martin, 2010).

Ideas from agent-based (or individual-based) models (ABMs) can also help understand how growth emerges at a local level. ABMs are computational models applied at the micro level to simulate the actions of autonomous, diverse agents (both individuals, organisations, and groups) and how they interact. ABMs are used in a range of subject areas including biology, ecology, and social sciences. ABMs were first developed in the 1940s, although they only become widely

DOI: 10.4324/9781003256205-2

applied in the 1990s with the development of computers (see e.g. Grimm and Railsback, 2005; Niazi and Hussain, 2011; Gustafsson and Sternad, 2010). However, ABMs do not consider the institutional or cultural context.

Institutional change is typically seen as incremental, which results in continuity of a technological path in a country, or radical change, leading to the breakdown of institutional configurations and the creation of new ones. However, a recent stream of literature calls for a reassessment of this binary view of institutional change. For example, Strambach (2008) argues that innovation can occur in non-favourable institutional settings even without radical institutional change. Linked to path dependency, this literature brings the study of institutions into evolutionary economy geography. It assumes that institutions and economic structure can co-evolve. Linked to the notion of "institutionally void contexts" which are especially prevalent in developing countries where institutions are generally weaker, the institutional voids refer to non-performing or under-performing organisations or individuals because of the institutional obstacles (Mrkajic, 2017; Boddewyn and Doh, 2011).

Plasticity as a notion was originally developed by Alchian and Woodward (1988) who argued that economic resources and investments were variable and subject to decisions made by actors. The role of individual, creative agents who can flexibly interpret institutions (the "rules of the game") is important here (Scott, 2011).

Actors use institutions as toolkits in many ways to solve new problems (Strambach, 2008). The local dimension is important because this is where we can see multiple institutional configurations forming (e.g. national institutions interacting with firm and industry-specific institutions). Many institutional configurations help to generate variation, which is important according to the EEG literature in processes of economic self-transformation. Path plasticity exists at the local level in the way actors can flexibly interpret institutions. New combinations of institutional configurations – not necessarily brand-new institutional forms – can arise because of interactions among people located in close geographic proximity (e.g. unplanned meetings, neighbourhood effects). Path plasticity also occurs at a macro level through the "elastic stretch of institutional configurations" (Strambach, 2008).

The idea of institutional hierarchy can help explain how it is possible to have some institutional change (plasticity) and simultaneously, stable institutional arrangements. One or a few institutions are more important than others. For example, a country may have multiple regional innovation systems with region-specific institutions which are absorbed by national-level institutional arrangements. Nevertheless, it is possible that a less important institution (e.g. a regional innovation system) can produce snowball effects on other institutions, leading to gradual evolution in the more important institutions.

The three-stage model

This book takes a co-evolutionary perspective and starts from the premise that economic growth and development are fundamentally **local processes** (Kogle, 2015).

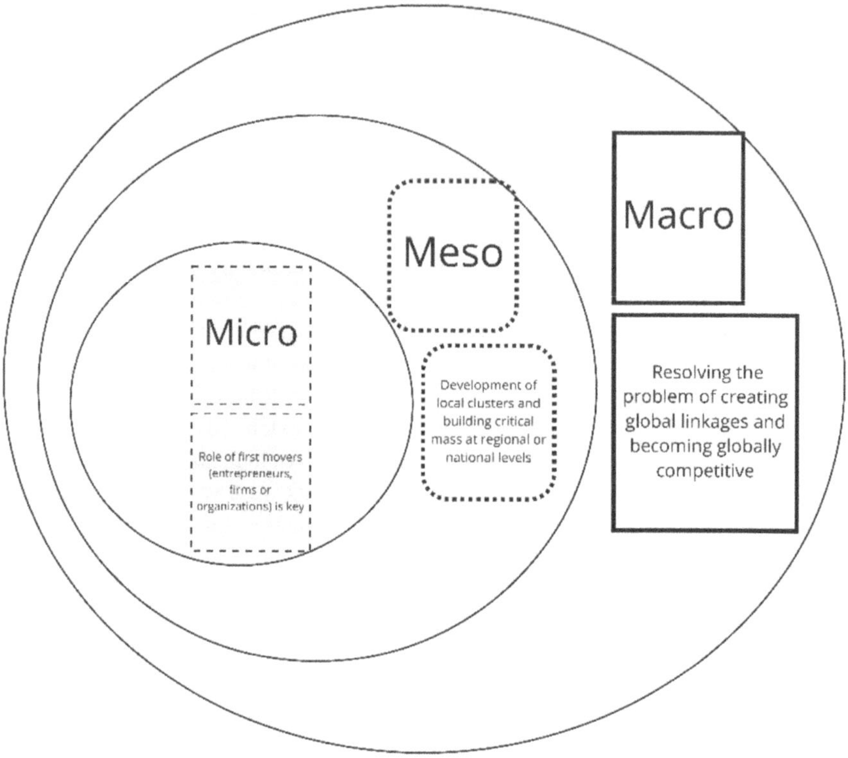

Figure 2.1 The three-stage stylised model of growth

Source: Author

Link to original diagram (editing rights via link): https://miro.com/app/board/o9J_l8jy9f4=/?invite_link_id=720221919781

These processes have several distinct, if overlapping, stages:

As Figure 2.1 shows, the three stylised stages are:

(a) Micro level (can be done by entrepreneurs or firms on their own or with the support of a national government) – key is the role of first movers (entrepreneurs, firms, or organisations);
(b) Meso level – development of local clusters and building critical mass at regional or national levels; and
(c) Macro level – resolving the problem of creating global linkages and becoming globally competitive.

Table 2.1 summarises these stages and outlines the main challenges that need to be addressed at each stage, as well as in the transitions between stages. The key

Table 2.1 Summary of three-stage co-evolutionary growth framework

Key dimension	*Stage 1*	*Stage 2*	*Stage 3*
	Problem of first movers and building an enclave	*Problem of critical mass*	*Problem of building global networks and becoming globally competitive*
Policy focus of the national state	R&D/knowledge generation/production capacity Absorptive capacity	Local networking and local demand	International networking (at or behind technological frontier)
Resources	Significant resources needed to start enclave and encourage people to move there and build infrastructure Physical space needed Firms need resources and capabilities to seek out new domains in a process of entrepreneurial self-discovery.	Ongoing support from state and good quality local management	Economic/fiscal mechanisms to incentivise firms' international orientation/networking Different resources needed for various kinds of global linkages: FDI, learning by exporting/importing, and upgrading in global value chains.
Institutions/ actors	One institution/organisation to lead on creating enclave. Informal grouping (bottom-up, firm led) or state-led initial "push" to create.	Sufficient variety of knowledge and production institutions needed to achieve critical mass.	Institutions should be open to foreigners and have absorptive capacity to take on new knowledge Need highly specialised and inter-related institutions
Obstacles	Firms/organisations need to have enough autonomy and resources to seek out new domains and become first movers. Corruption as a barrier to enclave gaining a positive reputation in society Regulatory or construction delays related to creating enclave in a new place (greenfield) or existing place (brownfield) Presence in a cluster may be an obstacle for firms to appropriate rents from innovation	Need to become economically relevant as a place, not just S&T pocket of excellence To do collective learning and experimenting, firms/state bodies need sufficient autonomy	Fear among state actors of loss of domestic control Sanctions can limit access to foreign knowledge/technology/customers

Source: Author.

dimensions are national policy focus, resources needed, institutions/actors involved, and the possible obstacles change at each stage. It is a complex, iterative process of moving from micro to macro levels. It is possible for a cluster or firm to go backwards from Stage 3 to Stage 2 or 1.

Stage 1

The first stage, at the micro level, is about overcoming the "first mover" problem. The "first mover" is a term that comes from the business studies literature. A classic "first mover" is an entrepreneur. Entrepreneurs often drive development because they do not only find opportunities for growth but also seek ways to overcome or lessen binding constraints or obstacles (Gonchar et al., 2017). A key idea of this discovery process is positive variations in performance (Gonchar et al., 2017).[1] In other words, there are diverse outcomes at a micro level and a positive outcome might be an entrepreneur creating a firm. Some – but by no means all – of these positive variations may reach the meso level by collectively forming regional agglomerations or the macro level by joining global value chains. The key conceptual problem is how some positive variations spread, reproduce, and connect or link up. Arising from that, the critical policy challenge is how to make micro level growth spurts or pockets of excellence (the positive variations in performance) become sustained drivers of growth.

To overcome the first mover problem, an entrepreneur, firm, or organisation needs to develop a proof of concept and a new investment project to test a new domain. For example, Israel's innovation cluster solved this first mover problem in the 1950s–1970s by the public sector giving horizontal grants for business sector R&D. This led to a diverse number of R&D performing companies. As a result, Israel's civilian high-tech industry was born (Teubal and Kuznetsov, 2012).

In this first stage, the focus of policy should be to help create R&D, knowledge, or production capacity. The capacity of firms or other organisations to absorb this new knowledge is also equally important.

First movers (positive variations in performance) may have greater chances to spread, reproduce, and connect or link up if they are geographically close together. An enclave could provide this geographical proximity and so is one possible way policy might trigger this first stage of growth to help first movers spread and link up.

Significant resources are needed to start the enclave and encourage people to move there and build infrastructure. Moreover, sufficient physical space is needed. Firms and other organisations that will reside in the enclave need to have sufficient resources and capabilities to seek out new domains in processes of entrepreneurial self-discovery (Foray, 2017). To ensure consistency, one institution or organisation should take the lead in creating an enclave although of course, other organisations would be involved. Setting up an enclave can happen in diverse ways, either through an informal grouping that is led from the bottom-up by firms or led by a state which gives an initiating push to set up the enclave.

Potential obstacles at the first stage include firms or organisations in the enclave lacking enough autonomy and resources to seek out new domains and become first movers, corruption tarnishing the reputation of the enclave, and regulatory or construction delays. Being in a cluster (enclave) may also hinder firms from appropriating rents from innovation because the interactions between firms co-located in the enclave or cluster help knowledge spillovers, making knowledge a semi-public good (Ferreira et al., 2012).

Moving beyond the enclave for successful technological development and economic growth

The term enclave has been relatively neglected by scholars since the 1970s, although it has seen recent renewed interest by researchers in economic geography and economics (Phelps et al., 2015). Development scholars in the 1960s and 1970s used the term economic enclave to analyse certain industries, especially resource and extractive ones, and the extent of their linkages between companies and economies (e.g. see Weisskoff and Wolff, 1977). Some economic geography scholars recently reassessed the idea of enclaves, drawing on the earlier literature in development and area studies. For example, Phelps et al. (2015) suggest that there are important overlaps between enclaves (e.g. mining company towns and satellite platforms) and industrial agglomerations (e.g. Marshallian pure agglomerations and social networks), with the differences lying in whether they can generate localisation economies, and how specialised and how integrated into the local economy they are. Enclaves and agglomerations are two sides of the same analytical coin.

An economic enclave is a physically, administratively, or legally bound territory whose geography or morphology is intimately related to the following economic characteristics: dependence on one or a few large firms (often a multinational enterprise); high specialisation in one activity; and weak integration into the local economy, which is used primarily to access some local factors of production (Phelps et al., 2015).

The literature on industrial or innovation clusters (clusters of firms) is relevant when looking at enclaves. Both enclaves and clusters are concerned with concentrating science or R&D geographically in a relatively small area (see e.g. Cooke et al., 2011). The difference between the two terms lies in the normative associations often tied to the idea of an enclave.

The word enclave is often used in a normative sense to describe a failing entity that has not managed to link up with its surrounding environment. While policy makers may initially want to create an enclave that is separated from its economic, legal, or political environment, in the long-term, they hope that the enclave will grow and evolve to generate linkages and, hence, economic growth.

Ideas from ecology may help us understand the concept of enclaves, in particular how enclaves evolve over time. An enclave is a bit like moss, a small species of plant that does not have any leaves and generally likes shady or moist places. Mosses form *closely packed* green clumps or carpets, for example covering a wide area of the ground at the base of trees in a wood. Most mosses also use the wind to spread their spores a big distance relative to the size of the moss plant, a key process in their reproduction cycle. It takes just a few years for a moss species to colonise a surface, given the right conditions and exposure to water and wind.

Limiting factors for the growth of moss include: (i) reduced water available (e.g. by introducing sand or gravel on top of the soil as these drain water away from the top soil); (ii) excessive light (e.g. direct sunlight); (iii) increasing the quantity of competitor plants (e.g. grass) that can crowd out moss; (iv) making the soil where the moss is growing more alkaline and hence less acidic by introducing lime; (v) disturbing the bed where the moss is growing by trampling or raking it; and (vi) introducing chemicals (e.g. ferrous sulphate).

Lichens are similar except they typically grow on rocks. Lichen is a composite organism that grows out of fungus and exists in a *symbiotic relationship* with fungus. Lichens colonise a small part of a rock first, and then with the right balance of water, sun, and nutrients and minerals, spreads to other areas of the rock.

These ideas from ecology have parallels with enclaves. First, for moss, lichen, and enclaves, the idea of evolution over time is important. It reminds us to take a long-term view of the creation and spreading process. Second, the *symbiotic relationship* between lichen and fungus is an insight that may be relevant when looking at enclaves. The resources put into a new enclave (e.g. funding from the central government) benefit the local area where the enclave is made, and the enclave benefits from any existing infrastructure (roads, housing, and transport), human resources (talent) in place there, although often enclaves are created from a blank slate, in a territory where previously there was just virgin forest. Third, the ecological ideas about how moss or lichen spreads over a surface help to elucidate the goals of enclaves, which are to support new firms to grow in the protected area and then spread outwards to the wider national and/or international economy, as well as to encourage the creation of new knowledge. Finally, all enclaves – and moss – have rules which govern their activity.

Stage 2

The second stage is about building critical mass by supporting complementarities, synergies, and coordination. The policy focus here is how to promote local networking and local demand for the new technologies or new processes created in Stage 1. Resources required are ongoing support from the state and quality local management. This stage is about how the first mover investment(s) can be transformed into a collective portfolio of diverse projects that deliver public and club goods. Such a collective portfolio needs a sufficient variety of functioning knowledge and production institutions to then form a critical mass in Stage 3.

This book argues that key to success in Stage 2 are the following:

(1) Institutions as well as meaningful cooperation between them.
(2) Mutual trust and communication between different actors (government, firms, and research institutes).
(3) Collective learning and experimenting with policies and in business sector.

(4) Linking or bridging institutions to connect government, firms, and research institutes.

The construction of institutions – firm associations, public agencies, design bureaus, certification, quality, standards, etc. – as well as meaningful cooperation between them affects outcomes in any given industry. Mutual trust and communication are important to reduce the risk of opportunism and increase positive synergies. Collective learning in the policy sphere and business sector involves reflecting on past experiences and thinking of possible ways of working differently. Experimentation in policies and the business sector helps generate the diverse institutions and firms that comprise the positive variations in performance (cf. Stage 1). Linking or bridging institutions can help build public–private and public-to-public coordination and cooperation, which is important for collective action.

One obstacle to reaching Stage 2 is not becoming economically relevant to the local economy. R&D institutes, firms, or clusters of firms (which may be co-located in an enclave) must find a balance between being a pocket of R&D excellence and being locally relevant, that is, meeting local demand from industry and being able to quickly respond to new scientific developments and enter emerging areas. These two outcomes are often contradictory. Central and Eastern European countries, for example, have had success in reforming their R&D systems so they are more open and autonomous but have struggled to make their R&D systems relevant to industry (Radošević and Lepori, 2009).

There are a few empirical examples of countries or a unit of infrastructure that initially functioned as an enclave and managed to resolve the problem of critical mass in Stage 2. In Israel, this stage was passed by the civilian high-tech industry doing lots of collective learning and experimenting with venture capital in the mid-1970s to early 1990s. A critical mass of approximately 300 start-ups was achieved by 1992 in Israel, with a few being of high quality and highly valued, for example they had initial public offerings (Teubal and Kuznetsov, 2012).

The case of Tsukuba science city in Japan illustrates the challenges involved in Stage 2. Tsukuba science city was first planned by the national Japanese state in the 1960s as a large-scale, top-down science and technology project. Like Akademgorodok in Novosibirsk (see Chapter 4) and Skolkovo on the outskirts of Moscow (Chapter 6), Tsukuba was initially created by the state as an enclave on a brownfield site, that is on farmland about 60 km from Tokyo. Tsukuba became operational in the 1980s. Since then, it has had some success in solving the problem of collective action at a regional level. By 1994, for example, Tsukuba hosted a total of 101 research institutes including national, university, public, and private types of institutes (Table 2.2).

Since the state relocated 43 national research institutes to Tsukuba in 1980, almost the same number (41) of private research institutes have co-located in the same place. This is important because in Japan, private industry carried out 70% of all R&D and played a crucial role in forming consortia and joint research associations (Park, 1999). Private research institutes in Tsukuba have increased their

Table 2.2 Research institutes in Tsukuba Science City, 1996

Research institutes, by type	*Number*	*Share (%)*
National	44	43.6
University	5	4.9
Public	11	10.9
Private	41	40.6
Total	**101**	**100**

Source: Park (1999: 305)

activity in joint R&D, patenting (both domestic and international), and technology transfer although the state research institutes performed significantly better in international patenting than private research institutes (68.6% versus 30.8% of all patent enrolments in Tsukuba) in 1994. Private research institutes have also created new jobs, thus contributing to the regional economy. In 1975, they employed 115 people; by 1994, this number increased to 1367 (Park, 1999).

Twenty years on, Tsukuba has further increased the number of research institutes located in its territory, so it now hosts a greater variety of knowledge and production institutions. By 2013, the total number of public and private research institutions and enterprises in Tsukuba was more than 300.[2] Of that total, more than 80 were private (corporate) research institutes, that is double the number in 1994.[3]

However, by the mid-1990s, Tsukuba science city had not generated sufficient local synergies between government, universities, and private industry nor generated sufficient industrial spin-offs from basic and applied research to solve the collective action problem of Stage 2 and move to Stage 3. Critics have cited its inefficient allocation of the large volume of resources it received and its excessive focus on investing in big facilities and hardware. They also felt that the science city was more oriented towards capital city regional development than national development. The city lacked urban amenities such as transport connections with Tokyo and entertainment, meaning that many researchers refused to live in Tsukuba which hindered its development as a vibrant and dynamic city. Indeed, life in Tsukuba has been described as "flat" and separate from urban life which hinders how well the science city can stimulate innovation (Garner, 2006). Since 2006, the city has made concerted efforts to make it a more "liveable" city, including building over 140 parks, organising seasonal cultural performances and festivals, and completing an express train service in 2005 that connects Tsukuba with Tokyo in 45 minutes.

While Tsukuba seems to be stuck in Stage 2 of our growth framework, it has made some efforts to internationalise (Stage 3). The 1985 International Science and Technology Exposition was a large-scale effort by the government of Japan to both raise awareness about the positive aspects of science and technology with the Japanese public and to make Tsukuba science city globally known. The exposition was held in Tsukuba and attracted 20 million domestic and international visitors, including President Mitterrand of France and Prime Minister Margaret Thatcher of the United Kingdom. It succeeded in raising the domestic and international profile of the science city, as evidenced by the sharp rise in land prices and a rush among private companies to build R&D labs in Tsukuba after 1985 (Castells and Hall, 1994; Park, 1999). Private companies with R&D labs in Tsukuba now include Intel Japan (1980–2016), the Japanese robotics company Cyberdyne Inc., and the Japanese software company SoftEther Corporation. In addition, Tsukuba-based corporate (private) research institutes can access as outside users several globally leading and large-scale experimental facilities, including the electron-positron Super Collider TRISTAN's and Photon Factory at KEK, High Magnetic Field and high voltage electron microscopy facility at NIMS.[4]

Nevertheless, this 1985 exposition was a one-off event which limits its effectiveness as a catalyst in the long term. Moreover, Tsukuba science city remains predominantly a place of regional and national importance, with the national research institutes outperforming the private research institutes in international joint research, publications, domestic and international patent enrolments, and technology transfer in 1994. The public and national research institutes in Tsukuba also did not face much competition from industry: in the mid-1980s, the government of Japan prioritised basic research yet systematically cut funding for hiring researchers, hoping that the private industry would hire these qualified staff and absorb scientific information and technology transferred from the public sector. However, the private sector was unwilling to act as a competitor of the public sector by fulfilling these hopes (Park, 1999). If Tsukuba science city did not face much competition from industry within Japan, then the likelihood of global competitiveness and deeply embedded global linkages and international networking is slim.

The government of Japan has been experimenting more in recent years with policies to make Tsukuba globally competitive. For example, in 2011, Tsukuba was designated a "Comprehensive Special Zone for International Competitiveness Development." This represents an important growth strategy in Japan and an opportunity to promote projects that might generate innovation by capitalising on Tsukuba's accumulated science, technology, and human resources. However, it is too early to assess the outcomes of this new policy approach.[5] Furthermore, in 2013, the Tsukuba Global Innovation Promotion Agency was set up to be a bridging institution to facilitate joint R&D and innovative projects of the research institutes, government, and private companies and to make Tsukuba more globally competitive and innovative. However, it is too early to assess the performance of this new agency.[6]

Stage 3

The third stage is concerned with creating global linkages, international networking, and becoming competitive on a global level. In other words, the policy focus here is on the international networking dimension. Economic or fiscal mechanisms should incentivise firms or organisations to develop and foster their international linkages.

Different resources are needed for a wide variety of global linkages that can exist. Such links with foreign partners include privatisation and setting up new firms by foreign investors, foreign direct investment (FDI), learning by exporting to foreign markets and/or importing advanced technologies, materials, equipment, and software, supplier relationships with foreign-owned firms in a host country, and upgrading in global value chains. These kinds of foreign links have been found to be vital sources of learning and innovation for domestic firms in EU10 countries (Havas et al., 2015).

For international networking to happen, the cluster of organisations or firms needs to have attained sufficient critical mass of specialised and inter-related institutions (such as venture capital and specialised business development services). There are increasing returns when these specialised institutions are created. In high-tech clusters, private support institutions (e.g. venture capital and specialised business development services) for technological entrepreneurship only *respond* to – not create – commercial opportunities in innovative start-ups. If these commercial opportunities (projects) are limited in number, the private support institutions will not emerge because the incentives for them to do so are absent. Yet, it is these same specialised business development services and funding mechanisms (such as early-stage venture capital) that can strengthen the technological and marketing capabilities of firms. Hence, the presence of specialised business development services and funding mechanisms is necessary for globally successful clusters to form.

This stage needs:

(1) public and private support structures working in synergy and co-evolving;
(2) global demand for the new technologies created;
(3) private specialised business development services and funding mechanisms (e.g. venture capital); and
(4) supportive government policies (customs, tariffs, and Western sanctions may be obstacles in case of Russia).

There are few real-life examples of clusters that have reached – and stayed at – this stage, all in high middle-income economies. The high-tech cluster in Israel, for example, reached this stage in the 1990s when the growth of R&D accelerated. Various innovation and R&D support policies and mechanisms (a venture capital programme, R&D grants, and innovation programmes) were continued and a fully developed private venture capital industry thrived, supporting entrepreneurship with finance from the initial stages of development (seed funding) to the more mature stages (initial public offerings and mergers and acquisitions).

Another example from Central and Eastern Europe of a cluster reaching the third stage comes from Slovenia. Technology Park Ljubljana was created in 1992 with the emphasis on real estate, which companies could lease out with the option of then buying. By 2018, the park's emphasis has shifted to providing tailored niche services to resident firms. The park hosts 300 companies, of whom 250 (83%) are new technology-based firms (NTBFs). It now partners with over 100 organisations across the world and assists its companies to forge global linkages through technology transfer agreements. Technology Park Ljubljana has not completely shifted to Stage 3, however, as it continues to build up a critical mass of firms and organisations and to help match regional supply with demand for new technologies (Kokorotsikos et al. 2018).

The stages of growth model and institutional context

This previous section of this chapter presented the three stages as a stylised (ideal type) depiction of growth processes that is rooted in the literature on evolutionary theory and evolutionary economic geography. However, the model does not consider the institutional context which strongly shapes these processes and level of development. The idea of rents – "who benefits from modernisation processes" – helps us understand the political economy of authoritarian political regimes. Gaddy and Ickes (2005, 2013) discuss the rent management system in Putin's Russia and Ledeneva's (2013) concept of *sistema* to help explain Russia's power system under Putin. Moreover, the book draws on ideas about innovation systems and neo-Schumpeterian and co-evolutionary growth approaches. An overview of what we mean by modernisation is helpful next, both in general and in Russia more specifically.

Overview of modernisation: globally and in Russia

Since the 16th century, scholars have taken interest in both the concepts of modernity as a desired outcome and modernisation as a process of social change. This section briefly reviews the literature on modernity and modernisation worldwide, then examines economic modernisation in general before giving a historical account of the episodes of modernisation that have occurred in Russia from the time of Peter the Great (early 18th century) up until the present day.

Modernity versus modernisation

The term "modernity" in English first appeared at the end of the 16th century and came from the Latin word for "at present" (Rutland, 2015). In other words, in Western countries, modernity was considered as a state different from the past and it first emerged as a concept during the period of the Enlightenment and Renaissance when religion and the state were separated. An alternative tradition of modernity can be found in China where, before capitalism took hold in Europe, modernity was about technology, monetisation of the economy, commerce, and consumerism. Furthermore, the Confucian system vested central authority in the secular state above religion (Rutland, 2015). Hence, it makes sense to talk about a "plurality of modernities" (Rutland, 2015: 3). Countries have different paths of modernisation as well as varying outcomes of that process, that is varying modernities. Modernisation and modernity are transnational and should not be considered synonymous with the Western world.

It is helpful to think of modernity as an outcome (the "present" state), while modernisation is a process of (often disruptive) social change through which a country can become "modern." This process needs actors (states and leaders) to carry it out, that is modernisation requires agency. Modernisation can be measured either absolutely or relatively. In other words, we can either analyse how modernised a country is in itself or how far a country has "caught up" with more advanced, or frontier countries (Rutland, 2015).

More recently, we have noticed a shift away from scholarly interest in modernisation in the west and a corresponding increase in China. This may be a result of the globalised international political economy, where the United States and EU countries no longer see a political, economic, or strategic need for a domestic modernisation project per se. These countries now feel they need to maintain their global competitiveness, not catch up. Hence, the policy dialogue is focused on innovation and competitiveness (Rutland, 2015). While it is true that innovation and development of competitive production capabilities increasingly dominate policy discourses in the United States and some EU countries (while the term modernisation itself is rarely mentioned), these issues are part of an industrial policy, which is a way of modernising. In China, in contrast, scholars have recently been very active in conceptualising and operationalising modernisation and, for example, have produced an annual cross-country "modernisation index" since 2001. Interestingly, Chinese and Russian scholars are collaborating in some of these endeavours (Rutland, 2015; Lapin, 2013).

Modernisation of the economy

Turning now to how modernisation occurs in the economic sphere, the role of industrial policy is key. Broadly defined, industrial policies (or technology policies) aim to help a country develop and adopt technologies and capabilities that raise social productivity (Khan, 2015). The literature identifies at least seven different approaches to industrial and innovation policy (for a good summary of these approaches, see Radošević, 2017: 9–29).

We know that there *is* scope for industrial policies to influence a country's comparative advantage, which in turn can boost its competitiveness. The experiences of Asia from the 1950s to the 2000s illustrate that well-designed industrial policies can make a difference (Amsden, 1989). Critical is that learning processes occur, that the industrial policies are experimental and trial-and-error in nature: they must enable developing, young firms to acquire the organisational and technological capabilities and thus to become more competitive. Some countries in Asia (notably Korea) achieved rapid growth and catch-up thanks to these kinds of modernisation policies, whereas other Asian countries (such as in the Indian subcontinent) failed in the 1960s–1970s largely because strong interest groups captured the rents for private gain. Hence, how well industrial policies fit with that country's political settlement, that is the distribution of organisational power in a society, is crucial (Khan, 2015).

This idea of interest groups capturing rents from modernisation leads is important and points to the issue of who controls modernisation processes. The innovative technology of cyberspace illustrates the dangers new technologies can bring when governments cannot control them (Demchak, 2017–2018). Demchak (1995) illustrates how modernisations of militaries in some countries of Central Europe made it harder for these countries' civilian governments to control and manage the military. However, the existing literature does not appear to analyse the role of domestic versus foreign actors' control in modernisations, something which is surprising given their importance.

Domestic actors (governments, civil society, etc.) may play the dominant role in modernisation, therefore "leading" the process(es); conversely, foreign actors (multinationals, international organisations, etc.) may lead to modernisation process(es). What are the benefits and drawbacks of foreign-led modernisation versus domestic-led modernisation? Here, the perspective of political economy is valuable. Radošević (2011a) proposes a useful typology summarised in Table 2.3 which shows that a modernisation process led by either foreign or domestic actors has pros and cons. Foreign-led modernisation may lead to rapid integration in international markets and production processes, fast improvements in productivity of businesses' operations, and a significant expansion in production volume, yet at the cost of less strategic autonomy, limited functional/technological upgrading, unchanged subsidiary mandates, and limited local networking. Overall, the prospects for foreign-led modernisation result in short term, fast growth but potential structural weaknesses in the long term.

Table 2.3 Political economy model of modernisation

	Foreign-led modernisation	*Domestic-led modernisation*
Pros	• Quick international market and production integration • Fast productivity improvements in production (operations) • Significant expansion in volume	• Broad strategic autonomy • Full functional autonomy • Local networking • "Preserved" national innovation system
Cons	• Reduced strategic autonomy • Limited functional/technological upgrading • Unchanged subsidiary mandate • Limited local networking	• Limited international market and production integration • Slow productivity improvements and low efficiency • Slow expansion in volume • Poor operational performance • Potentially high rent-seeking costs and "waste"
Prospects for economy	Fast growth in the short term but potential structural weaknesses in the long term.	Slow productivity growth in the short term but potentially a more advantageous situation in terms of economic structure in the long term.

Source: Modified by the author from Radošević (2011a)

In contrast, a modernisation led by domestic actors promises broad strategic autonomy, full functional autonomy, local networking, and the "preservation" of a national innovation system. The trade-offs of a domestic-led modernisation are limited integration in international markets and production, slow productivity improvements and low efficiency, sluggish expansion in volume, poor operational performance of enterprises, and potentially high rent-seeking costs and "waste." Overall, the prospects of a domestic-led modernisation result in slow productivity growth in the short term but potentially a more advantageous situation in terms of economic structure in the long term. Hence, there is a value in finding a balance of foreign *and* domestic actors' involvement (i.e. the importance of complementarities between them). However, there are few empirical studies applying this typology to, for example, Russia's technological modernisation processes.

There are several economic and business studies on foreign investment in different sectors of the Russian economy (e.g. Henderson and Ferguson, 2014, on the oil and gas sector; on how thick local networks "lock out" foreign investors, see Lankes and Venables, 1996; on how "local knowledge" is a key bargaining strength of domestic actors, see Kock and Gullien, 2001). From the 1990s until the present, key factors for successful foreign joint ventures in Russia's oil and gas industry have remained surprisingly consistent: good contacts with key individuals in the power structure and the presence of a strong domestic partner. Russian domestic investors in oil and gas have many bargaining strengths due to their ability to maximise the value of their local knowledge and avoid foreign competition in an uncertain investment environment. Bureaucrats favour the status quo because of the opportunities for rent-seeking (Henderson and Ferguson, 2014).

However, while the study by Henderson and Ferguson (2014) gives us many insights into the real functioning of foreign joint ventures in Russia's important natural resources sector and clarifies the power dynamics between foreign and domestic companies and political elites, the study only analyses the oil and gas sector. Are there similar dynamics in other sectors that are the target of Russia's diversification and modernisation programme of the early 21st century? Who controls this modernisation process? To what extent is it foreign led or domestic led? A political science approach is needed to analyse the configurations of power, the roles of interest groups, and different actors within the state (executive and legislative branches).

We also lack an understanding of how industrial policies – efforts of modernisation – have fared globally, including in the post-Soviet space. The idea of rents, as well as a discussion about Russia's current political economy model, will help us understand how these processes have happened in Russia. Processes of modernisation are essentially about how innovation rents are generated and how existing rents are redistributed towards innovation. Hence, the next section summarises Russia's historical experiences of technological modernisation, while the section after that discusses different kinds of rents and their implications for economic growth.

Historical overview of technological modernisations in Russia: from the 18th century to the 21st century

The challenges of economic (and social) modernisations are not new to post-Soviet Russia and have, in fact, existed since at least the late 17th century. Moreover, these modernisations have tended to alternate between policies directed from above by state officials and policies to change conditions for modernisation from below (Yakovlev, 2014). In this respect, Russia's technological modernisation in the 2000s continues historical patterns of a top-down modernisation policy. Before turning to analyse Russia's modernisation in the first two decades of the 21st century, a brief look back at Russia's historical modernisations will set the current modernisation policy in context.

Round I of modernising Russia: Peter the Great's imitation of Holland's economic structure

Peter the Great (born 1672–died 1725) ruled Russia from 1682 until his death and was arguably a "coercive modernizer" (Graham, 2013: 193). In other words, his approach to modernisation was top-down (Malle, 2013). Peter the Great's primary reason for modernising Russia was to strengthen national military powers and make Russia be on a par with other countries in Europe. He presided over a successful period of modernisation of armament factories and importing modern technologies from Western Europe, focusing on particularly on building up the Russian navy (Graham, 2013).

Peter the Great visited Holland and returned to Russia, determined to emulate Holland's success in creating national wealth, as many successful countries did during the Enlightenment. Peter the Great wanted to follow Holland's experiences in creating a diversified manufacturing sector and in forming economic synergies. The economy of Holland in the 16th century was also noted for a strong division of labour (manufacturing industry, navy, warfare, luxury goods production, scientific discovery, and the arts); this resulted in many economic synergies (Reinert and Kattel, 2010).

Round II of modernising Russia: Witte's industrialisation in the 19th century

Another successful episode of modernisation "from above" in Russia's history was during the reign of Tsar Alexander II (ascended to the throne in 1855–assassinated in 1881). Sergei Witte was an influential policy maker who worked under the last two Tsars of Russia (Alexander III and Nicholas II) and led on an extensive industrialisation programme. The goals of this modernisation were the same as those of Peter the Great's – to help Russia "catch up" with more developed countries of the world. Yet, the technological context (the techno-economic paradigm) had changed from the 18th century to the 19th century. In Witte's time, the key infrastructure was the railways, so this was the focus of his modernisation (Reinert and Kattel, 2010).

Like Peter the Great, Alexander II had an authoritarian style of government, yet he allowed private investment when he understood its potential benefits. The case of railway construction and expansion is an interesting case of state-sponsored modernisation with private investment. Tsar Nicholas I (born 1796–died 1855) vetoed private investment in the railways although Russia had been a pioneer in railway construction up until the 1840s. By 1855, however, there were just 653 miles of railways in the Russian Empire in contrast to 17,398 miles in the United States and 8,054 miles in England.

When Tsar Alexander II assumed the throne in 1855, an engineer named Pavel Melnikov (1804–1880), who had studied the rapid development of railways in the United States and Western Europe, tried again to persuade the state of the importance of greater funding for railways considering the railways' significant economic impacts. In Alexander II, Melnikov found a more receptive ear and persuaded him to allow private (foreign and Russian) investors to fund the railways together with the Russian state. Melnikov believed in "a combination of government and private initiatives, with the government retaining ultimate control" (Graham, 2013: 20–21). He felt that the Russian state (particularly the Tsar) needed to maintain tight control because of political, military, and financial factors (Graham, 2013).

The next spurt in railway modernisation occurred after only about three decades, with the construction of the Trans-Siberian railway in 1889–1891 under the supervision of the enlightened bureaucrat, Sergei Witte, and the support of Tsar Alexander III, who reigned from 1881 to 1894 (Graham, 2013: 22).

It is clear, then, that industrialisation and modernisation in Tsarist Russia can be characterised as top-down in nature, focused on the military, and intermittently supported by the state and private investors.

Round III of modernising Russia: early Soviet period, 1920s–1930s

Stalin transformed the USSR from a predominantly rural society into an industrial and urban society, albeit at the expense of millions of people who were the victims of his policies. Worried by growing trends of capitalism, religiosity, and nationalism in the late 1920s, Stalin implemented a series of measures that aimed to bring about rapid indigenous industrial growth and return total control of the economy and society to the state (Lenin's New Economic Policy, NEP, in the 1920s included some market mechanisms). Stalin long wanted the USSR to be an economic autarky, that is to be less dependent on foreign trade. Stalin gradually became frustrated with Nikolai Bukharin who was responsible for industrial policy until the late 1920s as Stalin wanted faster industrialisation. Thus, from 1928 and into the 1930s, Stalin presided over a very rapid process of industrialisation, collectivisation of agriculture, and greater persecution of the wealthiest group of peasants (the kulaks) and "nepmen" who grew rich while manufacturing only a little (Service, 2004).

In theory, the Stalin period of economic modernisation and industrialisation proceeded according to a top-down state plan that sets high targets. Officials were motivated by the growing technological gap between the USSR and Western countries and foreign military threats. In practice, however, there was no plan or strategy in place, with policies frequently changing or abandoned altogether and targets altered when it became clear that they were not being achieved. Because of the political system of the time, lower ranking officials in the Communist Party of the Soviet Union and government routinely misled their superiors over performance indicators. This systemic issue means that statistics on the Soviet Union's industrialisation in the 1920s and 1930s must be interpreted with caution. Reportedly, gross industrial output increased by 137% from 1928 to 1933, and industry's output of capital goods rose by 285% in the same period. Moreover, national income doubled from 1927 to 1928 and total employed labour force almost doubled from 11.3 million under the NEP of the early 1920s to 22.8 million by 1932–1933 (Service, 2004).

Round IV of modernising Russia: Gorbachev and Yeltsin periods

The next episode when Russia tried to undertake economic modernisation was in the last days of the Soviet Union at the end of the 1980s. Gorbachev carried out a series of reforms – notably perestroika, glasnost – that have most often been described as modernisation from above (Åslund, 2007; Nove, 1989). Yakovlev (2014), however, argued that Gorbachev's initiatives relied on initiative from below and as such, were a new kind of modernisation. One scholar described the political leaders under Gorbachev who tried to carry out this modernisation as "hesitant modernizers" (Amann, 1986: 491) because of the trade-offs in their views about economic development versus self-interest and their doubts about the practicability and the social desirability of modernisation.

Yeltsin aimed to implement another round of modernisation from above in the newly independent Russia, drawing on the extensive foreign funds and technical assistance from the IMF and allowing a small segment of entrepreneurs and factory owners to enrich themselves at the expense of society (the so-called oligarchs). However, the programme of modernisation was undermined by the weak and fragmented state and the poor condition of the economy due to shock therapy and rapid privatisation.

Round V of modernising Russia: 2000 onwards

Before turning to innovation specifically, it is important to look at Russia's broader economic modernisation drive of the 2000s. How do Russia's political and economic elites view modernisation? Since the turn of the 21st century, they have turned to modernisation policies as a way of catching up with more advanced countries. Modernisation has been used as a tool of economic, social, and political development.

In the late 1990s–2000s, Russia witnessed a shift in policy towards diversification, modernisation, and innovation, partly as a response to the economy's dependence on natural resources and increasing calls for diversification. Since

2000, the most senior political leaders in Russia have increasingly spoken of the need for Russia to catch up with other countries and for modernisation and diversification of the economic structure. They saw the potential of R&D and innovation in stimulating more diversified economic growth away from dependency on natural resources. The key actors – Putin, Medvedev, and Surkov – had two slightly different visions of modernisation although both visions were about state-led modernisation.

Putin envisioned a project to make Russia great again, which was initiated with his "Millennium Manifesto" published online on 29 December 1999 and in the national newspaper *Izvestiya* the following day. In this Manifesto, Putin declared the economic well-being of the people to be an ideological, spiritual, and moral problem (Slade, 2006 on the website "GeoHistory Today"). Ever since becoming Acting President on 31 December 1999, Putin aimed to restore Russia's greatness and bring prosperity after the chaotic 1990s. This "restoring greatness" project of Putin morphed into a modernisation programme to diversify the economy and develop an innovation-based economy a couple of years later.

From 2002, two years into his presidency, President Putin aimed to develop a knowledge-based and innovative economy, emphasising the direct role of the state in providing funds and infrastructure for innovation (Dyker, 2012). The government subsequently developed infrastructure, legal, and financial mechanisms, and a variety of new organisations to promote innovation. Some of these initiatives started in the 1990s, but their implementation was intensified from 1999 to 2000 (for a summary, see Graham and Dezhina, 2008). These initiatives include innovation technology centres and Special Economic Zones, innovation clusters, Innopolis city (an IT-focused technology park in the Republic of Tatarstan that was formed in December 2012 and officially became a town in December 2014), rejuvenating the Soviet-era science towns and technology parks. Yet, different groups or factions of political and economic elites have their own narratives of modernisation, that is they understand modernisation in varying ways, be it in an economic, technological, political, social, or political sense (Kinossian and Morgan, 2014).

Putin was succeeded as president by Dmitry Medvedev from 2008 to 2012 who advocated a more liberal modernisation. To make his mark, he vigorously pursued not only the economic "modernisation" agenda started by Putin but also political modernisation. Medvedev saw modernisation as a multi-sided process that eventually included ostensibly democratic reforms (such as the reinstatement of direct elections for regional governors and reforms to reduce corruption in public office). Medvedev called for economic diversification and development of a knowledge economy. He renewed the emphasis from the top of the "power vertical" on innovation-led growth, putting innovation in nanotechnology as a state priority (hence his nickname, "nano-president," which may or may not have been satirical).

In common with Putin's vision, Medvedev thus promoted a modernisation led by the state. The Skolkovo innovation centre set up on the edge of Moscow by the central government under President Medvedev (see Chapter 7) is the latest manifestation of Russia's "state-directed capitalism," following a trend found in many emerging economies in the last 15 years.

From early 2010, Vladislav Surkov promoted a view of modernisation that was somewhat like Medvedev's view. Surkov was the first deputy head of the presidential administration and deputy chair of the Commission on Modernisation as well as an influential ideologist in the Kremlin. He proposed that political modernisation was possible in a special Russian way: modernising politics while keeping a top-down system that controls the social, economic, and political system. Surkov believed that a strong state is needed to direct modernisation with an authoritarian government governing and managing technological change (Glikin and Kostenko, 2010).

So far, however, despite these two visions of modernisation from the most senior figures in Russia's "power vertical" and despite maintaining near constant spending levels on R&D since 2000, the results from Russia's modernisation agenda have been quite limited (as discussed in Chapter 3).

To understand why modernisations in post-Soviet Russia have had little real effect in terms of innovation outcomes, ideas from ethnographic literature on the ambivalence of technology and its development are useful as well as the notion of rents. Recent research has meticulously shown, through cases from across the world, how technologies can be ambivalent: ambivalent in terms of substance, norms, functions, or in the motivations behind the development of new technologies (Ledeneva, 2018a: vol. 1: 14). Motivational ambivalence may be prominent in Russia: this form of ambivalence operates through a double purpose, that is differences in the declared versus hidden agendas in co-optation (through carrots) and control (by sticks, e.g. the tool of informal governance in Russia known as "chernukha," which "refers to the creation and distribution of information as a means of undermining the reputation of a particular political or business figure") (Ledeneva, 2018b: vol. 2: 439–440). Motivational ambivalence is associated with concepts of patron-client relations, power networks, and informal governance. Moreover, economies of favour form important parts of informal economies (Ledeneva, 2018a: vol. 1: 107), governed by social capital and social interactions more than the shadow economy or black market are. An example of functional ambivalence is in how an object or technology is sometimes used by people in new or unintended ways (e.g. jugaad in India, which is "a way of solving problems by working around constraints and improvising with limited resources," Ledeneva, 2018b: vol. 2: 133). The insights from this literature shows the key role of informal versus formal governance and suggests that much social and cultural complexity, determined by ambivalence, surrounds technology and its developments; this may help to explain why the numerous economic modernisation and innovation agendas in Russia have had little real effect yet in terms of innovation outcomes (see e.g. Dyker, 2012: 259–263).

Another reason to explain the divergence between Russia's modernisation and innovation policy intentions and rhetoric and real outcomes lies in the political economy of rents. Rents are the benefits that some actors gain from modernisation processes of change or conversely, from situations of equilibria which hinder modernisation from occurring. The next section discusses this further.

Rents

There are various kinds of rents, including inefficient and inhibiting growth rents and growth boosting. The concept of rents helps understand a country's political economy model and can be understood as "incremental changes in incomes or benefits created by particular institutions" (Khan, 2017: 4–5). Another widely cited definition of rents as applied specifically to the resources sector concerns the surplus that is received from oil and gas production: rent is "the revenue received from sale of the resource minus the cost of producing it" (Gaddy and Ickes, 2005: 560).

The conventional economic literature on rents focuses only on monopoly rents and their negative implications for growth. However, recent research (e.g. Khan, 2017; Melville and Mironyuk, 2016) argues for a more differentiated view on rents to recognise the variety thereof and diversity of possible outcomes from rents for growth and efficiency depending on the social context. Indeed, the same kind of rent (e.g. monopoly rents) can indicate efficiency or inefficiency depending on the specific context (Khan, 2017). Table 2.4 summarises six kinds of rents, and how they can be growth inducing or inhibiting depending on the specific political context.

From Table 2.4, we see that rents from natural resources are different in nature and have diverse implications for growth compared to rents generated from innovation and learning. Because Russia's economy remains dominated by natural resources despite a policy shift to diversity in the economy since the year 2000, it will take a long time for the country to see more rents from innovation and learning than from natural resources. The Russian scholar Simon Kordonsky notes that the Soviet economy was totally resource based, as is post-Soviet Russia's economy. The USSR's planned economy was focused on getting rid of all threats to actual and potential resource shortages. The Soviet Union's success in technological development was one outcome of this policy strategic focus as the state mobilised all resources and planned the allocation of resources to remove threats that were associated with falling behind the country's principal ideological enemy, the United States, particularly in the military field. Distinguishing between a market economy which is based on social classes and a resource-based economy organised hierarchically as a system of social estates (the people, government, entrepreneurs, and diverse marginalised groups), Kordonsky argues that Russia has historically been a resource-based economy (Kordonsky, 2016). The Russian state's primary goal is to mobilise and manage resources, including people, education, land, health, and labour. In contemporary Russia, economic development is considered by the governing social estates to be secondary to activities that determine and neutralise factors considered a threat to state integrity and social stability; indeed, economic development – such as innovation and modernisation policy – plays a "service" role of helping to remove the threats to the state's integrity (Kordonsky, 2016: 37).

Table 2.4 Typology of rents

Type of rent	*Description*	*Consequences for growth*
Monopoly rents	• Opposite to competitive rent-free markets	• Sometimes produce economies of scale (super-profits create incentives for more investment) • Sometimes lead to lost output and growth opportunities
Economic*	• Rents from (scarce) natural resources, for example oil and gas, cotton (Uzbekistan), fishing waters, and pasture lands; • Rents from transportation of natural resources and preferential access to foreign markets; • Control over finances and financial flows, for example from labour migrants; • External rents (e.g. from foreign aid and various subsidies)	• Rents can indicate efficiency; maximising rents is socially desirable; • Often growth-enhancing; • Can also be inefficient if tragedy of commons exist (i.e. no property rights or ownership of natural resource). Rents accrued would be dissipated among many people.
Political	• Transfer of rights through political mechanism, for example redistributive transfers; • In post-Soviet autocracies, monopoly of political rent is necessary to get economic rents (Melville and Mironyuk, 2016).	• Efficient/inefficient depending on who beneficiaries are (whether they have incentive to transition to productive capitalism). Also depends on configuration of political forces in society; • Can quickly become inefficient.
Schumpeterian	• From innovation and information generation; • These rents create incentives to efficiently use a scarce resource, for example capability to find and use existing information/make new information; • Rent can be from an easily imitated innovation (i.e. public good in nature) so sometimes is protected by state through patents.	• Government policies can increase/decrease these rents (e.g. tax breaks to innovators, competition policies, patent laws); • Can lead to economic dynamic efficiency if innovation/information generating rents becomes freely available to all in future (but not immediately after innovation/information generated); • Can lead to inefficiency if innovation/information generating the rents is monopolised and not diffused.

(*Continued*)

Table 2.4 (Continued)

Type of rent	*Description*	*Consequences for growth*
Rents for learning (imitation of existing technologies and adaptation to local conditions, institutions, etc.)	• Artificially created by a developmental state to speed up learning in infant industries and to give producers in these industries time to catch up; • Take form of policy-induced conditional subsidies (i.e. rents given before beneficiaries have imitated/adapted, not afterwards as in case of Schumpeterian rents).	• Rents can incentivise reducing costs over time; • Easier for states to administer learning rents in early stages of catch up (when next steps on "technology ladder" are clear and easy to monitor the performance of rent beneficiaries). Harder as the technology gets more sophisticated and products more differentiated; • Depends critically on state's ability to issue and retract learning subsidies.
Rents for monitoring	• Can be created by state.	• Can be efficient and good for growth depending on monitors' ability to monitor and enforce.

Source: Adapted from Khan (2017: 1–38).

*Notion of "economic rents" from Melville and Mironyuk (2016).

Political and economic rents are intertwined, especially so in post-Soviet countries. Having a monopoly on political rents is a precondition for being able to extract economic rents. This is the essence of a "King of the Mountain" analytical model[7] to explain the persistence of post-Soviet authoritarian regimes which lack high quality institutions and high state capacity. There is an inverse correlation between the quality of institutions and the extraction of political and economic rents in post-Soviet autocracies. Reforms to make institutions "better" (better for property rights, rule of law, effective governance, control of corruption, etc.) would diminish the autocrat's rents. This explains why an autocrat lacks incentives to strengthen institutions through reforms (Melville and Mironyuk, 2016).

It is important to remember that powerful organisations and/or individuals exist everywhere, in all societies. They are always keen to enrich themselves at the expense of society. An authoritarian regime can produce broad-based (inclusive) growth just as a democratic regime can; what matters is the configuration of relative power, the "relative bargaining power of competing organisations" (Khan, 2017: 5), and the social context. If political institutions in an authoritarian regime are not "captured" by powerful organisations (e.g. firms), then they can create incentives for those institutions' leaders to take a long-term view which we could call "developmental." Institutions and policies with developmental aims can create new kinds of incomes (e.g. Schumpeterian and learning rents) and disrupt old ones. Equally, developmental institutions or rules could be undermined if they are perceived as too much of a challenge by powerful organisations:

> Institutions that threaten the rents of powerful organisations will be strongly contested and may be reversed, modified or distorted in different ways.
>
> (Khan, 2017: 5)

Looking at the checks and balances in place in a given context – the "rent management system" (Khan, 2017: 15; Gaddy and Ickes, 2013: 99 apply this concept to Putin's Russia) – helps us understand how rents are allocated and used. Understanding the system (*sistema* in Putin's Russia, cf. Ledeneva, 2013) and how it configures formal and informal power and allocates rents is also important. Are the organisations getting a certain rent the ones that are supposed to benefit from this rent? Are they held to account on what these organisations are meant to deliver? Which organisations constrain other organisations and hold them accountable in their work? How power is distributed across organisations and institutions affects the outcomes associated with specific institutions.

Political economy systems in authoritarian regimes

Research tends to agree that Russia has become increasingly more authoritarian since 2000.[8] By 2009, a majority of Russian and foreign scholars described the Russian polity as authoritarian, electoral authoritarian, or an authoritarian-oligarchic-bureaucratic hybrid (Brown et al., 2009). The authoritarian president Putin has arguably maintained his power through a co-optation strategy, the most common way of three possible ways used by authoritarian rulers to sustain their power (Haber, 2008). Co-optation occurs when an autocratic leader buys loyalty from the organisation that helped him/her acquire power, that is through ensuring they are better off thanks to revenues from rents cooperating with the political regime than overthrowing it. Gaddy and Ickes (2013) describe the rent-sharing arrangements between Putin and a small group of individuals ("oligarchs") who owned assets in the natural resources sector. This rent management system was an informal contract, also called the "Protection Racket" (Gaddy and Ickes, 2013: 97) whereby Putin protected the oligarchs' ownership of assets – chiefly in natural resources sector – and in exchange, the oligarchs shared some of the rents from the natural resources with the value-subtracting manufacturing sectors. Thus, this is a kind of co-optation strategy as outlined by Haber (2008) earlier as Putin demanded loyalty from the oligarchs in exchange for protection of their assets and sources of natural resources rents. The result of this system for managing rents was social and political stability. The rent management system comprises a complex mixture of vested interests (different groups and individuals in society), each of whom had a stake in the different components of rent, for example after-tax profits, informal taxes, costs of production (Gaddy and Ickes, 2005: 563). The rent management system between Putin and the oligarchs was challenged by the 2011–2012 public protests, which empowered a new "creative class" centred on Moscow and St. Petersburg that was independent of the "older" economic sectors (e.g., oil and gas).

Another important aspect of Russia's system of managing rent since 2000 is the concept of *Sistema*, a notable attempt to define how authoritarianism is sustained under Putin (Ledeneva, 2013). Ledeneva argues that what matters is not just political leadership but also the surrounding system, the vertical of power supported by informal networks. Putin's regime relies extensively on the use of informal networks to maintain power. While she does not explicitly mention natural resource rents, we can infer that these are the main source of power because they have been so important for Russia's economy for many decades. *Sistema* helps political and economic elites regulate access to these resources and appoint loyal people. *Sistema* enables the state to function despite its weak formal institutions. Hence, the concept of rents introduced earlier in this chapter underpins and sustains *sistema*. As discussed earlier (Table 2.4), there are key differences in the consequences for growth between rents from natural resources and from innovation. Russia's elites in the *sistema* continue to be more reliant on natural resources rents, which means that their vested interests are against any government policies or initiatives that try to promote innovation rents.

The idea of "political settlements" (Khan, 2017: 1) – the distribution of organisation power – helps explain the economic and political effects of Russia's technological modernisation programme in the early 21st century. The distribution of power is essentially about who controls rents. Yakovlev (2014) argues that the control of rents is key to understand how state actors and businesses have interacted in Russia since the early 1990s. In the 1990s, the principal sources of rents were privatisation (a political rent in Khan's typology, see

Table 2.4), a significant difference in price for the same goods in the domestic and world markets, and domestic and international borrowing. The main beneficiaries of these *temporary* economic rents were actors in both federal and regional bureaucracies and in oligarchic businesses. Hellman (1998) argued that these early winners of the first waves of privatisation in post-Soviet countries therefore had no incentives to continue reforms. The 1998 financial crisis brought an end to these rents.

The 2000s heralded the beginning of the reallocation of rents from natural resources to government bureaucrats and *siloviki* actors, which skyrocketed largely due to the rise in global oil prices. In the 1990s, natural resource rents primarily benefited oligarchs, businesspeople who often had close informal ties with state officials and were able to benefit from privatisation processes. From the early 2000s until 2003–2004, state-business relations in Russia were relatively equal and were based on constructive dialogue (Yakovlev, 2014). However, after the federal bureaucratic elites introduced a mineral resources extraction tax to try and redistribute some of these rents from oil exports to the state, the balance of power between these two groups of actors shifted. Big business (notably the YUKOS company) resisted the tax because they felt such a policy was encroaching on its profits (Yakovlev, 2014). This resistance from big business led to the state taking more control of strategic industries (e.g. natural resources), and subsequently state actors (federal bureaucracy and security agencies) came to dominate over business.

The 2008 financial crisis that severely affected Russia was an external trigger to some of Russia's political elites about the need for change in the economy and the way political elites governed the economy and society. Medvedev's calls for modernisation and the reforms carried out from 2004 to 2008 are evidence of this (Yakovlev, 2014). However, these calls for change "from below" (ibid.: 11) were countered by strong resistance to change from the elites from security agencies (siloviki), who dominated top management of the state-owned corporations, and extensive capital outflows from Russia due to policy uncertainty (Yakovlev, 2014).

Innovation systems and evolutionary approaches to economic growth

The issue of technological modernisation in Russia is informed by theories of innovation systems and innovation policies. The reason is that weaknesses in Russia's innovation system may help explain why science towns and science and technology parks have not performed very successfully to date.

According to the "linear" model of innovation which predominated until the 1980s, fundamental science (discovery and invention) was the starting point of the process; the process was therefore "pushed" or initiated by science and the technological opportunities presented by science. Many scholars and policy makers thought that there were various, distinct stages ending in full-scale production and eventual commercialisation (Figure 2.2). This model defined

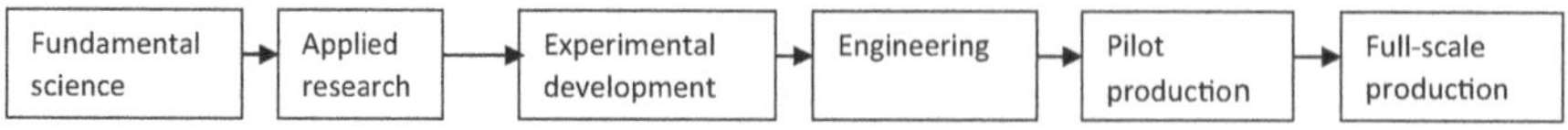

Figure 2.2 Linear model of innovation

Source: OECD (1992: 25)

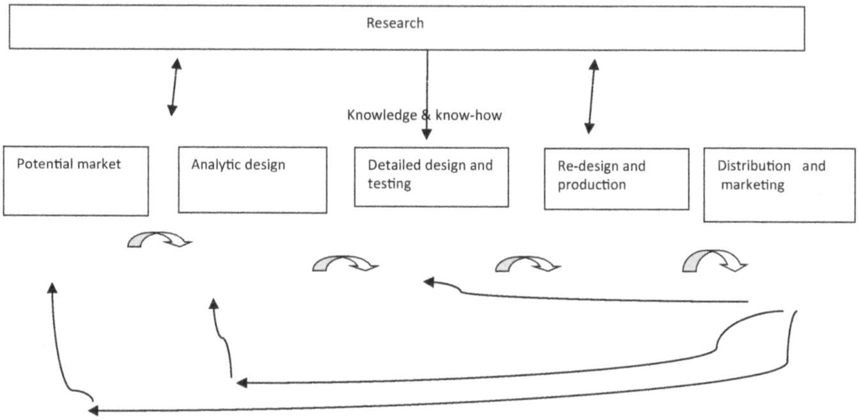

Figure 2.3 Interactive model of innovation

Source: OECD (1992: 25)

innovation in a clear, homogenous manner. The linear model was influential among policy makers in the Cold War context, and explains the large sums invested in R&D in the United States and the Soviet Union – policy makers believed that by investing more, they would see clear results in terms of outputs, for example patents, commercialisation of technological innovations (Cooper, 1998; Radošević, 2011b).

However, from the 1980s, this model began to be critiqued and led to an alternative "interactive" model (Figure 2.3). Since the 1980s, many researchers have pointed out the problems with the linear model of innovation: innovations usually occur because the innovators have perceived a demand for the innovation on the market. Moreover, the linear model ignores the important feedback loops that take place between the various stages of the process (Fagerberg, 2005).

The interactive model of innovation emphasises the social processes behind the new technologies and stresses an iterative interactive process between research, design, testing, production, and marketing of the finished product (Radošević, 2011b). According to this model, innovation is **uncertain** (the returns of investing in R&D cannot be known in advance), **collective** (innovation requires social interactions and learning), and **cumulative** – it takes a certain amount of time to learn and implement technological transformations (Lazonick, 2002). Many small, incremental innovations must be accumulated before a bigger, more radical innovation might occur, and innovation is a path-dependent process (Lazonick and Mazzucato, 2012). Inherent in the idea of interactive models of innovation is the fact that innovation processes are part of a system.

A well-designed innovation system is generally understood to mean one that has evolved over time, involves various interacting actors (firms, universities, and government agencies), and one that has well-functioning institutions that lay down the "rules of the game" (Woolthuis et al., 2005).

The concept of systems of innovation was first proposed by Christopher Freeman (1987). Freeman stressed the idea of networks in the system: "*network of institutions in the public and private sectors whose activities and interactions initiate, import and diffuse new technologies*" (Freeman, 1987: 1, italics added). Freeman's notion is based on much earlier works by List (1841) on the national system of political economy; List also emphasised the role of the state in coordinating and implementing long-term industrial and economic policies. The national system of political economy refers to the domestic structures and institutions that influence economic activities, of which one aspect is the national system of innovation. Because multiple significant developments in technology involve transformations in how production is organised, and in the wider socio-political relationships in an economy, many important features of society must be changed to develop or take advantage of new technology or production possibilities (Gilpin, 2001).

Moreover, Lundvall (1992) was a contemporary of Freeman and developed a theory of innovation as an interactive process. He stressed the need to look at the wider national system of innovation (NSI) beyond user–producer interactions (Lundvall, 1992). The "narrow" NSI comprises institutions which specifically aim to support knowledge gain and transfer (such as universities and R&D institutes). These institutions are embedded within the *broader* socio-economic system where many political, economic, and cultural influences shape the success of innovation.

The interactive or systemic innovation approach has been widely applied in policy making. An innovation system framework emphasises the flow of information and technology and the interactions between people, institutions, and enterprises which affect how and why an idea is transformed into a process, product, or service on the market. The notion of systems of innovation has been extended to the national, regional, local, technological, and sectoral levels.

Although national systems of innovation have been most discussed and applied in research and policy, innovations have existed and have influenced economic activity long before the dominance of nation-states since the 18th century. Freeman, like Adam Smith in *The Wealth of Nations*, has highlighted the importance of local innovation systems (such as Renaissance era city states and small principalities) for economic development (Freeman, 2002). Other scholars have argued that in the current "globalised" world, nation-states are less important than lower-level entities such as regions, provinces, industrial districts (or "clusters"), and cities in innovation processes (DeBresson, 1989).

Recent literature argues for the notion of an innovation **eco**system that drives innovation rather than NTBFs or large firms on their own (Su et al., 2018). The prefix "eco" emphasises the evolutionary nature of innovation and the environmental interdependencies that extend beyond the lead firm and other firms and R&D organisations in the system. A lead firm must coordinate the whole innovation process, from the development of a new idea to the manufacture of a novel/improved product and its introduction in the final market. Innovation ecosystems are based on some degree of co-specialisation among firms and other organisations. In other words, an ecosystem enables large firms (such as Apple) to interact with small technology-based firms (such as software companies developing apps for Apple products). The latter can then innovate based on the large firms' more stable technology platforms (Mandel, 2011).

Neo-Schumpeterian and co-evolutionary approaches to economic growth

Russia's technological modernisation programme of the first decade of the 21st century is fundamentally about **catching up** with Western countries: modernising Russia's economy to bring the country's technological and military level on a par with the world's most developed countries. Hence, evolutionary theories of economic growth that aim to explain the sources of technology and its dynamic development as well as elucidate the notion of the technology frontier are useful to understand Russia's economic and technological modernisation drive.

Economic growth and modernisation go hand in hand. What drives growth and modernisation are questions that have long fascinated economists, and more recently, political scientists and development practitioners. The mainstream (neoclassical) view of growth is that the initial conditions (or preconditions) need to be "right" – which for many decades in the 20th century was translated into policy as good governance (including "good" institutions), democracy, and free trade. Yet, the neoclassical (or Solow) growth model does not explain the sources of technology, leaving it as an unexplainable factor of growth. Endogenous growth theory (Romer, 1993) attempted to explain the drivers of technology within the neoclassical tradition, emphasising R&D as the main driver of innovation and growth. However, critics have questioned how relevant R&D is for countries trying to catch up with the high-income countries (Dominguez Lacasa et al., 2018).

To attempt to explain how countries can catch up with wealthier countries, the economist Aghion introduced the Schumpeterian-inspired notion of a **technology frontier** (Aghion, 2004). The technological frontier is the forefront of global knowledge and the latest technologies at any given point in time. The idea of catching up enables a distinction to be made between growth based on innovation (at the technology frontier) and growth from imitation (behind the technology frontier). However, catching up is not easy: Acemoglu et al. (2006) note that middle-income countries which are not yet at the global technology frontier risk falling into the trap of non-convergence if they do not switch from an investment-based growth strategy to one based on innovation. Interactions between R&D, innovation, and productivity are affected by the institutional context which differs depending on the country's position in relation to the technology frontier. We may expect countries (such as Russia) or firms behind the frontier to grow faster and catch up to the global technological frontier because they benefit from knowledge spillovers from countries or firms on the frontier by imitating technological activities. In contrast, those at the frontier must continually innovate to stay ahead. Moreover, policies and institutions that favour imitation are different from those promoting leading-edge innovation (Aghion et al., 2011).

In practice, the neoclassical approach has been very influential. Notably, it inspired the so-called Washington Consensus (WC) policies practised by the World Bank, International Monetary Fund (IMF), and United States Treasury (all organisations with their HQ in Washington, DC) from the mid-1980s until the 1990s. These policies advocated trade liberalisation, privatisation, and macroeconomic stabilisation (i.e. policies to get a free market) in state-directed economies and were inspired by events in Latin America in the 1980s. Washington Consensus policies were imposed in Latin American countries in the 1980s when it became clear that these countries' import substitution industrialisation strategies that drove their national development were unsustainable because they were driven by debt and reached a point where further growth was impossible.

Later, in the 1990s, the revised "Augmented Washington Consensus" added to this "policy recipe" for states the need to implement certain institutional reforms deemed crucial for growth. These kinds of economic reforms were recommended by Western advisors – notably, the IMF and Jeffrey Sachs – to countries in Central and Eastern Europe (CEE) in the 1980s–1990s. CEE countries at that time were thought then to be in the process of transition from socialism or communism to a market economy and democratic regime. There was a common assumption that the initial conditions at the beginning of the transition process would be short-lived because a market economy would be quickly set up and become operational, and these countries would thus then soon catch up with Western Europe (Berend, 2000). This justified the policy advice for rapid privatisation and liberalisation. WC-inspired reforms have been widely described as "shock therapy" with reference to their rapid implementation and lack of attention to institutional and cultural context (Stiglitz, 1999: 27).

In the new post-Soviet Russia, implementation of the WC-style reforms was carried out rapidly, and attempts to "superimpose" Western institutions on the country did not pay off; the country experienced a profound economic, fiscal, and social crisis. Russia's per capita income in purchasing power parity declined sharply between 1992 and 1998 (British International Studies Association, British International Studies Association, and Chatham House joint workshop, 4 June 2018). Science was far from immune from this general crisis: state-supported big science that existed in the Soviet Union virtually ceased because of the collapse of the state, meaning the state funding for science stopped. Moreover, ordinary Russians were the big losers of this general crisis and chaos; hence, it is not surprising that Western institutions came to be perceived negatively in Russia.

The preconditions were not short-lived in the 1990s as many Western advisors thought at the time because the transition did not happen in a linear, rapid way. Instead, path dependency and Soviet legacies persisted. This has led to a situation where post-socialist economies of CEE not only have some elements in their RDI systems that are like market economies of Western countries (e.g. emergence of specialised suppliers of R&D, especially small firms; universities have taken on greater roles in performing RDI) but also continue to have some other features that are socialist (e.g. R&D mainly done outside of industry) and post-socialist. Examples of post-socialist characteristics in RDI in CEE countries include the predominance of state-controlled R&D and innovation processes with emergent private ownership and the fact that enterprises are not the principal agents in funding or performing innovation (Radošević, 2011a).

How are evolutionary theories of growth relevant to Central and Eastern Europe (CEE)? Neo-Schumpeterian approaches assume that long-term growth in CEE countries will occur based increasingly on greater physical and human capital, innovation, and institutional change. Neo-Schumpeterian approaches build on the evolutionary school in economics (Nelson and Winter, 1982), which takes a dynamic perspective on the economy and sees history as constraining the present; in other words, the options available to firms and organisations (as well as states and markets) are path dependent.

Socialism was an institutional structure that was an obstacle to new organisational forms emerging. The Austrian political economist Joseph Schumpeter (1883–1950) assumed that big socialist firms could innovate, but he underestimated the role of the market in providing variety, and therefore in allowing for division of labour among firms which enabled them to specialise. Some socialist firms operated on the technology frontier: for example, the Zeiss company in East Germany managed to accumulate capabilities to innovate in response to demand within the constraints of the institutional context (Kogut and Zanader, 2000). Overall, however, socialism limited innovation because of the central planning system in the economy and because of the underdeveloped system of innovation and market.

Under a socialist system, firms did not have ways to learn through interacting with suppliers and customers. This kind of learning is emphasised in the literature on evolutionary economics of innovation as critical for firms to succeed. This knowledge stems from both R&D and non-R&D activities and from interactions with other firms and with other bodies (Havas et al., 2015; Edquist, 2011).

The role of policy and directed improvisation

One strand of the neo-Schumpeterian growth approach emphasises the co-evolutionary nature of economic growth and institutions and the essentially local nature of this process. A recent application of evolutionary theory to China's political economy model (Ang, 2016) is of relevance here. Ang argues that growth (markets) and institutions (states) co-evolve through continuous responses among local actors to changing problems. Key is actors' capacity to adapt to change. Rather than assuming institutions first need to be strengthened and then growth will follow, **Ang argues that weak institutions can be harnessed for growth and they will strengthen (formalise) over time, in parallel to economic growth.** To illustrate her argument, Ang takes the case of China and how the country managed to escape the poverty trap since 1978 by implementing a system of "directed improvisation": state-level bureaucrats directed (but not dictated to) regional and local bureaucrats to implement reforms to adapt to changing problems, allowing the regional and local bureaucrats to act flexibly and improvise while still following centrally issued mandates and instructions. This "directed improvisation" approach, which allows for some bounded policy experimentation at regional and local level, is at the essence of China's innovation and industrial policy (Kanellou et al., 2019: 10). Such an approach – contextualised by China's more decentralised political system – helps explain China's overall better innovation outcomes compared to Russia's.

This idea that weak institutions can be harnessed for growth and will strengthen over time, in parallel to economic growth, is interesting to apply to Russia. Many studies in the 1990s and 2000s have noted that Russia has weak institutions (EBRD Transition Reports and the OECD Reports on innovation policy). Acemoglu et al. (2006) and Rodrik (2008) show that where formal institutions are weak, the business environment can still foster growth if there are informal substitutes to weak institutions or improvements in dynamic incentives. This suggests that it is possible to counterbalance inefficient institutions. There is some empirical support for this idea in Russia: subnational institutional and economic variation (in wealth, consumer demand, skills, quality of infrastructure, and political stability) explain why FDI inflows into Russia increased from 2001 to 2010 despite a generally weak institutional environment. Foreign investors were attracted to regions of Russia which had a higher development level as that outweighed some institutional inadequacies, notably crime rate and corruption (Bessonova and Gonchar, 2015).

To sum up this section, neo-Schumpeterian theories of growth emphasise the role of innovation, institutional change, and physical and human capital for long-term growth. The concept of the technology frontier helps explain how countries can catch up with wealthier countries by pursuing economic growth through technological imitation. Countries that have reached the technology frontier can grow based on innovation, suggesting that for countries (such as Russia) in the catching up phase, imitation may be a more appropriate technological policy than innovation. Technological modernisation can also be understood by a neo-Schumpeterian approach emphasising the co-evolution of growth and institutions; this approach argues that rather than first reforming institutions, weak institutions can be harnessed for growth and can strengthen over time in parallel to economic growth. Thus, analysing cases at a regional and sub-regional level in a country can be illuminating to understand the nature and functioning of local institutions that are relevant for innovation and economic growth; this is what this book aims to do. The next section outlines how it attempts to show this.

How the book answers its questions

This section outlines the methodology used to answer the book's two main research questions:

(1) How has the authoritarian state of Russia addressed technology-based growth (as distinct from growth based on increasing inputs – labour, capital, etc.)?
(2) How does Russia's political economy model explain the problems it has faced in pursuing technology-based growth (substantial R&D investment yet comparative poor performance in innovation outcomes)?

The analysis is based on qualitative and quantitative data gathered from various sources: semi-structured interviews carried out during fieldwork in Russia; two original surveys carried out by the author of managers of science and technology parks and of entrepreneurs of small firms residing in STPs; government documents and other official documents; and media articles dating from the 1960s to the present.

The empirical material analysed in Chapter 4 (on science towns), Chapter 5 (science and technology parks), and Chapter 6 (on Skolkovo) was gathered through **fieldwork in Russia** (ten visits between 2011 and 2016). The author carried out **28 semi-structured interviews** during fieldwork visits with local and regional government officials, employees of state corporations (e.g. Rosnano) and regional agencies for innovation development, as well as with academics, scientists, journalists, entrepreneurs, and angel investors. These interviews were carried out in Obninsk and Akademgorodok as well as in Moscow and Tomsk. Respondents were found using the "snowballing" method, with many personal contact details provided by initial respondents and by academic colleagues in Russia, the United Kingdom, and the United States. A list of these interviews containing the town, professional role, and organisation where the respondent works as well as the month and year when the interview(s) took place is provided in Appendix 1; this list anonymises respondents such that personal details such as name, age, and gender are excluded to protect respondents' anonymity. The location of the interview (town) is included as the author felt it important for the research aims while not compromising on respondents' rights to anonymity. Most interviews were audio recorded with the oral informed consent of the respondent. During interviews not recorded at the respondent's request, the author of this book made extensive notes and asked the respondent to repeat several key points to ensure accuracy; further notes were made immediately after these interviews from memory by the author. The duration of the 28 interviews ranged from 20 minutes to nearly 3 hours (the interview lasting 3 hours was spread over 3 sessions), with most lasting between 30 and 60 minutes. Most interviews were in Russian; some interviewees preferred to speak in English or spoke in a mixture of Russian and English. Detailed summaries of all interviews as well as the author's immediate post-interview impressions of the interview were securely recorded in English and analysed with the help of the software NVivo. In addition, six interviews carried out by the author in Obninsk with scientists, local officials, museum staff, and a journalist and were transcribed as a verbatim text record by a native Russian speaker; this transcription was funded by an historical-ethnographic project called "Obninsk – the first Russian science city" with which the author collaborated between 2012 and 2014 (project coordinated by the Centre for Humanitarian Studies in the Russian Presidential Academy of National Economy and Public Administration, led by Professor Andrei Zorin of University of Oxford and Russian Presidential Academy of National Economy and Public Administration).

In addition, the empirical material analysed in Chapter 5 (science and technology parks) was also gathered through carrying out **two purposive surveys** of managers and resident firms **of science and technology parks** (STPs) designed by the author. In total, 17 STPs located across Russia responded to the survey of STP management (13% of the 125 parks in Russia, in 2017; survey covered 27% of Russia's regions with a STP). The second survey asked 11 resident firms located in three separate STPs in Russia about their reasons for moving to a STP and their experiences of the STP. Further information on the surveys' design and sampling frame can be found in Chapter 5.

Finally, the book analysed a range of **public documents, policy documents, and media articles** in both Russian and English relevant to the topic of modernisation and innovation in Russia.

Chapter 7 (Conclusions) will discuss how these perspectives shape or distort the stages of growth model and generate some facts on how the model operates in practice. Before that, this book turns to examine the empirical material (Chapters 4–6).

Notes

1 Israel Kirzner, an economist who followed the Austrian economics tradition, emphasised the central idea of the discovery process in entrepreneurship (Kirzner, 1997).
2 According to the official website of Tsukuba science city: www.tsukubainfo.jp/tsukuba/tsukuba.html [last accessed 30 December 2018].
3 According to the official website of Tsukuba science city network: www.tsukuba-network.jp/english/corporate.html [last accessed 30 December 2018].
4 Source: official website of Tsukuba science city network: www.tsukuba-network.jp/english/corporate.html [last accessed 30 December 2018].
5 Source: official website of Tsukuba science city: www.tsukubainfo.jp/tsukuba/tsukuba.html [last accessed 30 December 2018].
6 Source: official website of the Tsukuba Global Innovation Promotion Agency: http://tsukuba-gi.jp/en/about/organisation/principle/ [last accessed 30 December 2018].
7 The "King of the Mountain" model is a stylised model drawing on rational choice proposed by Melville and Mironyuk (2016) and Melville et al. (2014) that shows a desired state of authoritarian equilibrium when political elites in post-Soviet autocracies have guaranteed access to economic and political rents. It shows a curvilinear relationship between the quality of institutions and ability to extract rents. The "King of the Mountain" is the political elite(s) who has a monopoly on extracting rents from society, leading

to a "frozen equilibrium" where all political actors accept the rules and expected outcomes and a situation where they have no incentives to change the status quo or improve the quality of institutions. However, a post-Soviet autocratic leader is never "King of the Mountain" on his/her own as they must always try to build alliances and loyalties with different elite groups and they are always faced with the fundamental uncertainty of who will succeed him/her that is embedded in autocratic rule (Melville and Mironyuk, 2016).

8 There have been many terms used to describe this period in Russia's history. Some examples include Colton and McFaul's (2003) "managed democracy" to describe Putin's first presidential term in 2000–2004; semi-authoritarian regime (White, 2003); "stealth authoritarianism" (Hahn, 2004); bureaucratic authoritarianism (Shevtsova, 2005); electoral authoritarianism (Schedler, 2006). From Duncan, "Regime and Ideology in Putin's Russia," in Duncan (2007: 140–141). Andrew Jack, a journalist for the Financial Times based in Russia from 1998 to 2004, described Russia's political system in the early 2000s as a façade of democracy: it was "a system which had parties without ideas, debates without the most important participants, media without criticism" (Jack, 2005: 328).

References

Acemoglu, D., Aghion, P. and Zilibotti, F. (2006) 'Distance to Frontier, Selection, and Economic Growth', *Journal of the European Economic Association* 4/1 (pp. 37–74).

Aghion, P. (2004) 'Growth and Development: A Schumpeterian Approach', *Annals of Economics and Finance* 5 (pp. 1–25).

Aghion, P., Harmgart, H. and Weisshaar, N. (2011) 'Fostering Growth in CEE Countries: A Country-Tailored Approach to Growth Policy', in Radošević, S. and Kaderabkova, A. (eds.) *Challenges for European Innovation Policy: Cohesion And Excellence From A Schumpeterian Perspective*. Cheltenham: Edward Elgar Publishers.

Alchian, A. A. and Woodward, S. (1988) 'The Firm is Dead: Long Live the Firm: A Review of Oliver E. Williamson's The Economic Institutions of Capitalism', *Journal of Economic Literature* 26 (pp. 65–79).

Amann, R. (1986) 'Searching for an Appropriate Concept of Soviet Politics: The Politics of Hesitant Modernization?', *British Journal of Political Science* 16 (pp. 475–494). Available at: http://dx.doi.org/10.1017/S0007123400004531.

Amsden, A. H. (1989) *Asia's Next Giant: South Korea and Late Industrialization*. New York; Oxford: Oxford University Press.

Ang, Y. Y. (2016) *How China Escaped the Poverty Trap*. Ithaca: Cornell University Press.

Åslund, A. (2007) *Russia's Capitalist Revolution: Why Market Reform Succeeded and Democracy Failed*. Washington, DC: Peterson Institute for International Economics.

Berend, I. T. (2000) 'From Regime Change to Sustained Growth in CEE, Chapter 2, UNECE', *Economic Survey of Europe* 2/3. Available at: http://www.unece.org/ead/pub/surv_002.htm, http://www.unece.org/ead/pub/002/002_2.doc, http://www.unece.org/ead/pub/002/002_2.pdf.

Bessonova, E. and Gonchar, K. (2015) 'Bypassing Weak Institutions in a Large Latecomer Economy', *Journal of Institutional Economics*, February (pp. 1–28). Available at: https://doi.org/10.1017/S1744137415000041.

Boddewyn, J. and Doh, J. (2011) 'Global Strategy and the Collaboration of MNEs, NGOs, and Governments for the Provisioning of Collective Goods in Emerging Markets', *Global Strategy Journal* 1/3–4 (pp. 345–361). Available at: http://dx.doi.org/10.1002/gsj.26.

Boschma, R. A. and Martin, R. L. (eds.) (2010) 'Complexity Thinking and Evolutionary Economic Geography', in *The Handbook of Evolutionary Economic Geography*. Cheltenham: Edward Elgar Publishing.

Brown, A., Shevtsova, L. and Aron, L. (2009) 'Reading Russia', *Journal of Democracy Special Issue* 20/2 (pp. 1–29).

Castells, M. and Hall, P. (1994) *Technopoles of the World: The Making of Twenty-First-Century Industrial Complexes*. London: Routledge.

Colton, T. and McFaul, M. (2003) *Popular Choice and Managed Democracy: The Russian Elections of 1999 and 2000*. Washington, DC: Brookings Institution Press.

Cooke, P., Asheim, B., Boschma, R., Martin, R., Schwartz, D. and Tödtling, F. (eds.) (2011) *Handbook of Regional Innovation and Growth*. Cheltenham: Edward Elgar. Available at: https://doi-org.ezproxy.sussex.ac.uk/10.4337/9780857931504.

Cooper, J. (1998) *Role of the State in Promoting Technical Progress*. NATO Report. Available at: www.nato.int/docu/colloq/1998/23-cooper.pdf [last accessed 30 December 2018].

DeBresson, C. (1989) 'Breeding Innovation Clusters: A Source of Dynamic Development', *World Development* 17/1 (pp. 1–16).

Demchak, C. (1995) 'Modernizing Military Organizations and Political Control in Central Europe', *Journal of Public Policy* 15/2 (pp. 111–152).

Demchak, C. (2017–2018) 'Defending Democracies in a Cybered World', *The Brown Journal of World Affairs* (Fall 2017/Winter 2018) 24/1 (pp. 139–157).

Dominguez Lacasa, I., Jindra, B., Radošević, S. and Shubbak, M. (2018) 'Paths of Technology Upgrading in the BRICS Economies', *Research Policy* 48/1 (pp. 262–280). Available at: https://doi.org/10.1016/j.respol.2018.08.016 [last accessed 21 July 2021].

Duncan, P. (2007) 'Regime and Ideology in Putin's Russia', in Duncan, P. (ed.) *Convergence and Divergence: Russia and Eastern Europe Into the Twenty-First Century*. London: UCL SSEES (pp. 139–158).

Dyker, D. A. (2012) *Economic Policy Making and Business Culture: Why Is Russia so Different?* London: Imperial College Press.

Edquist, C. (2011) 'Design of Innovation Policy Through Diagnostic Analysis: Identification of Systemic Problems (or Failures)', *Industrial and Corporate Change* 20/6 (pp. 1725–1753). Available at: https://doi.org/10.1093/icc/dtr060.

Fagerberg, J., Mowery, D. and Nelson, R. (eds.) (2005) *The Oxford Handbook of Innovation*. Oxford: Oxford University Press.

Ferreira, M. P., Serra, F. R. and Maccari, E. A. (2012) 'When the Innovator Fails to Capture Rents from Innovation', *Latin American Business Review* 13/3 (pp. 199–217). Available at: http://dx.doi.org 10.1080/10978526.2012.730022.

Foray, D. (2017) 'The Economic Fundamentals of Smart Specialization Strategies', in Radošević, S., Curaj, A., Andreescu, L., Gheorgiu, L. and Wade, I. (eds.) *Advances in the Theory and Practice of Smart Specialization*. Oxford: Elsevier (pp. 37–50).

Freeman, C. (1987) *Technology Policy and Economic Performance – Lessons from Japan*. London and New York: Pinter Publishers.

Freeman, C. (2002) 'Continental, National and Sub-National Innovation Systems – Complementarity and Economic Growth', *Research Policy* 31 (pp. 191–211).

Gaddy, C. G. and Ickes, B. W. (2005) 'Resource Rents and the Russian Economy,' *Eurasian Geography and Economics*, 46/8 (pp. 559–583). Available at: http://dx.doi.org/10.2747/1538-7216.46.8.559 [last accessed 31 October 2019].

Gaddy, C. G. and Ickes, B. W. (2013) *Bear Traps on Russia's Road to Modernization*. Abingdon, Oxon, UK; New York, NY: Routledge.

Garner, C. (2006) 'Viewpoint: Science Cities: Refreshing the Concept for 21st-Century Places', *The Town Planning Review* 77/5 (pp. i–vi). Liverpool University Press. Available at: https://www.jstor.org/stable/41229022 [last accessed 21 March 2022].

Gilpin, R. (2001) *Global Political Economy: Understanding the International Economic Order*. Oxford: Princeton University Press.

Glikin, M. and Kostenko, N. (2010) 'Chudo vozhmozhno' [transl. 'Miracle is possible']. *Vedomosti* Interview With Vladislav Surkov. Vedomosti Newspaper, No. 26, 15 February. Moscow: Russia. Available at: https://www.vedomosti.ru/newspaper/articles/2010/02/15/vladislav-surkov-zovet-chitatelej-vedomostej-proektirovat-kremnievuyu-dolinu [last accessed on 7 December 2017].

Gonchar, K., Kuznetsov, Y., and Wade, I. (2017) 'Lessons for a Policy Maker From Real-Life Self-Discovery in Economies With Weak Institutions', in Radošević, S., Curaj, A., Andreescu, L., Gheorgiu, L. and Wade, I. (eds.) *Advances in the Theory and Practice of Smart Specialization*. Oxford: Elsevier (pp. 225–248).

Graham, L. (2013) *Lonely Ideas: Can Russia Compete?* Cambridge, MA: The MIT Press.

Graham, L. and Dezhina, I. (2008) *Science in the New Russia: Crisis, Aid, Reform*. Bloomington, IN: Indiana University Press.

Grimm, V. and Railsback, S. F. (2005) *Individual-based Modeling and Ecology*. Princeton, NJ: Princeton University Press.

Gustafsson, L. and Sternad, M. (2010) 'Consistent Micro, Macro, and State-based Population Modelling', *Mathematical Biosciences* 225/2 (pp. 94–107). Available at: https://doi.org/10.1016/j.mbs.2010.02.003. PMID 20171974.

Haber, S. (2008) 'Authoritarian Government', in Wittman, D. A. and Weingast, B. R. (eds.) *The Oxford Handbook of Political Economy*. Oxford: Oxford University Press (pp. 1–17). Available at: http://dx.doi.org/10.1093/oxfordhb/9780199548477.003.0038 [last accessed 4 June 2019].

Hahn, G. M. (2004) 'Managed Democracy?: The Establishment of Stealth Authoritarianism in St. Petersburg', *Demokratizatsiya* 12, 2/Spring 2004 (pp. 185–232). Available at: http://www.demokratizatsiya.org/bin/pdf/DEM%2012-2%20Hahn.pdf.

Havas, A., Izsak, K., Markianidou, P. and Radošević, S. (2015) *Comparative Analysis of Policy-Mixes of Research and Innovation Policies in Central and Eastern European Countries*. GRINCOH Working Paper Series, Paper No. 3.12. Available at: https://www.researchgate.net/publication/274060907_Comparative_Analysis_of_Policy-Mixes_of_Research_and_Innovation_Policies_in_Central_and_Eastern_European_Countries.

Hellman, J. S. (1998) 'Winners Take All, The Politics of Partial Reform in Postcommunist Transitions', *World Politics* 50/2 (pp. 203–234). Available at: http://dx.doi.org/ https://doi.org/10.1017/S0043887100008091.

Henderson, J. and Ferguson, A. (2014) *International Partnership in Russia. Conclusions From the Oil and Gas Industry*. London: Palgrave Macmillan.

Jack, A. (2005) *Inside Putin's Russia: Can There Be Reform Without Democracy?* Oxford: Oxford University Press.

Kanellou, D., Radošević, S. and Tseokuras, G. (2019) *The Trade-Off Between Accountability and Experimentation in Innovation and Industrial Policy: Learning Networks as a Solution?* Working Paper No. 24 for the GROWINPRO (Growth, Welfare, Innovation, Productivity) Project Funded by Horizon 2020, Grant Agreement No. 822781, November. Available at: http://www.growinpro.eu/wp-content/uploads/2019/11/working_paper_2019_24.pdf.

Khan, M. H. (2015) 'The Role of Industrial Policy: Lessons from Asia', in Bailey, D., Cowling, K. and Tomlinson, P. R. (eds.) *New Perspectives on Industrial Policy for a Modern Britain*. Oxford: Oxford University Press (pp. 79–98). Available at: http://eprints.soas.ac.uk/19849/ [last accessed 7 December 2017].

Khan, M. H. (2017) 'Introduction: Political Settlements and the Analysis of Institutions', *African Affairs* (pp. 1–20). Available at: https://doi.org/10.1093/afraf/adx044 [last accessed 7 December 2017].

Kinossian, N. and Morgan, K. (2014) 'Development by Decree: The Limits of "Authoritarian Modernization" in the Russian Federation', *International Journal of Urban and Regional* Research 38/5 (pp. 1678–1696). Available at: http://dx.doi.org/10.1111/1468-2427.12159.

Kirzner, I. M. (1997) 'Entrepreneurial Discovery and the Competitive Market Process: An Austrian Approach', *Journal of Economic Literature* XXXV/1 (pp. 60–85). Available at: https://search-proquest-com.libproxy.ucl.ac.uk/docview/839056138?accountid=14511 [last accessed 7 December 2020].\

Kock, C. F. and Gullien, M. F. (2001) 'Strategy and Structure in Developing Countries: Business Group as an Evolutionary Response to Opportunities for Unrelated Diversification', *Industrial and Corporate Change* 10/4 (pp. 77–113).

Kogle, D. F. (2015) 'Editorial: Evolutionary Economic Geography – Theoretical and Empirical Progress', *Regional Studies* 49/5 (pp. 705–711). Available at: https://doi.org/10.1080/00343404.2015.1033178 [last accessed 7 December 2017].

Kogut, B. and Zanader, U. (2000) 'Did Socialism Fail to Innovate? A Natural Experiment of the Two Zeiss Companies', *American Sociological Review* 65, April (pp. 169–190).

Kokorotsikos, P., Lund, E., Peretti, L. and Taylor, S. (2018) *Reshaping the functional and operational capacity of Sofia Tech Park*. Report by an Independent Panel of international experts. Brussels: European Commission Publication Office. Available at: https://knowledge4policy.ec.europa.eu/sites/default/files/report_reshaping_the_functional_and_operational_capacity_of_sofia_tech_park_2018.pdf [last accessed 22 March 2022].

Kordonsky, S. G. (2016) *Socio-Economic Foundations of the Russian Post-Soviet Regime: The Resource-Based Economy and Estate-Based Social Structure of Contemporary Russia*. Stuttgart: Ibidem-Verlag. Summary. Available at: https://publications.hse.ru/books/179279268 [last accessed 31 October 2019].

Lankes, N. H. and Venables, A. (1996) 'Foreign Direct Investment in Economic Transition: The Changing Pattern of Investments', *Economics of Transition* 4 (pp. 331–347).

Lapin, N. I. (2013) 'The Sociocultural Factors of Russian Stagnation and Modernization', *Russian Social Science Review* 54/4 (pp. 4–32), Available at: https://doi.org/10.1080/10611428.2013.11065517.

Lazonick, W. (2002) 'The Theory of Innovative Enterprise', in Warner, M. (ed.) *International Encyclopaedia of Business and Management*. Thomson Learning (pp. 3055–3076). Available at: www.uml.edu/centers/CIC/Research/Lazonick_Research/Older_Research/Theory_of_the_Firm/eibm.pdf [last accessed 15 June 2021].

Lazonick, W. and Mazzucato, M. (2012) *The Risk-Reward Nexus in the Innovation-Inequality Relationship: Who Takes the Risks? Who Gets the Rewards?* FINNOV Discussion Paper, March. Available at: http://steps-centre.org/wp-content/uploads/Mazzucato-STEPS-seminar-paper.pdf [last accessed 15 June 2021].

Ledeneva, A. (2013) *Can Russia Modernise? Sistema, Power Networks and Informal Governance*. Cambridge: Cambridge University Press.

Ledeneva, A. (ed.). (2018a). *The Global Encyclopaedia of Informality: Understanding Social and Cultural Complexity*, Volume 1. London: UCL Press. Available at: https://doi.org/10.14324/111.9781911307907.

Ledeneva, A. (ed.). (2018b) *The Global Encyclopaedia of Informality: Understanding Social and Cultural Complexity*, Volume 2. London: UCL Press. Available at: https://doi.org/10.14324/111.9781787351899.

List, F. (1841) *The National System of Political Economy*. London: Longmans, Green and Co.

Lundvall, B. A. (ed.) (1992) *National Systems of Innovation – Towards a Theory of Innovation and Interactive Learning*. London: Pinter Publishers.

Malle, S. (2013) 'Economic Modernisation and Diversification in Russia: Constraints and Challenges', *Journal of Eurasian Studies* 4 (pp. 78–99).

Mandel, M. (2011) *Scale and Innovation in Today's Economy*. Washington, DC: Progressive Policy Institute, Policy Memo, December.

Melville, A. and Mironyuk, M. (2016) 'Bad Enough Governance: State Capacity and Quality of Institutions in Post-Soviet Autocracies', *Post-Soviet Affairs* 32/2 (pp. 132–151). Available at: http://dx.doi.org/10.1080/1060586X.2015.1052215.

Mrkajic, B. (2017) 'Business Incubation Models and Institutionally Void Environments', *Technovation* 68 (pp. 44–55). Available at: http://dx.doi.org/10.1016/j.technovation.2017.09.001.

Nelson, R. R. and Winter, S. G. (1982) *An Evolutionary Theory of Economic Change*. Cambridge, MA: Harvard University Press.

Niazi, M. and Hussain, A. (2011) 'Agent-based Computing from Multi-agent Systems to Agent-Based Models: A Visual Survey', *Scientometrics* 89/2 (pp. 479–499). arXiv:1708.05872. Available at: https://doi.org/10.1007/s11192-011-0468-9.

Nove, A. (1989) *Glasnost in Action: Cultural Renaissance in Russia*. London: Routledge.

OECD (Organisation for Economic Cooperation and Development) (1992) *Technology and the Economy – the Key Relationships*. Paris: OECD.

Park, S-C. (1999) 'The Comparative Role of High-Tech-Oriented Public Institutions and Private Companies in Tsukuba Science City', *AI & Soc* 13 (pp. 301–311).

Phelps, N. A., Atienza, M. and Arias, M. (2015) 'Encore for the Enclave: The Changing Nature of the Industry Enclave with Illustrations from the Mining Industry in Chile: Encore for the Enclave', *Economic Geography* 2015-04, 91/2 (pp. 119–146).

Radošević, S. (2011a) 'Inaugural Lecture: Beyond Transition: Systems of Innovation, and Growth Perspectives in Eastern Europe', Presented at School of Slavonic and East European Studies, University College London. Available at: http://discovery.ucl.ac.uk/1326257/ [last accessed 15 June 2021].

Radošević, S. (2011b) 'Science – Industry Links in Central and Eastern Europe and the Commonwealth of Independent States: Conventional Policy Wisdom Facing Reality', *Science and Public Policy* 38/5 (pp. 365–378). Available at: https://doi.org/10.3152/030234211X12924093660435 [last accessed 7 December 2017].

Radošević, S. (2017) 'Assessing EU Smart Specialization Policy in a Comparative Perspective' in Radošević, S., Curaj, A., Andreescu, L., Gheorgiu, L. and Wade, I. (eds.) *Advances in the Theory and Practice of Smart Specialization*. Oxford: Elsevier (pp. 1–36).

Radošević, S. and Lepori, B. (2009) 'Public Research Funding Systems in Central and Eastern Europe: Between Excellence and Relevance', *Science and Public Policy* 36/9 (pp. 659–666).

Reinert, E. and Kattel, R. (2010) 'Modernizing Russia: Round III. Russia and the Other BRIC Countries: Forging Ahead, Catching Up or Falling Behind?' *A Preliminary Report Prepared by The Other Canon Foundation, Norway, for the Global Policy Forum* "The Modern State: Standards of Democracy and Criteria of Efficiency", Russia, Yaroslavl, 9–10 September 2010. Available at: http://hum.ttu.ee/wp/paper32.pdf [last accessed 22 March 2022].

Rodrik, D. (2008) 'Second-Best Institutions', *American Economic Review, American Economic Association*, 98/2 (pp. 100–104).

Romer, P. (1993), 'Idea Gaps and Object Gaps in Economic Development', *Journal of Monetary Economics, Elsevier* 32/3 (pp. 543–573).

Rutland, P. (2015) 'Competing Visions of Modernity: Reflections on the Russian Experience', Paper Prepared for a Conference on Modernization Sponsored by the Journal History and Theory and the Chinese Academy of Social Science in Guilin, China, 9–10 May 2015.

Schedler, A. (ed.) (2006) *Electoral Authoritarianism: The Dynamics of Unfree Competition*. Boulder, Colorado: L. Rienner Publishers, Inc.

Scott, B. R. (2011) *Capitalism: Its Origins and Evolution as a System of Governance*. New York: Springer.

Service, R. (2004) *Stalin: A Biography*. London: Pan Books, Macmillan.

Shevtsova, L. (2005) *Putin's Russia* (Revised and expanded edition). Washington DC: Carnegie Endowment for International Peace.

Slade, G. (2006) 'Deconstructing the Millennium Manifesto: The Yeltsin-Putin Transition and the Rebirth of Ideology', Article published on the website 'GeoHistory Today' maintained by The School of Russian and Asian Studies, Woodside, California, USA on 31 May 2006. Available at: https://geohistory.today/deconstructing-millennium-manifesto/ [last accessed 21 March 2022].

Stiglitz, J. E. (1999) 'Whither Reform? Ten Years of the Transition', in Pleskovic, B. and Stiglitz, J. E. (eds.) *Annual Bank Conference Development Economics*. Washington, DC: The World Bank (pp. 27–56).

Strambach, S. (2008) *Path Dependency and Path Plasticity: The Co-Evolution of Institutions and Innovation – the German Customized Business Software Industry*. IDEAS Working Paper Series from RePEc (pp. 1–31). Available at: http://ideas.repec.org/p/pum/wpaper/2008-02.html [last accessed 30 May 2019].

Su, Y. S., Kajikawa, Y., Tsujimoto, M. and Chen, J. (eds.) (2018) 'Innovation Ecosystems: Theory, Evidence, Practice, and Implications', *Technological Forecasting and Social Change* 136 (pp. 14–17). Available at: https://doi.org/10.1016/j.techfore.2018.08.009 [last accessed 21 July 2021].

Teubal, M. and Kuznetsov, Y. (2012) 'Sequencing Public Interventions to Support Techno-entrepreneurship', in de Mello, L. and Dutz, M. A. (eds.) *Promoting Inclusive Growth: Challenges and Policies*. OECD: Paris.

Weisskoff, R. and Wolff, E. (1977) 'Linkages and Leakages: Industrial Tracking in an Enclave Economy' *Economic Development and Cultural Change*, 1977-07-01, 25/4 (pp. 607–628).

White, S. (2003) 'Rethinking Postcommunist Transition', *Government and Opposition* 38/4 (pp. 417–435). Available at: http://dx.doi.org/10.1111/1477-7053.t01-1-00022.

Woolthuis, R. K., Lankhuizen, M. and Gilsing, V. (2005) 'A System Failure Framework for Innovation Policy Design', *Technovation* 25 (pp. 609–619). Available at: https://doi.org/10.1016/j.technovation.2003.11.002 [last accessed 21 July 2021].

Yakovlev, A. (2014) 'Russian Modernization: Between the Need for New Players and the Fear of Losing Control of Rent Sources', *Journal of Eurasian Studies* 5/1 (pp. 10–20). Available at: http://dx.doi.org/10.1016/j.euras.2013.09.004.

3 Science, technology, and innovation in the Soviet Union and Russia

An overview of key characteristics and performance

Introduction

To provide context for this book on innovation in Russia, an overview of research, development, and innovation (RDI) in the Soviet period and the post-Soviet era is important. How was science and innovation organised in the Soviet Union? Who provided the financial resources? What were the state's main goals? How did the collapse of the Soviet Union affect RDI? What have been the main trends in the 1990s and 2000s in relation to who funds and implements RDI? This is the national level framework in which the specific infrastructure projects analysed in the book were undertaken. Legacies from the Soviet era have effects on the operations and performance of innovation infrastructure in contemporary Russia, so understanding how the Soviet Union structured RDI and how Russia tried to restructure its economy and society after the collapse of the USSR is important.

The broad-brush strokes of science and technology in the Soviet Union are the following four statements: the prominence of big science (large volumes of resources allocated and many researchers employed); very centralised and hierarchical manner in which science and technology were organised; strong institutional separation of teaching, and fundamental and applied research; and focused heavily on the military as opposed to civilian R&D. Of course, there were differences across sectors. Moreover, there were reforms to the science and technology system over time. Following the economic stagnation in the 1970s and 1980s, late Soviet political leaders made efforts to introduce horizontal structures (e.g. production associations and science production-associations) and bring in commercialisation. They aimed to overcome the systemic weaknesses which were the cause of the underperformance of Soviet science relative to the large volume of resources allocated for science by the state (Graham and Dezhina, 2008).

This chapter is structured as follows. The following section briefly describes RDI in the Soviet Union. After that, the chapter surveys the key trends in RDI from the early 1990s up to 2016 examining R&D inputs, notably R&D funding and R&D performing sectors (particularly the predominance of the state in both financing and performing R&D), and the balance in Russia between R&D supply and demand. Next, chapter 3 then outlines Russia's science, technology, and innovation (STI) outcomes, focusing on trends in publications, citation practices, university–industry

DOI: 10.4324/9781003256205-3

collaboration, and patenting. The penultimate section gives an overview of R&D and innovation policies in the period from 1991 to 2015 and the new policy instruments and organisational structures that have been implemented in Russia since the early 1990s to support innovation. The final section concludes the chapter.

Science & technology and innovation in the USSR

To understand innovation in contemporary Russia, we need to understand the working and performance of R&D and innovation in the Soviet period. The Soviet legacies persist to this day in the way science and innovation are implemented in Russia (Cooper, 2008). The Soviet Union first developed a national policy for science in 1926, nearly a decade after the fall of the Tsarist Empire (Josephson, 1988). The Communist Party held ultimate power in the Soviet Union, both in the political and economic sphere. The Soviet state-planned science and technology (S&T) system drew on Marxist philosophical ideas and is still a benchmark for other state-planned S&T systems, for example in China since 1949 (Karaulova and Gershman, 2015; Klochikhin, 2013).

There were four key features of R&D and RDI in the USSR that help to understand the trends in the latter in post-Soviet Russia because of their legacy influences. These can be seen in Table 3.1.

First, since 1926, the Soviet Union conceived of **science on a big scale**. The state allocated significant resources and employed many researchers. This is reflected in a comparatively high ratio of spending on R&D to gross national product of 2.5%. Despite this investment, the USSR's achievements in technological innovation were overall unimpressive although it performed comparatively well in military industry (Cooper, 2008).

Second, the way R&D and innovation were managed was **very centralised and hierarchical**. It was centrally planned and funded; the aims and mission of science were issued in Moscow.

Third, there were **no linkages between the three main pyramids**: universities, the Academy of Science Research Institutes, and the industrial and defence sectors (Zaleski et al., 1969; Cooper, 2008). Universities were for teaching and did very little R&D. Academy of Science Institutes carried out fundamental R&D and some applied R&D, played a pivotal role in the overall science policy of the USSR, and held a position of prestige in society (Cooper, 2008). Meanwhile, the industrial

Table 3.1 Key features of research and development and innovation in the USSR

(1)	Big scale of science
(2)	Very centralised and hierarchical governance
(3)	Institutional separation of the three pyramids – universities (teaching), Academy of Science (primarily fundamental R&D, no teaching), and industrial and defence (primarily applied R&D although some fundamental R&D carried out)
(4)	Heavy military focus

Table 3.2 The state of Soviet Science (as of January 1991)

Indicators	*Total*	*Science sectors*			
		Academy of sciences	*Higher education*	*Branch sectors*	*Industrial sectors*
No. of organisations performing R&D, units	7,924	1,276	877	5,103	718
R&D expenditure, %	100	12.6	6.8	75.8	4.8
No. of highly skilled R&D personnel with higher education (% of total), including:	1,659,000	164,000 (9.9%)	300,000 (18.1%)	1,095,000 (66%)	100,000 (6%)
Doctor of Sciences	37,700	10,895	16,249	10,443	113
Candidates of Sciences	298,000	53,640	128,438	112,942	2,980

Source: Karaulova and Gershman (2015: 2) based on from *Science of the USSR in figures* (1990).

(engineering departments within industrial enterprises) and defence sector undertook applied R&D (and very little basic R&D). The industrial sector included branch sectors: research institutes, design bureaus, engineering research institutes, and experimental facilities of branch ministries. Most industrial enterprises lacked R&D facilities and the enterprise (industrial) sector employed very few researchers (Cooper, 2012) – just 6% of all highly skilled researchers in 1991 (Table 3.2).

Fourth, Soviet R&D was very **militarised**. In the 1960s–1970s, the USSR spent more than 70% of its R&D budget on military/space sectors, compared to less than 2% of R&D expenditure in Japan in the same period (Table 3.3). Moreover, the spillovers from defence and military sectors to the civil economy were extremely limited. General Secretary Gorbachev and his team introduced a special policy of "conversion" in the 1980s, but this was ineffective because of "organisational barriers, inadequate incentives and a marked quality gap between the military and civilian sectors" (Cooper, 2008: 2).

The operation of the S&T and innovation system in the USSR can be better understood if compared with Japan, a country sharing some similarities with the USSR (Table 3.3). First, in the 1960s–1970s, both countries were in the later stages of industrialisation after suffering extensive damage in the Second World War. Second, both had well-developed education systems with a high proportion of young people studying science and technology. Third, Japan and the USSR relied on technology imports from Western Europe and the United States, although the USSR restricted these imports more. Finally, both countries created long-term visions (missions) for their science and technology system (Freeman, 1987).

However, a key difference was that Japan's science and technology system strongly integrated R&D, production, and import of technology at the enterprise level and had strong linkages between users, producers, and sub-contractors (i.e. linkages between firms and external sources).

The strong role of the military in R&D in the Soviet Union has some continuities with the situation in Russia today. As a share of GDP, Russia has always spent

Table 3.3 National systems of science and technology in Japan and the USSR in the 1960s–1970s

Japan	*USSR*
High GERD/GNP ratio (2.5%). Very low share of military/space R&D (<2% of R&D)	Very high GERD/GNP ratio (approximately 4%). Extremely high share of military/space R&D (>70% of R&D)
High proportion of total R&D at the enterprise level and company-financed (approximately 66%)	Low proportion of total R&D at the enterprise level and company-financed (<10%)
Strong integration of R&D, production and import of technology at the enterprise level	Separation of R&D, production, and import of technology and weak institutional linkages
Strong user–producer and sub-contractor network linkages including R&D	Weak or non-existent linkages between R&D, marketing, production, and procurement
Strong incentives to innovate at the enterprise level involving both management and workforce	Some incentives to innovate made increasingly strong in the 1960s–1970s but offset by other negative disincentives affecting both management and workforce
Intensive experience of competition in international markets	Weak exposure to international competition except in arms race
Increasing amount of fundamental research in industry itself as well as in universities and government institutes	Fundamental research concentrated in Academy of Science Institutes, with poor communications with industry

Source: Freeman (1987: 10)

Table 3.4 Military expenditure as a share of GDP, 1992–2018, selected countries

Country	*1992*	*2000*	*2005*	*2010*	*2015*	*2016*	*2017*	*2018*
United States	4.7%	2.9%	3.9%	4.7%	3.3%	3.2%	3.1%	3.2%
China	*2.5%*	*1.9%*	*2.0%*	*1.9%*	*1.9%*	*1.9%*	*1.9%*	*1.9%*
India	2.7%	2.9%	2.8%	2.7%	2.4%	2.5%	2.5%	2.4%
Pakistan	*6.7%*	*4.2%*	*3.9%*	3.4%	3.6%	3.6%	3.8%	4.0%
Russia	***4.4%***	***3.3%***	***3.3%***	***3.6%***	**4.9%**	**5.5%**	**4.2%**	**3.9%**
France	3.2%	2.5%	2.4%	2.3%	2.3%	2.3%	2.3%	2.3%
Germany	2.0%	1.4%	1.3%	1.4%	1.2%	1.2%	1.2%	1.2%
United Kingdom	3.5%	2.1%	2.2%	2.4%	1.9%	1.8%	1.8%	1.8%

Source: SIPRI Military Expenditure Database. Available at: www.sipri.org/databases/milex [last accessed 1 December 2019].

Note: Figures in italics are SIPRI estimates. Data for the USSR unavailable.

comparatively big sums on the military since 1992, never falling below 3.3% and increasing to 5.5% in 2016 (Table 3.4). To put this in international perspective, China spent between 1.9% and 2.5% of GDP on military, India 2.4%–2.9%, and the United Kingdom 1.8%–3.5%. United States spent about the same as Russia on military as a share of GDP (ranging from 2.9% to 4.7% in the period 1992–2018).

One study by Western academics argued that from 2012, Putin attempted to co-opt the innovation and modernisation initiative (epitomised by Skolkovo) started by President Medvedev by linking it almost exclusively to modernisation of the defence sector. This would have included channelling Skolkovo's R&D results into the defence sector and creating new Skolkovos in Russia's regions that would be attached to defence conglomerates (Gaddy and Ickes, 2013: 97–98). However, the author of this book is not aware of other studies that confirm this in fact happened.

Science & technology and innovation in the post-Soviet period: inputs

What are the key distinguishing features of STI in the Russian Federation? A key feature of STI in post-Soviet Russia is the dominant role of the state both in funding and implementing R&D and innovation. This is a legacy of the Soviet period when the state was the exclusive actor.

Trends in overall expenditures on R&D: mid-1990s to the present

Russia had a relatively significant increase in R&D spending from 1996 to 2015 (Table 3.5). Since 2000, Russia's total share of GDP spent on R&D (basic research, applied research, and experimental development) in the four main sectors, that is business enterprise, government, higher education, and private non-profit has stayed consistently at around 1%, which nonetheless represents quite a substantial volume of investment. Russia had a slight increase in R&D spending as a share of GDP in the period from 2008 to 2010, which corresponds with President Medvedev's technological modernisation policies. Russia's R&D funding increase to around 1% from 2000 and its small rise from 2008 to 2010 correspond with trends in other emerging economies, which increasingly recognise the importance of

Table 3.5 Research and development expenditure (% of GDP) in the Russian Federation and in international comparative perspective: 1996–2015

Country Name	1996	2000	2005	2010	2011	2012	2013	2014	2015
Russian Federation	1.0	1.0	1.1	1.1	1.0	1.0	1.1	1.1	1.1
Israel	2.6	3.9	4.0	3.9	4.0	4.2	4.1	4.3	4.3
Germany	2.1	2.4	2.4	2.7	2.8	2.9	2.8	2.9	2.9
Belarus	1.0	0.7	0.7	0.7	0.7	0.7	0.7	0.5	0.5
Poland	0.6	0.6	0.6	0.7	0.7	0.9	0.9	0.9	1.0
Spain	0.8	0.9	1.1	1.4	1.3	1.3	1.3	1.2	1.2
Republic of Korea	2.2	2.2	2.6	3.5	3.8	4.0	4.1	4.3	4.2

Source: UNESCO Institute for Statistics. No data available for years 1990–1995. Selected years shown for purposes of brevity. Numbers shown to one decimal place.

Note: Gross domestic expenditures on research and development (R&D) expressed as a percent of GDP. They include both capital and current expenditures in the four main sectors: business enterprise, government, higher education and private non-profit. R&D covers basic research, applied research, and experimental development.

innovation for economic growth and has consequently put innovation on their policy agendas (GCI 2015: 86).

Yet, some other countries have not just maintained but doubled or nearly doubled their spending on R&D between 2000 and 2014 (Table 3.5). The Republic of Korea increased its share of GDP spent on R&D from just over 2% of GDP in 1996 to 4.2% in 2014–2015.

State predominance in R&D funding

State funding for R&D as a share of total R&D expenditure has predominated in Russia from the mid-1990s, a socialist legacy and element of divergence with more developed market economies of the OECD countries and East Asia (China, Japan, Korea, etc.) where R&D funding from the business sector ranged from 35% to 78% in 2017 (HSE, 2019: 281–283). As shown in Table 3.6, except for the period between 1995 and 2000 when the share of state funding decreased from 61.5% to 54.8%, the contribution from the state for R&D has grown in almost every year up until 2015 when it peaked at 69.5%. From 2015 to 2017, the state's share decreased slightly which can be explained by the greater share from business in this period. Business here includes small- and medium-sized enterprises as well as large firms.

As Table 3.7 shows, only just over a quarter (between 26% and 28%) of all spending on R&D came from business enterprises in the Russian Federation between 2011 and 2016. This is low compared to other countries (48% in Brazil, 49% in the United Kingdom, 62% in the United States, and almost 75% in China and Korea in 2015). Moreover, the share of R&D spending by business enterprises in Russia has barely changed since 2011.

However, the share of business enterprise expenditures on R&D of the total spending on R&D (BERD) masks the relatively elevated level of *public* funding to businesses for R&D. This means government subsidies to businesses. Combined direct and indirect public support to business R&D as a percentage of BERD in Russia was 62.7% in 2014 and 59% in 2016. That means that nearly two-thirds of BERD funding originally comes from the state budget. By comparison, combined

Table 3.6 Expenditure on R&D by source of funding and by year (in % of total), 1995–2017

	1995	**2000**	**2005**	**2010**	**2015**	**2017**
Total spending on R&D	100	100	100	100	100	100
State	61.5	54.8	61.9	70.3	69.5	66.2
Business	33.6	32.9	30	25.5	26.5	30.2
Higher educational institutions	0.3	0.3	0.4	0.5	1.2	0.8
Private non-commercial organisations	0.03	0.09	0.03	0.1	0.2	0.2
Foreign sources	4.6	12	7.6	3.5	2.6	2.6

Source: HSE (2019: 90).

Note: State includes resources from the budget and subsidies for maintenance of higher educational institutions, as well as resources for public sector organisations.

Table 3.7 Expenditures by business enterprises on R&D (BERD) in selected countries, 2011–2016

Country	2011	2012	2013	2014	2015	2016
Brazil	45.2	43.1	40.3	44.9	47.5	na
China	73.9	74.0	74.6	75.4	74.7	76.1
France	55.0	55.3	55.1	54.5	54.0	na
Germany	65.6	66.1	65.4	66.0	65.6	na
Israel	37.3	39.4	36.8	35.0	34.3	na
Republic of Korea	73.7	74.7	75.7	75.3	74.5	75.4
Russian Federation	27.7	27.2	28.2	27.1	26.5	28.1
United Kingdom of Great Britain and Northern Ireland	45.9	45.6	46.2	48.0	49.0	na
United States of America	58.4	59.5	61.1	62.0	62.4	62.3

Source: UNESCO Institute for Statistics, http://data.uis.unesco.org/# [last accessed 11 December 2018].

Note: Numbers shown to one decimal place.

direct and indirect public support to business R&D as a percentage of BERD in 2016 was 8.8% in France, 6.8% in the United States, 6% on average for all OECD countries, 3.7% in China, and 3.4% in Germany (OECD MSTI, 2018: 55).

State predominance in implementing R&D

Turning now to which actors perform R&D, Table 3.8 shows a clear and persistent trend of the dominance of Russian-owned organisations and, furthermore, of state-owned (mainly federal level but some regional government) organisations. In 1995, 99.4% of the 4,059 R&D organisations were Russian-owned (predominantly by the Russian state), while by 2016, this share had slightly decreased to 97.7% (of the total number of 4,032 R&D organisations).

Interestingly, the share of privately owned R&D organisations increased fourfold from 4.9% to 21.5% (from 198 organisations in 1995 to 865 organisations in 2016). This is most likely related to the changes in the total number of R&D performing organisations that were surveyed to compile this dataset (a particularly noticeable increase from 2014 to 2015) and the data not being re-weighted accordingly.[1] The share of foreign-owned R&D organisations also increased from 0.02% in 1995 to 1% in 2016, as did the proportion of combined R&D organisations owned by Russia and other countries (from 0.6% to 1.3% between 1995 and 2016).

Researchers in the science sector

It is also interesting to examine the dynamics since the 1990s in numbers of researchers in science as this indicates where the state has prioritised funding.

Table 3.8 Organisations that perform R&D by the type of ownership (1995–2016)

	1995	2000	2005	2010	2011	2012	2013	2014	2015	2016
Total, number	**4059**	**4099**	**3566**	**3492**	**3682**	**3566**	**3605**	**3604**	**4175**	**4032**
Total, %	100	100	100	100	100	100	100	100	100	100
Russian ownership	99.4	98.4	98.5	98.4	98.2	98.3	98.3	98.2	97.7	97.7
State	73.4	71.7	73.8	74.7	72.5	71.8	70.1	69.9	64.3	64.3
Federal	68.6	67.2	69.6	70.6	67.7	67	65.5	65.2	59.7	59.9
Regional	4.8	4.4	4.2	4	4.8	4.8	4.5	4.7	4.6	4.4
Municipal	0.2	0.3	0.2	0.4	0.5	0.4	0.4	0.4	0.4	0.3
Societal organisations	0.4	1.5	0.8	0.8	0.7	0.7	0.7	0.8	1	1.1
Private	4.9	9.5	11.8	13.5	14.4	15.3	16.8	17	21.1	21.5
Mixed (with some state ownership/other mixed)	20.5	15.5	11.8	8.7	9.2	8.4	8.3	8.2	8.6	8.1
Foreign	0.02	0.1	0.2	0.5	0.6	0.4	0.4	0.5	0.9	1
Combined Russian and foreign ownership	0.6	1.4	1.3	1.1	1.3	1.2	1.3	1.4	1.5	1.3

Source: Indicators of Science, HSE, 2018: 39–40. Some categories of ownership omitted from this table for the sake of brevity, including: owned by Russian citizens permanently living overseas, consumer cooperations, and state corporations.

Note: Some R&D organisations had multiple sources of ownership, which explains why the totals sometime exceed 100%.

While there has been a 30% fall in the total number of researchers from 1995 to 2017 (from 518,000 to 319,000), universities have increased the number of researchers they hire (from 35,000 in 1995 to 42,000 in 2017, i.e. an 18% increase). This suggests that the university sector has been the biggest beneficiary of state reforms of science in the 2000s (Table 3.9). Most universities in Russia are state-owned.[2]

On an international level, in comparison, Russia still performs well in terms of numbers of researchers. In absolute numbers of R&D researchers per million residents, Russia had 3,700 in 1996 and 3,250 in 2008. Comparative numbers for China were around 500 in 1996 and 1,000 in 2007 (EBRD, 2012: 71). By 2012, Russia still had a high number of researchers (3,096 per million population), which means it is in 19th place globally (Institute for Statistics, United Nations Educational, Scientific, and Cultural Organization). On this indicator, Russia is on par with the advanced transition countries of the Czech Republic and the Slovak Republic, the European Union average, and not far behind the United Kingdom, Germany, and Belgium (all had approximately 4,000 R&D researchers per million of the population in 2012).

Moreover, as Table 3.10 shows, for total number of researchers in full-time equivalent (FTE) per thousand labour force in 2016, Russia was some way behind the EU28 average (8.1), United States (9.1 in 2014), Japan (10.0), and Korea

Table 3.9 Numbers of Russian researchers by science sector (in thousands, head count)

Sector	*1995*	*2000*	*2013*	*2015*	*2017*	*2017/1995(%)*
Government	146.3	129.7	132.1	134.8	130.1	−11.1
Government academy	91.1	81.8	69.9	68.3	No data	−25.0
Universities	35.5	28.3	42.7	46.0	42.1	+18.6
Enterprises	336.7	267.6	193.7	198.1	186.3	−44.7
Total	**518.7**	**425.9**	**369.0**	**379.4**	**359.8**	**−30.6**

Source: HSE Science indicators (2018: 120); Nauka, Technologii, Innovatsii. Express-information, 22.11.2018. HSE. Available at: https://issek.hse.ru/data/2018/11/22/1141691897/NTI_N_111_22112018.pdf

Table 3.10 Total researchers in full-time equivalent per thousand total employment, selected countries, 2005–2016

Country	*2005*	*2012*	*2014*	*2016*
EU28 (OECD estimates)	6.2	7.5	7.8	8.1
Russian Federation	6.8	6.2	6.2	5.9
Korea	7.9	12.8	13.5	13.8
Japan	10.4	9.9	10.4	10.0
United States	7.6	8.7	9.1	..
Argentina	2.0	2.9	2.9	3.0
China	1.5	1.8	2.0	2.2

Source: OECD (2018)

(13.8) yet still comparatively well-endowed in this resource compared to Argentina (3.0) and China (2.2). Russia had 6.8 researchers FTE per thousand labour force in 2005, which declined to just 5.9 in 2016 due to funding cuts in the R&D sector (OECD Main Science and Technology Indicators, 2018).

However, the average age of Russian researchers is rising. In 2000, about 20% of all researchers were aged over 60; by 2008, this share had risen to 25% (Makarov and Varshavsky, 2013). Nevertheless, a relatively high number of researchers does not indicate productivity of a country's R&D or innovation system, as the following section on outcomes in STI will show.

Sectors performing R&D

Reviewing the institutional R&D systems of 27 countries worldwide using UNESCO data from 2007, Radošević (2011) notes that development is associated with a greater role of the business enterprise sector (BES) in both funding and performing R&D. Radošević (2011) shows a correlation between R&D organisational model and income level of countries in that countries with GDP per capita of USD 15,000 or higher tended to have BES dominated R&D systems (Model 1 in Table 3.11). Russia had a GDP per capita of USD 6,323 in 2003 and an R&D system predominantly performed by the BES sector and funded by the government or state (GOV) in 2007. This put Russia in that year in the same grouping in terms of R&D organisation as Belarus, Croatia, Hungary, Poland, Romania, and Slovakia.

What changes, if any, has Russia's R&D system undergone in the decade since 2007? The country's GDP per capita has increased sharply to approximately USD

Table 3.11 Models of institutional R&D system profiles in international perspective

Dominant performing sector < dominant source sector				
Model 1 – BES<BES	*Model 2 – BES<GOV*	*Model 3 – HES<GOV*	*Model 4 – GOV<GOV*	*Model 5 – GOV<BES*
United States	Slovakia	Portugal	Bulgaria	Kazakhstan
Ireland	Hungary	Estonia	Azerbaijan	
France	Poland	Lithuania		
United Kingdom	Belarus	Turkey		
Austria	Croatia			
Belgium	**Russia**			
Finland	Romania			
Germany				
Spain				
Korea (Republic)				
Slovenia				
Czech Republic				
Latvia				

Source: Radošević (2011: 369) based on UNESCO 2007 database. Own shading and bold highlights.

Note: BES – business enterprise sector. GOV – government. HES – higher education sector.

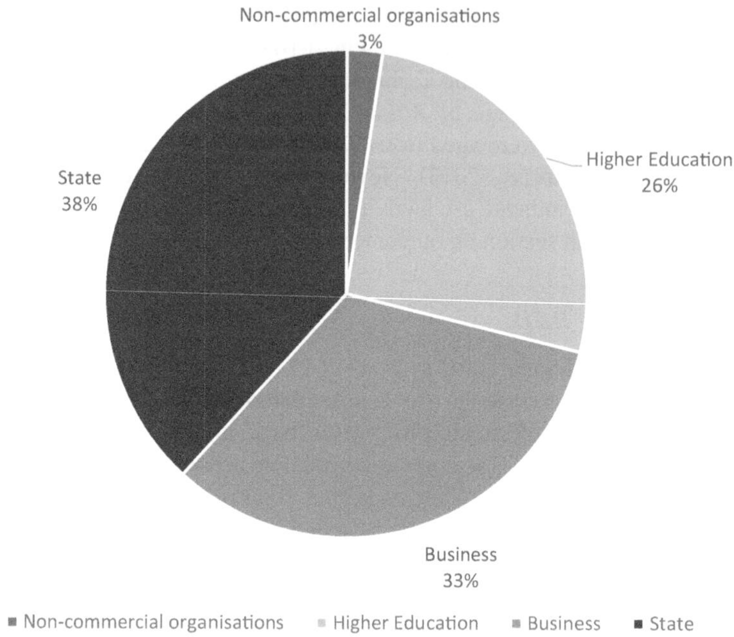

Figure 3.1 Sectors of science performing R&D in the Russian Federation in 2016 (in %)
Source: HSE Science Indicators (2018: 119).

26,000 per capita in purchasing power parity in 2017 (according to the World Bank), so if R&D organisational structure is a developmental or catching up issue as Radošević (2011) suggests, we would expect to see a greater role of BES in performing and funding R&D.

Table 3.11 showed that in 2016, the funding contributions of business enterprise sector remained small (28%). Furthermore, combined direct and indirect public support to business R&D as a percentage of BERD in Russia was relatively high (59% in 2016), indicating that nearly two-thirds of BERD funding originally comes from the state budget.

Figure 3.1 shows that in 2016, about 38% of R&D was carried out by the state, 33% by business, 26% by higher education institutions, and 2.4% by non-commercial organisations. However, since most higher education institutions in Russia are state-owned bodies, effectively nearly two-thirds (64.7%) of R&D is now performed by the government or state (as also shown in Table 3.11).

Quality of R&D supply greater than demand

Figure 3.2 shows an assessment of factors of demand and supply for R&D and technology in Russia. Although this is based on a subjective assessment of factors

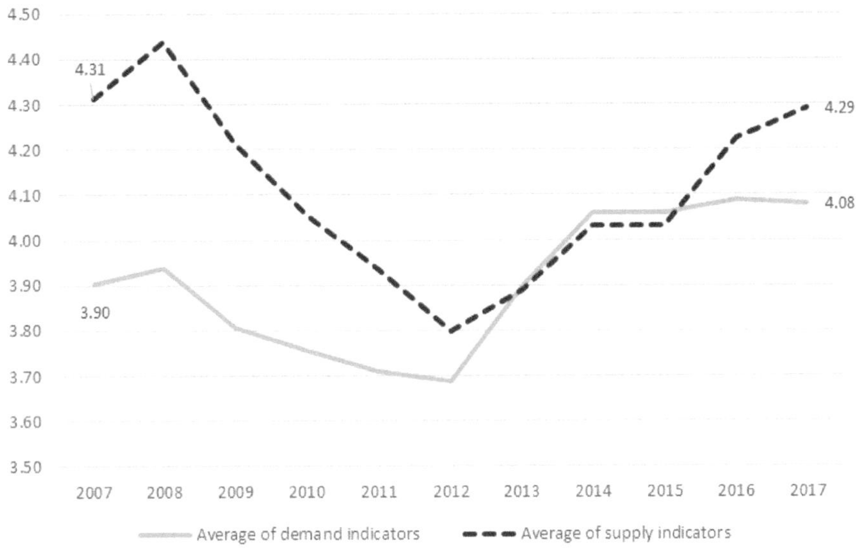

Figure 3.2 Supply and demand for research, technology, and development in Russia, 2007–2017

Source: Global Competitiveness Index, World Economic Forum (2018).

by the business community in Russia, it confirms that Russia – like other post-socialist economies – tends to have a relatively greater supply of research, technology, and development than quality of demand, that is they have supply surpluses and demand gaps. Interestingly, international sanctions imposed on Russia during the Ukraine crisis, which started in February 2014, seem to have contributed to improved demand for domestic research, technology, and development (although level of demand started to increase in 2012, it surpassed supply by 2014). Level of demand exceeded that of supply in 2014–2015. However, after 2015 the old gap between supply and demand reopened, suggesting that demand is the crucial constraint in the Russian research, technology. and development system.

Figure 3.2 shows the averages per year for a set of demand and supply indicators from 2007 to 2017 for the Russian Federation. The five supply indicators included in the analysis are as follows: (i) quality of the education system, (ii) quality of maths and science education, (iii) availability of research and training services, (iv) quality of scientific research institutions, and (v) availability of scientists and engineers. All these indicators were measured on a scale of 1–7 where 7 is the best.

The five demand indicators included in the analysis are as follows: (i) extent of staff training, (ii) on-the-job training, (iii) degree of customer orientation, (iv) buyer sophistication, and (v) firm-level technology absorption. All these indicators were measured on a scale of 1–7 where 7 is the best.

To sum up this section, it seems that Russia has not seen much structural change in R&D in the decade since 2007. This points to not only the effect of development or income levels but also institutional legacies on how R&D is organised. The Russian state continues to be the predominant funder of R&D in 2016. Moreover, if we assume that most higher education institutions in Russia are now state-owned bodies, the state continues to also be the predominant performer of R&D (nearly two-thirds of R&D). As a Soviet legacy, Russia tends to have higher quality of the supply of research, technology, and development (e.g. quality of maths and science education and availability of scientists and engineers) than demand (e.g. staff training in workplaces, on-the-job training, degree of customer orientation, and firm-level technology absorption).

Science & technology and innovation in the post-Soviet period: outcomes

Section 3.3 showed that on balance, Russia has sustained a relatively impressive level of funding of R&D as a share of GDP. What are the key outcomes of this investment? This section reviews the evidence in publications, citation impacts, university–industry collaboration, and patents.

Internationally indexed publications as indicator of scientific community global integration

Russia has made some progress in terms of greater integration into global scientific communities. One way of measuring this is to look at the share of scientific articles and reviews published by scholars based in Russia that are indexed in the international Web of Science and Scopus databases (Table 3.12). Russia increased its share of articles and reviews indexed in Web of Science from 1.95% in 2012 to 2.25% in 2016 (i.e. a 30% increase); Russia performed even better for articles and reviews indexed in Scopus where it increased its share to 2.77% in 2016 (i.e. a 90% increase since 2012). However, despite this improvement in international indexing performance, as of 2016 Russia had not fulfilled its own target set out in

Table 3.12 Increase in the share of Russian scientific articles and reviews indexed in Web of Science/Scopus

Year	*Web of science (articles + reviews), %*	*Scopus (articles + reviews), %*
2012	1.95	1.87
2013	1.94	2.01
2014	1.97	2.18
2015	2.18	2.52
2016	2.25	2.77

Source: Moed, H., Markusova, V., and Akoev, M. (2018). *Scientometrics*. Available at: https://doi.org/10.1007/s11192-018-2769-8

a May 2012 Presidential Decree of increasing its global share of publications in Web of Science to 2.44% by 2015.

Publications

In terms of total absolute number of published scientific and technical journal articles in the early 21st century, Russia does comparatively well. Russia nearly doubled its article output from 2003 to 2016 according to data from the World Development Indicators. Per capita volume of articles published almost doubled in the same period too (Figure 3.3). Such an increase can be explained by policies introduced during this period to boost scientific publications, notably the Project 5–100 programme introduced in 2013. It is important to remember, however, that this dataset only considers scientific and technical journal articles in a limited range of scientific and engineering fields: physics, biology, chemistry, mathematics, clinical medicine, biomedical research, engineering and technology, and earth and space sciences. These fields are ones in which Russia has long-held comparative strengths.

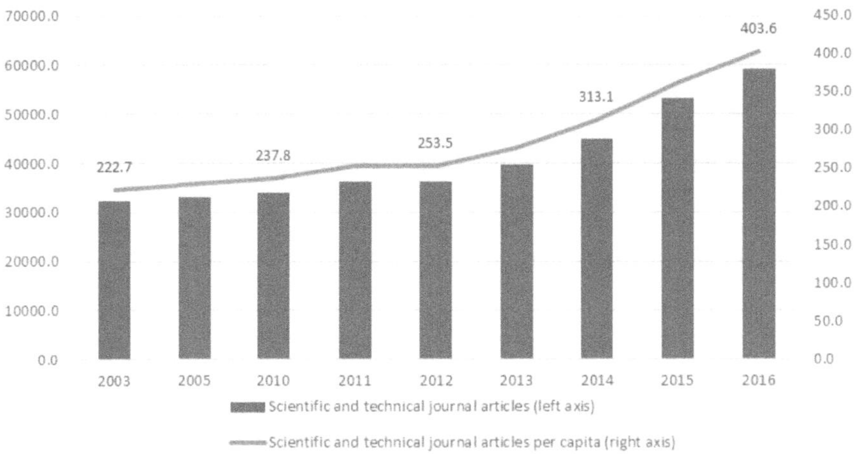

Figure 3.3 Number of scientific and technical journal articles with author(s) from Russia 2003 to 2016, in absolute numbers (bars) and per capita relative to total population (line)

Source: World Development Indicators, last updated: 21 September 2018.

Data for annual population of Russia are measured in millions of people and are taken from the Russian Federal Statistics Service. Available at: www.gks.ru/free_doc/doc_2016/rusfig/rus16e.pdf [last accessed 1 June 2019].

Note: Chart shows data gathered from National Science Foundation and Science and Engineering Indicators on total number of scientific and technical journal articles per country in a given year, that is the number of scientific and engineering articles published in the following fields: physics, biology, chemistry, mathematics, clinical medicine, biomedical research, engineering and technology, and earth and space sciences.

Table 3.13 Russia in international comparison for overall citation impact, 2017

Rank	*Country*	*Citations per document*	*H index*
1	United States	24.66	2,222
2	United Kingdom	22.43	1,373
3	Germany	20.29	1,203
4	Canada	22.6	1,102
5	France	19.91	1,094
6	Japan	15.55	967
7	Netherlands	26.46	957
8	Italy	18.49	953
9	Switzerland	27.38	919
10	Australia	19.83	914
13	China	8.27	794
17	South Korea	12.95	624
22	Russian Federation	7.24	540

Source: Scopus/Scimagojr (2018), Available at: www.scimagojr.com/countryrank.php?order=h&ord=desc&min=0&min_type=itp [last accessed 1 June 2019].

Citation impacts as indicator of global impact

Russian science has improved its international performance in terms of citation impacts from 1996 to 2016. As shown in Table 3.13, Russia was the 22nd country globally in terms of overall citation impact across all disciplines captured by the Scopus database in 2017. However, Russian federal universities and the group of 21 leading universities participating in the centrally run "Project 5–100" lagged far behind the C9 League of nine universities in mainland China and the Ivy League universities in the United States by 2016 in terms of aggregate field-weighted citation impact (Sterligov, 2018: 19).

Innovation – university–industry collaboration

The literature on innovation systems and policies emphasises the critical importance of linkages between universities and business or industry for innovation (Global Innovation Index, 2014: 49). Such collaboration is key for knowledge and technology transfer. From 2007 to 2017, Russia moderately improved how much collaboration occurs between universities and industry. Russia's average score in 2017 was 3.6 (where 7 is the best meaning "collaborates extensively") compared to 5.5 in Israel and 5.3 in Germany (Global Competitiveness Index, 2015).[3]

Innovation – patents

How does Russia compare on international patenting – a widely used indicator of innovation output – with other developing or emerging economies? Data from the World Bank show how Russia compares with Brazil, India, China, and South

Africa as well as Indonesia, Mexico, and Japan in terms of patent applications filed through the Patent Cooperation Treaty (PCT) or a national patent office over seven years between 2005 and 2012.[4]

Russia (followed closely by Brazil and India) saw the *biggest percentage increase* from 2005 to 2012 – a huge increase of 80% (Russia) and 75% (Brazil and India). Russia's increase may be associated with the government's modernisation and innovation policies which started around 2008.

Mexico and Russia had approximately the same number of PCT applications in 2012–14,020 for Mexico and 15,510 for Russia. The difference is that Russia saw a huge increase since 2005 while the number of Mexico's PCT applications remained relatively stable in this period. China saw a steady increase in PCT applications since 2005, from 79,842 to over 117,000 in 2012 (a 47% increase). Only Japan saw a percentage decrease (of 5.6%) in PCT applications between 2005 and 2012.

A longer-term perspective to understand Russia's international patenting from the 1990s up to the present shows that Russia slowly increased its total number of patent applications (direct and PCT national phase entries) from 1994 to 2016. Total patent applications (both direct and PCT national phase entries) from Russia increased slowly in the second half of the 1990s yet picked up from 2004 to 2005, reflecting the increased state spending on R&D and science from 2000. After the global financial crisis of 2008, patent applications from Russia rose more sharply to reach over 1200 in 2016.

From a comparative perspective, Russia in 2016 was in 5th position behind Korea, Germany, Israel, and Spain for total patent applications (Table 3.14). Korea, Germany, Israel, and Spain are all categorised as "innovation-driven economies" (Global Competitiveness Index, 2015). Hence, Russia's performance for total patent applications was relatively weak.

Russian patenting patterns

Patterns in patenting applications to the Russian patent office indicate the level of innovative technologies that are new for Russia but not necessarily novel for the rest of the world. These patents are, however, not a good measure of innovation outputs because many Russian firms (37%) prefer commercial secrecy to patents to protect their intellectual property and assets, according to the European Commission's "Community Innovation Survey 3" data from 1998 to 2000 (OECD, 2007).

As shown in Table 3.15, the number of submitted Russian patent applications nearly doubled from 1995 to 2016, of which 64% in 2016 were by Russian applicants. This indicates that the Russian research, technology, and development system does not have many foreign scientists or inventors. Not surprisingly, the total number of Russian patents *issued* was lower each year (except for 1995 when patents issued in exchange for invention certificates were included) because of the time needed to process patent applications. The total number of active Russian patents tripled from 1995 to 2016 (76,186 to 230,870 respectively), indicating

Table 3.14 Total patent applications (direct and PCT national phase entries, Russian Federation in international perspective, 1995–2016

Country of origin	1995	2000	2005	2010	2011	2012	2013	2014	2015	2016
Belarus	..	3	4	11	6	13	14	16	22	22
Czech Republic	14	52	81	288	271	388	403	469	474	566
Germany	11853	17706	20664	27702	27935	29195	30551	30193	30016	31201
Spain	357	549	701	1422	1501	1641	1707	1640	1671	1790
Hungary	70	107	131	246	235	280	273	321	311	293
Israel	1072	2508	3157	5149	5436	6455	7237	7352	7882	8253
Republic of Korea	2820	5705	17217	26040	27289	29481	33499	36744	38205	37341
Poland	19	33	102	185	197	307	377	463	507	496
Romania	7	12	18	82	93	94	124	147	165	142
Russian Federation	221	382	366	606	719	888	959	1007	991	1219
Ukraine	..	9	37	64	104	124	135	131	138	144

Source: WIPO statistics database. Last updated: May 2018.

Table 3.15 Russian patent applications and patents issued for inventions in Russia, 1995–2016

	1995	*2000*	*2005*	*2010*	*2011*	*2012*	*2013*	*2014*	*2015*	*2016*
Total submitted patent applications in Russia	22,202	28,688	32,254	42,500	41,414	44,211	44,914	40,308	45,517	41,587
of which, applicants are:										
Russian	17,551	23,377	23,644	28,722	26,495	28,701	28,765	24,072	29,269	26,795
Foreign	4,651	5,311	8,610	13,778	14,919	15,510	16,149	16,236	16,248	14,792
Total issued patents in Russia	31,556*	17,592	23,390	30,322	29,999	32,880	31,638	33,950	34,706	33,536
of which, applicants are:										
Russian	20,861	14,444	19,447	21,627	20,339	22,481	21,378	23,065	22,560	21,020
Foreign	4,772	3,148	3,943	8,695	9,660	10,399	10,260	10,885	12,146	12,516
Active patents in Russia	76,186	144,325	123,089	181,904	168,558	181,515	194,248	208,320	218,974	230,870

Source: HSE *Indicators of Science: Statistical handbook* (2018: 226). Moscow: Higher School of Economics.

*Including patents issued in exchange for invention certificates.

that obtaining patents from the Russian patent office is somewhat easier than from international patent offices.

Summary

Summarising this section on STI outcomes in post-Soviet Russia, the following are the key messages:

- Russia made progress in terms of greater integration into global scientific communities, as measured by the increased share of scientific articles and reviews published by Russia-based scholars that are indexed in the international Web of Science and Scopus databases from 2012 to 2016.
- In terms of citation impacts, Russia has increased its impact since 1996; however, Russian leading universities still lag far behind China's and the United States' leading universities on this indicator.
- Relative to other emerging economies of the BRICS grouping, Russia had the biggest percentage increase (80%) from 2005 to 2012 in patent applications filed directly through the PCT or indirectly via a national patent office. This growth in international patenting may be associated with the resources Russia invested in R&D, which since the year 2000 have consistently hovered around 1% – quite a substantial volume of investment.
- Controlling for population size, Russia has not seen much change in resident patent applications to all patent offices between 2000 and 2016.
- Patenting in the Russian patent office also saw a similar rising trend from 1995 to 2016, with the number of submitted applications doubled and a tripling of active patents in this 21-year period.
- However, we should remember that registered patents do not mean that the patents are used in industry (OECD, 2007) so Russia's performance in patenting in the last two decades does not tell us much about to what extent Russia's research, technology and development system is responding to, or shaping, industrial demand.
- Much evidence shows the importance of linkages (collaborations) between universities and industry for innovation because of the potential for knowledge and technology transfer. From 2007 to 2017, Russia only moderately improved how much collaboration occurs between universities and industry.

Science & technology and innovation in the post-Soviet period: policies (R&D and innovation)

The Russian state has evolved its STI policy since 1991. It has experimented with introducing a range of policies and organisational forms borrowed or imitated from other countries. Although imitated from abroad, the ways these initiatives have been implemented in Russia are shaped by Russia's post-Soviet institutional context. These efforts have gone some way to tackling the weaknesses of the national innovation system, principally the low levels of science – business linkages and low levels of private sector R&D funding (OECD, 2007).

This section gives an overview of the national policies introduced from the early 1990s to 2015 in Russia, classifying the policies as to whether they are focused on supply, demand, or linkages, or whether they are institutions or laws. It then gives an overview of the main organisational forms and new programmes that have been introduced since the 1990s, including science towns and science and technology parks.

Policy landscape at the national level

Overall, Russia's STI policies have predominantly focused on upstream R&D, that is on knowledge generation (research institutes, universities) and on public R&D. Policies for downstream R&D, that is diffusion, commercialisation and to support the private sector in being innovative, have been noticeably weaker or absent. We can observe three evolutionary stages in post-Soviet Russia's STI policy landscape (Table 3.16) from the early 1990s to 2015.

The first stage was the period from 1991 to 1999 during which the few S&T policies that were implemented were focused on providing economic stability and maintaining Soviet S&T capabilities (Gokhberg and Roud, 2016). Shock therapy and privatisation were implemented to try and transition the country to a market economy rapidly. There was an almost complete absence of a coherent or strong state. In this period, policy makers tried to preserve science in a crisis

Table 3.16 Summary of R&D and innovation policies in the Russian Federation by stage, 1991–2015

	1991–1999	*2000–2008*	*2008–2015*
Policies (R&D and innovation)	S&T policies focused on providing economic stability and maintaining Soviet S&T capabilities. Shock therapy and privatisation; an almost complete absence of a coherent or strong state.	STI policies focused on gradual increases of public R&D funding and preserving obsolete institutional structures and governance principles (Gokhberg and Roud, 2016).	"Contemporary" approaches (in line with international standards) to STI policy making adopted at a conceptual level only from 2009 (Gokhberg and Roud, 2016). Central state more prominent role in governing RDI. Concept of innovation first gained prominent place in policy discourses.

Source: Author (compiled from various sources).

state, continued to fund the highest priority S&T programmes, and introduced some new organisational mechanisms such as science foundations and technology parks (Graham and Dezhina, 2008).

The second stage of post-Soviet Russia's science and technology policy (2000–2008) was characterised by a greater number of STI policies, leading to a significant change in the institutional framework of R&D activity in Russia (Vercueil, 2014). This period saw STI policies that focused on gradual increases of public R&D funding and preserving obsolete institutional structures and governance principles (Gokhberg and Roud, 2016).

The third stage of post-Soviet Russia's science and technology policy begun after the global financial crisis of 2008, a shock that contributed to the concept of innovation first gaining a prominent place in policy discourses (Gokhberg and Roud, 2016). In this period, the government of Russia introduced many strategic, conceptual documents to create a long-term S&T policy (Table 3.17). Indeed, in just the four years between 2010 and 2014, 40 documents aiming directly to

Table 3.17 Institution building and policies in the R&D field, 1992–2014

Year introduced	*Policy/institution/initiative*	*Focus is on*
1992	Russian Foundation for Basic Research (RFBR)	Institution focused on funding fundamental R&D
1994	Russian Foundation for the Humanities (RFH)	Institution focused on funding fundamental R&D
1999	Federal law No. 70 on the status of *naukograds* in Russia (amended in 2015)	Law on fundamental R&D; Supply side
2000	Official creation of "science town" with legal status	Fundamental R&D; Supply
2001A	Presidential Council for Science and High Technologies created to provide strategic leadership and guidance for S&T	Institution
2001B	Patent Law amendment to intellectual property (IP) regulations – commercialised intellectual property rights to some extent	Law on patenting – demand side
2002A	First Federal Target Programme (2002–2006); "Science and Technology Development Guidelines until 2010 and beyond" – most important federal programme for funding applied research	Institution and state programme focused on applied research
2002B	Creation of the Russian Technology Transfer Network (2002–2006)	Institution, supply, demand
2003	Main Guidelines of Public Policy in Science and Technology	Institution and programme, supply
2004	Restructuring plan of R&D public organisations (2004–2008)	Supply
2006A	Federal programme for high-tech clusters ("Technoparks")	Institution, supply

Year introduced	*Policy/institution/initiative*	*Focus is on*
2006B	Creation of Russian Venture Company and 19 Regional Venture Funds	Institution, demand
2006C	Creation of open joint-stock company SEZ to develop Special Economic Zones	Institution, supply (downstream R&D)
2006D	Strategy for Development of Science and Innovation in Russia up to 2015 – aims to improve government funding programmes and foster science and industry linkages	Policy, supply and demand
2007A	2nd Federal Target Programme (2007–2012): innovation initiatives in higher education	Policy, supply
2007B	Creation of state corporations in high-tech sectors (Rosnano for nanotechnologies; Rostekhnologii for defence and high-tech industries; Rosatom for nuclear technologies)	Institution, supply
2008A	Long-Term Economic Development Plan ("Strategy 2020") published	Policy, supply
2008B	Restructuring of IPR legislation, tax treatment of R&D, and patenting activities	Supply
2008C	Creation of the status of National Research Centre	Institution, supply
2009A	Presidential Commission for Modernisation and Technological Development	Institution, supply
2009B	Regional Universities (7 universities granted) and National Research Universities (14 universities granted) created	Institution, supply
2009C	Restructuring of financing of Russian Academy of Sciences	Policy, supply
2009D	Launch of high-tech division of MICEX (Russia Stock Market)	Institution, demand
2010A	15 new universities given status of National Research University	Institution, supply
2010B	Creation of Technology Platforms	Institution, supply
2010C	Launch of Skolkovo innovation centre near Moscow	Institution, supply and demand
2010D	Restructuring of Government Commission on High Technology and Innovation	Institution, supply
2010E	Creation of Russian Defence Innovative Projects Agency	Institution, supply
2010F	Innovative Mega Projects	Policy, supply and demand (linkages)
2011A	Fully fledged S&T Foresight 2030 study initiated by the Russian Ministry of Education and Science to identify national S&T priorities	Policy, supply and demand
2011B	Programme for development of innovation in machine-building sector	Policy, demand
2011C	Government Development Scenario for the Russian Economy up to 2030 published	Policy, supply
2011D	Government Strategy for the Development of Innovation in Russia up to 2020 published	Policy, supply

(*Continued*)

Table 3.17 (Continued)

Year introduced	*Policy/institution/initiative*	*Focus is on*
2012A	Government long-term Programme for Shipbuilding industry	Policy, supply
2012B	Government approval of environmental programme up to 2020	Policy, supply
2012C	May (inaugural) presidential decrees – key directives on development of economy, science, technology, education, and other industries in social sphere. Contain both qualitative guidelines and target quantitative indicators to be achieved by 2018	Policy, supply
2013A	Reform of Russian Academy of Sciences (RAS) – very unpopular reform among scientists and researchers; brought RAS under more direct control of government; transferred management of RAS property to the control of a new state agency, the Federal Agency of Scientific Organisations (FANO)	Institution, supply
2013B	Project 5–100 programme aimed to make a select group of leading Russian universities more competitive in the global research and education market	Policy, supply and demand
2014	Federal Law No. 488 "On Industrial Policy in the Russian Federation" gives first official definition of concept of "industrial cluster" in Russia	Law, demand

Source: Vercueil (2014) based on BOFIT (2011), OECD (2011); additions to Vercueil (2014) by the author of this book; Sokolov and Chulok (2016).

regulate processes and relations in STI were adopted by the highest authorities, that is the Government, President, and the Russian Parliament (Gokhberg and Kuznetsova, 2015). The sheer number of policy initiatives initiated by the Russian state is an indication that the state authorities were prepared to try out an experimental approach in the STI field (Table 3.17).

The conceptual policy guidelines adopted since 2008 were in line with contemporary approaches to STI policy making followed by many other countries (Gokhberg and Roud, 2016). The period since 2008 is also characterised by the return of the central state in governing science and innovation (Klochikhin, 2012) and more intense efforts to develop a commercial culture in Russian science. A key policy that reflects the dominant role of the state in the economy is one that mandated large state-owned companies to innovate and cooperate with small and medium business as well as research institutions (Gershman, 2013).

Vercueil (2014) helpfully distinguishes between long-term policies that aim to make favourable conditions for innovation in specific sectors versus "public institutions designed to channel specific funding or implement particular tasks" (e.g. Russian Technology Transfer Network). Table 3.17 summarises the principal institutions, policies, and laws that Russia has implemented since 1992 in the area of STI and categorises them according to whether they are focused on supply of or demand for R&D or on linkages between various actors in the innovation system. Key new policies adopted since 2008 include competitive-based support for cooperation between companies, research organisations and universities (Gokhberg and Roud, 2012: 126–127), creation of new national research universities in 2009, support for regional innovation clusters (Kutsenko and Meissner, 2013), and the development of technology platforms (Proskuryakova et al., 2014). The chronology of modernisation in post-Soviet Russia puts the R&D institutions and policies as listed in Table 3.17 in a broader context (Appendix 1).

New organisational forms and incentives for innovation

Over the 70 years of the Soviet Union's existence and then in post-Soviet Russia, political and economic elites have initiated a wide variety of organisations and programmes to support the development of STI. Since 1991, some of these initiatives have sought to stimulate research–business linkages across Russia (Dezhina, 2018). This shows political elites have had a degree of willingness to experiment and "borrow" many institutional and organisational forms from abroad. The search for new forms may indicate that the system overall needed structural change. In borrowing institutional forms from abroad, political elites were to some extent doing a kind of institutional isomorphic mimicry: changing and adapting the outwards appearance and structures of institutions that are reasonably effective in other institutional contexts to hide their sustained lack of functional performance (Pritchett et al., 2013; Andrews et al., 2013). However, many of these location-based innovation initiatives were implemented in Russia because they were a "good fit" with the country's political economy. They were to some extent a continuation of STI policies of the USSR, for example some of the science towns created in the decade after the end of the Second World War were continued in the post-Soviet period and were given a new label, "*naukograd*." In addition, it is easier to politically control geographically concentrated areas for STI, which made these kinds of initiatives attractive for political elites in authoritarian Russia. This section outlines the aims and forms of these instruments, including those that will be analysed in Chapters 4–6 of this book.

In the past 15 years, some of these initiatives have re-oriented towards commercialisation of S&T. Figure 3.4 summarises the array of science and innovation state support mechanisms in Russia that have existed since 2000. They include the Academy of Sciences, technology transfer offices, research universities, innovation technology centres, special economic zones (SEZs), clusters, R&D funding bodies, science towns, and industrial and technology parks (sometimes called science and technology parks or technoparks). The Skolkovo innovation centre on the outskirts of Moscow is the newest addition to these initiatives, which has received a significant injection of resources from the state since it was created in 2010. This variety can help build up critical mass of institutions and actors engaged in S&T and innovation, although it can also lead to confusion and dispersal of state funding.

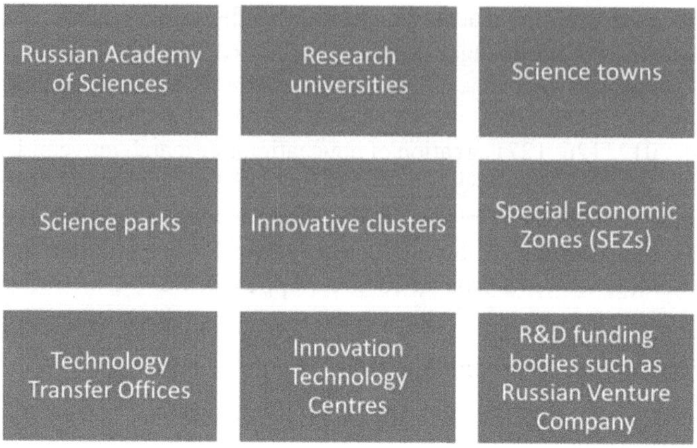

Figure 3.4 Russia's state support for science and innovation since 2000

Source: Author

The first **Innovation Technology Centre** (ITC) opened in 1996 in St. Petersburg. By 2008, Russia had 52 ITCs in total with more than 1,000 firms. ITCs overlap with the functions of science and technology parks in practice (both are often attached to a university) and suffer from low demand for high-tech products. Hence, we can think of ITCs as "de facto science and technology parks." Originally, ITCs aimed to help more established innovation enterprises (not start-ups). They received significant federal state funds (equivalent of approximately USD 50 million in 1997). However, a lack of strict criteria led to a situation where ITCs resembled STPs in practice.

Technology Transfer Offices (TTOs) were one of the first commercialisation mechanisms introduced in post-Soviet Russia. TTOs are a unit within research organisations that aim to bring together researchers with business people. TTOs were introduced in Russia in 2003–2004 and modelled on Western TTOs, particularly those found in the United States. They also have a Soviet "ancestor": patent departments in R&D institutes and higher educational institutions that evaluated innovations awarded to investors and applied to use patents by the institutions in foreign trade. Some of these Soviet patents departments still exist, with a few of them having been renamed as TTOs, but they are not that effective economically (Graham and Dezhina, 2008).

The post-Soviet TTOs introduced in the early 2000s are of two types: those in any kind of scientific organisations and those only in universities. The TTOs in universities have received more funding from the Ministry of Education and Science and the US Foundation Civilian Research and Development Foundation, although early evaluations suggest that they have been less successful than the other kind of TTOs. All the TTOs in Russia today face obstacles such as premature submission of R&D results for commercialisation (e.g. no economic feasibility studies done), scientists' negative attitudes towards commercialisation of their work, and legal hurdles in regulating researcher–business people cooperation (Graham and Dezhina, 2008).

Research universities were created in 2008 to better integrate teaching and research. In 2008, two leading technological universities were awarded this status by presidential decree; the following year, other universities were invited to bid for the status. The 2009 competition saw 110 applications, of which 12 were selected for the federal funding from the Ministry of Education and Science (approximately 10% success rate). Another 15 universities were selected in April 2010 (out of 128 applications, so a 12% success rate). The research universities policy programme is not an enclave by design, but rather a manifestation of the Triple Helix logic which emphasises interactions between universities, industry, and government.

Special Economic Zones were set up by presidential decree in July 2005 to focus on downstream R&D, that is on R&D that is nearly ready to be introduced onto the market. They aimed to provide direct and indirect stimuli for innovation. However, only a small number have been created (six hi-tech zones and two production zones by 2008 (Graham and Dezhina, 2008; Cooper, 2006).

The federal government of Russia launched a policy to support pilot **innovative clusters** in 2012. The 25 selected clusters (out of 94 applicants) aim to boost value-added production chains and economic growth in Russia's regions (The Innovation Policy Platform, OECD, World Bank).[5] All these clusters are in regions with existing centres of scientific excellence and/or industrial infrastructure, for example science towns, special economic zones (SEZs), and closed territories (HSE, 2018). This means that the clusters can benefit from path dependency and potentially also from knowledge spillovers. First launched in 2012 by the Ministry of Economic Development, clusters are focused more on the entity itself than its relationship with the outside world. Thus, this reflects the first stage in nurturing place-based innovation: creating and nurturing the place as an enclave, isolated from and protected against the external environment. According to official documents, an innovative cluster in Russia should have:

(i) a mechanism for coordination and cooperation *among the actors* of the cluster (horizontal linkages);
(ii) several companies and organisations, located in a limited territory, participating in *a value chain* in one or several key economic areas (vertical linkages); and
(iii) a synergy effect resulting from high levels of concentration and cooperation of these organisations which, in turn, raises their economic effectiveness and productivity.[6]

R&D funding bodies (development institutions in Russian)[7] are an institutional innovation the Russian state introduced since the early 1990s to provide financial assistance for science and innovation. Initially, they aimed to prop up science and help the existing scientific establishment survive the turmoil of the 1990s and collapse of the Soviet Union. Later, some of them shifted their focus to support innovation, meaning commercialisation of new technologies. The first of these institutions was the Russian Fund for Technological Development (RFTD), created in 1992 by the then Ministry of Science and Technology Policy to support "critical technologies" (government-defined priority technologies). The Fund for Assistance to Small Innovative Enterprises (FASIE) is another R&D funding body that has existed since 1994 and was modelled on the Small Business Innovation Research (SBIR) programme in the United States and the French state agency for innovation. It gets its budget from the federal government and redistributes the money via loans at preferential rates to small innovative enterprises that are at a later developmental stage and already doing civil (i.e. non-defence) commercial production. FASIE has seen some successes. A third development institution is the Venture Innovation Fund (VIF), created in 2000. It was modelled on Israel's Yozma Fund, a successful "fund of funds." Russia's VIF is a non-commercial organisation that sets up regional and industrial venture funds using government money on the basis of long-term shared financing.

Evaluating the efforts of the RFTD, FASIE, and VIF up until 2008, there are three main reasons why they have to date only enjoyed limited success. First, the Russian government has been unwilling to take on real risks and therefore, allocated relatively little money to innovation. Second, the potential rents from investing in innovation (the incentives) are limited when compared to those from investing in natural resources (oil, gas, and minerals). Third, Russia lacked experienced venture capital managers.

Other R&D funding bodies have been set up in Russia in the 2000s that are state corporations in form, meaning they are de facto funded and controlled by the state. Their goals are to foster the commercialisation of results from research. They include the Russian Venture Company (set up in 2006), Russian Technologies, and Rosnano (established in 2007).

Some scholars have criticised the effectiveness of these R&D funding bodies, claiming they are inefficient and only marginal actors in Russia's innovation strategy (Klochikhin, 2013). Other scholars have been more positive, pointing to their effects in regional development. For example, while Rosnano primarily aims to commercialise nanotechnology research by investment and by helping to build scientific and production infrastructure, its activity has introduced nanotechnology-related new specialisations in regions of scientific excellence, enabled the stronger regions to apply for other forms of federal funding, and has boosted local entrepreneurship (Gonchar et al., 2017).

Science foundations are relevant to this chapter because they are an example of a new kind of institution for Russia that has introduced new ways of funding fundamental R&D (i.e. upstream R&D) based on openness, competitive processes, and the peer review system rather than on state-directed missions.[8] The first government science foundation was set up in 1992, the Russian Foundation for Basic Research (RFBR). This was followed two years later by the Russian Foundation for the Humanities (RFH), which was explicitly for social sciences and the humanities. The RFBR and the RFH receive their budgets from the federal government as a fixed share of total government expenditures on civilian science (7% as of 2008).

The concept of a grant for science was a novel one in post-Soviet Russia and originated in the United States in the early 20th century when American large foundations were set up. Grants are commonly used to support basic research worldwide, and they tend to foster long-term research which brings indefinite results without direct assistance or profits in the short-term. Soviet researchers rather carried out R&D on a contract basis, that is they received money for very specific projects, often of short duration, targeted to – and requested by – the organisation funding the contract. Many Russian scientists, however, especially in the early and mid-1990s, disliked on principle the idea of having to compete for funding for their research. They were accustomed to essentially being given money for their research projects from the Soviet state, without having to apply on a competitive basis or show much initiative in generating and designing research projects.

The foundations to date have been limited by their modest budgets, complicated financial reporting procedures for grant holders, poor communication with researchers, a lack of anonymity during the selection process, and delayed and inadequate funding (Graham and Dezhina, 2008: 57–61).

Many – but not all – of these policy instruments began as enclaves separated from the surrounding institutional environment. This is because of the weak institutional environment, ambiguous property rights, the absence of a market economy in the USSR, and because it may be easier for state authorities to monitor and control the R&D happening in these places when it is an enclave compared to if it is fully open and integrated with the wider domestic and global economy. The initial function of enclaves, in other words, is to provide protection against hostile geographical and institutional environments.

Science towns first appeared in the Soviet Union in the late 1940s to early 1950s. Many of them were built at a considerable distance from Russia's capital city and/or in remote places; hence they were spatially isolated (Chapter 4 will discuss science towns in more depth).

The extent to which these organisations create a functioning system of innovation is debated. Some scholars argue that inefficiencies predominate (e.g. Klochikhin, 2012). Others emphasise the presence of strong vested interests in, for example, the Academy of Sciences and industry which have pursued their own survival strategies and undermined the Government's reform efforts. Hence, these vested interests may have prevented a functional system of innovation from taking root (Cooper, 2008).

Conclusions

The collapse of Communism in 1991 had a profound impact on Russian R&D and innovation, with some positive changes (e.g. end of ideological controls and censorship, and new freedoms for scientists and businesspeople to travel abroad) but more negative factors, principally the drastic reduction in state funding for science in the first half of the 1990s (Cooper, 2008).

Soviet legacies remain in present day Russia. These are a centralised science and innovation policy (although in the 1990s the state was very weak in governing science and innovation), few linkages between universities, the Academy of Science research institutes, and the industrial and defence sectors, and a high share of R&D spending on defence R&D that is almost as great as in Soviet times (23.8% in 2000 and 31.6% in 2004, Graham and Dezhina, 2008: 31). The role of business in funding and implementing R&D also remains weak, with the state playing the primary role.

Since the early 1990s, the government of Russia has made considerable efforts to reform the Soviet system of R&D and innovation. The Russian government has experimented with an impressive range of policy instruments and infrastructure to support R&D and innovation. Hence, we can say that Russian state has been activist in this regard, arguably pursuing the tool of institutional isomorphic mimicry to some extent although selecting institutions and organisations that were a better fit with the country's institutional context. These instruments include clusters, special economic zones, technology transfer offices, innovation technology centres, research universities, science foundations, R&D funding institutions, science and technology parks, and science towns. Some of the Soviet-era science towns have been reinvigorated with federal funding since 2000.

The subsequent empirical chapters of this book examine some of these initiatives – science towns and science and technology parks (Skolkovo is considered as a new, 21st century kind of science town with a STP located within it) – in terms of how successful they have been. These institutions will be examined because the concept of a science town has a long history in the USSR and elsewhere, and the core challenge many of Russia's multisectoral science towns have faced since the 1990s is how to convert their scientific and R&D capabilities into products and processes that can be commercialised. STPs were first introduced in Russia at the start of the 1990s. Hence, Russian policy makers and businesspeople have had the longest "exposure" to science towns and STPs relative to the other institutions for innovation and R&D discussed in this chapter. Given science towns and STPs have existed in Russia for longer compared to clusters, special economic zones, technology transfer offices, innovation technology centres, and research universities, Russia has had more time to adapt the former institutions to local contexts. With both institutions, Russia continues to have difficulties in supporting the networking elements, fostering the linkages and collaborations between science towns and STPs and other firms and organisations in the wider national and international economy. The empirical chapters look at science towns and STPs through the lens of a three-stage growth framework, examining to what extent they have extended beyond their enclave origins, are building critical mass, and forming linkages in their region and in the rest of Russia, and globally.

Notes

1 Former colleagues in the Institute for Statistical Studies and Economics of Knowledge, Higher School of Economics, Moscow – the institutional owner of the *Indicators of Science* datasets – provided useful commentary to help interpret the data presented here.

2 It is unclear how many state universities there are now in Russia but in 2005 there were 655 state universities versus 413 non-state universities according to an official source:

https://web.archive.org/web/20080531104416/www.ed.gov.ru/uprav/stat/1846/ [last accessed 11 December 2018]. It is likely that with reforms since 2005, the number of non-state universities has declined.
3 http://reports.weforum.org/global-competitiveness-report-2014-2015/rankings/ [last accessed 15 November 2021].
4 World Intellectual Property Organization (WIPO) – the World Intellectual Property Indicators – and published by the World Bank as part of the World Development Indicators.
5 The number of federally supported clusters later increased to 27 (HSE, 2018).
6 http://innovation.gov.ru/taxonomy/term/545
7 This sub-section on R&D funding bodies in Russia draws largely on Graham and Dezhina (2008: Chapter 5: 67–88).
8 This sub-section on science foundations in Russia draws largely on Graham and Dezhina (2008: Chapter 4: 45–66).

References

Andrews, M., Pritchett, L. and Woolcock, M. (2013) 'Escaping Capability Traps Through Problem Driven Iterative Adaptation (PDIA)', *World Development* 51 (pp. 234–244). Available at: http://dx.doi.org/10.1016/j.worlddev.2013.05.011.

BOFIT. (2011) *Bofit Yearbook 2011* [online]. Helsinki: Bank of Finland Institute for Emerging Economies. Available at: http://www.suomenpankki.fi/bofit_en/seuranta/viikkokatsaus/Pages/default.aspx [last accessed December 2018].

Cooper, J. (2006) 'Of BRICs and Brains: Comparing Russia With China, India, and Other Populous Emerging Economies', *Eurasian Geography and Economics* 47 (pp. 255–284).

Cooper, J. (2008) 'Soviet and Russian Research, Development and Innovation', in Durlauf, S. N. and Blume, L. E. (eds.) *The New Palgrave Dictionary of Economics*, 2nd edition. Basingstoke, Hampshire: Palgrave Macmillan (pp. 1–5). Available at: https://doi.org/10.1057/978-1-349-95121-5_2289–1 [last accessed 30 December 2019].

Cooper, J. (2012) 'Science-Technology Policy and Innovation in the USSR', Presentation at Workshop Russia's Skolkovo in Comparative and Historical Perspective, UCL SSEES, Wednesday, 13 June 2012

Cornell University, INSEAD, and WIPO. (2014) The Global Innovation Index 2014: The Human Factor In innovation. 2nd printing. Fontainebleau, Ithaca, and Geneva: World Intellectual Property Organization (WIPO). Available at: https://www.wipo.int/edocs/pubdocs/en/economics/gii/gii_2014.pdf [last accessed 21 March 2022].

Dezhina, I. (2018) 'Innovation Policy in Russia and the Development of University–Industry Linkages', *Industry and Higher Education* 32/4 (pp. 245–252). http://dx.doi.org/10.1177/0950422218774974.

EBRD – European Bank for Reconstruction and Development (2012) *Diversifying Russia: Harnessing regional diversity*. London: EBRD. Available online at: https://www.ebrd.com/news/publications/special-reports/diversifying-russia.html [last accessed 21 March 2022].

Freeman, C. (1987) *Technology Policy and Economic Performance: Lessons From Japan*. London: Pinter.

Gaddy, C. G. and Ickes, B. W. (2013) *Bear Traps on Russia's Road to Modernization*. Abingdon, Oxon and New York: Routledge.

Gershman, M. (2013) 'Programmy innovatsionnovo razvitiya kompanii s gosudarstvennym uchastiyem: perviye itogi' [trans. from Russian: 'Innovation programmes of state-owned companies: first results'] *Foresight and STI Governance* 7/1 (pp. 28–43). Available at: https://publications.hse.ru/en/articles/78735639.

Global Competitiveness Index (2015). *The Global Competitiveness Report 2014–2015*. World Economic Forum. Date of data collection or release, 3 September. Available at: http://reports.weforum.org/global-competitiveness-report-2014-2015/rankings/ [last accessed 15 November 2021].

Gokhberg, L. and Roud, V. (2012) 'The Russian Federation: A New Innovation Policy for Sustainable Growth', *The Global Innovation Index* (pp. 121–130).

Gokhberg, L. and Kuznetsova, T. (2015) *Russian Federation*. UNESCO Science Report: Towards 2030. Available at: https://en.unesco.org/unesco_science_report [last accessed 11 January 2019].

Gokhberg, L. and Roud, V. (2016) 'Structural Changes in the National Innovation System: Longitudinal Study of Innovation Modes in the Russian Industry', *Economic Change and Restructuring* August 49/2–3 (pp.269–288).

Gonchar, K., Kuznetsov, Y., and Wade, I. (2017) 'Lessons for a Policy Maker From Real-Life Self-Discovery in Economies With Weak Institutions', in Radošević, S., Curaj, A., Andreescu, L., Gheorgiu, L. and Wade, I. (eds.) *Advances in the Theory and Practice of Smart Specialization*. Oxford: Elsevier (pp. 225–248).

Graham, L. and Dezhina, I. (2008) *Science in the New Russia: Crisis, Aid, Reform*. Bloomington, IN: Indiana University Press.

Higher School of Economics (HSE) (2018) *Indicators of Science*. Moscow: HSE.

Higher School of Economics (HSE). (2019) *Indicators of Science* 2019 [*Indikatory nauki*: 2019] Available in Russian at: https://www.hse.ru/primarydata/in2019?fbclid=IwAR3WEU44jUPndEMUbTOUKMO4pB0XfsY1V-EyfA6rL6zkusq1xBPjnGDf32M [last accessed 06 June 2019].

Josephson, P. R. (1988) 'Science policy in the Soviet Union, 1917–1927', *Minerva* 26/3 (pp. 342–369). Available at: https://doi.org/10.1007/BF01096401 [last accessed 21 July 2021].

Karaulova, M. and Gershman, M. (2015) 'Russia: Nanotechnology Country Profile', Working Paper, Project on Emerging Technologies, Trajectories and Implications of Next Generation Innovation Systems Development in China and Russia, February. Manchester: Manchester Institute of Innovation Research, University of Manchester.

Klochikhin, E. A. (2012) 'Russia's Innovation Policy: Stubborn Path-Dependencies and New Approaches', *Research Policy* 41/9 (pp. 1620–1630).

Klochikhin, E. A. (2013) 'Innovation System in Transition: Opportunities for Policy Learning Between China and Russia', *Science and Public Policy, Oxford University Press* 40/5, February (pp. 657–673).

Kutsenko, E. and Meissner, D. (2013) 'Key Features of the First Phase of the National Cluster Program in Russia', April 18, 2013. *Higher School of Economics Research Paper* No. WP BRP 11/STI/2013. Available at SSRN: https://ssrn.com/abstract=2253377 or http://dx.doi.org/10.2139/ssrn.2253377 [last accessed 30 December 2019].

Makarov, V. and Varshavsky, A. (2013) 'Science, High-Tech Industries, and Innovation', in Alexeev, M. and Weber, S. (eds.) *The Oxford Handbook of the Russian Economy*. Oxford: Oxford University Press. Available at: https://doi.org/10.1093/oxfordhb/9780199759927.013.0026.

OECD (2007) 'Stimulating Innovation in Russia: The Role of Institutions and Policies', Economics Department Working Papers no. 539, Gianella, C. and Tompson, W. Available at: www.oecd.org/eco/working_papers [last accessed 31.12.2018].

OECD (2011) *Reviews of Innovation Policy: Russian Federation 2011*. Paris: OECD Publishing. Available at: http://dx.doi.org/10.1787/19934211 [last accessed 7 December 2017].

OECD (2018) *Main Science and Technology Indicators*, Volume 2018 Issue 1. Paris: OECD Publishing. Available at: https://doi.org/10.1787/msti-v2018-1-en.

Pritchett, L., Woolcock, M. and Andrews, M. (2013) 'Looking Like a State: Techniques of Persistent Failure in State Capability for Implementation', *Journal of Development Studies* 49/1 (pp. 1–18). Available at: http://dx.doi.org/10.1080/00220388.2012.709614.

Proskuryakova, L. N., Meissner, D. and Rudnik, P. (2014) 'A Policy Perspective on the Russian Technology Platforms', Higher School of Economics Research Paper No. WP BRP 26/STI/2014, 20 February 2014 (pp.1–27). Available at SSRN: https://ssrn.com/abstract=2398912 or http://dx.doi.org/10.2139/ssrn.2398912.

Radošević, S. (2011) 'Science – Industry Links in Central and Eastern Europe and the Commonwealth of Independent States: Conventional Policy Wisdom Facing Reality', *Science and Public Policy* 38/5 (pp. 365–378). Available at: 10.3152/030234211X1292 4093660435 [last accessed 7 December 2017].

Sokolov, A. and Chulok, A. (2016) 'Priorities for Future Innovation: Russian S&T Foresight 2030', *Futures* 80 (pp. 17–32).

Sterligov, I. (2018) 'Russian Federal Universities: A Bibliometric Comparison with 5Top100, C9 and Ivy League', *Higher Education in Russia and Beyond (HERB)* 1, Spring (p. 15). Available at: https://herb.hse.ru/data/2018/04/08/1164650223/1HERB_15_view.pdf [last accessed 15 November 2021].

Vercueil, J. (2014) 'Could Russia Become More Innovative? Coordinating Key Actors of the Innovation System', *Post-Communist Economies* 26/4, 30 October 2014 (pp. 498–521) http://dx.doi.org/10.1080/14631377.2014.964464.

World Economic Forum. (2018) *Global Competitiveness Index*. Available at: http://reports.weforum.org/global-competitiveness-report-2014-2015/rankings [last accessed 1 December 2018].

Zaleski, E., Kozlowski, J. P., Wienert, H., Davies, R. W., Berry, M. J. and Amann, R. (1969) *Science Policy in the* USSR. Paris: OECD.

4 Forever enclaves? Science towns in contemporary Russia

This first empirical chapter examines Russia's science towns.

These are towns or areas within a bigger city built after the Second World War with the explicit purpose of nurturing research and development. The chapter compares two contrasting science towns, focusing on the towns' historical evolution since the 1950s and main outcomes.

Introduction

Science towns are not unique to the USSR and Russia: they were established in Nazi Germany, the United States, and Japan, as well as in other places. The first science town[1] in the world started in 1937 in Peenemünde, Germany as a military research centre to produce missiles and rockets. The USSR, however, implemented the idea of science towns on a much greater scale than any other country (Ruchnov and Zaytseva, 2011).

The present chapter examines cases of two types of science towns, namely an *akademgorodok* and a *naukograd*. The justification for selecting only these two kinds of science towns is that these types still exist in contemporary Russia, unlike the *sharagi* and closed cities (although it is true that some closed cities still exist, they remain closed to foreigners so from a practical point of view are very hard to research). *Naukogradi* and *akademgorodki* remain on the modernisation and innovation policy agenda and so have policy relevance. The naukograd is Obninsk in the Kaluga region in Western Russia; Obninsk was the first science town to be selected for federal funding specifically for naukograds in 2000; thus, it has symbolic importance. The *akademgorodok* that this chapter will examine is located on the outskirts of the Siberian city of Novosibirsk. The Novosibirsk *akademgorodok* is arguably the largest, most well-known, and successful science town in the Soviet Union and Russia (Wainwright, 2016).

Historical evolution: 1950s–1980s

The histories of Obninsk and Novosibirsk, Akademgorodok are similar. Initially, both places were created and developed under the close supervision of the

DOI: 10.4324/9781003256205-4

highest state authority. However, while Obninsk officially became a town in 1956, Akademgorodok in Novosibirsk has never been an independent administrative unit. Rather, it was, and continues to be, a part of a district within Novosibirsk city. For much of its history, Obninsk was a "departmental" town largely dependent on the decisions taken in the Soviet Ministry of Medium Machine Building (*Minsredmash*) which was responsible for nuclear weapons production. On the contrary, Akademgorodok was an academic settlement – the "little academy town" – from the very beginning under the control and influence of the Siberian Branch of the Soviet Academy of Sciences.[2]

1950s–1980s

Origins

This section compares and contrasts the origins and development in the first three decades of the science towns of Obninsk and Akademgorodok.

First conceived in 1946, Obninsk was initially set up to produce R&D and carry out production in the nuclear sector. Specifically, it was created to help develop the Soviet Union's "big science" atomic bomb project. Obninsk received substantial resources for its first two decades because its economy aligned with the Soviet Union's big science policy and ideological support for science.

Officially, a town from 1956, Obinisk in fact developed around a single "Laboratory V" built in 1946 under the Ministry for Internal Affairs of the Soviet Union. It was part of the Soviet Union's atomic bomb project led by the scientist Igor Kurchatov. In 1960, this laboratory became known as the Institute for Physics and Power Engineering, the first institute built in Obninsk and still the most important, as shown by this excerpt from an interview:

> So, all these factors came together . . . and also the luck factor of course . . . immediately after the war [1941–1945], in 1946, a secret laboratory was established here. Besides, the river Protva was necessary for such production. So, all these circumstances came together, as well as a bit of chance too, of course . . . So that's why a secret laboratory was organised in this place . . . **many** converging factors. First builders came, then **German** scientists began to come – at first on contract – contracts that were very favourable for them. Right after them, from 1947, famous Russian scientists started to come.[3] [**emphasis** in original].

The geographic location was a key factor impacting the decision of where to build "Laboratory V" and the surrounding settlement. Although Obninsk is relatively close to Moscow (approximately 100 km), the founders of "Laboratory V" picked the location for the town precisely because of its isolation from Moscow. Obninsk was built as a town in the woods and is often described as a "green town" by various contemporary documents and residents' impressions of their town. The presence of nature encouraged many scientists to move there in the Soviet period, as shown in the following extract from an interview:

> Well, look at the map . . . it's all so green. This place used to be a place of summer country cottages. It's quite remote. There were several villages – you can see all the settlements marked here – . . . the station "Obninsk." There were good rail links with Moscow. . . . a good motorway too. . . . it was easy to get to Moscow. Then the only connections with Moscow were by car or train . . . At the same time, the area was remote and quite out-of-the-way[4]

Akademgorodok (located in a district of the Siberian industrial city of Novosibirsk) was founded 11 years after Obninsk in 1957. It was officially established by the Siberian Division of the USSR Academy of Sciences (henceforth SD SAS). In the beginning, the Soviet Council of Ministers described Akademgorodok's goal as:

> The main task of the Siberian Branch of the Academy of Sciences of the USSR is the all-round development of theoretical and experimental research in the field of physics and engineering, natural and economic sciences to address the most critical scientific issues and problems contributing the most to the successful development of forces of production of Siberia and the Far East.[5]

This citation from the Soviet Council of Ministers shows the importance this institution – one of the highest governing authorities of the USSR – ascribed to Akademgorodok for interdisciplinary fundamental science *and* for applying that knowledge for the development of Siberia and the Far East. The natural resources sector generated great interest for Akademgorodok's founders (Josephson, 1997).

A key actor who led Akademgorodok's creation was the academician Mikhail Lavrentiev. He had a close personal relationship with Nikita Khrushchev (First Secretary of the Communist Party of the Soviet Union, 1953–1964, and Chairman of the Council of Ministers, 1958–1964). This helped to secure the necessary state resources, policy documents, approvals, and permits for rapid construction, which meant that it was functional as a scientific centre by the mid-1960s. Lavrentiev effectively had an open pass to the Kremlin thanks to his friendship with Khrushchev (Josephson, 1997; Vodichev et al., 2007). An indicator of the political support Akademgorodok enjoyed in its first decade is the 2.6 billion roubles in capital investment the SD SAS received from 1959 to 1965, five times more than the rest of the Soviet Academy of Sciences received in the same period (Vodichev et al., 2007).

Yet, the creators of Akademgorodok (represented by Lavrentiev) did not just see the academy village as a centre for fundamental research. They had an ambitious vision to make a ring of concentric circles, fanning outwards from the core of fundamental research in the academy village's research institutes to industry located nearby that would absorb and apply the results of the fundamental science.

In the Soviet period, Akademgorodok had several research institutes that successfully cooperated with enterprises in the wider economy. Such research institutes include the leading Budker Institute of Nuclear Physics (founded in 1959), which even in the Soviet period "produced advanced experimental machinery that it then directly sold to other scientific institutions and to industries in the Soviet Union and abroad, using the funds to directly supplement its budget" (Castells and Hall, 1994: 53). The same institute built a linear collider in Moscow through direct cooperation with another institute of the Soviet Academy of Sciences and produced scientific equipment for European Organization for Nuclear Research. These high-profile international links that the Institute of Nuclear Physics maintains is expected given its broad profile in high-energy physics and particle physics dating from the Soviet era. However, this vision was only achieved to a limited extent.

The founders' vision was realised in the late 1960s with the creation of a new organisational unit in Akademgorodok: the "belt of introduction" (*poyas vnedreniya*). This was introduced in 1966 and consisted of construction bureaus and research institutes built around Akademgorodok to be intermediaries between science and industry. These design bureaus and research institutes were accountable in administrative and financial matters to different ministries and to the Academy of Sciences for scientific issues (Cherevikina, 2007). The design bureaus (part of the Soviet Union's branch sectors) had a dual affiliation. The Academy of Sciences provided the scientific leadership to the design bureaus while the political ministries funded the bureaus. These design bureaus were supposed to complement the basic R&D carried out in the Academy's research institutes, create new equipment and other experimental pieces of apparatus that the Academy research institutes could use, and accelerate the introduction of new R&D into the practical sphere.

However, the effectiveness of the design bureaus was reduced because of a lack of horizontal coordination within the vertically integrated system of science. This means that the R&D carried out by the Academy of Sciences mismatched the needs of the design bureaus. Moreover, Academy of Sciences research institutes increased the volume of R&D done to contract. Third, there were constraints imposed by the five-year and annual plans on the design bureaus from the ministries (part of the centrally planned system). Over time, the Academy of Sciences institutes were relegated to the role of consultants with minimal influence on science and technology policy implemented by the ministries and design bureaus (Evseenko and Untura, 2002).

The question of military R&D in the history of Akademgorodok is interesting. Akademgorodok benefited from military R&D resources indirectly. Some scientists and engineers who were imprisoned in Soviet sharagi (these were part of the Stalinist Gulag system and were prison camps where scientists and engineers had to work for the Soviet Union's military R&D) later joined Akademgorodok's research institutes. For example, Yury Rumer was a physicist who was imprisoned as part of the Great Terror of the late 1930s and then exiled to Siberia where he worked as an engineer in the aircraft-making Tupolev sharaga for 10 years. Upon release from the sharaga, Rumer joined the SD SAS and was a scientist in Budker's Institute of Nuclear Physics in Akademgorodok from 1964 until his death in 1981 (Josephson, 1997).

Some of Akademgorodok's research institutes also enjoyed greater societal and political prestige and reputation thanks to the scope for certain scientific disciplines to have a high potential for military application (e.g. nuclear physics). For example, the following quote shows how Akademgorodok's famous Computer Centre – hosted by the Institute of Mathematics – did contract work in the 1960s for a nearby industrial factory, which produced some electronic technologies for the military:

> In 1964 the Computer Center concluded a contract with the Barnaul Radio Factory for the introduction of an ASU [Automated Management System] as part of its research "in the area of the theory and practice of automated management of industrial enterprises." The Barnaul Radio Factory ASU was connected with inventory control and statistical analysis of production processes, norms, and quality control. Located in Barnaul, some 125 miles south of Akademgorodok, the radio factory produced a wide variety of electronics, including some for the military.
>
> (Josephson, 1997: 151).

Akademgorodok in Novosibirsk was created to deliver basic R&D in almost all areas of science, including chemistry, physics, mathematics, genetics, sociology, economics, geology, medicine, and other disciplines. Lavrentiev, conceptualised the place as a triangle, referring to the three core elements of Akademgorodok: basic science, human resources, and production. This idea, "Lavrentiev's triangle," became the science town's motto by the mid-1960s (Tatarchenko, 2013: 69).

Crucial to developing the human resources element of Lavrentiev's triangle was Novosibirsk State University (NSU). This university was set up as an integral part of the little "academy village" and was designed from the outset to engage in research and teaching across all scientific disciplines and maintain the close ties with Siberian Branch of the Russian Academy of Sciences (SB RAS) research institutes that its founders initiated. Such close ties between science and research on the one hand and education on the other hand was an organisational innovation in the Soviet Union.

Another innovation was Lavrentiev's idea to create a "feeder school" for Novosibirsk State University (NSU). This materialised in January 1963 when the Physical-Mathematical School was established as part of NSU. Graduates of this school went on to study in NSU and other leading universities in the USSR (Vodichev et al., 2007).

The Soviet state wanted to keep Akademgorodok as a place of physically concentrated science to isolate the strategically important basic R&D its scientists performed, far from the Soviet Union's Western border.

A crucial part of creating the new Akademgorodok lay in attracting the right balance of experienced and more junior researchers and scientists. The academy village was designed to be pleasant to live in as an incentive for scientists to move with their families so far from Moscow and Leningrad. Scientists were given good living standards (e.g. spacious flats or houses, leisure and social facilities, subsidised groceries). Many scientists were attracted by Akademgorodok's location because it was geographically distant (approximately 3,400 km) from the bureaucratic controls of Moscow and Leningrad. Indeed, Akademgorodok's founders promised novelty and scientific independence and freedom (Josephson, 1997).

Thus, Akademgorodok's development has always been linked with the Siberian Branch of the Academy of Sciences, a powerful organisation devoted to fundamental research. Like Obninsk, Novosibirsk Akademgorodok was deliberately created in a remote and sparsely populated area – its founders wanted to create a place devoted to science which would be a pleasant living and working environment for scientists and technicians. Akademgorodok was built from nothing in the middle of forest, while being only 20 km south of Novosibirsk.

In the 1960s–1970s, there was a specific atmosphere inside Akademgorodok. There were various forums where scientists, engineers, and students could relax and socialise away from home and work: music clubs, amateur theatres, and "the Integral" club. Such institutions helped to increase personal interactions between scientists working in different institutes; nevertheless, the diverse scientific disciplines maintained barriers on an institutional level.

In the early period of its existence (1950s–1964), Akademgorodok was open to foreign scientists, but these linkages were tightly controlled by the Communist Party of the Soviet Union. Indeed, in the Khrushchev era (1953–1964) foreigners were a key part of the political, cultural, and social life of Akademgorodok, and the controls widespread elsewhere in the USSR were less strict in the scientific town (Josephson, 1997). Despite Akademgorodok's location far from Moscow, it managed to establish connections not only with industry within the country, but also internationally with scientists. One example is the experience of the department of automatic programming in the Computer Centre of the Soviet Academy of Sciences, headed by academician Yershov from 1957 until his death in 1988 (Yershov online archive, date unknown). Yershov had access to the latest literature in the West and could consult with United States experts. He was later awarded various international prizes. In 1974, he was elected Distinguished Fellow of the British Computing Society (British Computer Society), and in 1980, he was awarded the International Federation for Information Processing's Silver Core medal (ibid., and cited in Tatarchenko, 2013). This example reminds us that Akademgorodok in Novosibirsk always had some degree of international linkages in the Soviet period.

However, such communication at the international level may be restricted to certain disciplines such as IT and programming which in many ways uses its own language, that of computing. Other evidence from the rest of Akademgorodok (as opposed to just the Computer Centre) shows a different story. A study conducted in the town by two researchers from Spain and the United Kingdom in 1990 highlights four factors why Novosibirsk Akademgorodok was unable to continue producing scientific excellence and productivity, despite having very high scientific excellence when it was created (Castells and Hall, 1994: 82):

(i) isolation from the rest of the economy and Western countries and between the science sector, economy, and society;
(ii) vertical control and organisation of the Soviet Academy of Sciences in the context of centralised planning; and
(iii) shortage of co-operation between researchers in different scientific research institutes within the town.

One scientist from Akademgorodok interviewed by the author has worked and lived in Obninsk for more than 30 years. In the quote from the following interview, he compares Obninsk and Novosibirsk Akademgorodok, noting the uniquely fundamental research activities in the latter, in contrast to the original goal of its founders:

> So that was the atmosphere in all towns with a concentration of science. Akademgorodok – the same . . . I was there, yes . . . even more . . . concentrated science and research. In Obninsk there is a small factory, and prototype production. Yet in Novosibirsk it's . . . solely fundamental science. And everyone who wanted to work in industry, business, or something else went to Novosibirsk. Akademgorodok is near a big city, which has everything. While only scientists stayed in Akademgorodok. That place had a higher concentration of scientists than even Obninsk.[6] [own translation]

The first decade of Akademgorodok's existence was, by all accounts, a successful period. A world-class, internationally known scientific centre had been created.

Moreover, most of the newly created research institutes had already produced world-leading research in the disciplines of mathematics (pure and applied), physics, chemistry, biology, geology and geophysics, and economics. Much of this new knowledge was a product of interdisciplinary collaboration.

The 1970s saw further development, albeit at a slower rate. An important policy for developing interactions between different research institutes came into effect in the 1970s and continued into the 1980s. This was the policy of Collective Use Centres, which enabled research groups from various research institutes in Akademgorodok to share expensive equipment. Some of the first such centres were in the Computer Centre, the Budker Institute of Nuclear Physics, and the Institute of Catalysis (Vodichev et al., 2007). The legacy of these Collective Use Centres can still be seen today, with entities of the same name and fulfilling the same functions in Akadempark. There was a general economic slowdown and stagnation in the USSR from the 1970s onwards. An illustration of this slower growth in Akademgorodok comes from the statistics showing the annual increases in numbers of researchers employed by the Siberian Branch of the Academy of Sciences of the USSR. As shown in Table 4.1, the initial very rapid growth in researcher numbers of more than 50% from 1958 to 1961 fell to just 2.7% in 1971–1975.

Table 4.1 Growth in researcher numbers in Akademgorodok

Period	*Average annual growth in numbers of researchers employed by the Siberian Branch of the Academy of Sciences of the USSR:*
1958–1961	50%
1961–1965	15%
1966–1970	4.3%
1971–1975	2.7%
1976–1980	3.2%

Source: Vodichev et al., 2007: 222.

The key strategic development priorities for Akademgorodok in the 1980s were to support the advanced development of fundamental R&D, accelerate the growth of a regional network of SD SAS, and create new research groups based in different Siberian towns. The policy priority to boost the regional network was successful as evidenced by the increase in capital investments given to SD SAS in the mid-late 1980s. However, the problem of applying R&D into practice remained an acute one in the 1980s (Vodichev et al., 2007). For example, when the political controls on technology assessments from the Brezhnev era were eased, economists in Akademgorodok created a lab to study the ecological and legal issues about Lake Baikal in 1988 (Josephson, 1997).

The first scientists arrived in Obninsk in the late 1940s, before the town formally existed. They came to a place without amenities and where the presence of the surrounding woodland was keenly felt. One scientist reminisced about how he arrived in the winter of 1947 with his family:

> there was one big building which afterwards was called the main building. It remained like that, then they were forced to build a lot . . . and as for accommodation . . . there was just one three-storeyed house where some of the scientists lived. But most of them lived in so-called "Finnish houses," which were built right in the wood . . . meaning the houses were made in Finland . . . and as part of reparations we got them . . . with all amenities . . . Yes . . . there was a bathroom but not immediately . . . they installed gas not immediately but quite quickly . . . I brought my family . . . it was . . . early in 1947 and the month of January . . . there was very little there . . . So, there was no running water, no sewage, no gas, of course (*laughs*) . . . So, we came . . . we brought our things . . . and so it turned out that there was a stove that was fuelled with wood. Well, thank God, the firewood was prepared and we came and lit the stove, and the house became warm.[7] [own translation from Russian transcript]

Another resident, who arrived 10 years later in 1958, also stressed how Obninsk was built from scratch and remembered the town's rapid construction:

> We left for Obninsk in 1958 . . . The city was special. People who were very high-flying came here, and quickly built homes and a meteorological tower.

> There was nothing else. People largely came from Chelyabinsk-40 . . . in 1959 here there was only the *Institute for Physics and Power Engineering and nothing else*. Only the Fedorov Tower was built.[8] [own translation from Russian transcript]

Some residents of Obninsk to this day still see their town's greenness, more than 50 years since it was founded, as a special feature. This idea of defining their town partly based on its connection with nature helps us understand the origin of the town. Its planners chose the location of the town precisely because it was woodland, sufficiently isolated from Moscow to be an enclave, but still relatively close to the capital city. Thus, in associating the town in the present day with greenery and nature, the residents interviewed create a link with their town's history.

Some residents' desire to keep their town green has been reinforced by the town administration's recent attempts to destroy the green forest and build new homes. One resident of Obninsk explained their position regarding greenness:

> Our Administration has entered into a deal with the "construction mafia" and wants to cut down all the forests around Obninsk by building multi-storey commercial buildings. Moreover, it is not Obninsk residents who are buying the new apartments but rather newcomers who have money. The science town [*naukograd*] is gradually becoming a torgograd [trading town]. We, a group of enterprising citizens, want to preserve the forests and nature of Obninsk by creating in the green zone of Obninsk a specially protected nature area. We have been fighting with the town administration over this for 4 years already.[9] [own translation from Russian transcript]

In contemporary Obninsk, the greenery and woodland are limited to a few places. For example, there is a large wood on the outskirts of the city where an Olympic-sized swimming pool and ice rink was completed in 2012, paid for largely by the regional budget. The old part of town conveys a sense of greenery all around. However, the rest of the town is less green, while the woodland remains on the edge of the town. The research institutes, enterprises, and universities are spread out across the whole town.

In the 1960s–1970s, there was a specific atmosphere inside Obninsk as in Akademgorodok. There were various forums where scientists, engineers, and students could relax and socialise away from home and work: music clubs, amateur theatres, etc. Such institutions helped to increase personal interactions between scientists working in different institutes; nevertheless, the diverse scientific disciplines kept barriers on an institutional level. One interviewee describes here the particular kind of social interactions in science towns in the 1960s–1970s:

> That was the atmosphere of a scientific town at that time. Freedom, openness, freedom of thought and sense of humour . . . First, those cities which had many intelligent and diverse people differed from other cities by their

> free-thinking spirit. And even in Soviet times . . . even in Soviet times, when there was a tough ideology and propaganda and all . . . people in Obninsk thought more freely.[10]

Moreover, in the early period of its existence (1950s–1970s), Obninsk was open to foreign scientists (apart from in the first few years), but these linkages were tightly controlled by the Communist Party of the USSR. This system of tight control by the centralised state ended when the Soviet Union collapsed.

The 1990s: a period of deep economic crisis and a search for solutions

The 1990s was a transitory period when the newly formed Russian Federation was moving away from the Soviet planned economy, undergoing intense learning about capitalist systems, and introducing shock therapy and a market system. This is quite important to understand the nature of Russia's current authoritarian political system.

Like many towns in Russia, Akademgorodok and Obninsk were badly affected by the economic, social, and political consequences of the break-up of the Soviet Union.

Akademgorodok

Akademgorodok was severely affected in economic, social, and political ways by the break-up of the Soviet Union. There was a perceptible crisis in funding for science and research from the late 1980s until the mid-1990s. Akademgorodok was particularly badly hit by the crisis for several reasons (Vodichev et al., 2007). First, historically, it had always been prioritised by Soviet rulers as a place of science. It was a symbol of "big science," and consequentially, it got preferential treatment. When the state collapsed in 1991, it was affected particularly badly by the sharp fall in state funding for R&D (an example of the sharp decline between 1990 and 2000 in the number of researchers employed in just one research institute is shown in Table 4.2). Second, being part of the Soviet Academy of Sciences meant Akademgorodok was isolated from other segments of the country's science and research community, such as higher educational institutions and institutes and enterprises under the control of particular ministries (e.g. nuclear energy), and it was isolated from industrial production systems. Third, it was heavily dependent on central funds because it has always been a place that specialised in fundamental research, not applied science, despite its founders' intentions to make it an "innovation beltway" linking research and production. Fourth, its own special system of training personnel to an advanced level meant that these people had to re-train if they wanted to work elsewhere in research or industry. Fifth, the community of scholars living and working in Akademgorodok has been described by some researchers as elitist: the community had its own ethics and culture of scientific work, partly due to its geographical isolation. This fact created problems for

Table 4.2 Publications of Institute of Computational Technology in Akademgorodok, Novosibirsk (1990–2000)

Year	*No. of staff (of which researchers)*	*No. of publications in Russian scientific journals*	*No. of publications in foreign scientific journals*
1990	300 (3)	Na	
1991	324	5	9
2000	100 (54)	42	46

Source: Institute of Computational Technology in Akademgorodok, Novosibirsk.

researchers and scientists when they tried to adapt to the new living and working conditions that emerged in the late 1980s and early 1990s.

Officials in the new Russian state begun to realise the negative consequences of the crisis in R&D on national security in the mid-1990s. Akademgorodok continued to be managed by the vertically organised Academy of Sciences, while the municipal authority that governed the Akademgorodok area (and a wider area of the district) played a more minor role, primarily focusing on housing and local amenities. This shift in understanding of the 1990s crisis among political and Academy of Sciences officials in Siberian branch led to a wave of new policy documents and strategies that attempted to redefine the role and future position of science in Russia as well as set out the financing arrangements for science (Vodichev et al., 2007). Chief among these new policies was a federal law introduced in 1996, "On science and science-technology policy." One article of this law (Article 6.4) explicitly mentioned the Siberian Branch of the Russian Academy of Sciences as being the "direct beneficiary and main custodian of resources of the federal budget" (Vodichev et al., 2007: 353–354). This provided some guarantee for SB RAS of state funding and hence a starting point to rebuild Akademgorodok's scientific reputation and capacity.

The emergence of a market economy in 1991–1992 where science and research played an important role in contributing to production geared for the market meant that new, very small innovative enterprises appeared in Akademgorodok. A law was passed in 1991 that allowed such enterprises to be created by individuals, but research institutes were not permitted to (co-)found them because they are state-funded institutions. There is a debate about why these enterprises emerged. On the one hand, some scholars argue that scientists enthusiastically created new enterprises and wanted to join in with the spirit of the early 1990s, a spirit which actually emerged in the mid-1980s under Gorbachev (Gordiyenko et al., 2000). On the other hand, others recall that scientists created these enterprises because of financial need: in other words, they were more concerned about survival and knew very little about enterprises. One interviewee in Akademgorodok, Novosibirsk, described what motivated her and colleagues from the Institute of Automatics and Electrometry (IAE) to create their own small company in 1991:

> When we were in the institute, we didn't even have such computers (PCs). Small enterprise was founded in 1991 not because of a "good life" . . . it

> was a necessary thing to do. The monthly salary of a researcher was about USD 20. So, it was a very low salary that you couldn't live off. We decided to start a company, and would work there alongside our jobs in IAE – would work extra and more. We didn't leave the institute on the one hand, but on the other hand we tried to work extra to earn more money on the side. It was a necessary step, which the political and economic situation in the country made us take. We didn't know anything apart from how to develop things using our brains. (author's own interview and translation, date of interview: 8 September 2014)

While the research institutes were not allowed to co-found the small innovative enterprises, they were involved in the enterprise in other ways. The research institute staff who set up the small enterprises took the R&D developed in the institutes and attempted to commercialise it. One of the successful, small innovative enterprises that grew out of SB RAS research institutes in Akademgorodok in the 1990s is Tairus, a firm created in 1989 that grows and processes crystals for jewellery using R&D developed in the Trofimuk Institute of Petroleum Geology and Geophysics (Cherevikina, 2007). Tairus further developed the technology and is now the only producer in the world of precious stones in hydrothermal conditions.

Another success case is the firm Institute of Chromatography EcoNova Ltd., a world-leading supplier of instruments called high-performance liquid chromatographs that was founded in 1991 to develop and commercialise R&D from the SB RAS Institute of Chemical Biology and Fundamental Medicine, the Limnological Institute, and the Budker Institute of Nuclear Physics (Cherevikina, 2007). EcoNova grew from having 22 employees in 2001 to 36 full-time employees in 2012, with another approximately 30 staff hired on temporary contracts when they have many orders to fulfil (author's interview with chair of board of directors, 6 November 2012, Akademgorodok, Novosibirsk).

In February 1999, SB RAS had a total of 77 research institutes under its management. Of those, nine were in the humanities. The majority of the other 68 institutes produced copyrightable goods of industrial property (SB RAS, 1999). Most of the registered intellectual property in SB RAS in the 1990s was for inventions. In fact, there was a substantial drop in the number of registrations for inventions in 1994 and 1995 (just 189 inventions registered in 1995), that is on average in 1995, there were just over two inventions per institute. The gradual increase in intellectual property (IP) registrations after 1995 is testament to Siberian researchers' slow adaptation to the new economic conditions and the new processes to protect IP (Cherevikina, 2007).

Moreover, 44 foreign patents were received for inventions and 6 licences sold abroad, which shows that even during the crisis years in the 1990s, Akademgorodok had links with the world beyond Russia and saw utility in patenting abroad. 23 licences were sold in Russia between 1993 and 1999. However, the low number of licences sold both in Russia and abroad indicates that the level of demand for new technologies produced by Akademgorodok researchers was quite low in the 1990s (Table 4.3).

Table 4.3 Intellectual property in the Siberian Branch of the Russian Academy of Sciences, 1993–1997

Indicators	*1993*	*1994*	*1995*	*1996*	*1997*	*Total*
Protection documents received in Russia for:						
- Inventions	601	410	189	235	308	**1743**
- Utility models	0	3	5	12	9	**29**
- Design inventions	3	1	0	0	1	**5**
- Trade marks	2	0	1	3	2	**8**
- Computer software	0	0	0	2	3	**5**
- Databases	0	0	0	3	1	**4**
Foreign patents received for inventions	11	7	7	11	8	**44**
Registered know-how	0	28	18	7	5	**58**
Licences sold in Russia	0	7	6	4	6	**23**
Licences sold abroad	2	3	0	0	1	**6**
Number of licences per one patent:						
- In Russia						**0.013**
- Abroad						**0.14**
Number of patent services	84	76	70	61	70	

Source: SB RAS (1999)

In addition, since 1990, the Institute of Automation and Electrometry and the Institute of Tomography of SB RAS in Akademgorodok, Novosibirsk, have sold their equipment to other industrial and scientific units. However, such a practice existed without the consent of the director of the institute and without the agreement of industrial ministries or the Academy of Sciences. Hence, such research industry links ensued directly through the researchers and enterprises. In other words, such linkages were not very sustainable (1994).

The late 1990s saw the beginning of a recovery in Akademgorodok as well as in the wider national arena of research and development. From 1997 to 2001, total funding for the SB RAS increased by three times. Of this, the resources from the federal budget grew by 2.7 times in this period. On average for the years 1997–2001, the share of federal funding on R&D in SB RAS's budget was 47.3%.[11]

Obninsk

The 1990s was a crisis period when many people – including scientists in state research institutes – lost their jobs or did not get paid for months on end. Many of them left their jobs in science and research, either going into business or moving abroad. In 1995, the number of people employed in the town's science sector fell by 9%, and Obninsk average salaries were four times less than the national average compared to the previous year (Chernykh, 2004). The quality of infrastructure, both in the research institutes and in residential housing, deteriorated.

The reason was a drastic decline in state funding for science and research and a sharp drop in state orders for science, circumstances which were, in turn, precipitated by Yeltsin's policies of shock therapy and rapid privatisation from 1992. The following quote illustrates the consequences of Yeltsin's policies:

> By late 1992, the domestic economic situation further deteriorated, as shock therapy reforms put most of the population on the brink of poverty. The high degree of corruption and the social and economy decay resulting from the reforms created widespread disillusionment with the pro-Western agenda. The country came close to becoming a failed state . . . preoccupied with survival as poverty, crime, and corruption made it a shadow of the industrialized country that it once was.
>
> (Tsygankov, 2014: 90)

Faced with this crisis period and a transformation from a planned, directed model of science governance to a more market-based model, the political elites of Obninsk took some key decisions to change how the town governed science and research. Like their peers in Russia's other *naukograds*, they pursued a strategy of "survival through development" in the 1990s whereby local scientists and political elites acted collectively to ensure their towns muddled through the crisis years rather than waiting for handouts from Moscow (Rabkin, 1997). They sought ways to emerge from the crisis years of the 1990s and to find new sectors for economic growth, including ICT, automobile, and pharmaceuticals industries. Hitherto, the town's economy had been very rooted in the nuclear industry.

One way which Obninsk officials found to take the town out of the crisis was by opening up to the rest of the world. This is epitomised in the start of a twinning arrangement (or sister cities) with Oak Ridge in 1992, a town of a similar profile to Obninsk in the state of Tennessee, United States. It is also a science town created by the state in 1942 for the Manhattan Project, an initiative by the United States, Canada, and Britain to develop the atomic bomb. A delegation from the Obninsk administration visited Oak Ridge from 15 to 25 January 1998 which was "not just an exchange of official delegations, nor a cultural or a tourist trip, but a working visit as part of a joint year-long project to learn from Oak Ridge's transition experience and adapt it for Obninsk" (McDaniel, 1998: 2).[12] The trip's costs were fully paid for by a grant that Obninsk and Oak Ridge received from Sister Cities International, a United States nonpartisan and non-profit organisation created in 1956 in an effort to spread "citizen diplomacy,"[13] and the US Information Agency (USIA).

Another way was by setting up a new team for science within the Obninsk administration. This team was composed of relatively young, trained scientists who favoured a technocratic and cooperative style of governing. This was in 1994, when a new head of the town's government – the mayor – took office. Mikhail Shubin was quite young when he took up the post (44 years old in 1994, mayor from 1994 to 2000). He was a technocratic politician with a research degree in economics ("candidate of science") and disliked giving press interviews or conferences or interacting much with local people (Chernykh, 2012). At the same time, Shubin strongly believed in local self-governance for municipalities, and he was a supporter of Boris Yeltsin: he was often quoted as saying the phrase "the street elected me!" (*menya vybrala ulitsa!*) in a reference to his popular mandate (Novaya Sreda, 2011). Shubin brought in a new team within the town administration to coordinate science policy and international cooperation. The head of this new team from 1994 until 2000 was Oleg Luksha, under whom they tried hard to implement a new way of governing science in Obninsk – a new, more "cooperative" style according to Luksha in an interview (interview with author, 2012).

This means they wanted to get the different research institutes and organisations to cooperate in order to recover from the crisis that had hit Obninsk hard at the start of the 1990s. The team faced serious obstacles in doing this as the town and its institutes had been built on a more directive, or top-down, governance style whereby the institutes fitted into a hierarchical, national structure. For example, Minsredmash, Rosatom, the Russian Ministry of Health, and the Ministry of Agriculture all had their own institutes in Obninsk which received funding and orders from the central direction of these structures, usually based in Moscow.

The mid-1990s was also the time when the process to make Obninsk Russia's first science town (*naukograd*) began. It was a long and political process, initiated by Obninsk politicians and scientists as well as some federal politicians and bureaucrats. The aim was to secure long-term, federal funds for Obninsk to help it recover from the crisis that began in the early 1990s, although economic malaise and stagnation actually started in the late 1970s. The idea to make Obninsk into a *naukograd* was first discussed as early as 1991 (Larina, 2006), yet the corresponding presidential decree was only passed in May 2000 (Presidential Decree of the Russian Federation No. 821, 6 May 2000). Under mayor Shubin, a referendum on the town's Charter held on 17 December 1995 showed that 80% of Obninsk's population wanted the town to develop as a place dedicated to science. Thus, Obninsk found a way out of the 1990s crisis period not just by applying for (and ultimately winning) federal funds but also by mobilising efforts by the local administration, population, research institutes, and other organisations.

The founder of the Russian Technology Transfer Network (RTTN) explained the process of getting the *naukograd* status and the role of Obninsk in, for example, passing a law on *naukograd*:

> Obninsk was, thanks partly to our efforts, a leader in the movement of naukogrady, in other words, besides Obninsk there were other towns . . . interested in copying our experience etc. In Obninsk, there were quite a lot of different conferences on these issues, we lobbied governmental bodies . . . the result was the law on *naukograd* because without legislation, getting this status [of *naukograd*] didn't mean anything. Only within the framework of the law was it possible to . . . foresee possibilities for budget funding, for development etc.[14] [own translation]

Mayor Shubin's beliefs about local governance and strong municipalities often led him into conflict with the regional administration, which ultimately led to his resignation at the end of 2000 when a new governor of Kaluga region (Anatolii

Artamanov) won the election against a rival candidate (Aleksey Demichev) whom Shubin supported. The year 2000 was the start of the "power vertical" era in Obninsk and more generally in Russia. The "power vertical" refers to reverse decentralisation and the subordination of municipal authorities to regional and they, in turn, to federal authorities.

The start of the experiment of Obninsk as a naukograd was in 1998–1999, run by the town assembly. The rationale for this experiment was the Decree of the President of the Russian Federation No. 1171, dated 7 November 1997. The goals were to develop a mechanism for the stable, unsubsidised development of the town and to ensure federal support for the town – two seemingly contradictory goals. The key policy areas of the experiment were:

- restructuring of the scientific-production complex;
- establishing the innovation infrastructure and attracting investment;
- international cooperation;
- IT development; and
- human resources training.[15]

While it is hard to achieve success in just one year, the experiment can be said to have had some success because it led directly on to a longer, five-year programme with the same aim of ensuring Obninsk developed as a science town in a sustainable and unsubsidised way. Particular achievements during 1998–1999 include:

- **As part of the sub-goal to create innovation infrastructure and attract investment:**
  - Association of Scientific Institutions formed.
  - Competition for basic research projects in materials, power engineering, and the environment run by the regional government and the national Russian Fund for Basic Research.
  - The town assembly adopted a document about investment support.
- **As part of the sub-goal to develop international cooperation:**
  - Russian–Dutch project began (called "Technological Cooperation between Kaluga region and the Netherlands"), which created a Kaluga regional agency to promote investments and technologies;
  - The "EuroAsia" Fund started to carry out a special programme in Obninsk, "Integrated Development of the City Community with EuroAsia Support";
  - A project called "Programme for the Solution of Municipal and Public Problems" was carried out in collaboration with Obninsk's twin city of Oak Ridge in the United States and with the support of the United States Information Agency (USIA – devoted to public diplomacy, the agency was dissolved in 1999).

- **As part of the sub-goal to develop the IT network and infrastructure:**
  - The Obninsk Computer Network was formed.
- **As part of the sub-goal to improve human resources training:**
  - "Energy 3000," a scientific and educational programme, began as part of the Federal Targeted Programme "State Support for Integrating Higher Education and Basic Research in 1997–2000" (Obninsk, 1999).

As can be seen from the aforementioned list, the first year of the naukograd experiment had some success. Most efforts went into developing international cooperation and bringing lessons learnt and experiences from other countries to Obninsk, while attempts to restructure the scientific-production complex were absent, or at least unreported by the town's authorities (i.e. not reported in the official publication about the programme, Obninsk, 1999). Restructuring an entire town's scientific-production complex is undoubtedly a long-term task. The formation of the Association of Scientific Institutions and the Obninsk Computer Network are examples of the town trying to resolve collective action problems and build up critical mass forming in the town, issues that will be further discussed in the following section of this chapter on interpretations.

As already mentioned, Akademgorodok and Obninsk were both badly affected by the economic crisis that started in the early 1990s. To try and help their places recover from the crisis, local and regional elites in the two localities chose explicit internationalisation policy strategies in the 1990s. Both places chose to reinstate contacts and networks internationally to learn from other countries' experiences and adapt them to their own town. Obninsk established a twin town arrangement, while Akademgorodok arranged for some directors of Akademgorodok-situated research institutes and top managers of programming companies to participate in international study tours (see the section "Learning from abroad," specifically the part on pp. 120–122 on "international study visits and the emergence of two business associations").

During the 1990s and 2000s, Obninsk sustained arguably more experiences of policy learning from Europe and the "West" in science and technology than Akademgorodok. Many local administration officials, as well as managers and scientists from Obninsk's research institutes and factories, participated in the EU TACIS programme and twin city projects with the United States (e.g. with the nuclear town of Oak Ridge in the state of Tennessee, United States – see p. 182 of this chapter) and several European countries. This programme included several study tours for businesspeople, scientists, and officials. Involvement in the TACIS programme led directly to the creation of the organisation "Russian Technology Transfer Network" (RTTN) in 2002 as the European Commission allocated some resources to set up the RTTN. The RTTN is a bottom-up network organisation by the Obninsk Centre of Science and Technology (OCST) and the Koltsovo Innovation Centre in the Novosibirsk region. Because it is based in Obninsk, the town and Kaluga regional administrations can draw on the RTTN's capabilities to help with urban and regional development. However, the RTTN is primarily a nationally focused organisation inspired by European experiences:

> We are focused on the national level. It is the problem of the administration . . . of the regional administration how best to make the most of us (based in the town). In other words, we . . . have certain competencies and if we feel that . . . or if the administration feels that our competencies can be judiciously used for urban or regional development then we are open to cooperation. But we don't have a problem, for example, with orders . . . and no problem with participation in various town programmes etc. Where we are needed, we are brought on board in other words, we are not focused at the moment on town and regional problems.[16] [author interview with chair of RTTN, 26.06.2012, own translation]

The years 2000–2010: the return of the state

Akademgorodok

The 2000s were characterised by a return of the state in terms of state funding for R&D in Akademgorodok. At the end of the 1990s, Akademgorodok slowly began to emerge from the crisis situation of the 1990s. The annual average of the share of federal funding for SB RAS over the 5 years from 1997 to 2001 was just over 47%. An average of 37% of the budget of SB RAS came from contracts for R&D; resources from contracts increased by 4.6 times from 1997 to 2001. Just under a third of the contract funding came from foreign contracts. By 2005, about half of revenues of SB RAS came from the federal budget; in 2010, this share had increased substantially to 71% (Table 4.4). This is evidence of the greater role of the state in funding R&D in Russia in this period. In contrast to the growth of federal funding, the income that SB RAS received from contracts almost halved from 2005 to 2010 (from 39% to 23%).

Table 4.4 Share of funding for SB RAS by source (%)

Year	*Federal budget*	*Contracts (international and grants)*	*Rent*	*Other (including Ministry of Education and Science, Russian Science Foundations)*	*Total*
5-year average for 1997–2001	47.3	37	na	Na	100
2005	49.2	39.4	2.5	8.9	100
2010	71.0	23.3	1.4	4.3	100

Source: SB RAS Annual Reports (in Russian). Available online: www.sbras.ru/ru/cmn/reports

Obninsk

Since 1991, there have been more governing institutions in Obninsk than ever before in the Soviet era. The key organisations controlling the town of Obninsk since 1991 are the city administration, regional administration, and the larger, federal structures regulating many of the town's research institutes and organisations.

A change in the town's ruling structure came in 2001. In relation to Obninsk's new status of "*naukograd*" that came into force in 2000, the new role of deputy mayor for science was introduced in April 2001. This shows that the town was more committed to supporting its science and research community. The local deputy and geography scholar, Alla Prosvirkina, was appointed to this position.

Another important part of the governance structure is the Kaluga regional administration. The regional governor heads this administration: in the 1990s (1991–1996) the governor was appointed by President Yeltsin; then, elections were introduced in 1996 until 2005 when all governors were again appointed by the President of Russia. Anatolii Artamanov won the 2000 gubernatorial election, a position he holds to this day, meaning he is one of only a handful of long-standing governors in Russia who have managed to combine loyalty to the President of Russia with popular loyalty to their subjects in their regions. Artamonov has therefore led Kaluga region's important policy agenda to boost science and innovation and promote foreign direct investment.

As for the affiliations of Obninsk's research institutes and organisations, there are clear patterns whereby most of them are part of larger, federal structures. Three research organisations and enterprises in the town now have the status of state research centre, a sign of prestige. Five of the 10 main research institutes or organisations in Obninsk are institutionally subordinate to the state corporation for atomic energy, Rosatom. One organisation is subordinate to the state corporation for technologies, Rostekhnologii. Meanwhile, three research institutes are subordinate to the Federal Agency "Roshydromet," the agency for hydrometeorology. Three research organisations are accountable to different federal ministries, while the "Geophysical Service" reports to the Russian Academy of Sciences. The group of companies called the OCST is a special case as it was founded in 1997 by several large enterprises in Obninsk and the town administration.

An important linkage between the town administration and the research institutes and organisations is the Council of Directors. This body consists of the heads of all the town's research institutes and organisations and factories. They meet regularly and play an important role in the governance of the town, for example, in early 2005 when the town had to decide who to appoint as the new mayor.

Hence, the scientific and research institutions in Obninsk have many links with the federal government. This chapter has already illustrated how many of the town's research institutes and organisations are affiliated with federal state corporations or agencies. Another link with the central state is official visits to the town by federal-level political elites. For example, President Medvedev made an official visit to Obninsk in April 2010, which was a politically and historically significant event. He came to Obninsk to convene the country's first meeting on modernisation by his presidential commission for modernisation. It was the first time a head of state had visited Obninsk, which shows that Obninsk figured prominently in top political elites' minds as a leading place of science and innovation. Nevertheless, the agenda of Medvedev's visit only included a federal-level meeting, not tours of the local enterprises or research institutes or talking with local residents (Chernykh, 2012).

Moreover, the official status of "science town" (*naukograd*) that Obninsk received in 2000 gives the town, in theory at least, access to significant federal funds for science and innovation. However, control in terms of funding for science and innovation will be discussed later (p. 192), in particular whether this status actually results in significantly more resources.

Four of Obninsk's top ten scientific institutions in terms of producing publications are a research production association, a scientific–production enterprise, an experimental centre, and a centre that acts as a focal point for the town's innovative businesses (Obninsk Centre of Science and Technology). This suggests that Obninsk is more oriented towards downstream research, or research which is closer to market, than Akademgorodok.

In the 2000s, the region of Kaluga – in which Obninsk is located – was one of the leading regions in Russia for volume of inward foreign investment. This positively impacted the policy of Obninsk town administration and other agencies' views on foreign investment and linkages.

In the 2000s, Obninsk saw renewed federal funding as a naukograd. However, this funding came with restricted usage. In 2011, Obninsk received approximately 2.1 million USD (59.5 million RUB, GBP 1.3 million) of federal funding in "additional expenditures" as part of the naukograd programme. This money was first and foremost allocated to the project to create an innovation zone in Obninsk, which is designed to accommodate small innovative enterprises in a compact area (Dudov, 2011). Obninsk's local budget steadily increased from 2009 to 2014. A large proportion of local expenditures was spent on welfare. Science and innovation were and continue to be (since 2014) primarily funded from the federal budget.

Owing to Obninsk's status as a formally listed naukograd in Russia, it has access to special federal funds. The Federal Law on naukograds (1999, with amendments of 20 April 2015 which took effect from 1 January 2017) states:

1. "Budgets of subjects of the Russian Federation, which contain municipalities with the legal status of naukograd, are given inter-governmental transfers from the federal budget for distribution to the corresponding local budgets in accordance with the rules set out in this article as regulated by the Government of the Russian Federation.

2. The inter-governmental transfers, as specified in point 1 of this Article are not counted when distributing other inter-governmental transfers from the federal budget and budgets of subjects of the Russian Federation."

(Article 8. State Support for the Development of Naukograds, original in Russian)

However, it seems that there are some contradictions between this Federal Law and the Budget Code of the Russian Federation, which is the legal document that controls intergovernmental transfers in the country. The Budget Code does not allow a science and technology project to be funded from different budgets, that is from federal, regional, and local authorities. The mayor of another naukograd (Fryazino) described the problems in a 2012 interview that was published online:

> However, it became clear quite quickly that "naukograd" financing is hard to receive due to bureaucratic inefficiencies at a federal level. The Budget Code of the Russian Federation, a key rule governing financial resources, prohibits the funding of the same project from budgets of different levels. "Naukograd" money is for the regional or municipal budget, and hence cannot top-up defence projects that are funded by the federal budget. Naukograd funding cannot be given to fundamental research that is financed by the Russian Academy of Sciences also from the federal budget. "Naukograd" money cannot be used for innovative development that is financed by the Federal Ministry of Industry and Trade. Neither can it be used for advanced studies or research that receive grants from the Ministry of Science and Education. Naukograd funding is only for local projects that are in the interests of the town or region, as a result of which the town (region) should get something of material nature such as a machine or instrument that will be used in the town (regional) economy. Moreover, the project should meet the priority areas as specified in the presidential decree. We did not have any projects that met this criterion.
>
> It turned out that "naukograd" funds could only be used to improve the town's infrastructure: social, housing, communal, etc. Thus, the town – thanks to naukograd funding – can provide for the town's enterprises and their employees worthy infrastructure, while the enterprises should secure their own funding for new R&D in the priority areas as specified by the presidential decree. If the enterprises could not fund the priority areas and ensure the town meets the criteria for naukograds, then the town would cease to receive additional "naukograd" funding for its development.
>
> (online published interview with Mayor of Fryazino, 2012, author's own translation from Russian)

The top research institute in Obninsk for publications (3436 publications), the Institute for Physics and Power Engineering named after Leypunsky (IPPE), also scored highest in that locality for citations (17,623 citations). This was the founding institute in Obninsk around which the town grew. This institute was established in 1956 and to date has a reputation for being the strongest and largest institute in the town. The publications and citations data confirm this reputation as the leading research institute of Obninsk.

The years 2011–2017

Akademgorodok continues to maintain and cherish its green location away from the hustle and bustle of a large city. It is near a large reservoir (known locally as the Ob "sea"), a popular summer-time location with residents for rest and relaxation. Despite some pressures from developers, the woods remain an integral part of Akademgorodok: research institutes, residential buildings, and shops are nestled between the trees and connected by dense networks of footpaths and bicycle tracks. Many people who live locally walk or cycle to work or school through the woods via well-signposted paths – getting around on these paths is often quicker than by taking public transport or a car.

Today, Akademgorodok in Novosibirsk has a total of 31 research and educational institutions managed by SB RAS. In addition, SB RAS runs four other entities in the little academy town: the Presidium of SB RAS (the management of SB RAS), the House of Scholars (a cultural and social meeting place), the Exhibition centre, and Akadempark, the technology park set up by SB RAS.[17] As shown in Table 4.5, Akademgorodok has a dense network of institutions which can be

Table 4.5 Institutional landscape for innovation in Akademgorodok and the wider city of Novosibirsk

Institutions for innovation, by type of focal activity	
New scientific knowledge	31 research institutes under the Siberian Division of the Russian Academy of Sciences (SB RAS); since 2013, SB RAS property and infrastructure were managed by the Federal Agency for Scientific Organisations (FASO) until it was abolished in 2018 by President Putin
	Novosibirsk State University (NSU)
	School attached to NSU (feeder school)
	Novosibirsk State Technical University
	Koltsovo *naukograd* focused on biotechnology in Novosibirsk city
	"Vector" state research centre of virology and biotechnology in Koltsovo, Novosibirsk
Technical knowledge and services (intermediary or bridging organisations)	Bottom-up business association of innovative enterprises "SibAcademInnovation"
	Bottom-up business association of IT firms "SibAcademSoft"
	Technology park ("Akadempark") under the institutional control of SB RAS
	House of Scholars managed by SB RAS (a cultural and social meeting place for SB RAS researchers)
Innovative activities	Spin-offs from institutes or universities
	Industries located near Akademgorodok in the city of Novosibirsk

Source: Author.

categorised into three groups depending on their primary purpose: (i) research and production of new knowledge, (ii) technical knowledge and services (intermediary or bridging organisations), and (iii) innovative activities.

The locality is no longer governed by the Academy of Sciences alone. There are four main "housekeepers" ("khozaiyin" in Russian) who play important roles in how the locality is run on a daily and strategic level. These institutional actors are as follows:

(i) Russian Academy of Sciences (RAS);
(ii) Federal Agency for Scientific Organisations (FASO, since the 2013 reform of the RAS; see Chapter 3 for a discussion of Russia's innovation system);
(iii) Novosibirsk State University; and
(iv) Regional, municipal, and private owners of property in Akademgorodok (Fateyeva, 2017).

In addition, the regional administration of Novosibirsk region plays a minor role. The political stability from a long-ruling regional governor and the mayor of Novosibirsk city ensures some continuity in science and technology policy although the real impact of regional authorities in STI is quite limited.

Akademgorodok's founders' vision of a ring of concentric circles from research to industry has today materialised in a successfully developing science park which has been active since 2011. It currently has 272 resident firms, of which 66 are based in the business incubator (see Chapter 5).[18]

Akademgorodok in Novosibirsk remains largely funded by the federal government. Table 4.6 shows that in 2015, 63% of all funding for SB RAS research institutions came from state subsidies (of which 59% was for specified state programmes). Thirty-seven per cent of their revenues was sourced by the institutions themselves, for example from licences, patent fees, rents of buildings. The story remained almost the same in 2018, although the share of revenues for state subsidies for state programmes declined by 2%.

A 2017 policy proposal from SB RAS, Novosibirsk State University, and regional administration is for the Novosibirsk scientific centre to be transformed into "Akademgorodok 2.0" by 2035, which could dramatically increase critical

Table 4.6 Revenues of SB RAS institutions accountable to the Ministry of Education and Science of Russia (in %), 2015–2018

Year	*State subsidies for state programmes/ missions*	*State subsidies for other goals*	*Own revenues*	*Total*
2015	59	4	37	100
2018*	57	4	39	100

Source: Report of the Chair of SB RAS, Valentin Parmon, on activities in 2018, April 2019. Available online in Russian: www.sbras.ru/report_2018 [last accessed 30 April 2019].

*2018 year includes medical and agricultural divisions of SB RAS.

mass of research and innovation at a regional level. It would incorporate several scientific, infrastructural, and social projects and would greatly expand Akademgorodok by integrating it with neighbouring research centres (Seliverstov, 2020). At the time of completing this book in mid-2021, the project was still being discussed by policy makers and business leaders and had not received any funding, neither from federal or regional authorities nor from the city of Novosibirsk.

This project would integrate Akademgorodok into a bigger entity with the nearby *naukograd* of Koltsovo that specialises in biotechnology, as well as with an entity that has an agricultural focus (Nizhniy Yeltsovka). In this sense, "Akademgorodok 2.0" is a project that aims to recreate the drive and vision of Akademgorodok's founders to create something new that will have long-term impacts on research and production both regionally and further afield.

The head of the science–educational complex and innovation in the Novosibirsk regional ministry of education, science, and innovation policy describes what had been achieved as of the summer of 2018:

> The hardest task was to bring together all the research, infrastructure, social, and engineering projects which would be appropriate to examine in this context. A coordinating council has been created under the control of the governor of Novosibirsk region [head of regional executive] and working groups set up to report to the coordinating council. As a result, 25 scientific projects, 15 infrastructure projects, and about 30 social and engineering projects have been included in the programme's plan of priority activities.[19] [author translation from Russian]

Obninsk's local economy: key features

Table 4.7 presents key socio-economic indicators for the naukograd of Obninsk from 2010 to 2017. The town has seen a small increase in population in the second decade of the 21st century. Official unemployment rates as a percentage of the labour force have fluctuated between 0.3% and 0.5%, which suggest that the town

Table 4.7 Socio-economic indicators for Obninsk, 2010–2017

	2010	*2014*	*2017*
Population	105,800	109,273	115,000
Unemployment (as % of labour force)	0.5%	0.33%	0.39%
Total employed in science and scientific services (% of town's labour force)	11,000 (21%)	11,100 (19.5%)	9,900 (20.6%)
Volume of scientific–technical outputs of town's research institutes	6.8 billion RUB	11.5 billion RUB (+8.4% higher than in 2013)	Na

Source: Obninsk local administration annual reports.

has high employment. A fifth of the town's labour force works in science and scientific activities – a share that has been stable since at least 2010. The volume of scientific outputs increased rapidly from almost 7 billion roubles (approximately 224.4 million USD as of exchange rate on 30 June 2010) in 2010 to 11.5 billion roubles (approximately 338.2 million USD as of exchange rate on 30 June 2014) in 2014.

According to official sources, the contribution to Obninsk's economy from science and R&D has grown slightly from 2011 to 2017 (Figure 4.1). In 2011, R&D contributed 11% to Obninsk's economy; by 2017, this had increased to 14%. This increased contribution of R&D to the town's budget may be associated with the policy shift from 2010 to see innovation as a mechanism for local and regional development. In 2010, the Kaluga region set up the Agency for Innovation Development, an organisation which acts as a specialised entity to manage innovative clusters and infrastructure projects for innovation and, thus, is an integrating force for innovative processes in the region.

Wholesale trade and retail decreased in relative importance in the town from 35% in 2011 to 28% in 2014 before rising moderately to 30% in 2017. Meanwhile, industry's contribution to Obninsk's economy was 38% in 2011, 44% in 2014, and 40.8% in 2017. The year 2014 also saw 6% of the town's economic GDP come from the construction industry (the share for other years was not reported in official sources). Overall, these statistics point to the slow evolution in economic structure in Obninsk over the last six years: the predominance of industry and the small but growing contribution of R&D since 2011.

Figure 4.1 Dynamics over time in contributions to the local economy, Obninsk naukograd, 2011–2017

Source: Obninsk local administration annual reports for 2011, 2014, and 2017

Institutions

As shown in Table 4.8, Obninsk has a dense network of institutions which can be categorised into three groups depending on their primary purpose: (i) research and production of new knowledge, (ii) technical knowledge and services (intermediary or bridging organisations), and (iii) innovative activities.

Obninsk currently has 10 research institutes and 13 tertiary educational institutions. The most well-known of these is the Obninsk Institute for Nuclear Power Engineering, which since 2009 has been incorporated into the MEPhI National Research Nuclear University (Moscow Engineering Physics Institute National Research Nuclear University). The town has a wide range of "bridging" type organisations that provide technical knowledge and services. These include the Russian Technology Transfer Network (RTTN), a bottom-up network organisation created in 2002 in Obninsk by the Centre for Science and Technology and the Koltsovo Innovation Center in Novosibirsk region. Other intermediary institutions are the Agency of Innovation Development-Centre of Cluster Development of Kaluga region (AIRKO), Obninsk Centre for Science and Technology, and the Council of Directors.

An interesting institutional parallel with Akademgorodok's two business associations (as described later in this chapter, pp. 120–122) can be found in Obninsk, in the Council of Directors. This Council was originally created in the 1980s but stopped being functional during perestroika. In January 1993, it was reconvened and "reborn" at the initiative of the then general director of the company "Tekhnologiya" (Alexander Romashin), who became its chairperson. Today, it exists

Table 4.8 Institutional landscape for innovation in Obninsk

Institutions, by the type of activity focused on	
New scientific knowledge	10 research institutes 13 tertiary educational institutions
Technical knowledge and services (intermediary or bridging organisations)	Russian Technology Transfer Network (RTTN) Agency of Innovation Development of Kaluga region Kaluga Regional Centre for Nano-industry Obninsk Centre for Science and Technology (OCST) Council of Directors of factories and institutes in Obninsk SCST state council for S&T as a local body
Innovative activities	Territory for innovative development, including a municipal industrial zone, Obninsk industrial park (for pharmaceuticals and food processing), and the Krasniy Zory innovation zone Technopark (planned since 2006, not yet operational) Research production associations Scientific production enterprises Two business incubators (hosting 29 companies in 2011, Dudov, 2011)

Source: Compiled by the author.

to provide a platform for dialogue and cooperation between the large enterprises and factories in Obninsk and the town administration. It is not only a place to discuss the town's most pressing issues but also to collectively find solutions to these problems. For example, in the year June 2011–June 2012, it met 12 times, examining 14 main issues, particularly social ones, such as affordable housing for younger employees, utilities in residential buildings, and how to preserve the town's science legacies and capabilities and capitalise on them to develop as a *naukograd* (Vperyod newspaper, 19.06.2012: 1).

The town's industrial cluster for pharmaceuticals and food processing has been operational since 2013.[20] There is some evidence that it has attracted foreign investment. For example, a Korean company, Lotte Confectionery Ltd., invested more than 3 billion roubles to open a factory in the park in 2010 that makes 300 brands of confectionery. The Serbian–Italian company, Palladio Zannini, also opened a factory there in 2017 that produces packaging for pharmaceutical and cosmetic goods. The large Russian pharmaceutical manufacturer, Niarmedic, opened a factory there in 2010 to make the drug Kagocel that is sold on the domestic market.

The third type of institutions active in Obninsk operates directly to produce innovative activities. These include some research production associations, scientific production enterprises, and two business incubators.

Thus, Obninsk has developed a dense network of institutions encompassing the following three groups depending on their primary purpose: (i) research and production of new knowledge; (ii) technical knowledge and services (intermediary or bridging organisations); and (iii) innovative activities. Some of these institutions are cases of isomorphic mimicry, copied in appearance from other countries yet not functional (e.g. the technopark). Other institutions are quite active, for example Russian Technology Transfer Network (RTTN) and the Agency of Innovation Development of Kaluga region.

The next section compares some key outcomes of Akademgorodok and Obninsk, looking at their respective performances in fundamental research (publications), research contracts with external organisations, and in clusters.

Outcomes in fundamental research: publications and citations

Akademgorodok in Novosibirsk is strongly oriented towards fundamental research. The number of publications between 1991 and 2016 is much higher in Akademgorodok Novosibirsk (5995–29,850 publications per organisation) than in Obninsk (21–4,793 publications per organisation). In addition, seven of the top ten performing organisations in Akademgorodok are research institutes affiliated with the SB RAS, with the other three organisations universities. In other words, Akademgorodok's top ten publication-producing organisations are all focused on upstream R&D, or fundamental research. This is not surprising given that the SB RAS founded Akademgorodok and given Akademgorodok remains a place of excellence in fundamental R&D.

The high-profile institute in Akademgorodok, the Budker Institute of Nuclear Physics, also published relatively widely in the period 1991–2016 (8392 publications) compared to other Akademgorodok research institutes and universities and had the highest number of citations of all the 20 organisations studied in Akademgorodok and Obninsk (123,338 citations). The Budker Institute of Nuclear Physics was founded just two years after its institutional twin (the IPPE in Obninsk) in 1958. The other institute in Akademgorodok concentrating solely on physics, the Ryzhanov Institute of Semiconductor Physics (founded slightly later in 1964), also had a high number of publications in the same time period (4361) and a large volume of total citations (22,030). This shows it is common practice to publish frequently and cite widely in physics (Roth et al., 2012). Moreover, it shows that these physics research institutes have built up strong organisational capabilities for undertaking and disseminating their research in the form of publications.

In Akademgorodok Novosibirsk (Figure 4.2), the most productive institutes as measured by Russian language **publications per staff member** for 1991–2016 were the Institute of Mathematics, Novosibirsk State Technical University, Institute of Catalysis, Novosibirsk State Medical University, and the Institute of Inorganic Chemistry.

Besides looking at publications per person, which relies on accurate and comparable statistics for numbers of staff or researchers (not available for all research organisations in the two science towns), we can also look at **citations per publication** as a way of evaluating the quality of research. Figure 4.3 shows the top 10 performing research institutes or organisations in Akademgorodok. The Budker Institute of Nuclear Physics had by far the highest number of citations per publication (13) on account of its very high absolute number of citations. The next top five institutions in Akademgorodok for citations per publication are active in research in the disciplines of cytology and genetics, catalysis, geology and mineralogy, semiconductor physics, and inorganic chemistry.

As shown in Table 4.9, the Geophysical Service of the Russian Academy of Sciences published at a much higher rate per member of staff than the other research organisations in Obninsk science town (24 publications per employee averaged over the period 1991–2016). The next most productive organisations as per publications by a number of total employees for the period 1991–2016 were the Research Institute of Radiology and Agroecology and the Obninsk Centre of Science and Technology.

Nevertheless, the numbers of publications per staff member in Obninsk research organisations are much lower than in Akademgorodok. This may well reflect differences between different disciplines, however, rather than varying levels of productivity.

Outcomes: research contracts

In addition to resources from state budgets for resolving the collective action problem and building critical mass, science towns can also benefit from contracts drawn up by their research institutes or companies. The number of contracts a research institute, organisation, or firm has with other firms or organisations to

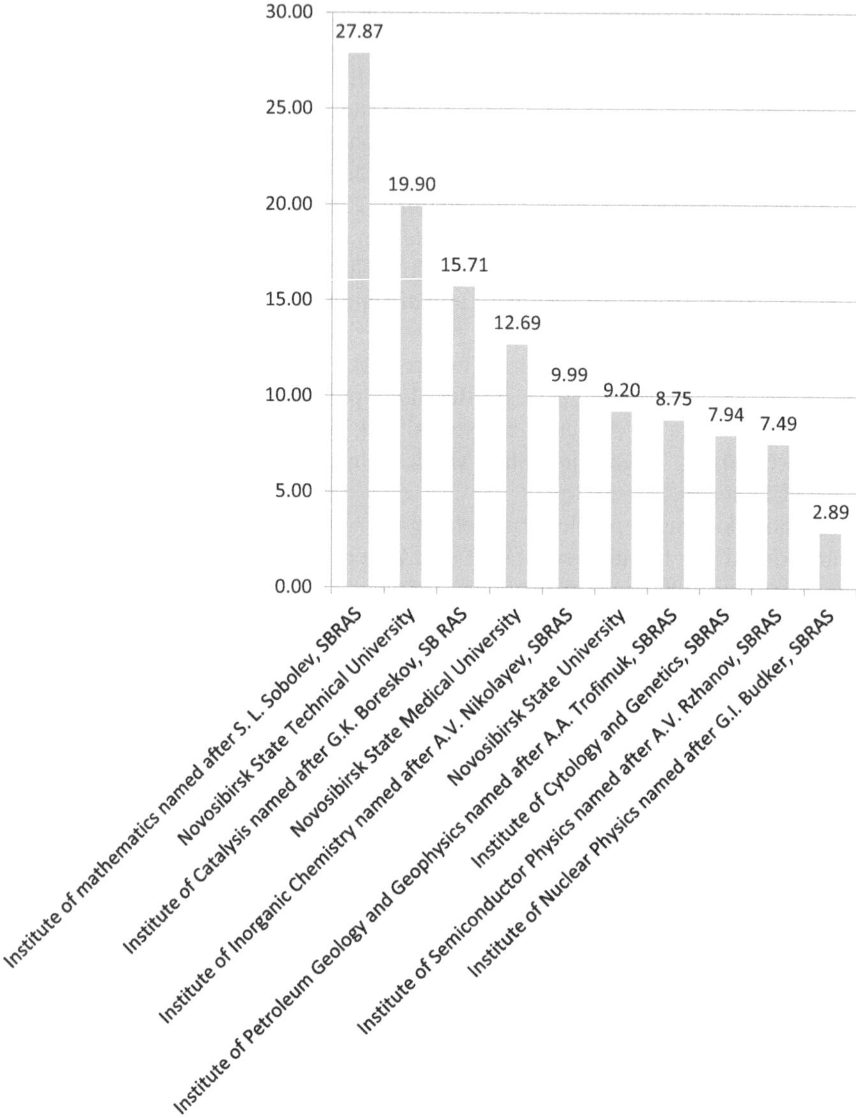

Figure 4.2 Number of publications per staff member of institutes and universities in Akademgorodok, Novosibirsk, 1991–2016

Source: www.elibrary.ru [last accessed 29 December 2018], compiled by author.

Note: To calculate the number of publications per researcher at each institute and university, the total number of publications between 1991 and 2016 was divided by the total number of staff (last year available).

Disciplinary publication bias was not controlled for here.

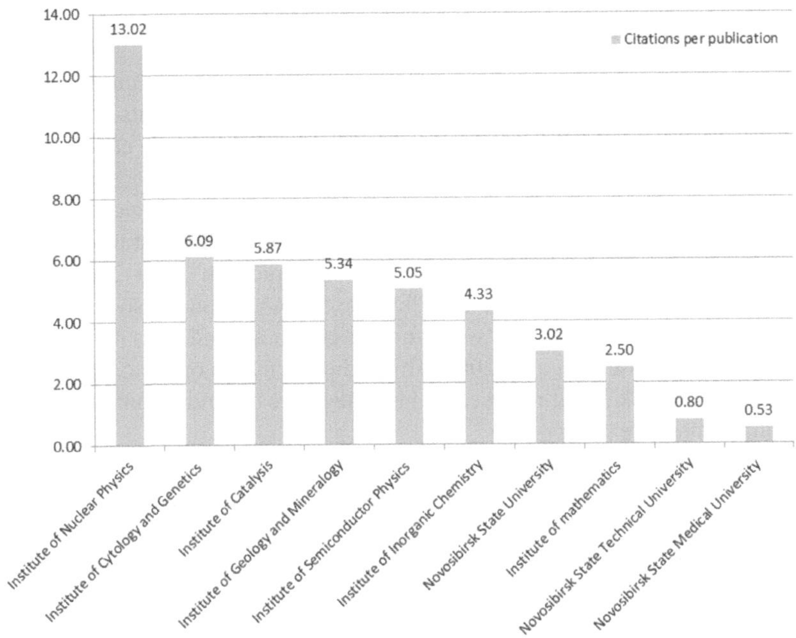

Figure 4.3 Citations per publication in Akademgorodok, 2005–2013

Source: www.elibrary.ru [last accessed 29 December 2018], compiled by the author.

Table 4.9 Number of publications per staff member of institutes and universities in Obninsk, 1991–2016

Name of research organisation (English)	*Publications/staff (for 1991–2016)**
Geophysical Service of Russian Academy of Sciences	23.97
All-Russian Research Institute of Radiology and Agroecology	1.61
Obninsk Centre of Science and Technology	1.17
Research Production association (RPA) "Typhoon" of Russian Federal Service on Hydrometeorology and Environmental Monitoring	0.76
State Scientific Centre of the Russian Federation – Institute for Physics and Power Engineering named after A. I. Leypunsky	0.74
All-Russian Research Institute of Agricultural Meteorology	0.49
National Research Institute of Hydrometeorological Information – World Data Centre	0.47
Experimental Scientific-Research and Methodology Centre "Simulation Systems"	0.37
Obninsk scientific–production enterprise "Technology"	0.17

Source: www.elibrary.ru [last accessed 15 May 2018].

Note: Shown in descending order by publications per staff member. To calculate the number of publications per researcher at each institute and university, the total number of publications between 1991 and 2016 was divided by the total number of staff (last year available). Data on numbers of staff in the Central Russian Humanitarian Engineering Institute in Obninsk were unavailable, so this institution was excluded here, despite being ranked seventh for number of publications.

sell certain products or services indicates how interconnected it is. Of course, this depends to a large extent on the discipline: some disciplines are closer to industry than others.

In the 2000s, Akademgorodok's "Institute of Catalysis" is arguably the flagship institute in terms of how successfully it has restructured itself since 1991 and adapted to the conditions of a market economy (Radošević et al., 2001). In 2000–2001, this institute received 75% of its budget from contracts (mainly foreign ones), with the remainder from the Russian state (Radošević et al., 2001). Similarly, another leading institute in Akademgorodok (the Institute of Atomic Physics) received 70% of its funding from contracts in 2000–2001. Another example is the Institute of Chemical Physics, SB RAS which also received 70% from contracts (of which 45% were foreign contracts) and just 30% of its revenues from the state budget in 2001. This indicates that in order to survive, some of Akademgorodok's leading research institutes were dependent on revenues from primarily non-state sources.

The Institute of Computational Technology in Akademgorodok, Novosibirsk was formed in 1990. In recent years, it has undertaken R&D work on contract for several external organisations and enterprises, including the Siberian State University and the enterprise "Information satellite systems named after Reshetnyov," a leading company in Russia in the space sector (multiple contracts). The institute has also done contract work for other Russian enterprises such as "Apatit," and Krasmash, and for a Siberia-based, non-commercial organisation called the "Ecological Centre for Sustainable Use of Natural Resources." In 2000, the institute started setting up contracts with foreign organisations as well as with Russian ones (Table 4.10).

The organisation "Obninsk Centre of Science and Technology" (OCST) had contracts with several federal organisations as of 2011: RosNauka (a federal agency created in 2004 that was accountable to the Ministry of Science until it was abolished in 2010) and the Ministry of Science. The OCST also had contracts with the leading technical university MEPhI and the leading State Research Centre of Russia, the "Institute of Physics and Power Engineering," named after

Table 4.10 Contracts of Institute of Computational Technology in Akademgorodok, Novosibirsk (1990–2017)

Year	*No. of staff (of which researchers)*	*Contracts with foreign organisations*	*Contracts with Russian organisations*
1990	300 (3)	No	Yes
1991	324	No	Yes
2000	100 (54)	Yes	Yes
2010	94 (58)	Na	Na
2012	114 (73)	Na	Na
2017	289 (107)	Na	Na

Source: Annual reports of the Institute of Computational Technology in Akademgorodok. Compiled by the author.

Leypunsky which is based in Obninsk. As the OCST does not carry out production itself, it also drew up contracts with several research institutes within the RAS and with suppliers of production.

From 2012, the OCST decided to transfer all specialised production (non-mass) to a newly formed daughter company it sets up, the "production-technical centre of OCST." The OCST has the trademark for the four-letter abbreviation "OCST" (registered with Rospatent in 2012). This means that OCST receives a payment for the use of this abbreviation by companies that sell OCST products.

In Obninsk, the connectedness of research institutes to federal structures – particularly in the 2000s – impedes internationalisation. Evidence of this comes from the lower number of United States patents held by Obninsk-based researchers. International linkages in Obninsk seem to be limited in scale and scope to only cover exchanges of researchers and local government officials. One explanation could be that the federal government is afraid of losing control of the town's strategic key assets in strategic industries.

How does Obninsk fare in having international contracts for technological production? The scientific–production enterprise "Technology" is a holding company now forming part of the state corporation "Rostekhnologii" and which has held the prestigious status of a Russian state research centre since 1994. It developed out of an experimental factory to produce silicate glass for the aviation sector that was formed in 1959 in Obninsk. "Technology" now partners with 60 companies that are based in 20 countries globally, including the United States, United Kingdom, Norway, Denmark, Germany, Belgium, the Netherlands, Switzerland, Austria, Israel, Uzbekistan, Kazakhstan, China, and Vietnam.

Another example of international linkages that Obninsk has is the Obninsk-based "Medical radiological scientific centre" (affiliated to the Ministry of Healthcare, hence a federal state budget institution) which was founded in 1962 with the purpose of developing better methods for radiation diagnoses and radiation therapy. Today, it is a leader in its field and, since 1995, has maintained a World Health Organisation centre for scientific work in radiation epidemiology.

Learning from abroad

Three aspects of learning from abroad will be examined in this section: scientists going on international trips and foreign scientists visiting Russia; project collaborations with international partners; and foreign study visits for local scientists and businesspeople.

Scientists' foreign visits

Visits made to other countries and foreign scientists visiting Akademgorodok are examined here. In the 2000s, researchers in Akademgorodok institutes regularly travelled abroad to visit colleagues and to explore the potential for new collaborations. A smaller number of foreign specialists visited Akademgorodok each year.

Table 4.11 Foreign cooperation in and with Institute of Catalysis

	2004	*2009*	*2010*	*2011*
Total no. of foreign specialists to BIC per year	79	125	89	58
No. of countries from which foreign specialists to BIC came	15	31	18	14
Total no. of visits made by BIC specialists to foreign institutions	171	203	263	193
No. of countries visited by BIC specialists	24	31	33	31

Source: Boreskov Institute of Catalysis (BIC) Annual Reviews in English for 2004, 2009, 2010, 2011. Available at: www.catalysis.ru/block/index.php?ID=1&SECTION_ID=1254 [last accessed 1 January 2018].

The most high-profile research institute in Akademgorodok, the Boreskov Institute of Catalysis (BIC), will be looked at here. Table 4.11 shows the extent of linkages BIC had over seven years (2004–2011). The number of foreign researchers' visits to BIC peaked in 2009, while most BIC researchers went on work trips abroad in 2010. It was much more popular for BIC researchers to go abroad than foreign researchers to visit BIC.

Local political officials and managers in the SB RAS in Akademgorodok supported and promoted international linkages among its scientists and young companies in the 2000s. The SB RAS had quite a patriotic policy, as illustrated by the following excerpt from an interview with an employee of the Centre for Public Affairs, SB RAS:

> now Russian scientists can go on expeditions abroad . . . Scientists are in principle citizens of the world but nevertheless, because of patriotic considerations it is preferred that as many as possible effective . . . scientists spend most of their time in Russia, work in Russia, are interested in Russia, receive Nobel prizes for Russia.[21]

This quote shows that officials remain a bit wary of scientists travelling abroad even though it is allowed, which may be associated with fears that scientists will emigrate in search of better job opportunities or living conditions abroad.

International scientific collaboration

International collaboration in research is important for innovation because it can be a source of potential knowledge exchange with other countries. Previous literature (Grupp et al., 2001; Kotsemir et al., 2015) has analysed bibliometric data to examine international collaborations through co-authoring journal articles and other academic outputs. While this large topic is beyond the scope of the present book, it could be the subject of future research to understand the trends in international co-publications among researchers in Russia's science towns.

Participation in foreign projects is another common form of research collaboration that was supported by the SB RAS in the 2000s. The Boreskov Institute of Catalysis has long-standing international links. The institute has benefited from foreign investment before 2004. In 2001, for example, the institute collaborated with foreign partners who invested in equipment, computers, and repairs and renovation in the institute (Radošević et al., 2001).

The BIC frequently participates in joint international research projects, including on the use of synchrotron radiation, with leading international centres in Europe and the United States (e.g. BESSY, ESRF, and others). In addition, it collaborates with universities and research centres in Germany, France, the Netherlands, Spain, Italy, Greece, United States, and other countries as part of projects supported by diverse international foundations, including with the International Association for Cooperation with Scientists from the former Soviet Union (INTAS), NATO ("Science for the world"), NWO, and the European Framework Programmes.

A particular case in point is the Institute of Catalysis' joint cooperation on catalysis research with scientists in India, a project which has been ongoing since 1987 when an Integrated Long-Term Programme of Cooperation in Science & Technology between India and the Russian Federation was signed. Another example of the Institute's international cooperation was the Seventh European Framework Programme on science and technology from 2007 to 2013 concentrating on nanoscience, nanotechnologies, materials, and new production technologies. As a final example of international linkages held by the BIC, some of its 1779 staff (of whom 310 are researchers) are regularly invited to participate as experts representing Russia in UN bodies.

As shown in Table 4.12, since the early 1990s, the Institute of Computational Technology has greatly increased the number of publications in Russian and foreign journals. Interestingly, the number of publications in foreign journals seems to have peaked in 2000 (46 publications) and then declined to just 27 in 2012. Its count of publications in Russian journals, meanwhile, continued to increase from 1991 to 2012. This suggests a policy of *less internationalisation* of research from 2000, perhaps a factor of more national funding for research that required publishing in Russian journals, although it should also be remembered that research universities in Russia have introduced internationalisation policies and incentivised researchers to publish in global journals with high impact factors. At the same time, the institute's staff headcount nearly trebled after 2012, having remained

Table 4.12 Publications of Institute of Computational Technology in Akademgorodok, Novosibirsk (1990–2017)

Year	*No. of staff (of which researchers)*	*No. of publications in Russian scientific journals*	*No. of publications in foreign scientific journals*
1990	300 (3)	Na	
1991	324	5	9
2000	100 (54)	42	46
2010	94 (58)	Na	na
2012	114 (73)	68	27
2017	289 (107)	Na	na

stable at around 100 between 2000 and 2012. That means that by 2017, it had nearly returned to the size it was when it was founded in 1990, that is after nearly two decades, it had recovered from the 1990s crisis which dramatically reduced the numbers of employed scientists across Russia.

The Institute of Nuclear Physics in Akademgorodok, Novosibirsk increased the number of collaborative research projects with foreign scientific laboratories between 2006 and 2014. In 2006, the institute had 23 such collaborations, while in 2014, the number went up to 37. These collaborations tend to be long term, with the oldest dating back to 1977 (with the Daresbury laboratory in the United Kingdom). Moreover, the institute has collaborated with labs from many countries including the United States, the United Kingdom, Germany, Italy, Switzerland, the Czech Republic, Kazakhstan (from 2007), Korea, Japan, and China. This points to institutional sustainability and maintenance of the institute's international collaborations over several decades, including throughout the turbulent 1990s.

International study visits and the emergence of two business associations

Novosibirsk Akademgorodok has an interesting example of bottom-up industry participation in governance of science, technology, and innovation triggered by an international study visit. This experience is a case of businesses attempting to resolve collective action problems. In the 2000s, two local business associations emerged in Akademgorodok.

The stimulus for creating the two associations was a month-long study visit to the United States in 2000, funded and organised by the US programme called SABIT (run by the US Department of Trade).[22] A group of research institute and small company directors was formed from different towns of Russia and former CIS countries. Eighteen people were selected from Novosibirsk Akademgorodok alone (directors of research institutes and top managers of programming companies). Representatives from the companies that initiated the two associations were both present. While in America, they learnt about US businesses and business associations and saw how industry associations can enable solutions to be found collectively. Upon their return to Russia, these representatives collectively agreed that they needed to make their own associations. During this US study visit in 2000, the participants from Russia observed first-hand how commercialisation works in the United States and decided to apply the idea in Russia. One interviewee who was on that study trip emphasised that the structures and principles of the business associations founded in Akademgorodok as a result of the US trip were completely Russian; only the idea was *borrowed* or copied from the US (interview with director of association "SibAcademInnovatsiya," Akademgorodok, Novosibirsk, 16 September 2013). Drawing on the concept of institutional mimicry, this suggests that while the institution of a business association was indeed imitated from the West by Russia, the way it was set up and functions is influenced by the Russian institutional context.

Both associations were very important to the emergence and development of Akadempark, the high-tech park officially created in July 2006 under the framework of the 2006 federal programme (according to the park's statute).[23] The two associations of innovative enterprises in Akademgorodok – SibAcademSoft (association of IT companies in region) and SibAcademInnovatsiya[24] – are examples of bottom-up successes, where local industry successfully grouped together in a show of collective action to lobby for their interests in front of local, regional, and federal authorities. The heads of both associations were interviewed by the author of this book in 2013–2014.

A holding company called "Mediko-biologicheskiy soyuz" was the initiator – or first mover – for the "SibAcademInnovatsiya" association. It was created in 2001 because of a perceived lack of dialogue and understanding between authorities, science, and entrepreneurship about the role of small- and medium-sized enterprises (SMEs) in commercialising scientific research and because of widespread perceptions that SMEs were stealing intellectual property and preventing the survival of science. Another aim of the association was to better represent the interests and needs of SMEs to local and regional authorities. The authorities, in turn, liked the association because it made it convenient and clear with whom in industry they could talk. Initially, the association interacted with regional authorities and the administration of Novosibirsk city; later, the association started to also have a dialogue with federal authorities through the president of association, who also sat on the Presidential Council on Modernisation (interview with director of association "SibAcademInnovatsiya," Akademgorodok, Novosibirsk, 16 September 2013). That the association was received positively by the local authorities was confirmed by another interviewee who previously worked in the science department of Sovetsky district: the district officials had friendly relations with the two associations of innovative firms in Akadamgorodok in 2002 and stressed their roles in helping to build the technology park (interview with the former head of science department in Sovetsky district administration, 2002–2007; and current senior researcher in a research institute of SB RAS, Akademgorodok, Novosibirsk, 17 September 2013).

The head of the other association, SibAcademSoft (which represents and brings together IT companies in the region) confirmed in an interview what the head of "SibAcademInnovatsiya" association reported. She described how by the year 2000, a critical mass of programming (software) companies had built up in Akademgorodok and that these companies were growing fast. The two associations were founded with the support of the chair of SB RAS and the regional administration (interview with the chair of SibAcademSoft association, Akademgorodok, Novosibirsk, 8 September 2014).

As for the technology park "Academpark," both associations played key roles in pushing the park project through bureaucratic hoops. The interviewee from SibAcademSoft association explained:

> Originally, the park was for IT technology companies. We were actively working with SibAcademInnovatsiya, which appeared after SibAcademSoft.

> SibAcademInnovatsiya brought together the other (non-IT) companies and they said "we also need a place where our companies can develop." So, they decided to work together on the park. Thus, SibAcademInnovatsiya signed up to the idea and was quite active in helping us push the project.
>
> (interview with the chair of SibAcademSoft association, Akademgorodok, Novosibirsk, 8 September 2014)[25]

These two business associations have thus helped generate interest in the technology park among small companies and helped to create a critical mass of software companies in Akademgorodok.

Clusters

As already discussed, around 40% of Obninsk's GDP comes from industry, a share that has been quite stable since 2010. The town and regional authorities have been active in pursuing policies to support and develop a range of industrial sectors, notably through the implementation of clusters. Obninsk currently has nine distinct clusters, including in the automotive, composites, IT, nuclear, agricultural, logistical, and pharmaceutical sectors. As shown in Table 4.13, as of 2017, the IT cluster hosts the greatest number of companies (125), followed by the pharmaceutical cluster (63) and the composite materials and aerospace cluster (19 companies). These clusters are managed by a regional agency of innovative development – Centre for cluster development of Kaluga region (known by its Russian abbreviation, AIRKO), a dynamic organisation that has been very active since its founding in 2010 by the regional government. The goal of AIRKO is:

> To create the conditions for the emergence and promotion of innovations, to find new sources of growth, to develop a high-tech sector of the economy and territorial clusters of Kaluga region.
>
> (AIRKO website, last accessed 1 May 2019)

Overall, the nine clusters in Kaluga have had some impressive results over a recent 5-year period (2011–2016). As shown in Table 4.14, they have brought together 169 SMEs as of 2016 – over a 600% increase since 2011. The number of companies using the clusters' services (e.g. the use of advanced equipment, consulting and accounting services, etc.) increased by 1400% in the five years to 2016,

Table 4.13 Obninsk industrial clusters: key results in 2017

Cluster industrial sector focus	*Number of companies resident in cluster*
ICT	125
Pharmaceutical	63
Composite materials and aerospace	19

Source: Obninsk town administration annual report for 2017.

Table 4.14 Key performance results of Obninsk's clusters (2011–2016)

	2011	*2012*	*2013*	*2014*	*2015*	*2016*
Number of SMEs in clusters	23	69	107	130	149	169
Number of SMEs using services provided by clusters	12	108	118	133	177	180
Number of new jobs created by the activity of clusters	39	52	62	68	45	50

Source: AIRKO 2016 Annual Report, p. 5. Available in Russian at: www.airko.org/information/shareholders [last accessed 1 May 2019].

resulting in 180 service users. According to the literature (e.g. Wessner and Howell, 2017), perhaps the most significant indicator of economic impact of these clusters is the effect on job creation. There was a 28% increase in new jobs created by the clusters from 2011 (39 new jobs) to 2016 (50 new jobs created). However, when compared to the Albany nanotechnology cluster called in New York state in the United States, the effect of Kaluga region's clusters on direct job creation remains limited. Just over 3500 local jobs (and another 17,000 indirect jobs when calculated using the industry multiplier method) were created by the investment to create the Albany cluster in its first 8 years of operation (Wessner and Howell, 2017: 171).

Furthermore, a new cluster for nuclear and radiological technologies was formed in 2017 in collaboration with the state corporation Rosatom and the Association "Kaluga cluster of nuclear technologies." The strategic development priorities for this cluster were identified in April 2017 regarding civil use of nuclear technologies.

Two micro case studies of the two clusters (in IT and pharmaceuticals) in Kaluga region with the greatest number of companies will be discussed next to understand how they function and what kind of companies participate in them.

MICRO CASE STUDY OF THE IT CLUSTER IN OBNINSK AND KALUGA REGION[26]

Created in 2013, the IT cluster in Kaluga region has the highest number of firms participating of all Kaluga region's clusters. This is probably associated with the fact that the ICT sector tends to have many very small firms as the barriers to entry are low in this sector, although the cluster also hosts branches of a handful of large Russian companies. The cluster's goal is to form an ecosystem, as shown in the following statement published on the AIRKO website:

> to create a full-scale ecosystem in Kaluga region to develop the ICT sector by consolidating the knowledge-based, production, scientific, innovative, organisational, and administrative potential of members of the ICT cluster; the cluster aims to make ICT production and the regional economy more competitive.[27]

In early 2019, the ICT cluster of Kaluga region had 128-member organisations so three more than in 2017 (Table 4.14). The lead or anchor firm was ZAO Kaluga

Astral, a closely held company under the laws of the Russian Federation and an established Russian software company since 1993 with over one million clients across Russia and 500 employees. ZAO Kaluga Astral hosts a free IT school for children and implements the pilot project called "Yandex Lyceum" (an initiative of Yandex) to teach schoolchildren the fundamentals of coding. This is evident that the ICT cluster is helping to upgrade ICT skills in the local workforce.

The core of the ICT cluster is made up of a handful of big Russian companies, including OOO "NPF Sigma," a research-and-production firm created in 1991 that specialises in developing and implementing automated systems integrated security and life support facilities. Other ICT cluster members are AO Kraftway Corporation plc, "OAO KEMZ" ("Kaluga electromechanical factory"), a publicly owned joint-stock company created in 1917, and the Kaluga regional branch of OAO Rostelekom, a partly state-owned company and largest provider of digital services and solutions in Russia. Moreover, the cluster also hosts large IT firms from other regions in Russia as well as organisations of higher professional education. These educational organisations play a key role in the cluster to supply a developed educational system with qualified workers.

Thus, in its first six years of activity, the ICT cluster in Kaluga region is performing well in that it has brought together a significant mass of firms and educational institutions. Many of the cluster participants are large and established Russian firms so forming linkages with such firms is one way the regional ICT sector and the wider regional economy could become more competitive. It is also contributing to boosting the regional population's level of ICT skills through organising educational opportunities for young people.

MICRO CASE STUDY OF THE PHARMACEUTICAL CLUSTER IN OBNINSK AND KALUGA REGION[28]

The pharmaceuticals, biotechnology, and biomedicine cluster was created in 2011 and is spread over seven sites in Kaluga region, including Obninsk town which has the largest concentration of resident companies (Table 4.15). At its root is a non-commercial partnership which was formalised by the ten largest resident firms to manage the cluster. The cluster cooperates with federal, regional, and local governments.

Table 4.15 Growth of Obninsk Pharma Cluster, 2010–2017 (number of participating organisations)

Year	*No. of participating organisations*
2010	0
2015	56
2016	62
2017	65

Source: www.pharmclusterkaluga.ru [last accessed 16 March 2018].

It aims to be a high-tech science-production complex, which co-locates interacting and complementary production facilities and infrastructure organisations for the development, production launch, and release of innovative, new generation pharmaceutical and medicinal products: medicines, pharmaceutical substances, radiopharmaceutical agents, and medical equipment that meets WHO standards of good manufacturing practice (GMP) to raise the safety of medicines.

This cluster is one of 25 innovation clusters across Russia supported by the Federal Ministry of Economic Development since 2012. In October 2016, the cluster was successful in a competitive process run by the Ministry of Economic Development of the Russian Federation and was included as one of the innovative clusters to get funding from the Ministry under the programme "Developing innovative clusters – leaders of investment attractiveness of a global level." While the Kaluga pharmaceutical cluster received state subsidies from 2012 (Dezhina, 2013; Kutsenko and Meissner, 2013), it started as a regional initiative before building on existing capacity in Obninsk's infrastructure, equipment, and human capital.

To date, the cluster has attracted more than 60 firms, research organisations, and innovation-supporting organisations. Since 2010, the number of organisations taking part in the pharma cluster has increased rapidly to reach 65 in 2017 from 0 in 2010 (Table 4.15). These 65 organisations include large international firms (such as the British–Swedish ventures AstraZeneca, NovoNordisk, and Stada CIS), Russian large- and medium-sized firms (Niarmedik Plus, Mir-Pharma, PharmVilar, and Bion), and 38 small innovative and engineering enterprises (comprising more than half of all the firms in the cluster).

From 2012 to 2016, four factories were opened in the cluster offering integrated production following international GMP standards. The four factories were built by resident companies: Niarmedik-Pharma (Niarmedik group), "Berlin-Pharma" ("Berlin-Hemi Menarini group"), "AstraZeneca" (AstraZeneca Industries group), and "NovoNordisk" ("NovoNordisk AB" company). The companies invested a total of 51 billion RUB (approximately 832 million USD as of 31 December 2016 exchange rate) in these construction projects.

2018 saw two of the cluster's leading participants expand their production facilities in the cluster. On 19 September 2018, "NovoNordisk" launched production of the complete cycle of insulins in the cluster's industrial park called Grabtsovo (preparation of ready-to-inject forms of insulin using the company's original substance. On 31 October of 2018, Niarmedik-Pharma begun production in Obninsk of the complete cycle of reactive chemicals for genetic identification of individuals and establishment of kinship. The set of reactive chemicals is the company's own unique asset, significantly different from Western analogues.

As shown in Table 4.16, the cluster had approximately 6,400 employees in 2012. At the end of 2016, 9020 people were employed by organisations that are part of the cluster, of which 3626 worked in pharmaceutical companies. This is, however, not an increase in employees but rather a reflection of new organisations joining the cluster. The cluster also has among its participants leading Russian state research centres in the sphere of development, production, and application of

Table 4.16 Kaluga Pharmaceutical Cluster: results to date (2007–2017)

Criteria of cluster effectiveness	*Criteria value*
Total number of organisations in the cluster (2017) of which no. of small innovative companies	65 38
Members (shareholders) of cluster's managing organisation	Ten of the largest cluster residents grouped together to form the shareholders of the non-commercial partnership "Kaluga Pharma Cluster" in February 2012
Total revenue from sale of production by organisations of cluster between 2007 and 2011	*Large pharma enterprises:* 11.2 billion RUB (incl. 3.4 billion RUB in 2011); *Small and medium enterprises (incl. R&D sector):* 3.0 billion RUB (incl. 0.9 billion RUB in 2011)
Average number of employees (2012–2016)	2012: 6,400 people, of which: 400 *in large pharma enterprises in cluster* Approximately 1,000 *in small and medium enterprises* More than 5,000 *in research centres* 2016: 9,020 employees in total (of which 3,626 in pharma companies)
Total volume of private investment for production, development (prototypes), and market promotion of new products	4.1 billion RUB (approximately USD 128 million) in 2011 27.5 billion RUB (approximately USD 448 million) in 2016

Source: www.airko.org/clasters/farma-claster/information [last accessed 16 March 2018].

radiopharmaceutical agents [including Obninsk's Institute for Physics and Power Engineering named after Leypunsky (IPPE) and the Karpov institute].

Total production by cluster members equalled 27.5 billion RUB (approximately USD 448 million) in 2016, rising to 35.3 billion RUB (approximately USD 521 million) at the end of 2017. Another success in the Obninsk cluster is the rapid increase in total private investment for production, development (prototypes), and market promotion of new products: from 4.1 billion RUB (approximately USD 128 million) in 2011 to 27.5 billion RUB (approximately USD 448 million) in 2016. This indicates that the management organisation for the cluster was very effective in bringing private investors on-board and leveraging inward investment for the cluster (Table 4.16).

Building a network across organisations and firms is one of the cluster's main goals (including partnerships with universities and research institutes across Russia), which is a good first step to creating an innovation system with a diverse range of institutions and actors. In addition to some real economic impacts, Obninsk's pharmaceuticals, biotechnology, and biomedicine cluster has also engaged with influencing state policy. For example, in 2013, it advised the government of Russia on state inspections of pharmaceuticals and set out the case for legal clarity of the concept "produced in Russia" (Agency for Innovation Development in

Kaluga region, 2013). Hence, as well as clear successes in innovation, Obninsk's cluster also has political capital to influence policy makers, similar to the two business associations in Novosibirsk discussed earlier in this chapter.

As a sign of its emerging global relevance, the Kaluga pharmaceutical cluster became the first in Russia to be given the Quality Audit Silver Label of the European Cluster Excellence Initiative (ECEI) by the European Secretariat for Cluster Analysis in 2017.[29] The Silver Label of the ECEI is a quality label in its own right, assuring that the cluster has successfully implemented the improvement processes which were initiated following a Bronze label benchmarking.

To sum up, the pharmaceutical cluster in Kaluga region has developed rapidly since 2011 to attract a critical mass of high-tech firms in the pharma sector spanning large Russian and international enterprises as well as small innovative and engineering firms. It has achieved quite impressive regional impact to 2017 in terms of number of jobs created, revenues generated, and private investment leveraged.

Interpretations

The two case studies presented in this chapter showed how two contrasting science towns have evolved over the last 50 years. This section aims to interpret these case studies considering the three-stage growth model outlined at the end of Chapter 2.

Given their importance, there are two main reasons justifying the study of science towns. One reason science towns deserve scholarly attention is because they used to form – and continue to nowadays – a crucial part of both R&D and innovation policies in many countries. Geographically concentrating R&D in a science town, and housing R&D employees and their families in the same locality, makes sense because it can enable collective action problems to be resolved, can enable critical mass to build up, and can encourage complementarities and knowledge spillovers among the various R&D actors in the town.

Moreover, political regimes can easily control the scientists living and working in the science towns. Globally, many – but far from all – science towns had restricted access or were closed entirely to foreigners, particularly those that did defence R&D. For example, Los Alamos in the US state of New Mexico was created in, or soon after, 1942 by the US government which was looking for a top-secret, closed location for the state-sponsored atomic bomb programme called the Manhattan Project (active 1942–1946). At that time, information about Los Alamos was highly secretive and classified, and incoming and outgoing correspondence was censored.

Similar regimes of censorship and control existed in Soviet science towns. Since the dissolution of the USSR in 1991, many of Russia's science towns have opened up to bring in investment from large foreign and Russian firms, carry out R&D and production under contract with "outsider" firms and organisations, and co-publish or collaborate in other ways with researchers elsewhere in Russia or abroad.

A second reason why an historically informed understanding of Russia's science towns matters is that they contribute to the debate concerning the limitations of the linear model of innovation as compared to the interactive model of innovation. Science towns (and science and technology parks, as will be discussed next in Chapter 5) developed based on the logic and assumptions of a linear model of innovation. These entities aim to concentrate all the steps in a single geographical area that, according to the linear model, lead smoothly and predictably from new (fundamental) knowledge to applied R&D and then to full-scale production which can be sold in markets. However, much literature has shown that this linear view is misleading because of the interactive, cumulative, and uncertain nature of innovation processes (Lazonick, 2002). Such processes involve linkages and feedback loops for growth and a dynamic economic system, as well as numerous changes in a total system including the market environment, production facilities and knowledge, and the social context (Block and Keller, 2011; Kline and Rosenberg, 1986). Interactions which have been shown to be so important for innovation do not automatically emerge once a science town or science park has been built.

From the two case studies, this chapter has found that the science towns of Akademgorodok and Obninsk (the latter albeit to a lesser extent) have been quite successful in producing fundamental research (as seen by publications data). The number of publications between 1991 and 2016 is much higher in Akademgorodok Novosibirsk (5,995–29,850 publications per organisation) than in Obninsk (21–4,793 publications per organisation). A similar story comes from the data presented here on citations per publication between 2005 and 2013 – publications with at least one author from Akademgorodok had generally higher citation rates than those with an author from Obninsk. Akademgorodok's superior publication record is consistent with its founding mission of being a centre of research excellence in Siberia (Stage 1 of the growth model).

However, they have had less success in building on their knowledge and R&D capabilities by commercialisation. The two science towns have also been less successful in building national and inter-regional linkages through helping to increase the number of new firms created, using patents to bring new products to market, or forging global linkages through value chains (Stage 2).

Obninsk's experience with building industrial clusters since 2010 has had some success in creating new jobs and attracting large Russian firms (e.g. Russian pharma companies). In this way, the clusters have helped to build a critical mass of commercial interactions, primarily at an intra-country level (Stage 2). However, the number of direct new jobs created is very small when compared to other clusters, for example Albany nano-cluster in New York state, United States (Wessner and Howell, 2017).

Some of the leading research institutes in Akademgorodok, notably the Institute of Catalysis, have maintained long-standing international research collaborations (e.g. through visits and joint projects) into the present. This is evidence that this science centre is internationally oriented to an extent. International linkages in Obninsk seem to be more limited in scale and scope in the 1990s and 2000s, including exchanges of researchers and local government officials and some foreign investment by companies, notably in the pharmaceutical industry (Stage 3 of the growth framework).

Why do we not see more critical mass of innovation actors and activities in Obninsk and Akademgorodok that could help achieve economic impact from their R&D and innovation? And why are these two places not more globally connected? I argue that the reasons are connected to the institutional context in Russia.

The institutional context in Russia centres on the nature of the power structure. President Putin does not exercise absolute control over the country as many Western commentators assume. Rather, Putin's power is constrained by competing bureaucracies and interest groups (Higgins, 2017). This competition explains why there is a discrepancy between what Putin says in public discourse and what happens in reality; for example, Putin proclaimed the importance of entrepreneurial freedom in a speech in 2015:

I believe free enterprise to be the most important aspect of economic and social well-being. Entrepreneurial freedom is something we need to expand to respond to all attempts to impose restrictions on us.

In parallel, the recent case of Michael Calvey, a US investor who has lived in Russia for nearly 30 years, illustrates the actual treatment of entrepreneurs and investors. Calvey founded the Baring Vostok private equity group and was imprisoned before trial for 2 months in early 2019. On 6 August 2021, Calvey was given a 5.5-year suspended prison sentence after having been found guilty of embezzlement – a crime he denies.[30]

Notes

1 "Science town" is more commonly used although the term "science city" is also found in some countries. For example, the science city in Kolkata, India is a large area on the outskirts of Kolkata city that opened in 1997 and is home to science museums and educational exhibits for the general population. Because the cases examined in this chapter are relatively small in terms of population and would not be considered a city on this basis, I have chosen to use the label "science town."

2 Although Novosibirsk Akademgorodok also received funding from *Minsredmash* for its initial construction at the end of the 1950s (Josephson, 1997), it was not fully financed by *Minsredmash*.

3 Interview from Obninsk project archive, June 2012, carried out by present author. Original transcript in Russian, transcribed as:

> a srazu posle voyni [1941–45], v sorok shestom godu, zdyes' razmyestilas' sekretnaya laboratoriya. Da k tomu zhe escho reka Protva, neobkhodimaya dlya takovo proizvodstva. Vot vsye eti obstoyatelstva vmeste splyelis', nu i . . . factor sluchae tozhe, konyechno . . . Poetomu zdyes' i organizovali sekretnuyou laboratoriyou – imenno zdes' . . . MNOGO bylo skhodyaschikhstya v odnom mestye obstoyatelstv. Priyekhali snachala stroiteli, zatem stali priyezhat' NEMETSKIYE uchoniye – ponachalu po kontraktu – ochen' vygodnomu dlya nikh kontraktu. No srazu zhe . . . s sorok syedmovo goda stali priyezhat' i russkiye uchoniye s imenyem.

4 Interview from Obninsk project archive, June 2012, carried out by author. Original transcript in Russian, transcribed as:

> Nu, posmotrite na karte . . . na kartu – ona vsya zelyonaya takaya. Zdes' . . . byla dachnaya mestnost'. Dovolno glukhaya. Neskolko derevyen' – vot oni tozhe vsye oboznacheny – naselyonniye punkty. Vot . . . stantsiya "Obninskaya". Po zheleznoy doroge khoroshee soobscheniye s Moskvoy . . . Shosse, shosseynaya doroga . . .

do Moskvy dobratsya lyogko bylo. Togda yezdili zho tol'ko na avtomobilyakh ili poyezdakh. Vot. A v to zhe vryema myestnost' takaya ooyedinennaya, dovolno . . . glukhaya.

5 Source: O sozdanii Sibirskogo otdeleniya Akademii nauk SSSR: postanovleniye Soveta Ministrov SSSR, 18 maya 1957 goda. Available at: www.prometeus.nsc.ru/science/sbras50/03.ssi [last accessed 21 March 2014]. Original citation in Russian, transcribed as:

> Schitat' osnovnoy zadachey Sibirskovo otdeleniya Akademii nauk SSSR vsemernoe razvitiye teoreticheskikh i eksperimentalnykh issledovanii v oblasti fiziko-tekhnicheskikh, yestestvennykh i ekonomicheskhikh nauk, napravlennykh na resheniye vazhneishikh nauchnykh problem sposobstvyouschikh naibolee uspeshnomu razvitiyou proizvoditel'nykh sil Sibiri i Dal'nyevo Vostoka.

6 Interview from Obninsk project archive, carried out by I. Wade, 22 June 2012. original transcript in Russian: «И вот такая атмосфера была во всех городках с концентрацией науки. Новосибирский академгородок – то же самое. Это . . . Я был там, да. Новосибирский академгородок – он ещё более . . . там ещё более концентрирована наука. Обнинск – он всё-таки . . . здесь есть и небольшой завод, и опытное производство. А в Новосибирске это . . . исключительно академическая наука. И все, кто хотел работать на производстве, в бизнесе, там в чем-то ещё – ехали в Новосибирск. Он же рядом, большой город, там есть всё. А в академгородке оставались только ученые. Там концентрация ученых была ещё больше, чем в Обнинске.»

7 Interview from Obninsk project archive, June 2012, carried out by G. Orlova and A. Zorin, 30.03.2012. Original transcript in Russian: ' . . . Значит, была . . . единственный большой дом, назывался у нас потом «главный корпус». Он так и остался, потом заставили, заставили много . . . А жилья . . . был один трёхэтажный дом, где жили . . . ну, кто-то из учёных жил. Но большинство учёных жило в финских домиках, были построены вот в этом самом лесу, в котором вы находитесь . . . были построены финские домики . . . ну финские домики – в смысле, они были изготовлены в Финляндии . . . по репарации достались нам и эмм . . . со всеми удобствами . . . да, ванна была, но не сразу . . . газ не сразу, но довольно быстро было сделано . . . А в начале, мы приехали, это был . . . Вот семью я перевёз . . . это был . . . было начало сорок седьмого го-да, январь месяц был . . . значит, ещё . . . мало что было там . . . Значит, не было ни воды, ни канализации, ну ни газа, конечно *(смеётся)* . . . Значит, мы приехали . . . привезли нас, наши вещи . . . ну и оказалось так, что есть печка, которая топилась дровами, ну, слава богу, дрова были приготовлены, и мы приехали, затопили печку, стало тепло . . .'

8 Interview from Obninsk project archive, carried out by xxx, 2 December 2011. Original transcript in Russian: "Bolshe nichevo ne bylo. V osnovnom iz Chelyabinska-40 priyezhzhali . . . v 1959 krome FEI nichevo ne bylo. Stoit tol'ko Fedorovskaya bashnya."

9 Addition to interview from Obninsk project archive, carried out by Z. Vasiliyeva, 24 April 2013.

10 Interview from Obninsk project archive, carried out by I. Wade, 22 June 2012. original transcript in Russian: "Во-первых, вот такие города, где много умных и разносторонних людей, ещё отличаются свободомыслием. И даже в советские времена . . . даже в советские времена, когда была жесткая идеология и пропаганда и всё . . . – люди в Обнинске мыслили более . . . вольно."

11 SB RAS Annual Report for 1997–2001. Available online (in Russian) at: www.nsc.ru/win/sbras/rep/2001/fso.html [last accessed 1 May 2019].

12 Original quotation in Russian: "визит команды из Обнинска в Окридж был не просто очередным «обменом» официальными делегациями, культурным обменом или

туристическим вояжем, а являлся рабочим программным мероприятием в рамках совместного годичного проекта по адаптации в Обнинске опыта экономического развития Окриджа. Кроме того, что тоже впервые, расходы на визит полностью покрывались бюджетом полученного гранта."

13 See the official website of Sister Cities International: www.sister-cities.org/about-sister-cities-international [last accessed 4 March 2015].

14 Original quote in Russian, transliterated as:

> "Obninsk byl, blagodarya, v tom chisle i nashim usiliyam, opredelyonnym liderom vot takovo dvizheniya naukogradov, to yest' tam i Obninsk byl I drugie . . . zainteresovanniye goroda, kotoriye pytalis' perenimat' nash opyt, to yest', i tak dalee. V gorode provodilos' dostatochno mnogo razlichnykh konferentsii, kotoriye byli posvyashcheny etim voprosam, zanimalis' my lobbirovaniyem pravitelstvennykh struktur . . . chto, nu, sobstvenno, rezultatom stal zakon o naukogradakh, potomu chto bez zakonodatelnovo oformleniya, prisvoyeniye takovo statusa nichevo ne davalo, tol'ko v ramkakh zakona mozhno bylo, tak skazat', predusmotret' vozmozhnosti byoudzhetnovo finansirovaniya, dlya razvitiya i tak dalee."
>
> (Author's interview with O.L., location: Obninsk, date: 9 November 2011)

15 Obninsk, 1999.

16 "мы, как бы, заточены на . . . эээ . . . национальный уровень. Это проблема администрации, проблема региональной администрации, как нас использовать лучшим образом, то есть, мы . . . обладаем определенными компетенциями, и если, мы считаем, что . . . или администрация считает, что наши компетенции могут быть разумно использованы, да, для целей . . . эээ . . . городского, регионального развития, то мы открыты для участия, но у нас нет проблемы, допустим, с заказами, да . . . и проблем, с точки зрения . . . как сказать, участия в городских каких-то программах и так далее. Там, где мы нужны, нас привлекают, то есть, мы не сфокусированы сейчас на городские и региональные, вот конкретные, региона, проблемы." [Author's interview with chair of RTTN, 26 June 2012].

17 SB RAS website: www.sbras.ru/files/files/2018-atlas_sbras_4-7.pdf [last accessed 1 May 2019].

18 www.academpark.com/ [last accessed 29 December 2018].

19 Original quote in transliteration: "Samym slozhnym okazalos' sobrat' vsye nauchniye, infrastrukturniye, sotsialniye, inzhenorniye proyekty, kotoriye tselesoobrazno rassmatrivat' v etom kontekstye. Byl sozdan koordinatsionny soviet pri gubernatorye Novosibirskoy oblasti i rabochiye gruppy v yevo sostave, gdye sovmyestno s SO RAN prokhodilo rassmotreniye etykh proyektov. Kak itog – 25 nauchnykh, 15 infrastrukturnykh i okolo 30 sotsialnykh i inzhenornykh proyektov my vklyouchili v plan pervoocherednykh meropriyatii." (Klyoushnikova, 2018, 27 August 2018, 'Akademgorodki 2.0: kontsepsiya, razvitiya, kadry' (transl. from Russian: 'Akademgorodok 2.0: Concept, Development, Human Resources') [www.sib-science.info/ru/sbras/akademgorodok-2-0-kontseptsiya-24082018].

20 Investment Portal website of Kaluga Region, maintained by the Government of Kaluga region. Available at: http://investkaluga.com/industrialnyy-park-obninsk/#1 [last accessed 30 December 2018].

21 Author interview date 1 November 2012, own translation.

22 For more information on the SABIT programme in Russian, see www.sabitprogram.org/index.php?option=displaypage&Itemid=50&op=page&SubMenu= [last accessed 27 March 2015].

23 See Chapter 5 for further analysis of this technology park.

24 Both association names in English are transliterations from the Russian names, which are contractions for 'Siberian Academy Software' (SibAcademSoft association) and 'Siberian Academy Innovation' ('SibAcademInnovatsiya' association).

25 The text cited above is a direct quote from the transcript written in English and in summary style (not verbatim) shortly after the interview, which was conducted in Russian and audio recorded with the orally informed consent of the interviewee.
26 Material Taken from AIRKO website, www.airko.org/clusters/ikt
27 Source (Russian original): AIRKO website, www.airko.org/clusters/ikt [last accessed 31 May 2019].
28 Source (in Russian): AIRKO website, www.airko.org/clusters/farma-cluster [last accessed 31 May 2021].
29 The attainment of Silver label could not be verified by the author of this book on the website of the European Secretariat for Cluster Analysis, https://cluster-analysis.org/benchmarked-clusters/?complete=1 [last accessed 31 May 2019].
30 www.rferl.org/a/russia-calvey-suspended-sentence/31397581.html [last accessed 6 August 2021].

References

Block, F. L. and Keller, M. R. (eds.) (2011) *State of Innovation: The U.S. Government's Role in Technology Development*. London: Routledge.

Castells, M. and Hall, P. (1994) *Technopoles of the World: The Making of Twenty-First-Century Industrial Complexes*. London: Routledge.

Cherevikina, M. Y. (2007) 'Innovatsionnaya sistema SO RAN: Ot planovoy modeli k rynochnim otnosheniya', *Nauka. Innovatsii. Obrazovanie*, Moscow, str. 240–280 [transl.: 'Innovation System of SB RAS: From Planned Model to Market Relations', *Nauka, Innovatsii, Obrazovanie* (Russian journal name in translation: *Science, Innovations, Education*)] (pp. 240–280).

Chernykh, N. (2004) *Obratny otschot* [transl. *Reverse counting*] Moscow: Vash poligraficheskiy partnyor.

Chernykh, N. (2012) *Obninsk. Perezagruzka* [transl. *Obninsk Reboot*] Moscow: Vash poligraficheskiy partnyor.

Dezhina, I. (2013) 'Technology Platforms in Russia: A Catalyst for Cluster Development?', Paper Presented at Triple Helix 11th International Conference, London, 8–10 July 2013 (unpublished).

Dudov, A. (2011) 'Razvitiye goroda Obninska: problem iresheniya' [transl. 'Development of the Town of Obninsk: Problems and Solutions']. Report in Russian by Senior Specialist in the Department for Innovative Development, Administration of Obninsk. Available at: http://www.admobninsk.ru/administration/report/report2011/ [last accessed 8 March 2018].

Evseenko, A. V. and Untura, G. A. (2002) *Evolyoutsiya novosibirskoy modeli innovatsii* [transl.: *Evolution of the Novosibirsk Model of Innovation*] Novosibirsk: Working Paper of the Siberian Branch of the Russian Academy of Sciences [in Russian]. Available at: http://lib.ieie.su/~novikova/PublEIE/Untura_Galina_Afanasevna_(d_e_n_).htm#Year2002 [last accessed 30 December 2019].

Gordiyenko, A. A., Yeremin, S. N. and Tyuganov, Y. A. (2000) *Nauka i innovatsionnoe predprinimatelstvo v sovremyennom obshchestvye: sotsiokulturnyi podkhod* [Science and innovative entrepreneurship in contemporary society: a socio-cultural approach]. Novosibirsk, Russia: Institute of Archaeology and Ethnography of SB RAS Publishing house (in Russian).

Grupp H., Schmoch U. and Hinze S. (2001) 'International Alignment and Scientific Regard as Macro-Indicators for International Comparisons of Publications', *Scientometrics* 51/2 (pp. 359–380).

Higgins, A. (2017) 'In Russia, innovators beware', *New York Times International*, 17 August. Available at: http://www.nytimes.com/images/2017/08/17/nytfrontpage/INYT_frontpage_global.20170817.pdf [last accessed 7 December 2017].

Josephson, P. R. (1997) *New Atlantis Revisited: Akademgorodok, the Siberian City of Science*. Princeton, NJ: Princeton University Press.

Kline, S. J. and Rosenberg, N. (1986) 'An Overview of Innovation', in Landau, R. and Rosenberg, N. (eds.) *The Positive Sum Strategy: Harnessing Technology for Economic Growth*. Washington, DC: National Academy Press (pp. 275–307).

Klyoushnikova (2018) 'Akademgorodki 2.0: Kontsepsiya, razvitiya, kadry' [transl. from Russian: 'Akademgorodok 2.0: Concept, Development, Human Resources'], 27 August 2018. Available at: www.sib-science.info/ru/sbras/akademgorodok-2-0-kontseptsiya-24082018.

Kotsemir, M., Kuznetsova, T., Nasybulina, E. and Pikalova, A. (2015) 'Identifying Directions for Russia's Science and Technology Cooperation', *Foresight and Sti Governance* 9/4 (pp. 54–72). Available at: https://doi.org/10.17323/1995-459X.2015.4.54.72.

Kutsenko, E. and Meissner, D. (2013) 'Key Features of the First Phase of the National Cluster Program in Russia', April 18, 2013. *Higher School of Economics Research Paper No. WP BRP 11/STI/2013*. Available at SSRN: https://ssrn.com/abstract=2253377 or http://dx.doi.org/10.2139/ssrn.2253377 [last accessed 30 December 2019].

Larina, T. M. (ed.) (2006) *Obninsk – perviy naukograd Rossii: istoriya i sovremyennost* [trans. from Russian: *Obninsk – Russia's first naukograd: history and present day*]. Obninsk: Resource.

Lazonick, W. (2002) 'The Theory of Innovative Enterprise', in Warner, M. (ed.) *International Encyclopaedia of Business and Management*. University of California, USA. Thomson Learning (pp. 3055–3076). Available at: www.uml.edu/centers/CIC/Research/Lazonick_Research/Older_Research/Theory_of_the_Firm/eibm.pdf [last accessed 15 June 2021].

McDaniel, B. (1998) *White Book: Economic Development of Oak Ridge* [*Belaya kniga: ekonomicheskoe razvitiye Okridzha*], trans. from English by Latynov, V. Foreword and edited by Luksha, O.

Novaya Sreda (2011) 'Sudby merov' [transl. 'The fates of the mayors'], Article in *Novaya Sreda* Newspaper of Obninsk, in Russian, Published Online September 28, 2011. Available at: http://newsreda.ru/?p=5425 [last accessed March 4, 2015].

Obninsk (1999) *The Program for Development of Obninsk As Naukograd (Science City) 1999–2004*. In English. Obninsk: Obninsk town administration.

Rabkin, Y. M. (ed.) (1997) *Diffusion of New Technologies in the Post-Communist World*. Proceedings of the NATO Advanced Research Workshop on Marketing of High-Tech Know How St Petersburg, Russia June 1994. NATO Science Partnership Subseries: 4 (Closed), Vol. 13. Dordrecht, Netherlands: Springer. 1st ed.

Radošević, S. et al. (2001) *NATO Project Supported by NATO Science for Peace Program*. New York: Springer.

Roth, C., Wu, J. and Lozano, S. (2012) 'Assessing Impact and Quality From Local Dynamics of Citation Networks', *Journal of Informetrics* 6/1 (pp. 111–120). Available at: https://doi.org/10.1016/j.joi.2011.08.005.

Ruchnov, K. M. and Zaytseva, Y. G. (2011) 'Krizis naukogradov Rossii' [transl. 'Crisis of naukograds of Russia'], Published on the Official Website of The Free Economic Society of Russia as an Entry for the Competition 'Future of the Economy 2011'. Available at: http://www.mosveo.ru/images/stories/00008.doc [in Russian] [last accessed 20 March 2022].

SB RAS, Siberian Branch of the Russian Academy of Sciences (1999) Presentation at the Scientific Seminar 'Intellectual Property: Protection, Defence of Rights,

Commercialization, and Education', February 18–19, 1999, SB RAS, Novosibirsk City. Available at: http://www.sbras.nsc.ru/intellectual/result/analiz.htm [last accessed 01.03.2018]

Seliverstov, V. E. (2020) 'Akademgorodok 2.0 Megaproject: Are Dreams Coming True?', *Regional Research of Russia* 10/1 (pp. 107–116).

Tatarchenko, K. (2013) '"A House with the Window to the West": The Akademgorodok Computer Center (1958–1993)', PhD Dissertation, Princeton University, November (unpublished).

Tsygankov, A. P. (2014) *The Strong State in Russia: Development and Crisis*. New York, NY: Oxford University Press.

Vodichev, E. G., Krasilnikov S. A. and Lamin V. A. (2007) *Rossiyskaya akademiya nauk. Sibirskoye otdeleniye. Istoricheskiy ocherk* [Russian Academy of Science. Siberian Branch. Historical Essay]. Novosibirsk, Russia: Nauka, SO Publishing (in Russian).

Wainwright, O. (2016) 'Step into Silicon Forest, Putin's Secret Weapon in the Global Tech Race', *The Guardian*, 5 January. Available at: www.theguardian.com/artanddesign/2016/jan/05/silicon-forest-putin-secret-weapon-global-tech-race-siberia-russia [last accessed 19 July 2021].

Wessner, C. W. and Howell, T. R. (2017) 'Smart Specialization in the US Context; Lessons From the Growth of the Albany, New York Nanotechnology Cluster,' in Radošević, S., Curaj, A., Andreescu, L., Gheorgiu, L. and Wade, I. (eds.) *Advances in the Theory and Practice of Smart Specialization*. Oxford: Elsevier (pp. 157–181).

5 Science and technology parks in post-Soviet Russia

Introduction

Science and technology parks (STPs) have been a popular, location-based innovation policy worldwide since the 1950s and in Russia since 1990. Much literature exists examining STPs globally. The present chapter contributes to this literature by offering empirical evidence on contemporary Russian STPs. It analyses the role of these as instruments of innovation promotion in Russia, which is part of Russia's modernisation policy agenda. By analysing data from a new survey of park managers and resident firms, and from an examination of four cases of parks, this chapter argues that 21st century Russian STPs are largely internally focused – like most STPs are worldwide. This internal focus is expressed through parks' emphasis on supporting the creation and growth of small, high-tech firms by providing new infrastructure and access to specialised equipment at below market rates. These STPs have a high level of public sector involvement (federal and regional authorities) in terms of initial funding and ongoing support, although there is a new trend of privately funded parks emerging. In contrast to the 1990s generation of STPs, the current STPs rarely have close linkages with universities. STPs in Russia do cooperate with external actors so they are not fully closed enclaves. However, they have few global linkages as defined as having multinational companies or large domestic firms among their resident firms. They are globally networked through a rapidly growing membership among Russian STPs of the International Association of Science Parks and Areas of Innovation (IASP) since 2014.

Before turning to examine Russian STPs specifically, this chapter gives an overview of STPs globally by outlining the policy motivations for forming science and technology parks in many countries of the world, the variety of labels that different parks have, and the key features shared by most parks. The next section presents a historical evolution of STPs in Russia from the 1990s to the present. Then, the chapter describes the methodology of the two surveys that form the basis for the empirical results presented in this chapter. Subsequently, it analyses four STPs in Russia in more detail. The final section interprets the results in light of the three-stage model of economic growth processes (see Chapter 2) that is rooted in evolutionary theory and evolutionary economic geography (ECG) and views economic growth as a fundamentally local process.

DOI: 10.4324/9781003256205-5

Science and technology parks in the world: evolution and policy motivations

STPs have been a popular policy option for many governments globally since the 1950s and 1960s. We can divide the establishment of STPs into two main periods (Table 5.1). In wave 1 (1960s–1970s), STPs developed in the United States (Research Triangle Park, North Carolina, formed in 1959) and in Europe including Sophia Antipolis and Inovallée (France), Cambridge and Edinburgh (United Kingdom). These are generally considered the successful pioneer parks. Wave 2 (1980s to present) expanded STPs to Central and Eastern Europe and East Asia. For example, the Technopolis programme began in Japan in the early 1980s and aimed to develop STPs (Ivanov et al., 2006).

The 21st century has seen a rise in interest globally among policy makers, governments, businesses, and universities in setting up STPs. This is evidenced by the doubling of members of the IASP, a global membership, and network organisation established in 1984, from 200 in 2000 to 400 in 2013 (Figure 5.1). However, since 2013, the total number of IASP members has steadily declined to 350 members worldwide in 2021.

Table 5.1 The two main "waves" when STPs were established globally from the 1960s onwards

Wave 1 (1960s–1970s)	**United States: Stanford research park in Stanford University (1951); Research Triangle Park, North Carolina (formed in 1959)** **Brazil, Mexico, and Dominican Republic:** industrial parks started to be built (1960s)* **France:** Sophia Antipolis, near Nice (1969); Inovallée near Grenoble (1972, until 2005 known by acronym ZIRST) United Kingdom: Cambridge Science Park (1973) and Heriot-Watt University Research Park in Edinburgh (1971)
Wave 2 (1980s-present)	**Central and Eastern Europe:** Armenia, Azerbaijan, Belarus, Bulgaria, Croatia, Czech Republic, Estonia, Latvia, Lithuania, Macedonia, Poland, Romania, Russia, Slovakia, Slovenia (all created in 1990s–2000s)** **Central Asia:** Kazakhstan (late 1990s to early 2000s)*** **East Asia:** Technopolis area programmes, Japan (1983 Technopolis Law); high technology industrial park, Beijing, China (1988); Hsinchu Science Park, Taiwan (1980). **South Asia:** India± **Latin America (especially Brazil and Mexico):** science and research parks began to be developed in the 1980s and 1990s, with more built in the 2000s*

Source: Based on Rodriguez-Pose and Hardy (2014).

** These countries had at least one science park that is a member of the IASP, as of May 2015 (list of current IASP members available at www.iasp.ws).
*** Radošević and Myrzakhmet (2009).
± Audirac, 2003.

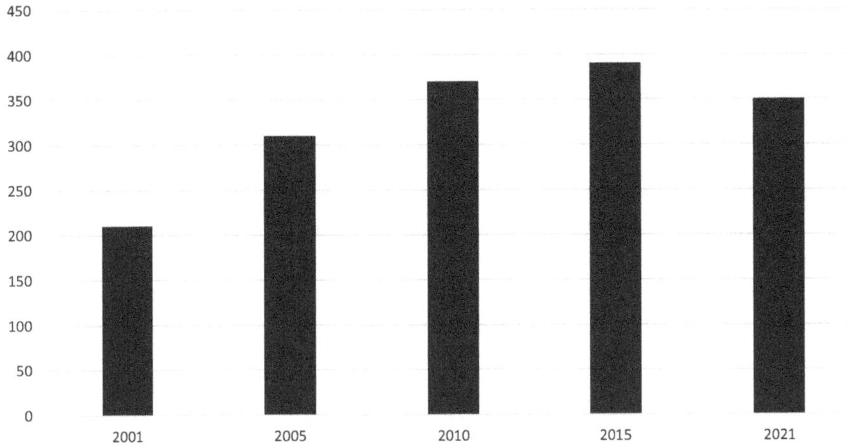

Figure 5.1 Growth in IASP membership, 2001–2021

Source: International Association of Science Parks and Areas of Innovation (IASP). Available at: www.iasp.ws/about-us/facts-and-figures [last accessed 30 June 2021].

STPs are often considered to have economic impacts at meso and micro levels. At a meso (regional or national) level, many governments, universities, and firms consider STPs to be places which facilitate interactions between young firms, older firms, research professionals, potential investors of research and innovations, as well as other actors of innovation processes. They are often seen as "intermediary organisations" between industry and research. At a micro (small- or medium-sized firm) level, STPs sometimes help firms residing in the parks be more innovative or help in the creation or nurturing of small firms.

Policy makers have been motivated to set up STPs for a variety of reasons. They may be convinced of the meso- and micro-level benefits, as outlined earlier. Alternatively, they may have been more persuaded by skilled marketing professionals of the potential gains from STPs or by the promise of receiving national subsidies or grants to promote the development of STPs or innovation in their own region or city.

Whether STPs achieve these goals in practice is, however, another question. The evidence globally is mixed. One critique of science parks and high-tech campuses that have been set up rapidly in India and Mexico in the 2000s describes them as remaining enclaves or "islands" with infrastructure provided by foreign investors themselves, surrounded by its absence. The central role played by large multinational IT companies in Bangalore, India and Guadalajara, Mexico (often described as new "silicon valleys") highlights how these places have forged close links with the global system of electronics production. At the same time, the new IT-driven economies created in these two localities have excluded and disenfranchised the urban poor, pushing them further into the "new geographies of marginality" (Audirac, 2003: 28). While it is not clear from these cases whether, in the absence of multinational IT companies in these two urban "silicon valleys," the urban poor would still be excluded and marginalised, they nevertheless contain lessons about the dangers of globally integrating into production systems.

What's in a name?

What exactly is a science or technology park? Indeed, is a science park different from a technology park or are the two used interchangeably? Often, they are used interchangeably yet sometimes they reflect different aims, set-ups, and geography. There are several other kinds of parks beyond science or technology parks. Table 5.2 summarises the main varieties of parks across the world based on varying levels of technological intensity (whether the focus is low, intermediate, or high tech) and the degree of support from management to park residents. This table shows that whereas an industrial park is low tech and provides low levels of management support, a science park is high tech but offers little management support. A technology park/centre, in contrast, is the most high tech and provides most management support. In between these extremes, there are other forms such as business incubators, managed workshops, and enterprise zones (Rodriguez-Pose and Hardy, 2014).

Another interesting point concerns the global variation in the prevalence of different kinds of parks. Hobbs et al. (2017) found that research parks are more common in the United States, science parks (focused on more high tech than research parks, see Table 5.2) are found more often in Europe, and technology parks (high-tech focused, with greater management support than in science parks) predominated in East Asia. In China, meanwhile, the most common form of parks are districts or areas for high-tech and industrial development (Kostyunina and Baronov, 2012). Moreover, all science parks in the United Kingdom are based in a university (Siegel et al., 2003). Often, these different terms are used to categorise what are essentially similar in design and scope (Rodriguez-Pose and Hardy, 2014). Massey et al. (1991) found that in the 1980s, the term science park was most common.

Table 5.2 Framework showing the varieties of park models across the world

		Technology level		
		Low	*Intermediate*	*High*
Management support	**Low**	Industrial Park	Business Park	Science Park
	Intermediate	Managed Workshop	Enterprise Zone	**Innovation Centre**
	High	Business Incubator	**Business and Innovation Centre**	**Technology Park/Centre**

Source: Rodriguez-Pose and Hardy, 2014: 16.

There are many kinds of parks operating in the world, all called by different terms. Sometimes the labels are used interchangeably, and sometimes not. Therefore, it does not matter much what the predominant label used in Russia is. It is more important to look at all types of aims which Russian parks have, their design, the level of management support provided, technological intensity, and industrial focus.

According to the IASP, STPs are organisations, managed by specialised professionals, that primarily aim to increase the wealth of its community by promoting the culture of innovation and the competitiveness of its associated businesses and knowledge-based institutions. It seems that a science park is, by definition, an organisation with an internal focus.

The IASP also specifies the following broad objectives of science parks:

- to stimulate and manage the flow of knowledge and technology between universities and companies;
- to facilitate the communication between companies, entrepreneurs, and technicians;
- to provide environments that enhance a culture of innovation, creativity, and quality;
- to focus on companies and research institutions as well as on people: the entrepreneurs and "knowledge workers";
- to facilitate the creation of new businesses via incubation and spin-off mechanisms and accelerate the growth of small- and medium-sized companies; and
- to work in a global network that gathers many thousands of innovative companies and research institutions throughout the world, facilitating the internationalisation of their resident companies.

The services that IASP provides to its members are a mixture of face-to-face and virtual services. These include networking at events, training, and consultancy, access to an e-platform to share new technologies and solutions with other companies, access to statistics and research on science park management and performance globally, advice on company online marketing and promotion, and access to proprietary software developed by IASP experts for analysis and strategic advice on science park development (Table 5.3).

Similar to the IASP definition, the UK Science Park Association defines a science park as an entity for supporting business and technology transfer that:

- encourages and supports the starting up and incubation of innovation-led, high-growth, knowledge-based businesses (*same as IASP*);
- provides an environment where larger and international businesses can develop specific and close interactions with a particular centre of knowledge creation for their mutual benefit (*same as IASP*); and
- has formal and operational links with centres of knowledge creation such as universities, higher education institutes, and research organisations (*similar to IASP objectives*).

Table 5.3 Services provided by the IASP to its members

Service	*Mechanisms*
International networking	Help members meet the right people face to face at the right time at major global and regional events, including conferences, seminars, and workshops. Virtual networking through member-only section of IASP website.
Open innovation support	POINT service enables members and their resident companies to share knowledge of their technologies and solutions with other companies, including other innovative companies and multinational corporations searching for new technologies.
Sharing best practices in knowledge and mutual learning	Webinars, publications, producing own research and collating others' research on STPs, news on recent developments and initiatives in science parks and areas of innovation.
Global visibility	Help members strengthen their global online presence (using social media) and share their new developments and successes (via IASP monthly e-newsletter).
Training and consultancy	Organising regular seminars on science park and innovation management for members, as well as ad hoc trainings and individual advice. Putting members in touch with experts for feasibility studies and concrete consultancy projects.
Strategic profiling	Proprietary software (IASP Strategigram©) available online to help science park managers analyse their park's strategy and development and compare it with other parks.

Source: www.iasp.ws/activities/services [last accessed 30 December 2019].

In both the IASP and the United Kingdom Science Park Association (UKSPA) definitions of science parks and their objectives, the management roles, and emphasis on promoting an "environment" conducive to innovation distinguish science parks from property companies. In the United Kingdom and elsewhere, however, there is evidence that property companies have begun to buy up increasing numbers of science park sites.

Thus, a science park is fundamentally about the proximity of firms. Parks physically locate resident firms near each other in a relatively small area, which is thought by park planners to facilitate the exchange of knowledge and interactions. Theoretically, too, proximity had benefits which many supposed would bring added value to organisations and firms. However, these theoretical benefits often have not materialised. Globally, STPs tend to share four features, although of course there are variations. It is also striking that these features have remained remarkably constant since the 1980s, when science parks first appeared globally. A UKSPA document from 1985 spelled out the criteria for its membership, criteria which look very similar to the aforementioned criteria and characteristics used today by the IASP and the UKSPA (cited in Massey and David, 1991: 14):

STPs globally tend to share the following characteristics:

(i) they are a property-based initiative;
(ii) they have formal operational ties with a university or other higher educational or research institution;

(iii) they have an active role for management in facilitating the transfer of technology and business skills to businesses; and
(iv) they typically aim to foster the creation and growth of knowledge-based businesses and organisations that are normally resident on the site of the park.

STPs in the Russian Federation

Historical evolution of STPs in Russia: a tale of two generations

This section distinguishes between two "generations" of STPs in Russia, the first of which was created in the 1990s and the second after 2007. Both focused on providing state funding for the construction of infrastructure in STPs. The first policy to allocate resources for STPs was the five-year programme called "Technoparks of Russia," which was introduced in 1990. This programme sought to increase the returns from Soviet-era R&D by allocating targeted financing to the first generation of parks. Tomsk scientific–technical park was the first park to open in 1990 (Kostyunina and Baronov, 2012). This park in Tomsk did well in its first few years because of strong support to introduce the market economy and entrepreneurship from local actors, an entrepreneurial management team, and strong local knowledge capacities (universities and research institutes of the Academy of Sciences). It generated significant wealth. However, by the mid-1990s, this park collapsed financially, primarily because it was over-reliant on imported goods (e.g. importing tea from India) and because the federal government ran into financial difficulties, meaning many public sector workers in Tomsk and across the country faced unpaid wages and salaries for a prolonged period (Comins and Rowe, 2008). Overall, federal resources from this programme were too limited for it to have much sustainable success (Kostyunina and Baronov, 2012).

By 1995, the year the first federal programme for STPs ended, there were 42 technoparks across Russia and 900 innovative firms in these parks. This means that, on average, each park hosted 21 firms. However, the 1990s was a crisis period for small firms, with a high turnover of small companies. Technoparks were no exception: in 1999, Russian parks had about 35% fewer resident firms than in 1995, or only about 590 firms in Russian parks. Moreover, while the 19 most developed parks in Russia had on average 28 resident firms, the remaining 50 parks had on average just one resident firm. Hence, 72% of technoparks in the late-1990s were in an embryonic state, and this explains why many scholars argued that the 1990s was a period when there was a "crisis of technoparks in Russia" (Zaitsev and Okorokov, 2002: 65).

Russia's federal state seemed to forget about STPs in the late 1990s and early 2000s. There was an absence of federal-level programmes or policies, with the corresponding resources, for STPs in this period. Nonetheless, since the early 1990s, some regions and local governments in Russia continued to invest in their own technology parks and business incubators or supported the creation of privately funded parks or incubators. Research by the Higher School of Economics suggests that there are between 80 and 100 of these regional/local/private technology parks and approximately 300 business incubators (reported in Yugrinova, 2014). These regional or local infrastructure initiatives were never thoroughly evaluated or monitored so many of them are operating ineffectively or have ceased to exist (Yugrinova, 2014).

It was not until 2005 that more state sponsored STPs were built, driving the creation of the second generation of Russian parks. Federal funds were provided for building infrastructure on a co-financing basis with regions. Originally, these STPs emerged as a kind of "second rate" alternative to another innovation policy tool – special economic zones (SEZs).

In 2005, the Russian government passed a federal law on SEZs, which are entities focused on supporting R&D that is nearly ready to be launched onto the market. By 2008, six hi-tech SEZs and two production SEZs had been created (Graham and Dezhina, 2008). SEZs are hence another policy tool used in post-Soviet Russia to promote innovation, distinguishable from STPs by their technological focus and by their superior level of federal funding. In the handful of Russian regions that did not get selected to have a SEZ, technoparks were built instead. The regions that got the chance to build a technopark in 2005 were Novosibirsk, Tyumen, Sarov, Kazan, and Obninsk. Firms resident in these technoparks were not entitled to the tax discounts or financial compensation that firms in SEZs could have. The only financial support from the federal state for technoparks lay in the form of funding for infrastructure construction – on a 50–50 basis, with the other 50% of the funding from regional budgets. Furthermore, while 2 billion roubles (approximately GBP39 million, USD 76 million, EUR 58 million as of currency rates on 1 January 2007[1]) were earmarked in the 2007 federal budget for infrastructure construction in the five technoparks listed previously, the SEZ in Zelenograd received 23.8 billion roubles (approximately GBP 462 million, USD 905 million, EUR 686 million) for construction. That is almost 12 times more than the amount given to the five technoparks (Kostyunina and Baronov, 2012).

Until 2006, the governance framework at a federal level for parks was very weak, signalling a lack of political interest in technology parks as a tool for innovation policy. The initial impetus for state policy on technology parks came from the very top of the political vertical, after President Putin visited the technology parks – mainly focused on the ICT sector – in the Indian city of Bangalore as part of his official visit to India between 3 and 5 December 2004. Inspired by Bangalore's state-funded technology parks, Putin called for Russia to emulate India (Yugrinova, 2014). Putin's vision was put into motion by the federal bureaucracy in 2006: the Government of Russia approved a programme specifically for STPs. The programme, called "Creation of technoparks in the sphere of high technologies in the Russian Federation" (10 March 2006, No. 328), aimed to create seven hi-tech parks (later revised to nine and then 12: see Karetin, 2010), secure state funding, and diversify sources of funding for the STPs. Because the Ministry of Telecom and Mass Communications of the Russian Federation was the coordinator of the programme, all the parks were originally meant to have an ICT focus. This focus was soon expanded to include more hi-tech sectors (e.g. nanotech, biotech, information technologies, and others). Between 2007 and 2009, nine parks were built under this programme using federal and local (regional) funds on a co-funding basis. A park in Kemerovo region was included at the last moment, in December 2007 (Karetin, 2010).

The Governmental Commission for transport and communications under the Ministry of Telecom and Mass Communications evaluated these state-funded parks in early 2009 and concluded that they were not developing in line with the government's expectations, the regions lacked capabilities for setting up parks, and there was occasional duplication of projects and a shift towards creating *infrastructure for engineering*. Unfortunately, this evaluation is not publicly available. The evaluation led to the suspension of funding for four parks in 2009–2010 (in Tyumen, Moscow region, Kaluga region, and Saint Petersburg) and a reduction of resources for the remaining five parks in Tatarstan Republic, Novosibirsk, Kemerovo, Nizhny Novgorod, and the Republic of Mordovia (Karetin, 2010).

Since 2007, two more technoparks joined the Ministry of Telecom and Mass Communications programme to bring the total number to 11. As of October 2013, however, only eight of these parks were operational (Kuzbass in Kemerovo Oblast, Academpark in Novosibirsk, IT park and Himgrad in Kazan, Republic of Tatarstan, IT park in Naberezhnye Chelny, Z-Valley in Samara region, and other centres in Tyumen and Mordovia). Moreover, only three of the 11 parks that received technopark funding since 2007 had achieved 75% of their targets (Hopkins, 2013). Another official source states that federal funding for three parks has been discontinued since 2009 (parks located in St. Petersburg, Moscow region, and Tyumen region), pointing to a mechanism for federal authorities to exercise some control over the development of STPs (GoR information sheet, date unknown).

In this light, only Samara and Novosibirsk regions (home to the Z-Valley and Akadempark technoparks) had their funding guaranteed by the government in the autumn of 2013 up to the end of 2014, while the other nine parks were forced to compete in order to secure further funding. The winners of this competitive funding to allocate USD 65 million of federal money were Moscow city (USD 10 million), Sverdlovsk Oblast and Penza Oblast (USD 22 million each), and Republic of Mordovia (USD 11 million). Mordovia's technopark received USD 40 million from the federal budget between 2007 and 2012, while Penza had got USD 13 million in technopark funding prior to 2013. It seems that past success is a necessary (but not sufficient) condition of state funding for technoparks (Hopkins, 2013).

Overall, federal funding for technoparks between 2007 and 2014 comprised 13 billion roubles (approximately USD 379 million, GBP 221 million, EUR 277 million as of currency exchange on 1 July 2014).[2] This money came from federal coffers and was transferred to regional budgets on condition that regions co-financed the construction of infrastructure.

In Russia, STPs represent a stage of Russia's STI policy that was introduced in 1990. Russia borrowed the policy instrument of STPs from other countries and adapted STPs to the Russian context. It was only after 2005 that the Russian state introduced a strategy for STPs and regulation governing their activity.

In 2014, the Association of Clusters and Technology Parks of Russia published a "national standards for technology parks" to help state (federal and regional) and local authorities increase the performance of Russian STPs and ensure STPs develop effectively and create favourable conditions for resident firms. This document was updated in 2021. The standards document contains a list of requirements that STPs must meet to gain official recognition as a STP. Accordingly, the official definition of an STP in Russia is:

> a technology park is a property portfolio, which includes innovation, engineering, and technological infrastructure and provides a full cycle of services to create, accommodate, and develop high-tech companies. The complex is managed by one operator – a specialised management company.
>
> (Association of Clusters and Technology Parks of Russia, 2021: 6)[3]

This definition contrasts with a broader one that encompasses all kinds of innovation clusters, for example science cities, technopoles (Rodriguez-Pose and Hardy, 2014; Kostyunina and Baronov, 2012).

We lack sufficient scientific evidence on the performance of Russian science parks. There are some studies about the "first generation" of parks set up in the 1990s (see e.g. Batstone and Westhead, 1996; Bruton, 1998; Kihlgren, 2003). However, there is surprisingly little published research on Russia's "second generation" STPs set up since 2000. Considering the substantial state funding these parks have received since 2006, this is surprising and perhaps an oversight that deserves to be addressed. The post-2006 generation of STPs is not only better funded by the state, but simultaneously largely internally focused on construction of infrastructure and somewhat internationally linked, through membership of the IASP. Is the 2000s generation of science parks in Russia performing with any more success than the 1990s generation of STPs? Is there any evidence to suggest that lessons have been learnt among policy makers and businesses regarding the failures of the 1990s parks?

The first STPs appeared in Russia in the early 1990s supported by the Federal Ministry of Education (Table 5.4). This mirrored a similar global trend in the 1980s: by 1990, there were over 300 STPs in the world, approximately 50% of which were in the United States (Larina, 2006). The idea of STPs gained traction in the late Soviet Union, and the experiences of Western STPs began to be discussed in Russian scientific journals from 1988 (Kihlgren, 2003).

The rapid rise in IASP membership among Russian STPs between early 2014 and 2015 is proof of a renewed interest in STPs among policy makers and businesses in Russia and partly motivates this chapter. The increase in IASP membership among Russian STPs is arguably a sign of a policy shift in Russia towards greater internationalisation of STPs. STPs are a distinctive, post-Soviet, and foreign-inspired stage of Russian research, development, and innovation policy because they are one mechanism for supporting innovation and technological commercialisation. In early 2014, IASP had nine members from Russia; by mid-2015, there were 37 Russian members (email communication with IASP staff, 14

Table 5.4 Number of STPs in Russia (all kinds including state-funded, public–private initiatives, and privately funded parks)

Year	*Number of technology parks*
1990	2
1991	8
1992	24
1993	43
1995	42
2000	76
2008	80
2014*	80–90
2017**	125

Source: RA Expert (2011); Zaitsev and Okorokov (2002).

These figures are broadly confirmed by other sources although with small variations by year, including Kostyunina and Baronov (2012).

* As of March 2014, according to Ernst & Young Global Limited and Russian Venture Company (2014).
** Hundred and twenty-five parks that meet all the criteria for an official technology park. *Source*: 2017 *III Annual Review of Technology parks of Russia*, Association of Clusters and Technology Parks of Russia (pp. 192–195).

May 2015). Moreover, Moscow hosted IASP's 2016 World Conference. What explains this exponential growth in Russian members? Becoming a member of the IASP is not cheap (EUR 1700 for full membership as of 2015). Therefore, the STPs in Russia must feel that the benefits merit the membership fee. Arguably, the rise in members shows that Russian parks are still interested in international collaboration despite the increasingly tense geopolitical relations between Russia and Western countries since early 2014. Russian policy makers and young businesses may see membership of IASP as a mechanism to evade Western sanctions on Russia or continue operational links with the international business community. Alternatively, the Russian government might have pressed more Russian STPs to join IASP in 2015 to guarantee a bigger Russian presence at the 2016 world conference of IASP hosted by Moscow and ensure its success. It could also equally be explained by state-funded parks' need to spend funds within a certain timeframe, and IASP membership offered a convenient way to help achieve this goal independent of construction schedules.

In fact, STPs were not created on entirely blank slates. Instead some STPs have been developed in regions which previously had strong industries or research and scientific strengths, such as closed towns [closed administrative-territorial entities ("zakrytye administrativno-territorialnye obrazovanye") or ZATO] and science towns. Of the six or so "pioneer" STPs set up in the early 1990s, half (in Moscow, Zelenograd, and Tomsk) had a science city or ZATO. The generation of STPs set up in the 2000s, however, does not have such a strong association with closed cities or science towns. The geographical spread of STPs in Russia today is broader, encompassing most regions of the country; Western Russia (west of the Urals mountains) is particularly well-endowed in STPs. There are many formerly closed towns and science towns that do not have a STP today. Moreover, while many parks have old, "Soviet-era" specialisations (e.g. engineering, machine learning, ICT), there are also significant numbers of STPs with newer specialisations (e.g. biotech, biomed, nano). This shows that path dependency, historical experiences, and legacies have a small role to play in explaining the appearance of STPs – particularly the STPs of the 1990s. Other factors such as the actions of local and regional elites and federal and regional funding are perhaps more important.

Quite quickly, regional authorities saw the potential benefits of technology parks for local economic development. They provided support by allocating funds, providing vacant industrial or office buildings, or – in some cases – by pursuing a non-interference policy.

As Table 5.5 shows, Russia is like other countries in having a wide range of kinds of STP. The most common kind in Russia in the 1990s was university-based technoparks (Chistyakova, 2010).

By looking at the variety of firms in STPs in Russia, we can gain insights into what the system of innovation is like in Russia and how (if at all) STPs contribute to the operation of such a system. Table 5.6 shows that the 17 STPs that responded to the author's survey had an ***arithmetic mean of 134 firms (all kinds)*** in 2015. The arithmetic mean number of firms in the sample of STPs excluding Skolkovo technopark was 64 in 2015. Skolkovo technopark is an outlier because it is on such a bigger scale compared to the other STPs in Russia with 1200 resident firms in 2015. Of the total number of firms in Russian STPs, the majority were ***production firms***. The parks also reported a high proportion of "other" types of firms, which could mean park residents (research teams developing a project or start-ups) that are not yet in the production stage but rather still in development or prototype stages. The service firms often provide ICT services or catering to STP residents, so are not necessarily innovative. Moreover, ***STPs in Russia have a small number of foreign and Russian big firms*** meaning that they are focused on supporting start-ups, small- and medium-sized firms. This focus on start-ups and small firms makes them like most STPs in other countries.

Another kind of parks in Russia is those that are privately funded. These types of STPs are a very recent phenomenon in Russia, with one source stating that they first appeared in 2010, two years after Medvedev became president (Volkonitskaya and Lyapina). Indeed, by 2015, as many as 33% of Russian parks that responded to IASP's survey (5 of 15) claimed they did not receive any financial support from the public sector or governments (Figure 5.2).

How effective were the 1990s generation of STPs?

Analysis of Russia's STPs summarises the key features of Russia's ten most successful STPs according to a 2000 evaluation. It examined the following variables: year in which the park was founded, the number of resident firms, the extent of links with the local university, founders and growth patterns of the small innovative enterprises, sources of financing, managers' qualifications, training for

Table 5.5 Types, aims, and features of STPs in Russia

Type	*Aims when park created*	*Features*	*Examples*
University based	✓Commercialisation of R&D; ✓Increase the attractiveness of the founding university; ✓Keep valuable talent and R&D in the university.	✓Land given by university; ✓New buildings constructed or existing buildings allocated to park; ✓Offices rented out to small innovative firms; ✓University's scientific facilities and library collections made available to park residents;	Scientific park of Moscow State University; Technopark of MIFI.
Regional sector based	✓Introduce new technologies to regional industrial enterprises; ✓Develop science and technological potential of the area; ✓Create more jobs.	✓Regional or city authorities, universities, research centres, enterprises, and other interested parties involved in setting up park; ✓Anchor university carries out R&D as contracted by park; ✓Small firms in park do own R&D or R&D for large firms.	Tomsk technopark, Mordovia technopark, Udmurtia technopark.
Industrial based	✓Organise new production; ✓Promote new technologies.	✓Created taking into account of the needs of potential residents; ✓Production facilities built for industrial production; ✓Infrastructure built, for example hotels, office and logistic facilities.	North–West technopark, "Na Ryzhyevke" technopark in St. Petersburg (under construction in 2010).
Network based	✓Distribute innovation across the region to existing actors (research centres, enterprises, etc.); ✓Commercialisation of R&D.	✓Technopark facilities created in existing research centres.	Agrotechnopark "Sibirsky" (under construction in 2010).
Science town based	✓Capitalise on the intellectual potential of science towns; ✓Commercialisation of R&D.	✓Creation of engineering, transport, and social infrastructure; ✓Construction of technopark modules; ✓Construction of housing.	Technoparks in Pushchino, Chernogolovka, Troitsk, Dubna, and Novosibirsk's Akademgorodok (under construction in 2010).

Source: Chistyakova (2010).

Table 5.6 Types of firms that are based in 17 technology parks in Russia (2015)

Name of technology park	*Total number of firms (2015)*	*Number of production firms*	*Number of service firms*	*Number of big foreign firms*	*Number of big Russian firms*	*Number of other types of firms (SMEs or leaseholders)*
KNIAT	60	12	6	0	1	41
Tyumen Technopark (State Budget Organisation "West Siberian Innovation Center")	51	38	4	0	3	6
FABRIKA	33	0	33	0	2	0
Zhiguli Valley	141	2	18	4	6	98
Sapfir	3	3	0	0	0	200*
Yakutia	79	14	10	0	0	79
Ingria	70	5	65	0	0	0
Sarov	57	3	15	0	3	25
NP ITC "InTeh-Don"	40	40	3	1	2	0
Strogino	54	24	4	0	0	17
Akadempark	175	175	80	1	1	0
Kazan IT park	150	120	15	1	5	0
Technopolis "Moskva"	34	33	5	3	11	na
ITMO University technopark	35	5	5	2	1	0
Skolkovo technopark	1200	30	30	0	60	1080
Navigator campus	14	3	3	1	0	7
Slava	90	70	20	0	0	4

Source: Author's survey of STP managers, 2015–2016. n = 17.

Note: * Sapfir technopark has 200 lease holders listed as "other kinds of firms." These were not counted by the park's management as resident firms because they are not innovative or high tech, but simply rent out office space. The fact that the number of leaseholders is so high in Sapfir park indicates that this privately funded park set up in 2014 relies on these property rents as revenue sources.

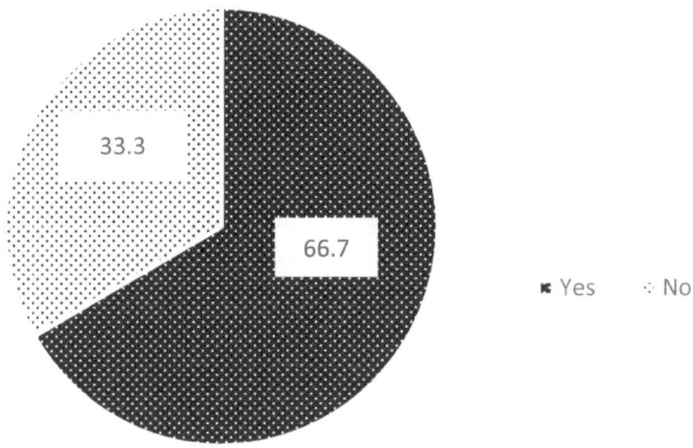

Figure 5.2 Does your park/area receive financial support from the public sector/ governments?

Source: IASP 2015 survey of 15 full IASP Russian members.

employees, and the main problems as perceived by managers of STPs ("Technoparks in Russia," RA Expert, date unknown).

Batstone and Westhead (1996) provided the earliest assessment by Western scholars of the effectiveness of STPs in Russia. They used the concept of new competition as a framework – following Best – which sees the decline of "old competition," based on large-scale industrial production and in its place new forms of competition based on small firms which act as strategic agents in national and international markets (Best, 1990). A shortage of this kind of new competition leads, according to Best, to technological stagnation. In socialist economies, low economic growth since the 1970s was a result of weaknesses in technology and innovation relative to Western, more capitalist economies. Such a conceptual framework may be considered rather than ideological and pro-market; nonetheless, despite its limitations, Batstone and Westhead (1996) is useful because of its research design, questions posed, and findings.

Batstone and Westhead (1996) argued that new small- and medium-sized enterprises (SMEs) in post-socialist Russia were significant in providing competition to older, larger firms and saw the new science park "movement" as a potential avenue to success for SMEs and entrepreneurs. Support to new technology-based firms (NTBFs) in the new STPs was part of the government's small business strategy in the early days of transition from a centrally planned economy. However, with the benefit of hindsight, SMEs supported by the nascent science parks in the early 1990s could not seriously compete with the older, bigger firms.

Survey results

This section briefly describes the methodology used to obtain the empirical evidence analysed in this chapter. Next, the main results from the surveys are presented.

Methodology

The empirical basis of this chapter comes from two original surveys. One purposive survey was conducted on a sample of 17 managers of STPs in Russia. The selection mechanism for this survey was to invite all 37 Russian member parks of the International Association of Science Parks and Areas of Innovation to complete the survey as it was assumed that parks who were members of this association would be more likely to be established and organised and hence perhaps more likely to have international linkages; the random element was which of the 37 parks responded to the invitation.[4] This survey asked the managers about the reasons why firms chose to locate to their park, the type of location within an urban area where the park is (out of town, university, enterprise, or research institute), when the park was founded, numbers of resident firms and the different kinds of firms, and the main barriers facing firms in Russian technology parks.

The survey was conducted by the author in online format (questionnaire written using google forms and a link to the survey sent via email) or face to face in Russian between May and August 2015 and in May 2016. In total, the survey invitation was sent by email to managers of all 37 Russian member parks of the International Association of Science Parks and Areas of Innovation (IASP) using the contact details available on the IASP website. The author followed up within a few days of sending the managers' survey invitation by email by phoning all recipients to increase response rates. In the end, the response rate for the managers' survey was 46% (17 out of 37 parks).

The survey of park management garnered responses from 17 different technology parks across Russia. This is 13% of the 125 technology parks that existed in 2017 according to the Association of Clusters and Technology Parks of Russia (see Table 4). The sampled parks are in 12 regions of Russia out of a population of 44 regions with a technology park, meaning that 27% of regions with a technology park as of 2017 are sampled. The mean number of firms in the sample of technology parks is 59 as compared to 34 firms in the total population of 125 parks in 2017 (this was calculated by dividing the total number of resident firms by the total number of recognised parks in 2017, that is 4317 divided by 125).[5]

The second survey was carried out with 11 resident firms within three different Russian technology parks to understand firms' perspectives on reasons for moving to technology parks, the services they use in the park, and cooperation patterns with other firms in the park and located outside the park. The survey was conducted by the author during face-to-face interviews in Russian with a representative(s) of the firm's management between May and August 2015.

The English language versions of the two surveys were translated into Russian by the author of this book and by native Russian speakers. The English and Russian versions of both questionnaires can be found in Appendix 3.

Table 5.7 details the 17 technology parks that were included in the survey, which region they are in, and these parks' sectoral focus. These sectors include those that are "traditional" for the USSR and Russia (ICT, instrumentation, machine-building, chemistry, civil engineering, computer science, and energy) as well as

Table 5.7 Technological sectors of 17 surveyed technology parks in Russia

Name of technopark	*Region of Russia*	*Main sectors of focus*
IT park FABRIKA	Astrakhan Oblast	ICT & communications
Sapfir JSC Science and technology park	Moscow city	Civil engineering, electronics, optics, services for business and industry, software engineering
Kazan Hi-Technology Park "IT Park"	Republic of Tatarstan	ICT & communications
Navigator Campus	Republic of Tatarstan	Electronics, medical equipment, mobile and wireless solutions, robotics and plant automation, other electricity/electric science and technology
Non-commercial partnership innovative technological centre (NP ITC) "InTeh-Don"	Rostov Oblast	Chemistry and chemicals, energy saving and conservation, ICT & communications, other materials
Technopark Zhiguli Valley	Samara Oblast	ICT & communications, energy saving and conservation, transport and space, chemistry and new materials, and biotechnology, health & pharmaceuticals
Technopark Ingria	Saint Petersburg	Education, health & pharmaceuticals, ICT & communications, robotics and plant automation
Joint Stock Company Technopark of industrial technologies "innovation-technology centre" (KNIAT)	Republic of Tatarstan	Aeroplane construction, machine-building, instrumentation
Technopark of ITMO University	Saint Petersburg	Biotechnology, ICT & communications, telecommunication, new materials, optics
Akadempark (technopark of Novosibirsk Akademgorodok)	Novosibirsk Oblast	Biotechnology, informatics and telematics, sensors and instrumentation, micromachines and nanotechnology
Technopark Sarov (private limited company)	Nizhny Novgorod Oblast	Energy, environment, health & pharmaceuticals, ICT & communications, materials
Technopark Skolkovo LLC	Moscow city	Informatics and telematics, space technology, energy saving and conservation, biomedical science and technology, nuclear science and technology
Moscow city government-owned Technopark Strogino	Moscow city	Civil engineering, computer science and hardware, materials, micromachines and nanotechnology, optics

(*Continued*)

Table 5.7 (Continued)

Name of technopark	*Region of Russia*	*Main sectors of focus*
Technopark Yakutia	Republic of Sakha (Yakutia)	Biotechnology, construction engineering, ICT & communications, land transportation, other energy science and technology
Technopolis Moscow	Moscow city	Biotechnology, ICT & communications, micro- and nanoelectronics, robotics and plant automation, new materials
Tyumen Technopark (State Budget Organisation "West Siberian Innovation Center")	Tyumen Oblast	Oil/gas recovery, environment, health & pharmaceuticals, ICT & communications, other materials
Technopark Slava	Moscow city	ICT, biomedicine, energy, instrumentation, nanotechnology, robotics

Source: Author's survey of STPs (2015–2016).

newer areas (robotics, biotechnology, biomedicine, new materials, optics, and nanotechnology). This shows that these STPs are open to hosting firms that are active in many different sectors, potentially allowing fruitful cross-collaborations and interdisciplinary R&D. Unfortunately, it was not possible to get a comprehensive overview of the sectoral focus of all the technology parks in Russia so we do not know how representative this sample is according to sectoral focus.

Main findings from the surveys

(1) Science and Technology Parks in Russia are mostly internally focused

One key finding from the surveys is that STPs in Russia are largely focused on internal development, that is on nurturing NTBFs. This is in line with the main objective of STPs across the globe. According to the author's survey of park managers, most respondents stated that – on a strategic level – their parks were founded to be a source of new businesses entering markets, that is as mechanisms to encourage diversification and competition. This is important because it suggests that Russian STPs are not just perceived as an enclave with shiny new infrastructure and equipment. As shown in Figure 5.3, most managers of STPs said that their parks were founded to help create new firms, support new firms to produce or develop new technologies, and help with R&D and technological development. Six parks (35%) chose the reason "assist with technology transfer" (in the online survey).

When asked more concretely why firms choose to move to an STP, managers who responded to the survey selected reasons that reflect the more prosaic reality rather than the high-level, strategic reasons why STPs are founded. For example, one way of achieving the high-level goal for STPs "to support the creation and development of new firms" is by providing firms with infrastructure and access to specialised equipment. Infrastructure in this context means office space for firms, laboratories or other areas for machinery, prototype-production, and specialised equipment.

Infrastructure creation in STPs is supported by some evidence from the author's survey of Russian STP managers. All park manager respondents selected infrastructure and specialised equipment of the park as one of the most important reasons why firms moved to the STP (Figure 5.4). However, other reasons frequently cited by STP managers included "opportunities to cooperate with other firms in the park" (65%), "access to finance (venture capital, grants, loans, etc.)" (53%), and "boosting the image of the firm" (47%), **suggesting that park management does not exclusively see their park's infrastructure as the only attraction for firms choosing to locate to the park.**

To summarise, Russian technology parks tend to have prioritised building new infrastructure in conjunction with developing other elements of parks such as supporting resident firms to network and access services such as finance and accounting.

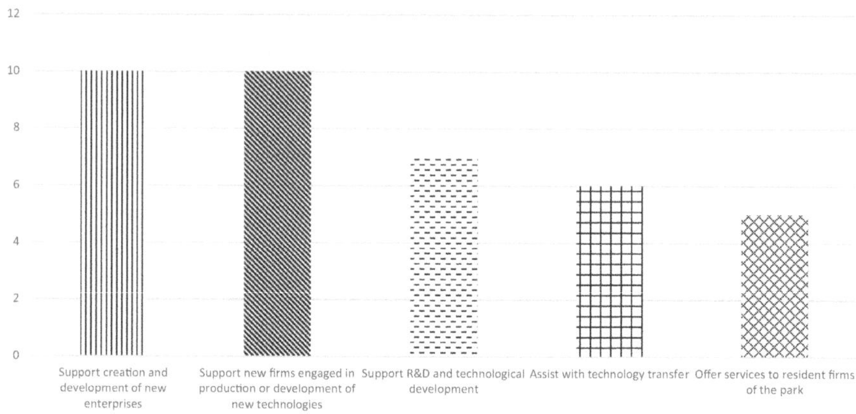

Figure 5.3 Five top reasons for creating STP in Russia (according to managers of STPs)

Source: Author's STPs survey carried out in 2015–2016 (n = 17).

Note: Respondents could select multiple answers. Graph shows the number of respondents who selected each answer. Original question asked in Russian was: "Nazovitye, pozhalysta, osnovniye-prichiny sozdaniya tekhnoparka, v kotorom vy rabotayete."

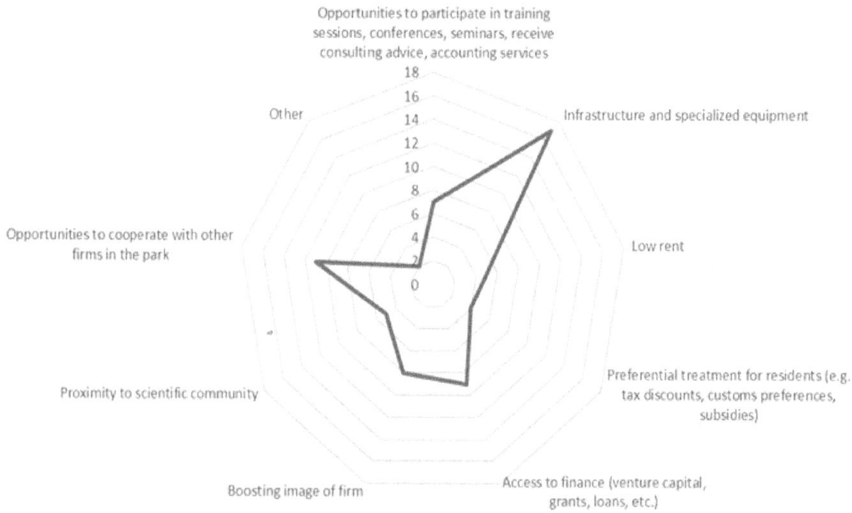

Figure 5.4 Reasons firms chose to move to a science and technology park (STP managers)

Source: Based on 17 respondents to author's survey of science and technology park management (2015).

Notes: Respondents were asked to select up to three reasons they feel are most important for their park. Chart shows the number of resident firms selecting this reason. Original question: "Please select the main reasons why firms move into the science park?" (original question in Russian: "Nazovitye, pozhalysta, osnovniye prichiny po kotorym firmy pereyezhayout na territoriyou technoparka?") % calculated as proportions based on total number of answers selected by respondent and converted into % – for example six answers selected means each answer gets 16.7%.

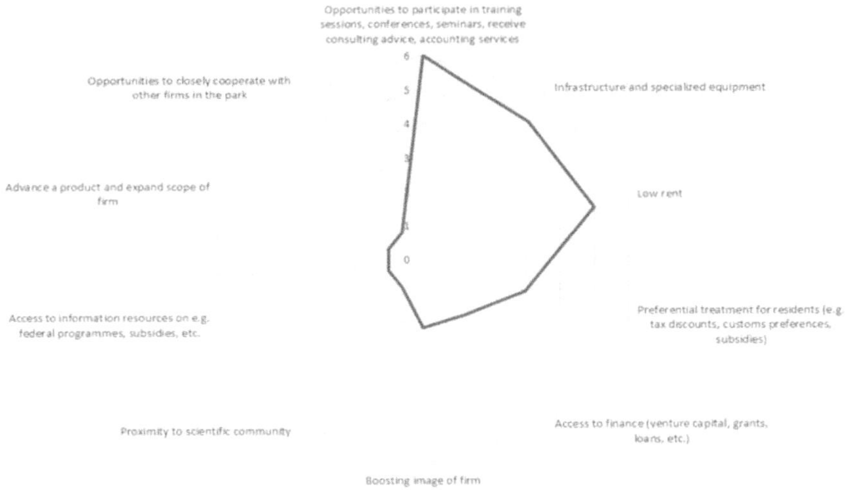

Figure 5.5 Reasons firms chose to move to a science and technology park (firms' views)

Source: Based on ten respondents to author's survey of science and technology park firm residents (2015).

Note: Respondents were asked to select up to three reasons they feel are most important for their firm.

STP managers' views tally to some extent with those of resident firms on why they moved to a STP (Figure 5.5). Both resident firms and STP managers agreed on the importance of infrastructure and specialised equipment for attracting firms. Yet, firms also reported that ***low rent and opportunities to take part in training sessions, conferences, and seminars as well as receive consulting advice and accounting services were important for them***. Interestingly, access to finance was perceived to be a more important attraction by STP managers (53% of respondents selected this reason) than by the resident firms (only 20% of respondents). This could point to differences in views about the technological readiness of firms' products or services, that is how close they are to entering a market. More finance is needed, the further a product or process is from market.

Thus, there is some disconnect between what STP managers feel are the main factors attracting firms to locate in STPs and what resident firms say are the main reasons they located to the park.

(2) But firms resident in Russian STPs do often cooperate with entities outside STPs

An important mechanism for building up critical mass is by resident firms cooperating with firms or other organisations outside STPs. When STP resident firms cooperate with firms outside STPs, they are forming linkages in the real economy

Table 5.8 Cooperation by firms resident in Russian STPs

With whom firm cooperates (e.g. joint contracts, internships etc.):	*No. of STPs who selected this entity (note: respondents could select as many options as they wanted):*
Other firms *not* in the science park	10
Other firms *in* the science park	7
Universities	6
Foreign organisations or firms	6
Research institutes	4
Federal government bodies	2
Russian non-commercial organisations	2
Municipalities	2
Regional government bodies	2
Federal government bodies	2
Other: international, annual exhibition	1

Source: Questionnaire to managers of firms in STPs, May–June 2015, n = 11. Respondents could select all answers that apply and/or add "other" option. Original question in Russian: "Sotrudnichaet li vasha firma (naprimer, sovmyestniye kontrakty, stazhirovki togda li/s drugimi firmami ili organizatsiyami?"

and thus, creating the potential for the STP to have real economic impacts. For example, a firm in a STP may have a joint contract for R&D work with a firm located outside STPs.

Table 5.8 presents data from the survey showing which firms or other organisations STP firms cooperate with in some way, including via joint contracts, internships, etc. Interestingly, ***other firms located outside the STP were the most commonly cited cooperation partner***, followed by other firms in the STP, universities, and foreign organisations or firms.

(3) Level of public sector involvement is very high, although privately funded parks have recently emerged

As shown in Figure 5.6, more than half of the sample of technology parks – 10 parks (59% of the sample) – were funded by the state (federal and/or regional governments, including one park that was funded by the research institute of aviation technologies where it is located). None of the sampled parks were funded by local authorities, an indicator of the weak status of this level of government in Russia. Three of the parks (18% of sample) were funded by a combination of public and private resources. Finally, four parks (23% of sample) were set up with private sector funding. It is a relatively new trend in Russia for the private sector to take the initiative to create parks. These four private parks are specialised in ICT, electronics, and energy: all sectors in which technology parks tend to have higher levels of private sector participation in other countries (Rodriguez-Pose and Hardy, 2014: 69). Three of these privately funded parks are in big cities (Moscow, Kazan, and Astrakhan) and were created since 2011; the fourth private park

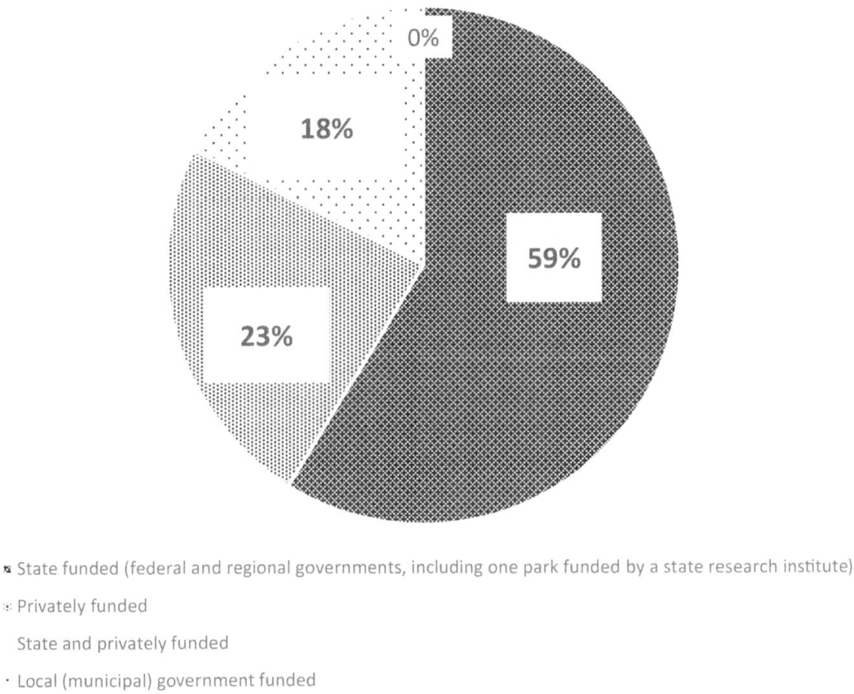

Figure 5.6 Sources of funding of 17 Russian technology parks

Source: Based on 17 respondents to author's survey of science and technology park management (2015).

was created in 2004 in a relatively big town called Novocherkassk with a population of 160,000 in the southern region of Rostov.

This shows that Russian STPs tend to be created with state resources although there is a relatively new trend of the private sector setting up parks.

(4) Universities are rarely involved as co-founders or partners in the post-2000 generation of STPs in Russia

ITMO University technopark in Saint Petersburg is the only one of the 17 surveyed STPs in Russia that is located on the territory of a university. ITMO University technopark was created with subsidies from the federal government. This is a notable shift in technology park policy since the 1990s, when university-based technoparks were the most common kind of park in Russia (Chistyakova, 2010).

The apparent lack of contemporary Russian STPs located in universities may be a barrier to the development of STPs. Close university–industry linkages have been crucial factors driving the world's most successful STPs (Rodriguez-Pose and Hardy, 2014). Key in the latter cases has been linkages with world-leading universities, which are scarce in Russia as in other emerging economies.

(5) Knowledge-intensive "anchor tenants" (often foreign multinational firms) are not present in Russian STPs

Some STPs globally have attempted to attract subsidiaries of multinational enterprises as "anchor tenants" as an alternative strategy for knowledge building to forming linkages with local universities or research institutions. This strategy has only been successful in a few cases, however, because of problems related to the small size of the anchor tenant, their motivations for investing in the STP, and the lack of competitive advantages offered by STPs to potential anchor tenants (Rodriguez-Pose and Hardy, 2014). In the few cases globally where STPs have had success from subsidiaries of multinational enterprises being "anchor tenants," these anchor tenants were large firms with special R&D units that they relocated to the STP. These STPs were in regions with access to big new markets or with competitive advantages such as skilled labour, lower transaction costs, or proximity to the multinational firm's home market (Rodriguez-Pose and Hardy, 2014).

The results from the two surveys of Russian STPs indicate that Russian parks have generally not managed to attract large foreign or Russian firms as "anchor tenants." This could be an obstacle to creating linkages between small and large firms (e.g. creating buyer-supplier relationships). Figure 5.7 shows that only 11 of ***the 17 STPs sampled (65%) had any big Russian firms as tenants in 2015–2016***. Skolkovo technopark had the greatest number of big domestic firms (60), far ahead of the other 11 STPs which hosted between 1 and 11 large Russian firms.

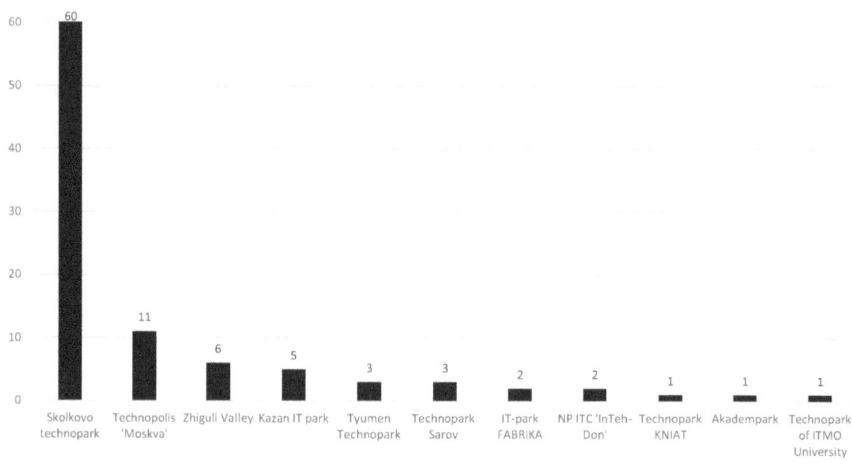

Figure 5.7 Number of big Russian firms in Russian STPs

Source: Author's survey of STP managers, 2015–2016; n=17.

Note: Six STPs surveyed reported 0 big Russian firms hence they are not included in this Figure.

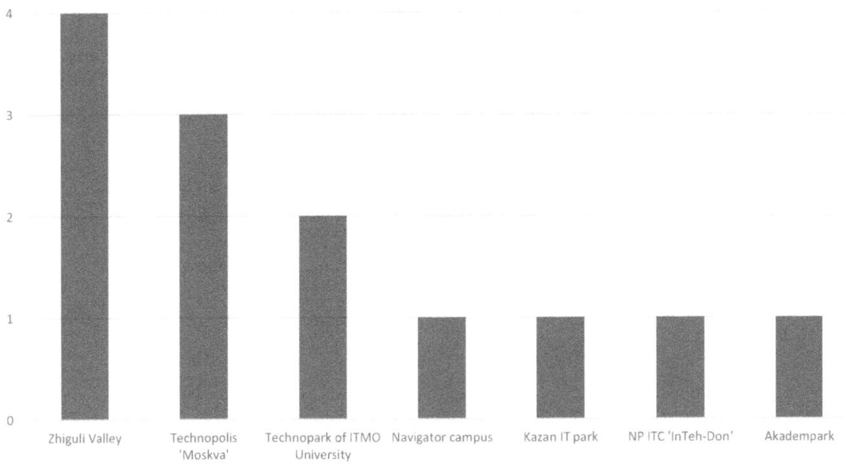

Figure 5.8 Number of big foreign firms in Russian STPs

Source: Author's survey of STP managers, 2015–2016; n = 17.

Note: Ten STPs surveyed reported 0 big foreign firms hence they are not included in this figure.

Figure 5.8 shows that the highest number of ***large foreign firms*** was 4, in just one park (Zhiguli Valley park in Tolyiatti town, Samara region). Zhiguli Valley park is in a town and region with long-established links with the Italian automobile industry and a proactive, pro-business regional government.

The observed lack of big companies (whether foreign or Russian) in Russian STPs is a worrying signal for the development of an innovation ecosystem in which STPs play an important role.

(6) Management of STPs quality is pretty high

Previous research finds that the quality of STPs' management is critical to the success of parks through increasing tenants' intangible capabilities, notably managers' skills and business and entrepreneurial experience, capabilities in knowledge and technology, and the amount of training they get (Rodriguez-Pose and Hardy, 2014).

The author's survey results indicate that Russian STPs tend to have skilled and experienced management teams. A 2000 evaluation of the effectiveness of Russian STPs found that the most successful ones had managers with professional training, very often abroad where they studied Western experiences countries (Graham and Dezhina, 2008: 75). What about in 2015? Do many STP managers have personal experience of Western and/or East Asian STP experiences? According to the survey of STP managers carried out for this book, a large majority (82%) of the 17 STP managers had travelled abroad for their work in the STP

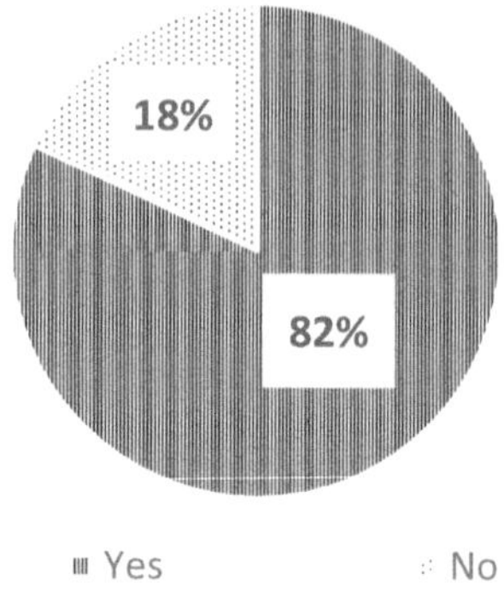

Figure 5.9 Have managers travelled abroad for their work in the STP?

Source: Author's survey 2015–2016; n = 17.

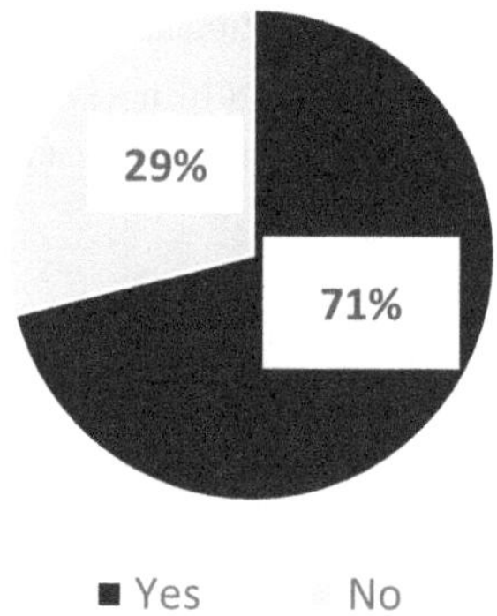

Figure 5.10 Does the science or technology park have an expert council? Evidence from Russia

Source: Author's survey of STP managers, 2015–2016; n = 17.

(Figure 5.9). Foreign exposure is an important source of managerial skills and training but does not necessarily mean that those managers who have travelled abroad for work increased their skills.

One indication of competent management of STPs is if the parks follow international good practices in the way tenant firms are recruited. The STPs surveyed for this book mostly do follow international good practices in recruiting resident firms. For example, 71% (12 of 17 STPs surveyed by author) had an expert council which is primarily responsible for assessing applications by firms to become a resident of the park (Figure 5.10). Hence, the expert council is the critical mechanism that decides how many firms join the park.

Table 5.9 describes the role of the expert council across several STPs in Russia. Across the 12 STPs that described what their expert council does in the survey of

Table 5.9 STP managers' views on the role of the expert council

Expertise on innovative projects. Developing recommendations for accepting residents to the STP.
Selection of projects proposed by firms, entrepreneurs, and researchers.
Advisory body. Main tasks are: to carry out expert assessments, prepare professional recommendations based on analysis of applicants' documents, and to take decisions about who to accept as residents of the STP.
Expert assessment of applications for residency of STP. Participation in editing of the journal "High-tech business."
Identifying the innovativeness and potential of projects submitted to the business incubator. Making decisions about entry to the business incubator.
Making decisions about financing of projects; contributing to the strategic development of the STP.
Strategic planning of the STP's activities. In reality, our STP is territorially spread out, with firms located in different areas but often structurally and technologically inter-related and interconnected.
Expertise; mentoring
Expert council is an advisory, consultative body that makes recommendations.
The main functions of the expert council are to carry out expert assessments and prepare professional recommendations based on the following documents submitted: (1) Application contract with STP management body to engage in hi-tech activities in the STP and to acquire the status of STP resident. (2) Application contract with the foundation about participating in support and development programmes for residents of the business incubator of the STP and about acquiring the status of resident of the STP incubator. (3) Internal regulatory documents of the STP, development programmes of the STP, including support programmes for innovative activities of STP residents. (4) Results of monitoring activity of STP residents.
Expert council makes decisions about the significance, need for, and innovativeness of the products/processes made by companies resident in the STP.
Evaluation of applicants for residency of STP, supporting and helping develop residents' projects.
Evaluation of the innovativeness and environmental impacts of the products/processes made by companies resident in the STP. Additional information: 25 people in the pool who can be called on as needed to form the expert council (although not all are called on for every meeting). This pool of people includes university professors and representatives of the STP administration. They do not get a salary for their work in the expert council. A general meeting occurs 1–2 times per year and approximately once per month on an "as needed" basis (five to six people from expert council meet for these monthly meetings to assess candidates). On average, the STP receives three applications per month.

Source: Author's survey of STP managers, 2015–2016; **n = 12**.

Note: Respondents were asked to describe – in written form in their own words – the role of the expert council if one exists in their STP. Their answers have been translated into English by the author.

park managers, the expert councils are tasked with providing expertise on applications from teams of researchers or firms for projects to develop as a resident of the STP. Often the expert councils are a consultative body that advises on decisions taken by the STP managers. In a couple of STPs surveyed, the expert council also act as mentors to support and help develop residents' projects.

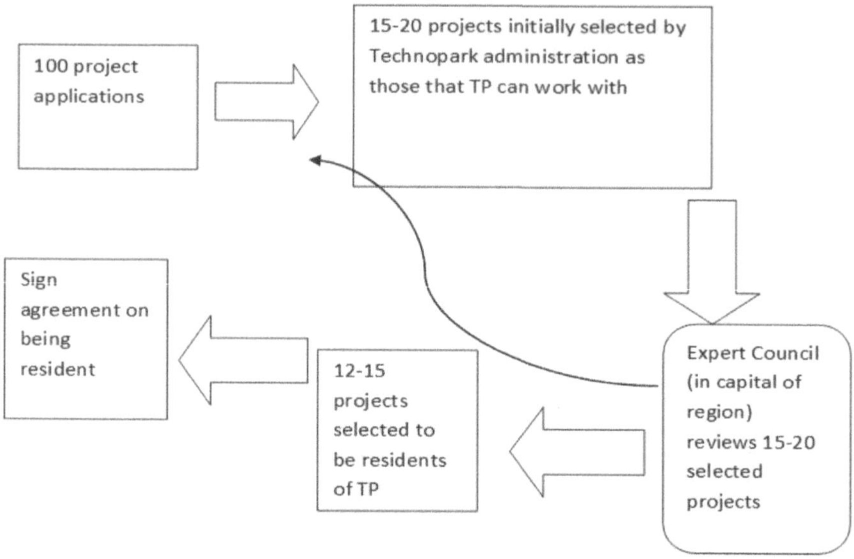

Figure 5.11 Selection process in a state-funded science park in Samara region, Russia (2015)

Source: Author's interview with the STP's administration managers, 9 July 2015.

Note: The numbers refer to one quarter, that is over a three-month period.

The first stage in a firm becoming a resident of a science park in Russia is to submit a formal application. A package of technical, economic, and legal documents is needed. In one case, 11–12 separate documents had to be submitted.

How does the expert council mechanism work? Figure 5.11 illustrates the mechanism for one state-funded park in Russia, showing that out of 100 project applications (one company can submit more than one project if desired) received in any given three months, 15–20 projects will be preliminarily selected by the STP administration and put forward for consideration by the expert council. The expert council then reviews these applications – both on paper and by inviting the applicant firms to orally present their projects – and selects 12–15 of them to become residents. At each stage, the teams behind applications that are not selected to proceed are invited to revise their application in line with the comments from the STP administration; hence, it is quite an interactive process that allows firms to learn from the application process and reapply if they desire. Thus, the success rate of becoming a resident in this particular park is 12%–15%. This indicates tough competition and a high demand for places in this STP in Togliatti, Samara region. Perhaps, the shortage of new infrastructure, shared use specialised equipment, and modern office space for young firms in the town of Togliatti are reasons why this STP has such a competitive selection process. Zhiguli Valley high-tech park was built on a greenfield site on the edge of Togliatti and has five industrial sectors. The presence of Avtovaz, an increasingly crisis-ridden large company (the biggest car manufacturer in Russia), next door to the park may also help explain why small and medium firms are keen to move into the park as this proximity may help them secure supplier contracts with Avtovaz. The author's fieldwork suggests that it is easier to become a resident of other STPs in Russia, although the data are not available to confirm this at present.

(7) Firms in STPs are often not ready to launch products or processes on the market

As shown in Table 5.10, the most commonly cited barrier to STP firms' growth and development was the lack of technologies ready for market. Firm owners' lack of experience in selling on the market and a lack of finance were the next most often cited obstacles. More finance is needed when a technology is not ready for the market, so it is not surprising that firms mentioned both finance and technologies not ready to go to market. This finding suggests that STPs in Russia are largely places for the development of new technologies and processes before they are ready for the market. Overall, all but two of the cited barriers to firm growth are factors internal to the firm and park. The legislative framework was cited as a barrier to STP firms by four STP managers, and the activity or inactivity of regional state authorities was perceived as an obstacle by two STP managers in the survey.

Nevertheless, according to the author's survey of resident firms, 82% of them claimed to have products or services that were ready for sale (Figure 5.12). This does not mean that the firms are actually making sales. One interpretation could

Table 5.10 Main barriers for firms in Russian STPs according to STP managers (number in right hand column indicates number of parks that selected that barrier

Barriers	Internal to firm	Technologies firm produces not ready for market	**11**
		Firms owners' lack market sales experience	**10**
		Lack of financing	**9**
		Lack of qualified workers	**3**
		Lack of consulting services	**1**
		Lack of researchers/scientists	**1**
		Location of park	**1**
	External to firm and park	Existing legislation at federal/regional/local levels	**4**
		Activity or inactivity of regional state authorities	**2**

Source: Q17 of author's questionnaire to managers of STPs, May–June 2015, n = 17.

Note: Respondents could select all answers that apply and/or add "other" option. Original question in Russian: "Nazovite osnovnyie baryery dlya razvitiya firmy v tekhnoparke" ("Please state the main barriers for firm development in the technopark").

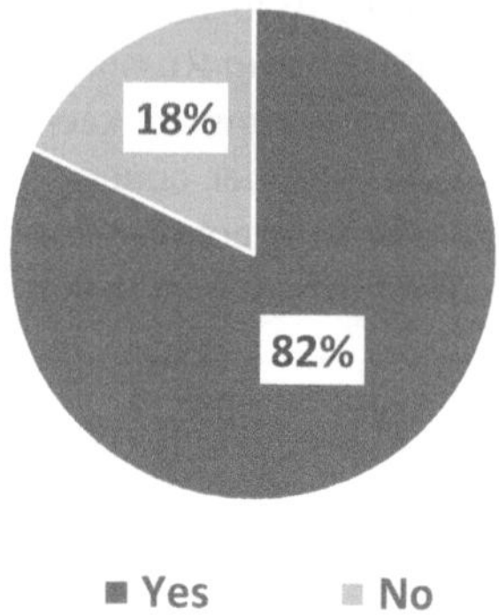

Figure 5.12 Number (and share) of firms in STPs that have products or services ready for sale (on local/regional/national/international markets)

Source: Author's survey of firms in STPs, 2015–2016. n = 11.

be that this indicates that firms in STPs lack knowledge and experience of market sales, a common barrier cited by STP managers (Table 5.10). Because they are inexperienced, the firms' managers overestimate how market ready their products or services are.

Mini case studies of four STPs

This section analyses four STPs to complement the survey results presented in the previous section of this chapter. Four STPs are profiled here in more depth because they could be considered as pioneers among Russian STPs in showing signs of creating local, regional, or international linkages. Three of the STPs discussed in this section – IT park, Zhiguli Valley park, and Akadempark – had the highest number of resident firms in 2015 (according to author's survey) and therefore had the most potential for growth and forming linkages.[6] Ingria park in St. Petersburg has been selected for analysis here because of its unusual strategic focus for Russia on helping its resident firms to network and providing services and support to new firms.

IT park, Kazan, Republic of Tatarstan

IT park was initiated in 2009, making it part of Russia's second generation of technology parks that are supported by the federal government. It has received subsidies from both the federal and regional governments. Its main site in the city of Kazan has been working since 2009, while a second site opened in 2012 in the second largest city of Tatarstan, Naberezhnye Chelny (approximately 225 km or 140 miles east of Kazan, with a population of approximately 0.5 million in 2010).

In 2015, IT park had 150 resident companies; as of January 2018, it had 151 companies. This shows relative stability in the numbers of companies in the park.

In terms of outcomes, revenues from park residents in 2017 totalled 12 billion RUB (approximately 208 million USD), and the volume of residents' exports in the same year was 364 million roubles (6.3 million USD as per exchange rate on 1 January 2018). The park overall got the highest rating (A+) in a national Russian rating of technology parks in 2017.[7]

Since 2014, the IT park has offered a variety of training and educational courses via its IT Academy. These courses teach the basics of IT software, programming, etc. and are open to all adults, children, and employees of firms in the region. In 2018, 939 people completed training courses at the IT Academy. This total number included 272 schoolchildren who did coding classes, 341 people who completed "i-Land" educational courses, and 326 adults who graduated from one of the Academy's other courses.

The experience of IT park's IT Academy illustrates how the IT park has formed linkages with the local and regional economy and society and is helping to upgrade ICT skills in the local workforce.

Zhiguli Valley, Tolyiatti city, Samara region

This park was created in 2010 with funding from the federal government. It now consistently ranks highly in several Russian ratings of STPs (e.g. the rating by the Association of clusters and technology parks of Russia). Zhiguli Valley park generates an economic impact as demonstrated by its total tax revenues of its residents (approximately 500 million RUB or 8.7 million USD) in the third quarter of 2017.

Of note are the international and national linkages that this park has managed to forge. In 2015, it had four big foreign firms and six big Russian firms among its 141 residents. Who were these big firms? The German multinational company Bosch is one of the foreign firms that has a presence in Zhiguli Valley park to develop and adapt electronic stability control systems for domestically produced cars. The proximity to Avtovaz, the biggest car manufacturer in Russia, as well as the company's long experience in the Russian market (since 1904) were key factors in moving some of its high-tech manufacturing production to Zhiguli Valley. As Norbert Klein, the president of Bosch for Turkey, the Middle East, Africa, Russia and CIS countries, said in a media interview in September 2015, Bosch expanded its investment in Russia because of the potential market growth and was not concerned by the impact of international sanctions on doing business in Russia. The crisis since 2008 in Russia has, however, meant that Bosch increased the share of its Russian-made production for export (from 50,000 items for export from its Russian factories in 2013 to a planned 90,000 items in 2015).[8]

Akadempark, Novosibirsk city, Novosibirsk region

Akadempark park is a case where a local university as well as numerous research institutions have been closely involved in its operations from the outset. It started in 2010 thanks to a combination of state and private funding totalling 250 million USD (Kim, 2017). A publicly traded (joint stock) company was set up to manage the creation and operational affairs of the park, which has received some state funding (federal and regional) for infrastructure yet is considered a privately operated park by the management (author's interview with a member of Akadempark's management, September 2014).

The park's comparative advantages include its proximity to a big city and a large pool of skilled labour including students, staff, and alumni of two leading universities. Table 5.11 shows that in the 7 years from 2012 to 2019, the number of resident firms fluctuated between 175 and 356. There is no limit on how long firms can stay in the park, although the youngest firms in the incubators must move out of the incubator after three years. The number of employees in resident firms increased by 49% over this period; because there are only 79 more firms in 2019 compared to 2012 (295 versus 216 firms), this indicates that on average the firms have grown quite substantially. The data on sales revenue are incomplete and because they are only available up until 2015, can only give a rough idea of dynamic growth in the park.

Akadempark is notable because it has more than doubled the number of residents in three years from 2015 to 2018 (from 175 to 356 residents, as of September 2018 according to the park's website). Of the 356 resident firms in 2018, 134 are new start-ups housed in the incubator within the park. Even though the number of firms fell again to 295 in the first half of 2019, such a big increase in resident numbers in just three recent years points to the park's high level of dynamism, which can be attributed to effective management of the park, high level of political support for the technology park from local and regional administrations, and effective relations with federal political structures and with the Siberian Branch of the Russian Academy of Sciences.

Similar to IT park's IT Academy discussed earlier in this section (pp. 164–165), Akadempark in Novosibirsk strives to help upgrade the local population's skills in entrepreneurship, innovation, and technology. This practice illustrates how

Table 5.11 Key performance indicators of Akadempark, 2012–2019

	Number of resident firms (total)	*of which, no. of firms in a business incubator*	*No. of employees in resident firms*	*Sales revenue from resident firms' products/processes/services in RUB (and USD)*
2012	216	37	6,214	3 billion
2013	289	76	7,700	13.5 billion (385 million USD)
2015	175	Na	~9,000*	17 billion*
2018	356	134	Na	Na
2019 (May)	295	95	9,244	Na

Source: Akadempark annual reports and website; author's site visits and interviews with management figures.

* "The companies [in Akadempark] now employ almost 9,000 people between them, generating an annual income of 17 billion RUB (£175 million)." (Wainwright, 2016).

Akadempark has formed linkages with the local and regional economy and society. It organises month-long innovation schools twice a year: one in the summer and one in the winter. To date, more than 1,000 participants have taken part in their training schools.

These training schools fulfil the function of "pre-incubation" phases lasting 3–4 months that many business incubators have worldwide but Akadempark does not have. Instead, the summer and winter schools are the "pre-incubation" phase through which budding entrepreneurs or researchers are trained and coached on their innovative projects; the best are invited to move into one of the park's four incubators (specialising in ICT, instrumentation, biotechnology, and nanotechnology). Each school lasts a month in which time the participants have an intensive programme of lectures and seminars followed by a period when they work independently in their small teams on their projects. The culmination is the semi-final round and the grand finale. There is tough competition to be a participant in the schools. On average, each school gets about 300 applications from individuals (two people per project, so 150 projects). 100–120 people (50 projects) get selected to participate in the school. Of these, almost 50% (23 projects) are selected to go into the semi-final round and 12 winning projects go through to the final. Thus, the success rate (reaching the final) for projects is around 8%. Those reaching the final are invited to join one of the park's business incubators. As an indicator of the close links between the summer and winter schools and the rest of the technology park, 80% of the residents in Akadempark's incubators as of September 2014 were past winners of the summer/winter schools (author's interview with a member of Akadempark's management, September 2014).

These training schools are one way the park develops linkages with local universities. Many final year undergraduate and graduate students from local universities (Novosibirsk State University, Novosibirsk State Technical University, and others) take part in their training schools. As of September 2014, 20 graduates had been accepted to work on an innovative project in one of Akadempark's business incubators and then became a full-fledged resident of the park. Scientists of the universities also act as experts to evaluate applicants' projects to join the incubator or the technology park.

Akadempark has limited linkages with big Russian companies. As of September 2014, three large Russian companies had an office in the park: the software company "Center of Financial Technologies," the internet company Yandex, and "Sberbank-tekhnologii," the division of the large domestic bank Sberbank that maintains the company's IT systems.

In the autumn of 2014, no international companies had a presence in the park. As of May 2015, one large foreign company had R&D facilities in the park according to the author's survey.

Ingria, St. Petersburg city

Ingria is a rare example of a business incubator within an STP in Russia that is more focused on services and connecting its residents with each other and with potential investors, suppliers, etc. than on providing infrastructure. In fact, Ingria began before the technology park of which it is a part became operational and exists to help researchers and entrepreneurs develop their business ideas into commercially viable projects and attract external investment.

The initial investment to create Ingria was in 2007 in the form of a subsidy from the regional government. From the start, it has aimed to attract innovative technology start-ups that are registered as businesses in St. Petersburg. Ingria now hosts over 80 resident start-up companies, of which nearly 30 rent additional office space. Seventy per cent of its residents are in the IT software sector, with the remaining 30% in medical technology, materials science and nanotech, machine tools, etc. Over 100 companies have "graduated" from Ingria already, some having served the maximum permitted term of 3 years, some simply outgrowing the facility. A typical innovative start-up comes to Ingria as a team of three to six people, while before leaving their personnel grows to 40–60 people. The churn rate is about 25%–30% per year (Rozhdestvenskiy and Barchenko, 2015).

The management team of Ingria was able to leverage from the state resources (in the form of a regional government subsidy) to quickly attract private venture investment, which has enabled Ingria to scale up and generate some local and regional impact. In 2012, the incubator attracted USD 15.3 million for 18 of its resident companies, which represented 850,000 USD on average per company. In total since 2009, Ingria has attracted 2.1 billion RUB. In the first four months of 2014, Ingria had already secured 4 million USD in confirmed deals (Rozhdestvenskiy and Barchenko, 2015).

Other performance outcomes that illustrate how Ingria has managed to scale up and build up a critical mass include a sixfold increase in the number of firms resident at any one time in the incubator from 2009 to 2015. Moreover, Ingria has almost doubled the number of staff employed by its resident firms and more than tripled the number of organised events from 2009 to 2012 (Table 5.12).

Ingria is also noted for its focus on the international dimensions of innovation. Benefiting from its proximity to Finland (150 km to the Russian–Finnish border), it maintains partnerships with several organisations in various regions of Finland. Together with Ingria's partner organisations in Israel, its Finnish partners

Table 5.12 Key performance outcomes of Ingria incubator, 2009–2015

	No. of resident firms	*Revenues of residents, USD million*	*Investment attracted, USD million*	*No. of employees in resident firms*	*No. of events organised in Ingria*
2009	12	2.3	na	Na	59
2010	63	5.4	3.4	416	128
2011	70	11.2	12.6	597	129
2012	86	20.2	15.3	776	205
2014	75	Na	Na	Na	na
2015	70	Na	Na	Na	na

Source: Rozhdestvenskiy and Barchenko (2015).

participate in Ingria's educational and technology transfer activities. Ingria also has partners in Silicon Valley, United States (the nestGSV business incubator) and South Korea (Gen3 company). Moreover, Ingria also helps foreign start-ups enter the Russian market. In 2014, Ingria's management initiated a "soft-landing" programme to assist small companies interested in the potential of Russia's market but struggling to enter the market due to cross-cultural business differences and legislative obstacles. The "soft-landing" programme includes a range of services: a fully equipped workplace for the company representative, a comprehensive consulting package, and assistance to obtain a tourist visa for Russia since the start-up is not doing business in Russia yet. Ingria staff guide the project through their extensive international network of partners, helping to find, if necessary, clients, investors, resources, government contacts, and future staff. The foreign start-up usually takes 2–3 months to decide whether to proceed with a Russian venture or not. Thanks to the "soft-landing" programme, the start-ups face lower risks of failure in their market exploration phase. Data on the effectiveness of this initiative are unfortunately unavailable (Rozhdestvenskiy and Barchenko, 2015).

Interpretation and conclusions

This final section aims to interpret the findings of this chapter from the perspective of the three-stage model of economic growth processes outlined in Chapter 2. As a reminder, this model is rooted in evolutionary theory and ECG and views economic growth as a fundamentally local process. These processes have several distinct, if overlapping, stages:

(a) micro level – key is the role of first movers (entrepreneurs, firms or organisations such as the management company of a STP);
(b) meso (regional and national) level – development of local clusters and building critical mass; and
(c) macro (global) level – resolving the critical mass problem and the problem of how to create global linkages and become globally competitive.

The fact that Russia has enthusiastically initiated a wave of STPs since the early 1990s – since the 2000s with strategic support from the state – is evident that there are some first movers in this area who are acting as entrepreneurs to find opportunities for growth and seek ways to overcome or lessen binding constraints or obstacles to innovative entrepreneurship (Stage 1). The first movers in this context are the specialised management companies organising STPs in Russia and some firms residing in these STPs. To some extent, the presence of 125 officially recognised STPs geographically spread across Russia as of 2017 means that there are strong possibilities of creating diverse outcomes at a micro level. Moreover, the diversity of founders of STPs (state, private, and public–private actors) increases the chances of varying outcomes or "positive variations of performance" (Stage 1). Such regional variation in the organisation and impacts of STPs in Russia is also evidence of the "institutional hierarchy" concept

(Chapter 2). This refers to a situation whereby the national level of institutions and rules remains fairly constant, while at a regional and local level, there is more dynamism as actors experiment with different policy approaches and are able to flexibly interpret institutions.

However, Russia's economic modernisation agenda that began in the early 2000s (see Chapter 1) arguably gave too much attention to the construction phase of STPs, neglecting the creation of linkages with external organisations (Stage 1). This meant that the incentives for officials, universities, enterprises, or private businesses to create STPs lasted only for the initial construction phase. Parks in Russia were founded primarily to be a source of new businesses entering markets. To attract new businesses and teams of researchers or entrepreneurs with ideas for a new business project to locate to the STP, park managers said in the survey that providing high quality infrastructure and specialised equipment was one of the most important "draw factors."

Nevertheless, data from the survey presented in this chapter showed that firms residing in STPs cooperate most often with other firms located outside the STP, followed by other STP resident firms, universities, and foreign organisations or firms. This is an encouraging sign because it indicates that STPs are open to their residents cooperating externally even if the initial resources to build STPs were not explicitly targeted for cooperation (Stage 2).

Are Russian STPs economically relevant entities for their local or regional economies, or merely developer projects? A few of the STPs profiled in this chapter have local or regional relevance that are developing dynamically to not only nurture new innovative firms but also build linkages with local universities and the regional economy (Stage 2). For example, IT park in Kazan and Akadempark in Novosibirsk provide training and educational opportunities to boost the skills of the local labour force and to constantly help generate a critical mass of innovative start-ups that can take up residence in the parks. However, few of the post-2000 generation of STPs in Russia have strong linkages with globally leading universities which limits the scope for knowledge transfer (Stage 2). Moreover, the evidence presented here showed that firms in 11 of the 17 STPs surveyed by the author lack ready for market technologies. This indicates that STPs are not responding to demand for new technologies (or creating the demand) and hence, have some way to go before they are relevant to their local and/or regional economy. This is an example of how the institutional context of post-Soviet Russia shapes the functioning of STPs.

Russian parks have generally not managed to forge global linkages. The exception is in the sharp rise in Russian STPs' membership of an international STP industry association in 2015; while membership in this association gives the STPs more exposure globally, it gives limited opportunities for international production links (Stage 3).

Zhiguli Valley park in Samara region and "Technopolis Moskva" in Moscow are exceptions here because in 2015 they had four and three big foreign firms respectively as anchor tenants. The park in Samara region was able to draw on the region's historical links with foreign automobile manufacturing companies, while "Technopolis Moskva" benefited from its location in the urban agglomeration of the capital city. Ingria in St. Petersburg is another exception in that it has an extensive international network of active partners with whom it collaborates. The management of Ingria incubator also initiated a programme in 2014 to support foreign start-ups wishing to enter the Russian market. Overall, however, Russian parks have generally not been very successful to date in creating global linkages, which hinders the development of an innovation ecosystem in which small and large firms cooperate and which helps Russia become more globally competitive.

National level factors (e.g. legislative framework, customs regimes) are serious obstacles to Russian STPs scaling up and "going global," that is moving to stages two and three of the three-stage model. Four out of 17 STP managers who completed the author's survey reported that the legislative framework at federal/regional/local levels was a principal barrier to the development of firms in their STP.

The survey results and mini case studies described in this chapter highlight a problem of many Russian STPs – in common with several parks in the periphery of emerging economies of the world – whereby managers and political elites hide behind "conspicuous statistics" for parks. These statistics include number of firms, export value generated, number of local jobs created, and volume of sales revenues generated by park resident firms to boost the social and political reputation of the parks. Focusing on these kinds of indicators can lead to a neglect of more important development indicators of parks' development such as their technological level (high, medium, or low) and the quality of economic growth they produce (Rodriguez-Pose and Hardy, 2014).

Notes

1 Xe, an online currency converter tool showing historical rates. Available at: www.xe.com/currencytables/?from=RUB&date=2007-01-01 [last accessed 15 August 2018].

2 Budget on the official website of the Ministry of Telecom and Mass Communications of the Russian Federation (since 2018, called the Ministry of Digital Development, Communications and Mass Media of the Russian Federation), available at: http://minsvyaz.ru/ru/activity/directions/445/#section-budget [last accessed 15 August 2018]. Currency conversions from Xe, an online currency converter tool showing historical rates. Available at: www.xe.com/currencytables/?from=RUB&date=2014-07-01 [last accessed 15 August 2018].

3 Original Russian definition: "3.1 технопарк: имущественный комплекс, включающий в себя, в том числе, объекты инновационной, инженерной и технологической инфраструктуры, обеспечивающий полный цикл услуг по созданию, размещению и развитию высокотехнологичных компаний, и управляемый единым оператором – специализированной управляющей компанией."

4 The survey was designed as purposive because the goal was to focus on a sub-sample of all STPs in Russia. However, because no strata within those 37 STPs were constructed, the result was a biased sample of those 37 STPs because it is possible that the more established and organised STPs were more likely to respond to the survey. This can only be confirmed by testing.

5 2017 *III Annual Review of Technology parks of Russia*, Association of Clusters and Technology Parks of Russia (pp. 192–195). Available online in Russian at: www.akitrf.ru/technoparks/analiticheskie-materialy/ [last accessed 1 May 2019].

6 Skolkovo technopark was an outlier because in 2015 it had 1200 “resident” firms. However, it is not presented here because it is part of Skolkovo innovation centre, which is the subject of Chapter 6 of this book. Moreover, the building for Skolkovo technopark was under construction in 2015 and firms got the status of technopark resident without being required to be in residence in Skolkovo.
7 Report of the year 2017 on IT park website, www.itpark-kazan.ru/ru/node/2968 [last accessed 1 April 2019].
8 Interview with Norbert Klein by Ivan Nechepurenko, *The Moscow Times*, 9 September 2015. Available at: www.themoscowtimes.com/2015/09/09/sanctions-dont-matter-on-russian-market-says-germanys-bsh-ceo-a49468 [last accessed 1 May 2019].

References

Association of Clusters and Technology Parks of Russia (2021) *Tekhnoparky – trebovaniya: natsionalniy standard Rossiiskoy Federatsii 56425–2021* [transl. *Requirements for technoparks: national standard of the Russian Federation 56425–2021*]. Moskva: Standartinform. Available to download as a PDF (in Russian) from: https://akitrf.ru/upload/medialibrary/266/46ku94ptqceb96dkdv2y1ayilrdssepn.pdf and https://www.akitrf.ru/technoparks/base_for_technoparks/ [last accessed 20 March 2022].

Audirac, I. (2003) ‘Information-Age Landscapes Outside the Developed World Bangalore, India, and Guadalajara, Mexico’, *Journal of the American Planning Association* 69/1 (pp. 16–32). Available at: https://doi.org/10.1080/01944360308976291.

Batstone, S. and Westhead, P. (1996) ‘The Development of Science Parks and New Technology-Based Firms in Russia’, in Brezinski, H. and Fritsch, M. (eds.) *The Economic Impact of New Firms in Post-Socialist Countries: Bottom-Up Transformation in Eastern Europe*. Cheltenham: Edward Elgar (pp. 72–93).

Best, M. H. (1990) *The New Competition: Institutions of Industrial Restructuring*. Cambridge: Polity.

Bruton, G. D. (1998) Incubators as a Small Business Support in Russia: Contrast of University-Related US Incubators With the Zelenograd Scientific and Technology Park. *Journal of Small Business Management* 36/1 (pp. 91–94). Available at: https://search-proquest-com.libproxy.ucl.ac.uk/docview/221004145?accountid=14511.

Chistyakova, O. V. (2010) ‘Rol’ tekhnoparkov v razvitii innovatsionnoy infrastruktury regionov [transl.: ‘The Role of Technoparks in the Development of Innovation Infrastructure in Regions’]’, *Izvestiya IGEA 2010* 3/71 (pp. 103–106).

Comins, N. and Rowe, D. N. E. (2008) ‘Success Factors for Science Parks in the Developed World and Emerging Economies’, Abstract submitted for the 2008 IASP World Conference in Johannesburg, South Africa. Available at: www.warwicksciencepark.co.uk/wp-content/uploads/2011/03/SuccessFactorsforScienceParks.pdf [last accessed 30 December 2018].

Ernst & Young Global Limited and Russian Venture Company (2014) *Problems and Solutions: Business Incubators and Technoparks of Russia*. Report [In Russian: *Problemy i resheniye: biznyes-inkubatory i tekhnoparky Rossii*]. Moscow: Ernst & Young Global Limited and Russian Venture Company.

Graham, L. and Dezhina, I. (2008) *Science in the New Russia: Crisis, Aid, Reform*. Bloomington, IN: Indiana University Press.

Hobbs, K. G., Link, A. N. and Scott, J. T. (2017) ‘Science and Technology Parks: An Annotated and Analytical Literature Review’, *Journal of Technology Transfer* 42 (pp. 957–976). Available at: https://doi.org/10.1007/s10961-016-9522-3.

Hopkins, B. (2013) ‘Four Regions Secure $60 Million technopark Funding up to 2014’, *East-West Digital Network* (EWDN), Published 30 October 2013. Available at: http://

ewdn.com/2013/10/30/4-regions-secure-60-million-technopark-funding-up-to-2014/ [last accessed 30 April 2015].

Ivanov, V. V., Klesova, S., Luksha, O. P. and Sushkov, P. V., eds. (2006) *Kommertsializatsiya rezultatov nauchno-tekhnicheskoy deyatelnosti: evropeisky opyt, vozhmozhniye uroki dlya Rossii* [Commercialisation of results of science and technology: European experience and possible lessons for Russia]. Moscow: Tsentr issledovanii problem razvitiya nauki RAN [Moscow: Centre for the Study of the Problems of the Development of Science, Russian Academy of Science], pp. 13–263.

Karetin, A. N. (2010) 'Public Policy in Management of Innovation: Problems and Future Development', *Management of Innovation* 01/09 (pp. 84–88) [Original in Russian: Karetin, Alexandr Nikolayevich, 'gosudarskvennaya politika v sferye upravleniya innovatsiyami: problemy i perspektivy', *Menedzhment innovatsii*, 01(09)2010 (pp. 84–88).

Kihlgren, A. (2003) 'Promotion of Innovation Activity in Russia Through the Creation of Science Parks: The Case of St. Petersburg (1992–1998)' *Technovation* 23 (pp. 65–76).

Kim, L. (2017) 'In Russia's Siberian Silicon Valley, Business is Good But Risks Can Be High', *NPR*. Available at: https://www.nps.org/sections/parallels/2017/07/04/535401305/in-russias-siberian-silicon-valley-business-is-good-but-risks-can-be-high [last accessed 7 December 2017].

Kostyunina, G. M. and Baronov, V. I. (2012) 'Technoparks in Foreign and Russian Practice (original in Russian: Tekhnoparky v zarubezhnoy i rossisskoy praktike)', *Ekonomika (MGIMO Review of International Relations)*, 3/24 (pp. 91–99). Available at: https://vestnik.mgimo.ru/jour/article/view/1882/1445.

Larina, T. M. (ed.) (2006) *Obninsk – perviy naukograd Rossii: istoriya i sovremyennost* [trans. from Russian: *Obninsk – Russia's first naukograd: history and present day*]. Obninsk: Resource.

Massey, D. and David, W (1991) 'STPs; a Concept in Science, Society, and "Space" (a Realist Tale)', *Environment and Planning D: Society and Space* 10 (pp. 411–422).

Massey, D., Quintas, P. and Wield, D. (1991) *High-Tech Fantasies: Science Parks in Society, Science and Space*. London: Routledge.

Radošević, S. and Myrzakhmet, M. (2009) 'Between Vision and Reality: Promoting Innovation in Kazakhstan Through Technoparks', *Technovation* 29 (pp. 645–656). Available at: https://doi.org/10.1007/978-3-319-07992-9

RA Expert (2011) Available at: www.raexpert.ru/researches/technopark/part3.

Rodriguez-Pose, A. and Hardy, D. (2014) *Technology and Industrial Parks in Emerging Countries: Panacea or Pipedream?* New York: Springer International Publishing.

Rozhdestvenskiy, Y. and Barchenko, E. (2015) 'University Science and Innovation Business: A Case of Successful Russian Business Incubator' [unpublished paper].

Siegel, D. S., Westhead, P. and Wright, M. (2003) 'Science Parks and the Performance of New Technology-Based Firms: A Review of Recent U.K. Evidence and an Agenda for Future Research', *Small Business Economics* 20/2 (pp. 177–184).

Wainwright, O. (2016) 'Step into Silicon Forest, Putin's Secret Weapon in the Global Tech Race', *The Guardian*, 5 January. Available at: www.theguardian.com/artanddesign/2016/jan/05/silicon-forest-putin-secret-weapon-global-tech-race-siberia-russia [last accessed 19 July 2021].

Yugrinova, N. (2014) 'Parkovaya zona [transl.: 'Parking zone']', *Biznes-zhurnal* [transl.: *Business Journal*], December (pp. 24–29).

Zaitsev, I. V. and Okorokov, V. R. (2002) 'Analiz urovnya razvitiya rossiiskikh tekhnoparkov' [trans. 'Analysis of the level of development of Russian technoparks'] *Materials for the inter-university scientific conference, 6/65*. St Petersburg: St Petersburg State Technical University (pp. 65–66).

6 Russia's Skolkovo as a new kind of innovation centre

Between science town and technology park

Introduction

Launched in 2010, Skolkovo is Russia's latest high-profile manifestation of a policy shift towards diversification and innovation-based growth. This shift in policy can be seen in the way innovation has been given more prominence on the federal policy agenda and in greater state funding for R&D and innovation since 2008. This chapter aims to analyse the initial success of the Skolkovo project a decade after it started. At the first glance, this may seem premature; however, on reflection, the analysis of Skolkovo is interesting for a broad policy and academic audience as well for Skolkovo's managers. Learning by doing and learning from failure are widely recognised in the literature as important dimensions for succeeding in organisational innovation (e.g. see Karo and Kattel, 2015).

Skolkovo is described here as a kind of hybrid between a science town and science and technology park. It is designed as a self-contained town with a technology park on-site (like Akademgorodok in Novosibirsk as seen in Chapter 4) and housing for those who work there and their families. At the same time, it is significant as one of the highest-profile entities in the country's innovation landscape, having to date received the most state resources compared to other science towns and STPs in Russia. It was designed to be a physically concentrated and enclosed place to support homegrown hi-tech development and innovation on the outskirts of Moscow while at the same having many global linkages.

This chapter analyses new evidence collected through multiple site visits, semi-structured interviews with managers in Skolkovo, resident entrepreneurs, and academics among others, online sources of information (e.g. press releases, social media), and grey literature (official and unofficial reports). The chapter also asks how Skolkovo is performing in its first decade, drawing on the three-stage model of economic growth processes (see Chapter 2). Gel'man (2018) argues that Skolkovo was only briefly a success story during Medvedev's presidency (2008–2012), after which it stalled and lost its status as a priority project supported by the state (Gel'man, 2018: 7). This chapter interrogates this claim and argues it is premature to conclude that Skolkovo is already a failure.

To date, Skolkovo has been developing along a route described here as "mission-oriented innovation ecosystem." This is interpreted in the chapter to

DOI: 10.4324/9781003256205-6

mean following a clear mission (core or priority technologies) directed by the central state and created in a physically concentrated place, *while simultaneously* trying to create an innovation ecosystem that brings together start-ups, large firms, researchers and scientists, venture capitalists and other investors, students, universities, and state actors. The concept of innovation ecosystem has become very popular in both academic and policy discourses in the last 20 years, drawing on theories about the systemic, interactive, cumulative, and evolutionary nature of innovation (see Chapter 1 for overview).[1]

The Skolkovo project forms part of Russia's broader political agenda to modernise the country's economy, political system, and society. This latest modernisation project began in earnest in 2007 when the Ministry of Economic Development initiated a federal, long-term strategy on social and economic development up to 2020, which aimed to make Russia an innovation and knowledge-based economy by focusing on the long-term national priorities of dynamic economic development, better quality of life, national security, and strengthening Russia's global position (Government of the Russian Federation, 2008). International experts, however, have criticised this long-term programme because of its emphasis on promoting innovation rather than imitating world-leading technologies: they argue that a country behind the technological frontier, such as Russia, needs to first imitate new technologies and processes to reach the frontier level before innovation makes sense (e.g. Connolly, 2011: 452). Whether Skolkovo manages to imitate world-leading technologies and adapt them to the Russian context or whether Skolkovo will only focus on innovative technologies and processes remains to be seen.

The political support for economic modernisation and innovation increased during Medvedev's presidency (2008–2012). Indukaev argues that Skolkovo was a core part of Medvedev's modernisation programme (2018: 179). Gel'man (2018) goes as far to argue that Skolkovo's fate is (was) only dependent on Medvedev. Medvedev repeatedly stressed the need for modernisation to reduce Russia's dependency on natural resources and drive sustainable economic growth. His 2009 speech to the Federal Assembly, for example, outlined the five new priority spheres in science and technology (S&T): energy efficiency, telecommunications, space technologies, nuclear energy, and pharmaceuticals. Shortly after that speech in the same year, Medvedev added nanotechnology to the state's S&T priority list, just two years after the creation of Rosnano, a state corporation responsible for implementing state policies on nanotechnology.[2]

The importance of Skolkovo stems from vastly different views on prospects for modernisation of Russia. From an optimist's perspective, the increase in macroeconomic, political, and social stability since the turn of the 21st century has generated many pockets of vitality in the Russian economy (Adelaja, 2012). On the other hand, pessimists point out that capital flight is rampant and administrative barriers to growth are high (Åslund, 2007; ERBD, 2012; Åslund et al., 2010). In view of such divergent assessments, understanding the context matters and hence Skolkovo cannot be viewed in isolation from the larger social and economic landscape of Russia. Moreover, diverging views are due to the nature of social change which emerges through the accumulation of micro projects by actors who seek to challenge incumbents, dominant practices, and established "day-to-day routines" of organisations (Karo and Kattel, 2015). It is inevitable that actors' views on this process will significantly differ.

This chapter analyses the performance of Skolkovo innovation centre as the most recent manifestation of Russia's economic modernisation project that is directed and governed by an authoritarian political system. It assesses the extent to which Skolkovo is functioning as an enclave pocket of excellence and how far it is contributing to an innovation ecosystem in the country by making external linkages nationally and globally. External linkages could include events for students, researchers, and entrepreneurs, fostering a network of other innovation centres across Russia, and hosting multinational and large Russian companies as partners with R&D divisions based in Skolkovo, thus building critical mass, and the extent to which it is fostering global linkages. How far can it contribute to strengthening Russia's system of innovation? The conclusions are relevant for countries undertaking, or planning to undertake, similar modernisation projects.

The importance of Skolkovo stretches well beyond its boundaries. Namely, Skolkovo expresses a view also strongly present in more developed countries, whereby supporting innovation via new technology-based firms (NTBFs) is believed to be a key driver of growth and structural change (OECD, 1998). Hence, the lessons from Skolkovo may have broader implications that go well beyond Russia and other so called "emerging economies."

On Skolkovo as a "sistema" project?

Skolkovo has often been called Russia's "Silicon Valley" by global media (The Economist, 2012; Rice-Oxley, 2015). However, by design Skolkovo is far from Silicon Valley in California: Silicon Valley emerged organically over a long time with its roots traceable back to the radio technology spin-off firms from the Federal Telegraph Corporation in the Palo Alto area between 1910 and 1940. Later, the founding of the company Hewlett-Packard in 1938 as well as the role of Frederick Terman (Dean of the School of Engineering at Stanford University) in attracting military R&D funding to the area during the Second World War also proved critical to the creation of Silicon Valley (Sturgeon, 2000).

In contrast, Skolkovo is a mega project initiated and funded entirely by the federal level of the Russian government. It encapsulates the latest, most visibly international stage in Russia's STI policy and was initiated quickly by the federal state in a top-down manner in 2010. Hence, it is a project of the "sistema" that characterises Putin's regime ruling Russia since 2000 and also helps to sustain this "sistema."

Main organisations and governing bodies

This section outlines the main organisations and governing bodies in Skolkovo to set the context for the rest of the chapter.

Skolkovo main entities

The Skolkovo innovation centre comprises the following main entities[3]:

- Created in 2011, **Skolkovo Institute of Science and Technology (SkolTech)** does graduate teaching and research within the innovation centre's focal five technology areas or research clusters.[4] Through an operational partnership with the Massachusetts Institute of Technology (MIT) in the United States, on which SkolTech is modelled, it aims to integrate research, education, innovation, and entrepreneurship. SkolTech initially aimed to have 15 research centres (each with 3–4 labs) although by 2021 it had 9 Centers for Research, Education and Innovation (CREIs) that each focus on a critical challenge in energy, space, IT, etc.[5] In 2020, it had 147 faculty members (78% of whom were employed on a full-time basis), 140 postdocs and researchers, 520 research and engineering personnel, and 1,000 Masters and PhD students from 45 countries. As of 2020, Skolkovo noted 1,000 alumni who graduated from Skoltech between 2015 and 2020 (Skoltech Annual Report, 2020).
- **The Open University Skolkovo** (OpUS) is directly accountable to the Skolkovo Foundation and was set up in 2011. It aims to attract and develop young and talented engineers, inventors, and entrepreneurs so that they create successful, technological companies or go on to contribute to the "ecosystem of Skolkovo" in other ways such as by studying in Skoltech or working for the OUS. It also aims to help them be integrated into the wider Russian innovative ecosystem.[6] The OUS is run by a small management team of seven people, the small size of which is a limiting factor to its future growth. It is ambitious for its future development (interview with a deputy executive director of Open University of Skolkovo, May 2016). Its latest venture, for example, includes the launch of the Skolkovo Ed Tech Hub ("Edtech Sk") in July 2021, which aims to support start-ups in educational technologies by providing them with co-working or rented office space.[7]
- The **International Gymnasium** opened in September 2015 and provides schooling from pre-school up to 18 years of age.
- **Corporate partners**, including several multinational companies and many large Russian companies.
- **Infrastructure for start-ups** (such as a technopark that provides supporting infrastructure for new, innovative companies and assist in commercialising new technologies). These new companies should be NTBFs, which are commonly defined as types of small- and medium-sized enterprises that are more innovative in developing or using new technologies and newer than a "typical" firm (OECD, 1998);
- While not formally part of the Skolkovo innovation centre, the **Moscow School of Management SKOLKOVO** is privately owned and run and next door to the state-run Skolkovo. This has led to some confusion in the media. This business school is not part of the state-created Skolkovo but

is rather a privately funded business school established before the state-created Skolkovo, so has somewhat different motivations and ideological background. Nevertheless, both Skolkovos share aims of training new graduates in business and innovation management. Both have the potential to be powerful agents in the innovation ecosystem that the Russian state is trying to create from nothing to the west of Moscow city, if the mutual organisational, cognitive, social, institutional, and geographical barriers can be overcome. It is not only ideologically but also physically separate from the state-run Skolkovo innovation centre, being 4 km away on foot (10 km by car or public transport due to the absence of a direct road between the management school and innovation centre).[8] The School of Management has existed since September 2006 (the date of a ceremony to lay the foundation stone on the future site) and accepted its first students on the Executive MBA course in January 2009. It was the brainchild of a team of Russian oligarchs and international business leaders, with the support of top-level politicians including Putin and Medvedev. Its founder (and president from 2006 to 2011) is the Armenian businessman Ruben Vardanyan, in whose words the school aims to: "create a new educational centre in Moscow that will train leaders and entrepreneurs for emerging markets and that will be known for its innovative approach to teaching" (The Times, 2008).

Skolkovo governing bodies

Governance of the Skolkovo hub ecosystem takes place through the following bodies:

Skolkovo Foundation:

1. Skolkovo Foundation is the executive body responsible for the day-to-day management and strategic governance of Skolkovo. It is in charge of constructing and managing the innovation centre, and encouraging talented researchers and scientists to set up start-ups or spin-offs via grants, tax benefits, and simplified bureaucratic procedures, etc.
2. Often reported by the media as "Medvedev's baby," Skolkovo started out reporting to President Medvedev (2010–2012). Then, when Medvedev became prime minister in 2012, it switched its accountability reporting to the government and the PM.
3. Its founding President and current Head of the Board of Trustees of SkolTech is the businessman, Viktor Vekselberg. Vekselberg is a Russian oligarch who became very wealthy in the 1990s and is now president of the Renova Group. Until May 2018, Vekselberg was concurrently the chair of the Foundation Council; since May 2018, the former vice-president of the Government of Russia, Arkady Dvorkovich, took over the chair position of the Foundation's council.

Board of Trustees:

1. The is the highest-level body that has decision-making powers and is closest to the president and prime minister.
2. Consists of 15 top Russian politicians and bureaucrats, including three representatives of the Presidential Administration, four Ministers, the President of the Russian Academy of Sciences, Mayor of Moscow, head of the Association of Innovative Regions of Russia, the general director of the Russian Venture Company, and the Chairman of the State Corporation "Bank for Development and Foreign Economic Affairs" (Vneshekonombank) (Skolkovo Foundation, 2016c).
3. Chaired by Prime Minister Medvedev.
4. It meets once per year to review performance (in combination with the Foundation Council) and approve the most major investment decisions.

Skolkovo Foundation Council (Board):

1. The Council is like a corporate board of directors and meets quarterly to approve budgets, review performance (together with the Board of Trustees), and to approve major investments (if not subject to Board of Trustees approval).
2. Seventeen members who have senior positions in the Russian government and the Russian and global private sector, of whom the majority (as of mid-2019) are Russian and two are from the United States and Finland. As of mid-2019, there was one woman on the board (Oksana Tarasenko, a Deputy Minister of Economic Development of the Russian Federation).[9]
3. Co-chaired by Craig Barrett (Retired CEO/Chairman, Intel Corporation) and Victor Vekselberg (Chair of the Council of Directors of the Skolkovo Foundation); other members include John T. Chambers (Chairman and Chief Executive Officer of the Cisco Systems, Inc.), Eric E. Schmidt (Executive Chairman of Google Inc.), Suresh Prabhu (Chairperson, Council on Energy, Environment and Water, India), and Esko Aho (Prime Minister of Finland, 1991–1995, and Executive Chairman of the Board, East Office of Finnish Industries Ltd) (Skolkovo Foundation, 2016c).

The Board of Trustees and Foundation Council are, by some accounts, less engaged than could be expected from the board of a start-up. A start-up board aims to actively support and give guidance to the new company rather than simply approving budgets and decisions (anonymous interview with employee of Skolkovo Foundation, June 2012, Moscow).

Skolkovo Industrial Advisory Board (IAB):

1. The IAB is a feedback mechanism for major companies and monitors how the corporate partners are interacting with the rest of the "ecosystem of Skolkovo."

2. Current members of the board consist of representatives of 29 foreign companies and large Russian innovative enterprises.
3. It is currently chaired by Esko Aho, Prime Minister of Finland from 1991 to 1995 and current Executive Vice President of Corporate Relations and Responsibility in Nokia.

Scientific Advisory Council:

1. This body sets the priorities for R&D at Skolkovo and is composed of leading Russian and international scientists.
2. Consists of 27 leading scientists of which just over a third (ten) are from outside Russia. Only one woman is a member of the Council, a professor from the United States (Skolkovo Foundation, 2016c).

Urban Planning Advisory Board:

1. This body is responsible for advising on town planning issues.
2. As of 2014, it consisted of 21 members of whom almost half (ten) were practising Russian and international architects, six were academics, four were journalists, one was a representative of the Moscow city government, and one was a representative of Renova Group (Kinossian and Morgan, 2014: 1687).
3. By mid-2016, however, the size of this board had decreased by nearly half to 13 members, suggesting that its influence has decreased within Skolkovo decision-making.
4. Of the current 13 members, ten are practising architects, one is the Director of the Polytechnic Museum in Moscow, one is the Director of the open-air exhibition and entertainment space "VDNH," and one member is a representative of the Moscow city government.
5. Five of its members were foreign architects, with the remaining eight members Russian nationals in mid-2016.

Assessing Skolkovo's performance through the lens of the three-stage growth model

This section analyses Skolkovo's performance to data drawing on the three-stage model of growth.

Stage 1 – enclave

There are three aspects of Skolkovo that suggest it functions as an enclave of innovation: its policy motivation or the state's reasons and strategic aims for creating Skolkovo (although the actors do not have distinct policy aims related to each stage); its technological orientation or focus; and the substantial state resources devoted to setting Skolkovo up.

Strategic focus

In terms of the strategic policy guiding Skolkovo, we can see strong mission-oriented elements. Mission-oriented innovation means a kind of industrialisation in which the state plays a dominant role in shaping the direction of innovation investment. The mission is the purpose, or strategic aims, guiding where state investment for innovation should be allocated. A mission is related to an enclave nature because both indicate how a policy is operationalised. An innovation hub such as Skolkovo aims to become is arguably easier to set up as a physically concentrated and enclosed place. Skolkovo became operational very quickly, arguably because of the political economy of the authoritarian state in which it is located (Gel'man, 2018). Starting in late 2009, three key political actors began to discuss the idea of Skolkovo. These figures were Dmitry Medvedev, then President of Russia, Arkady Dvorkovich, advisor in the presidential administration, and Vladislav Surkov, then First Deputy Chief of Staff to the President and known at the time as the "grey cardinal" of the Kremlin. These discussions took place in the context of Medvedev's political and economic modernisation agenda. A key part of this agenda was the emphasis on openness of state policy, as this quote from Medvedev's speech at a meeting of the Commission for Modernisation in April 2011 shows:

> Skolkovo is not a closed-door deal; it's a public project. Moreover, it's a project around which ultimately all our modernisation efforts should develop. Hence, our citizens should be kept fully informed of developments and how these programmes are funded. The information must be absolutely open and public: about what's been done and what's in the pipeline.[10]

Medvedev's emphasis on openness of Skolkovo as a project contrasts sharply with the secretive missions to create Soviet science towns (such as Akademgorodok and Obninsk analysed in Chapter 4). Hence, Skolkovo is a post-Soviet phenomenon. Nevertheless, although Medvedev called for transparent and public information about its development, Skolkovo still functions to some extent as an enclave and is shaped by the nature of the authoritarian state, in particular the configurations of informal and formal power known as *sistema*.

Skolkovo was officially born in the spring of 2010. Its governing body, the Skolkovo Foundation, was formed at that time. Victor Vekselberg, an oligarch and owner and president of Renova Group (a large Russian conglomerate), has been the President of Skolkovo Foundation and co-chair of the Skolkovo Foundation Council since the beginning. The first components of Skolkovo innovation centre have been operational since early 2011.

The high-level support from Medvedev, Dvorkovich, and Surkov was critical to Skolkovo becoming a reality relatively quickly (Gel'man, 2018). First, the necessary presidential decrees and laws on Skolkovo were signed off within 6 months of its creation (Government of the Russian Federation, 2010b). It is governed by its own federal law, which gives it direct federal budgetary money and special tax discounts for companies associated with it. This makes it clearly an enclave in nature, at least at the outset, that is separate and different from the rest of the country.[11] The political economy environment and state-dominant capitalism in Russia in the 2000s is one where the President, Prime Minister, the uppermost federal bureaucracy, and military and security forces (known as *siloviki*) have much more power and control compared to the legislative bodies of authority. Moreover, since June 2000, big business and the state have followed a kind of "informal contract" whereby the former agreed not to meddle in politics in exchange for the latter not amending the outcomes of the privatisations of the 1990s (Yakovlev, 2014: 14).

Since it became operational in 2010, it has been perhaps the most high-profile manifestation of a policy shift in Russia towards diversification and innovation-based growth. It is designed to be a fully functioning "city" with complete urban infrastructure where scientists, researchers, and entrepreneurs can live, work, and interact, although without its own municipal government. A French architecture firm won a contract to design the buildings and landscape, and construction began in the summer of 2012 on land formerly used for cucumber farming. Skolkovo therefore was built on a greenfield site (former agricultural land) although there were discussions about locating it in an existing science town. Both Obninsk and Tomsk, the largest university-based town in the Siberian part of Russia, were on the cards. Yet in the end, the small village of Skolkovo on the outskirts of Moscow – with its single storey houses, a golf course, agricultural fields, and a private business school called "Skolkovo" – was named as the site of the *innograd* ("innovation town") in March 2010. In this way, Skolkovo became the existing science towns' biggest problem because they feared that the newest innovation centre would swallow up federal funds which might have been allocated to them (Ruchnov and Zaytseva, 2011).

Technical orientation

In addition to the policy motivations for creating Skolkovo which show mission elements, the technological orientation or focus of Skolkovo also suggests it is operating as an enclave directed by key actors in the central state. Since its beginning, Skolkovo has had five clusters that correspond with the national priority industries: ICT, biomedical science, energy-efficiency, space, and nuclear technologies.[12] This corresponds to some extent to Amsden's Stage 1 characteristic of the "late industrializers" countries: the diversification stage, when the state takes entrepreneurial decisions about which new industries to support and how much to invest (Amsden, 1989).

The space and nuclear energy industries grew from strong capabilities in the Soviet Union and was an example of successful mission-oriented R&D, supported by the state. The Soviet Union was the first country to launch an artificial satellite into space (Sputnik 1) in 1957 and the first to successfully put a human in space in 1961, accomplishments that are testament to the stronger human capital capabilities compared to the United States (BBC4, 2014). The other three sectors supported by Skolkovo – biomedical science, energy-efficiency, and ICT[13] – are relatively new for Russia and hence are examples of the state attempting to diversify its strategic industries and make in-roads into global emerging and high potential sectors. In this way, the federal state has steered Skolkovo in focusing on five core technologies that policy makers believe are of most strategic importance for the country.

Resources

Third, in terms of its available financial and political resources, Skolkovo shows aspects of mission-oriented innovation policy to create it rapidly as an enclave.[14] It aims to give its resident companies and scientists significant financial resources and office space or land where the companies can build their own R&D facilities. Data on actual investments and operational expenditures of Skolkovo are hard to find, despite Medvedev's calls for openness surrounding the Skolkovo project in 2011. The figures given here come from a variety of Russian and international media sources, which differ substantially.

The government of Russia committed approximately 3.9 billion roubles to Skolkovo in 2010 (127 million USD or 81 million GBP[15]), which represents a sizeable 0.007% of Russia's GDP (Government of the Russian Federation, 2010a; World Bank, 2011).[16]

As announced in 2010, the original amount of federal funding for Skolkovo was 54 billion roubles (approximately 1.7 billion USD) between 2011 and 2013, divided annually as 15 billion roubles in 2011, 22 billion roubles in 2012, and 17.1 billion roubles in 2013. The Ministry of Finance had back in 2010 emphasised that state funding for Skolkovo would only be for the centre's "early stages" of development, without specifying the duration of those early stages. The Ministry of Finance hoped that beyond its early stages of development, Skolkovo would start to attract resources from the private sector (Kommersant, 2010).

However, in 2013, Skolkovo got assurance that it would continue to receive some state funding up until 2020. In the summer of 2013, the government of Russia approved a sub-programme ("Creating and developing the Skolkovo innovation centre") as part of the state programme, "Economic development and the innovation economy." This meant that Skolkovo's financial future was more secure as it could count on continued state financing until 2020. However, the actual amount of financing fluctuated as follows.

In August 2013, it was announced that Skolkovo would get 135.6 billion roubles from the state budget (about 4.1 billion USD or 2.6 billion GBP according to exchange rates of that time) between 2013 and 2020 (Kouzbit, 2013). This ended months of uncertainty about the future of Skolkovo amid allegations of corruption.[17] Yet, by October 2013, the figure for total state financing between 2013 and 2020 had been reduced to 125.2 billion roubles or approximately 3.9 billion USD (RIA Novosti, 2013).

Assuming the financing was disbursed to plan in October 2013 (which is not definite given policy uncertainty in Russia), this would mean that Skolkovo would receive about 20 billion roubles per year until 2020. That is around 2 billion roubles per year more than it has received from the state in its first four years (2010–2014), as discussed later.

Turning now to actual funding that Skolkovo has received, in its first four years (2010–2014), Skolkovo Foundation received 74.7 billion roubles (approximately 1.3 billion USD) from the state and 43.5 billion roubles (approximately 742 million USD) from private and non-budgetary sources. Therefore, Skolkovo Foundation's total income to date from all sources equalled 118 billion roubles or approximately 2 billion USD (Reyter and Golunov, 2015: 8).[18] It should be noted that the 118 billion RUB does not include 5.98 billion RUB, which has been earmarked in the state budget for construction in Skolkovo but not yet allocated. As Table 6.1 shows, around two-thirds of the total has been spent on construction so far (64–67% depending on whether the 5.98 billion RUB is included); 6% has so far been spent on administrative expenses.

According to an interview conducted with an employee of Skolkovo Foundation in November 2015, the 8 billion roubles spent on administrative expenses includes the salaries of the more than 800 people working on administrative tasks in Skolkovo Foundation and its subsidiaries (such as the Centre for Intellectual Property) These 800-plus people work with Skolkovo start-ups, plan the construction, and other activities. The 8 billion roubles also includes all the expenses for events and consulting services, which make up substantial shares of the budget. For example, the architects and urban planners in the advisory councils have been paid consultant fees totalling tens of millions of USD (over 1 million RUB in current prices).

By the end of June 2012, almost 8.1 million roubles (approximately 260,000 USD or 160,000 GBP as of exchange rate on 30.06.2012) had been approved to be distributed via 135 grants.

To summarise these arguments, Skolkovo has rapidly secured significant volume of state resources. This is due to broad political support from senior policy makers (Gel'man, 2018). However, more political conflict over Skolkovo between different elite groups was noticeable after 2012 as evidenced by various media stories alleging corruption (see the section "How institutional context affects Skolkovo").

Four hundred hectares of land has been set aside for Skolkovo about 20 km to the west of the centre of Moscow city. This is an area where land available for building is extremely scarce. As of early 2012, the master planning for the city had been completed and construction begun. The first part of the city was planned to be ready in 2014. However, by September 2015 while some real progress had been achieved with some areas of Skolkovo completed and functional, many buildings still needed to be built according to publicly available information and site visits.[19] In November 2015, officials of the Skolkovo Foundation publicly stated that the main building of the technopark (which they claimed would be the largest park in Europe), several other buildings, as well as most of the landscaping would be complete in time to host the annual conference of the International Association of Science Parks and Areas of Innovation in mid-September 2016. Skolkovo did manage to meet this deadline.

Table 6.1 Skolkovo income categorised by major items of expenditure, 2010–2014

Expenditure item	**Amount from state budget (billion RUB)**	**Amount from private and non-budgetary sources (billion RUB)**	**Total financing (billion RUB)**	**Share of total income of Skolkovo Foundation (in %, rounded to one decimal point)**
Construction	45	35.6	80.6	64.7
SkolTech	12.1	0.6	12.7	10.2
Grants to resident start-ups	10.4	7.9	18.3	14.7
Administrative items	8	0	8	6.4
Marketing	3.4	0	3.4	2.8
Centres of collective use	1.7	0	1.7	1.4
		TOTAL (including the unallocated 5.98 billion RUB from construction)	**124.7**	
		TOTAL (without the unallocated 5.98 billion RUB from construction)	**118.72**	
Note: the sum given under state funding for construction includes 5.98 billion RUB which has not yet been allocated.				

Source: Reyter and Golunov (2015: 8), which cited ministerial documents, Audit Chamber of the Russian Federation, and Skolkovo own reports; calculations by RBC.

Table 6.2 summarises the state of construction at Skolkovo with planned completion dates and area in square metres for all the different parts of Skolkovo "city" for the period 2015–2018. Overall, this shows that while there were some delays in construction and the size of some of the different buildings and areas was smaller than planned, Skolkovo managed to rapidly deploy its resources and

Table 6.2 Planned construction completion dates of Skolkovo's different areas, 2015–2018

Element	*Expected year of completion*	*Total planned area (sq. m)*
Teachers' campus	2015	10,000
Renova Lab	2015	27,000
Residential flats	2015	51,000
Business centre Skolkovo "Matryoshka"	2015	30,000
Business centre "Galereya"	2016	78,000
Family campus	2016	22,000
Key partners zone	2016	126,000
International aviation academy	2015–2017	9,000
Technopark	2015–2018	160,000
Skoltech	2016–2018	215,000
Total planned area:		**728,000**

Source: http://sk.ru/city/p/main_objects.aspx [last accessed 30 January 2019].

construct a significant volume of infrastructure in a relatively short period of time. Phase I of Skoltech was due to be finished in 2016 and Phase II in 2018, giving a total area of 215,000 sq. m. The technopark meanwhile would cover 160,000 sq. m by 2018 – 95,000 sq. m of which was due to be finished by the end of 2015 and the rest by 2018. In fact, by mid-2017 only 96,228 sq. m was built and in use in the technopark. Phase I would provide office and common space for 4,000 people in the technopark, to be joined by an additional 3000 people once Phase II is ready. The technopark's office centre was completed in 2015, providing 43,000 sq. m office space for those running the projects supported by the park.

Three hundred and fifty-four residential flats provide accommodation for 1,400 people in total. The "family campus" in the D2 district of Skolkovo has accommodated 700 children of nursery and school age since it opened in 2016. In September 2015, a private gymnasium (international gymnasium "Skolkovo") opened its doors to its first pupils aged 3–18; initially, it was housed in Zaitsevo, another settlement in Moscow region, but it relocated to the family campus in Skolkovo. In the 2017–2018 academic year, it had 366 pupils enrolled.[20] The business centre Skolkovo "Matryoshka" – providing space for exhibitions and offices – was due for completion at the end of 2015 but was actually finished in 2016. Renova Lab is a scientific technical lab for the R&D division of the firm Renova (part of the Renova Group of which Vekselberg is president) that was ready for its first tenants in June 2016, six months later than planned. The business centre "Galereya" (78,000 sq. m) is for use by Skolkovo participants and partners and was completed in 2016. The "key partners' zone" (for Skolkovo's large firm partners, including CISCO, TMX-ALSTOM, and partners of the IT cluster) covers 126,000 sq. m and was completed in 2016. The international aviation academy is an educational centre spread over 9,000 sq. m. Finally, the teachers' campus provides residential accommodation for professors and lecturers of Skoltech.

The rapid mobilisation of such large quantities of financial and land resources is an impressive achievement, which is due in large part to the authoritarian political system characterised by a high concentration of power held by the most senior politicians (president and prime minister) in Russia. It is a particularly rapid mobilisation of resources when compared to the time required to launch a similar initiative in a Western democratic country, where bargaining and negotiations between the political executives, parliament, and state agencies can drag on for several months or years. Thus, in terms of mobilising financial and land resources, key elements of a mission-oriented innovation policy, Skolkovo undoubtedly has seen early success.

Performance of Skolkovo, 2009–2013

There are some aspects of Skolkovo's results so far that indicate its mission-oriented nature. Few academic studies have been published to date about Skolkovo; one of the few is by an employee of Skolkovo who heads up the robotics centre in the ICT cluster and in parallel completed a PhD on Skolkovo at an institute of the Russian Academy of Sciences. In a paper published in a Russian journal, Efimov (2014) proposes a dynamic typology of performance indicators of state support for innovation based on the case of Skolkovo. Moreover, he compares actual performance with target indicators. He argues that the performance indicators should change as Skolkovo evolves and divides the period since Skolkovo started into three distinct time periods: 2009–2011 (initial phase), end 2011 to mid-2012 (rapid growth phase), and mid-2012 to mid-2013 (rethinking the mission of Skolkovo phase). So, how has Skolkovo performed from 2011 to 2013 in terms of mission-oriented activities? In this chapter, mission-oriented activities are understood as the following: funding (both revenue and expenditures in the form of grants and construction), co-financing, adherence to the timetable and budget for construction, construction of infrastructure such as collective use centres and computer training centres, R&D centres rented out to corporate partners, as well as procedural indicators such as the average time taken to make decisions on participant status and on grants.

In the initial phase (end 2009 to end 2011), Skolkovo over-achieved its targets for co-financing from third parties. However, it gave out less than half of the total planned funding in grants in 2011 and had 20 fewer holders of grants compared to the planned number (77% of target). Skolkovo was also behind schedule for construction, achieving just 66% of its target progress level between 2009 and 2011 (Table 6.3).

In 2012, Skolkovo did better compared to the previous phase in approving grants with 85% of the 120-target number of grants approved (Table 6.4). However, it did not fare so well in terms of actually allocating the grant monies. The average share of co-financing of projects (including by state corporations, venture capital partners, and Skolkovo participants) as a percentage of total financing was above target in this rapid growth phase. Moreover, Skolkovo saw a good utilisation rate by firms of equipment it rented or acquired (59% of the equipment). However,

Table 6.3 Planned and actual indicators of mission-oriented activities of Skolkovo: end 2009 to end 2011 (initial phase)

Key performance indicator	*Target*	*Achieved*
Total financing from third parties, volume of co-financing of Skolkovo projects*, million RUB	2,500	2,736
Total grants given in 2011, in RUB (USD as of 2011 rates)**	7 billion RUB (approximately 218.8 million USD)	2.8 billion RUB (approximately 88 million USD)
Number of grant holders	More than 90	70
Adherence to timetable and budget for construction (considering excluded or postponed items originally planned), % of approved norms	More than 85	66

Source: Efimov (2014: 26)

*Includes financial resources of Skolkovo's partners allocated to Skoltech as well as resources of accredited co-investors of projects with the status of Skolkovo participant.
** Xe, an online currency converter tool showing historical rates. RUB > USD exchange rate as of 31 December 2011 used here. Available at: www.xe.com/currencytables/?from=RUB&date=2011-12-31 [last accessed 30 December 2019].

Table 6.4 Planned and actual indicators of mission-oriented activities of Skolkovo: end 2011 to mid-2012 (rapid growth phase)

Key performance indicator	*Target*	*Achieved*
Total number of grants approved in 2012 as per Skolkovo Foundation's grant policy, units	Minimum 120	103
Of which: total grants planned to be allocated, in RUB (USD)*	Minimum 6.3 billion RUB (approximately 194 million USD)	3.4 billion RUB
Of which: total grants needed to be allocated, in RUB (USD)*	4.9 billion RUB (approximately 151 million USD)	2.9 billion RUB
Average share of co-financing of projects (including by state corporations, venture capital partners, and Skolkovo participants), % of total financing	Not less than 40	48
Adherence to construction schedule in 2012: area given over for exploitation, sq. m	6,136	6,100
Adherence to construction schedule in 2012: total spending on construction, billion RUB (USD) *	20.9 billion RUB (approximately 645 million USD)	5.6 billion RUB (approximately 172.8 million USD)
Utilisation rate of equipment either rented or acquired by Skolkovo, %	Not less than 50	59
Number of collective use centres and computer training centres created	3	3

Key performance indicator	*Target*	*Achieved*
Area of R&D centres rented out to corporate partners of Skolkovo according to tenancy agreements, sq. m	More than 15,000	0
Average time for decision on award of participant status by provisional approval procedure, number of days	No more than 45	40
Average time for decision on award of participant status without provisional approval procedure, number of days	No more than 31	29
Average time for decision on grant award, number of days	No more than 100	67
Quality of operational plan and budget execution of Skolkovo Foundation in 2012, % of variations from targets	Not more than 10	40**

Source: Efimov (2014: 27)

* Xe, an online currency converter tool showing historical rates. RUB > USD exchange rate as of 15 June 2012 used here. Available at: www.xe.com/currencytables/?from=RUB&date=2012-06-15 [last accessed 30 December 2019].

**The significant variation from the target was caused largely by delays in constructing the innovation centre.

no R&D centres were rented out to corporate partners of Skolkovo: presumably caused by the delays in construction. Only 5.6 billion roubles (approximately 172.8 million USD) out of a planned 20.9 billion roubles (approximately 645 million USD) was actually spent on construction in this period. Nevertheless, three collective use centres and computer training centres were created as planned. In terms of procedural indicators of the time required for decision-making on participant status and grants, Skolkovo achieved better than its target indicators.

The period from late 2012 to the end of 2013 was one when the leadership of Skolkovo shifted the approach of the innovation centre from one based on rapid growth and quantitative performance indicators to one focused on qualitative changes related to commercialisation of R&D. In other words, in its first two phases Skolkovo tried to accumulate the necessary competencies, projects, and partners by rapidly increasing the number of participant companies and grant holders and by running various events and hosting conferences. Yet, in 2013 Skolkovo did a certain amount of re-thinking of its core goals and which indicators would be best to measure these goals (Efimov, 2014). This followed the publication in late 2012 of Skolkovo's new strategy, which increased the number of performance indicators from 9 to 14 and introduced some new economic indicators (to measure how attractive Skolkovo is for investors and how effective it is as a platform for commercialisation, e.g. total profits generated of Skolkovo-supported projects and number of jobs created). This rethinking phase may have related to the corruption allegations about Skolkovo that emerged in the media from February 2013 (see later section of this chapter entitled "How institutional

Table 6.5 Planned and actual indicators of mission-oriented activities of Skolkovo: mid-2012 to mid-2013 (rethinking the mission of Skolkovo phase)

Key performance indicator	*Target*	*Achieved*
Average share of external co-financing of Skolkovo participants' projects, % of total financing	50	60
Volume of private investment in Skolkovo for the creation and development of an innovative environment, including investment into Skolkovo participants' projects, billion RUB (cumulative)	4.2	3.2
Skolkovo participant-companies' profits from research activities, billion RUB	2.0	14.6*
Total number of jobs created	7,400	2,800
Venture investors: share of total investment from accredited venture investors, %	20	21
Average time for decision on award of participant status by provisional approval procedure, number of days	40	32
Average time for decision on award of participant status without provisional approval procedure, number of days	30	28
Average time for decision on grant award, number of days	70	69
Adherence to budget of Skolkovo Foundation (excluding budget for construction of the innovation city and payments under the contract with MIT), %	+10	−42

Source: Efimov (2014: 28–29).

*The significantly above target profit is explained primarily by the fact that approximately half of the total profits is from the only company that has the status of Skolkovo participant and is fulfilling all the requirements of Skolkovo project and the Federal Law No. 244 of 28.09.2010 ('On the innovation centre of "Skolkovo").

context affects Skolkovo"). Skolkovo's leadership felt the need to counter these allegations by somewhat changing Skolkovo's approach.

As shown in Table 6.5, the average share of external co-financing of Skolkovo participants' projects as a share of total financing continued to increase as in the second phase (60% by the end of 2013). Total profits of Skolkovo participant-companies from research activities was seven times higher than planned, although half of the 14.6 billion RUB came from a single company. Skolkovo also further reduced the time required for decision-making on participant status and grants, continued from the previous phase 2012. However, the amount of private investment in Skolkovo was only 3.2 billion roubles in 2013 compared to a planned 4.2 billion roubles; this shortfall was presumably a prolonged effect of the financial crisis and high capital outflows from Russia in 2011–2012. Moreover, only 2,800 jobs were created in 2013 as opposed to the 7,400 planned new jobs; the budget of Skolkovo Foundation in 2013 was also extremely negative (excluding the budget for construction and payments under contract with MIT).

This section has found some convincing evidence that Skolkovo exhibits mission-oriented elements that have helped the innovation centre develop as an enclave, including in its rapid development from idea to implementation, its goals and technological orientation, resources, and in some aspects of its performance to date. Thus, some of the conclusions have been confirmed of a recent study of Skolkovo based on an analysis of public documents and speeches by Russian politicians, which characterises Skolkovo as a mega-project "delivery vehicle" for the Russian state's implementation of its "authoritarian modernisation doctrine." The study also argues that Skolkovo is a case of "development-by-decree" (Kinossian and Morgan, 2014: 1691).

We may expect much stronger structural constraints on a "technologies push" project such as Skolkovo given Russia's relatively unfavourable institutional conditions for innovation. Namely, Russia's current dual state is characterised by a constitutional state, on the one hand, and an administrative regime that subverts the rule of law and genuine electoral competition, on the other hand (Sakwa, 2010; Kinossian and Morgan, 2014). Even though Skolkovo is regulated by its own federal law, the nature of the dual state and sistema (Ledeneva, 2013) mean that the institutional context is a constraint for Skolkovo. The enclave approach seems to be the natural first step to influence the landscape of Russian S&T which still largely operates as a post-Soviet system, characterised by legacies from the Soviet period (Radošević, 2003). Like any other national S&T policy, Russian S&T policy cannot fully compensate for deficient framework conditions. Often, the key solutions lie not in narrowly focused S&T and innovation policy but in the broader economic environment in "non-technological" areas such as entrepreneurship and the business context. Mechanisms of "creative destruction" or industry dynamics in Russia are still weak and are compounded by weak market demand for knowledge intensive services. A developed innovation and technology policy is indispensable for changing unfavourable framework conditions, but its effects may be too weak when confronted with strong rent-seeking opportunities from natural resource-based sectors.

Stage 2 – resolving problems of critical mass

Now, we turn to examine whether Skolkovo has managed to form any institutions (e.g. firm associations, public agencies, design bureaus, certification agencies, quality or standards institutions) and build a critical mass of start-ups. This is important to create an ecosystem of innovation, one of Skolkovo's aims.

Initiatives like Skolkovo, as well as others in the innovation sphere such as the state agency for nanotechnology "Rosnano," innovative clusters and research universities, coupled with the growing exports of Russian software, offer potential to reorient the Russian economy towards innovation-based growth. These initiatives may generate a momentum of their own and create pockets of growth in Russia, independent of natural resources. There may be some potential for these changes to generate new linkages in the Russian innovation system, which, at present, is characterised by a lack of interactions between the main pillars of the "triple helix" model (university–industry–government relations) – the Russian Academy of Sciences and the Universities, government, and industrial institutes (e.g.

Leydesdorff and Meyer, 2006). Indeed, some scholars prefer to label the Russian and Ukrainian innovation systems, for example, as a "double helix." This term reflects the lack of linkages between government, industry, and academia as well as the weak presence or complete absence of industry (Dezhina, 2013; Yegorov and Koretsky, 2013).[21]

Skolkovo aims to co-locate new knowledge production and NTBFs, thereby enabling access to a critical mass of researchers. Skolkovo Foundation is actively trying to recruit Russian scientists who are studying for higher degrees or working abroad. Skolkovo Foundation managers hope that by concentrating researchers and scientists in one geographic place and by facilitating interactions between them, Skolkovo will facilitate interactions between companies (both established and start-ups) so that knowledge can flow more freely. This is encouraging for attracting talent, yet the question remains as to whether Skolkovo is in practice doing so.

Strategic focus

Skolkovo may seem to be a mission-oriented policy that is governed in a top-down way following the logic of the linear innovation model. However, this view is too simplified and neglects the fact that Skolkovo's main objective is to create an "innovation ecosystem" which, by definition, requires elements of diffusion policy and a critical mass of actors. In this respect, Skolkovo can be considered as a project between mission and diffusion-oriented initiatives (Ergas, 1987). Hence, it seems more appropriate to define Skolkovo as a "*mission-oriented innovation ecology*" which is historically quite a new challenge for Russia. As pointed out by Loren Graham (2010) "mission-oriented initiatives of the past (nuclear weapons, launching a satellite into space) had 'a sharply focused goal, so sharply focused that the Russians knew exactly when they had reached it.'" This is much less possible for Skolkovo which aims to be a hub of science and innovation for the whole country.[22]

Moreover, Skolkovo has set itself ambitious targets to train schoolchildren and skilled graduates. A gymnasium opened its doors in the academic year 2015–2016 to pre-school and school age pupils. SkolTech was set up to provide graduate education modelled on the MIT experience. Thus, Skolkovo has some potential to contribute to Russia's economic growth. However, to achieve this goal, some important conditions must be met. Students or researchers at Skolkovo would need incentives to stay in Russia for work or further study if Russia's economy is to benefit from their skills and knowledge; recent trends indicate that a high proportion of Russia's graduates and postgraduates leave Russia in search of better opportunities (EBRD, 2012).

New or mature firms based in Skolkovo could help fuel growth through being networkers. In this sense, they would help to create the networks and social interactions which Salter and Martin (2001) claim can lead to growth. There are certainly many firms (1809 resident start-ups including a few dozen foreign firms as of late 2018) that have signed up to the Skolkovo initiative.[23] In addition, SkolTech and the school of management provide "clusters" of researchers and students. The Foundation Board, Foundation Council, and Advisory Council act as channels for politicians, bureaucrats, and international leading scientists to provide their inputs and interact with the other actors of the new Skolkovo "ecosystem" of innovation. This mass of firms, researchers, and others gives the potential for networking and interactions. However, due to the delayed construction progress firms are still not obliged to have a physical office on the Skolkovo site. So, they may decide never to relocate their employees to Skolkovo. Start-ups may choose instead to only apply for a grant or just be a participant of the Skolkovo project virtually or for marketing purposes. In other words, there is scope for opportunism which should be countered by incentives for commitment.[24]

Physical and virtual cluster goal

As mentioned earlier, some of Skolkovo's goals can be ascribed to a mission-oriented innovation policy. However, at the same time, Skolkovo also has some goals more akin to becoming an ecosystem – its wish to be a physical and virtual cluster to promote technological innovation and enable research community, businesses, and state bodies to interact.

These goals can be seen in the policy documents and speeches by Skolkovo officials made in Skolkovo's early days. According to the former Vice President for International Partnership Development in Skolkovo Foundation, the mission of Skolkovo is fourfold (Lenihan, 2012):

- diversify the Russian economy through innovation and entrepreneurship;
- integrate Russian science and technology into the global economy;
- develop human capital through world-class research; and
- nurture competitive knowledge-based companies.

Skolkovo conceptualises itself as a new "ecosystem" of innovation (Figure 6.1). It aspires to become a "basis for a vast ecosystem that spans all of Russia and brings together researchers, entrepreneurs and investors in five clusters" (The Economist, 2012).

In addition to a physical presence in a specific territory, it also plans to have a virtual sphere by connecting with other innovation centres across Russia and by being the hub for a "pan-Russian network" of science that incorporates former closed cities and state companies (Lenihan, 2012). This goal of creating a pan-Russia network started recently via a 2017 initiative of regional operators of Skolkovo. This is a network of innovative companies located anywhere in Russia that meet the criteria for residents of Skolkovo and gives them access to the same services and support structures as provided in Skolkovo innovation centre without requiring them to move part of their business to Skolkovo. By mid-2018, five regional operators had been approved (Akadempark in Novosibirsk, IT park-74 in Chelyiabinsk, "Lenpoligrafmash" technopark in St. Petersburg, University technopark in Yekaterinburg, and the IT park in Kazan and Naberezhniy chelny)

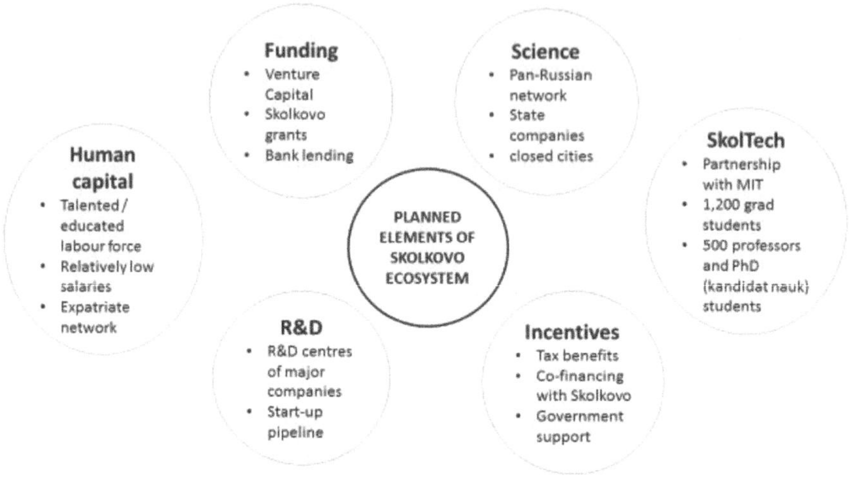

Figure 6.1 Skolkovo's ecosystem as initially conceived

Source: Adapted from Lenihan, 2012.

(Skolkovo Annual Report, 2018). While promising, this regional networking initiative is too nascent to evaluate.

In addition to providing funding and other support to start-ups, Skolkovo wants to attract big Russian and foreign companies to relocate some of their R&D in Skolkovo. The innovation centre provides quite generous financial and political incentives (made possible through its special federal budgetary and tax status) to companies in exchange for relocating some of their R&D to Skolkovo.

Skolkovo wants to foster interactions between business, students, researchers, and investors. As we saw earlier, interactions between different actors in an innovation system are crucial for a successful innovation ecosystem because these relationships can stimulate demand for innovation. This demand is not known in advance but rather will be discovered through interactions by private firms, government bodies, and researchers. Skolkovo's conceptual model as an innovation ecosystem makes it fundamentally different from the Soviet model of R&D and innovation, which focused on high spending on specific technologies that were needed by specified, known users (primarily, the military).

Skolkovo may contribute to growth by acting as a catalyst. It could increase the stock of useful knowledge (one of Salter and Martin's ways R&D can contribute to growth [2001]) by improving the standard and increasing the international integration of the Russian R&D system. Through helping to create new technologies – defined not only as technological hardware but also tacit knowledge, techniques, and methods for design and development – the innovation centre may create opportunities for knowledge spillovers across the Russian economy and internationally. Researchers attached to Skolkovo might move to other organisations, maintain existing affiliations, or carry out joint projects with researchers in other places in Russia or abroad. In this way, we would expect to see two-way knowledge exchanges and networks, both from and into the innovation centre. However, to do this effectively Skolkovo still needs to overcome numerous institutional and organisational barriers such as the still widespread opposition from some members of the Russian Academy of Sciences, who resent the significant financial resources and political support afforded to Skolkovo (Kinossian and Morgan, 2014).

Number of participating firms

As of the summer of 2012, there were 400 start-ups, or NTBFs, registered as participants of the Skolkovo innovation centre. NTBFs are commonly defined as particular types of small- and medium-sized enterprises that are more innovative in developing or using new technologies and newer than a "typical" firm (OECD, 1998: 219). About 25% of this number had received a grant from Skolkovo by 2012.[25]

As of June 2015, there were 1,070 projects with the status of "Skolkovo resident" (one start-up can have more than one project in Skolkovo). Of these 1,070 "residents," 45% had a profit in the 2014 financial year, of which 3% got more than 100 million roubles in profit (Romanova, 2015).

By the end of 2015, the number of participating projects had increased dramatically to 1,432, of which about a third were in the IT cluster (334). There were four other clusters in addition to IT: energy (334 projects), biomedicine (287), nuclear (191 projects), and space (450 projects). By 2020, there were 2,248 participating projects in Skolkovo across the full spectrum from developing an idea to ready to launch on a market (Figure 6.2). Most of these projects are in the IT cluster (37% of the total), with the nuclear, space, and advanced manufacturing technologies cluster the smallest (18% of total projects).[26] This is evidence that Skolkovo has continued to build up a critical mass of R&D and start-up activity between 2015 and 2020.

However, not all these firms were physically resident in Skolkovo. Until 2016, the companies selected to be a participant of Skolkovo were not compelled to have a physical office or lab space in the technopark of Skolkovo. This was partly justified by the lack of completed buildings and other infrastructure for the companies on the site, yet it does not help to build a viable ecosystem, which relies on regular and frequent physical proximity between the different actors as well as virtual proximities and communication. Reports in the Russian language media from the summer of 2015 indicate that 141 firms had their Skolkovo status revoked. Representatives of Skolkovo reported that the majority of these 141 firms were "dead souls," that is they were running projects that were insufficiently developed and the firms voluntarily decided to leave the Skolkovo project. Media cited the vice-president for grants and expertise at Skolkovo Foundation, Kirill Bulatov, as saying that the reasons for depriving 141 firms of the title of Skolkovo resident included a lack of understanding about why they applied to Skolkovo for the grant (they counted on getting a grant regardless of whether they actually did any work) and difficulties in the firms' R&D processes (Romanova, 2015).

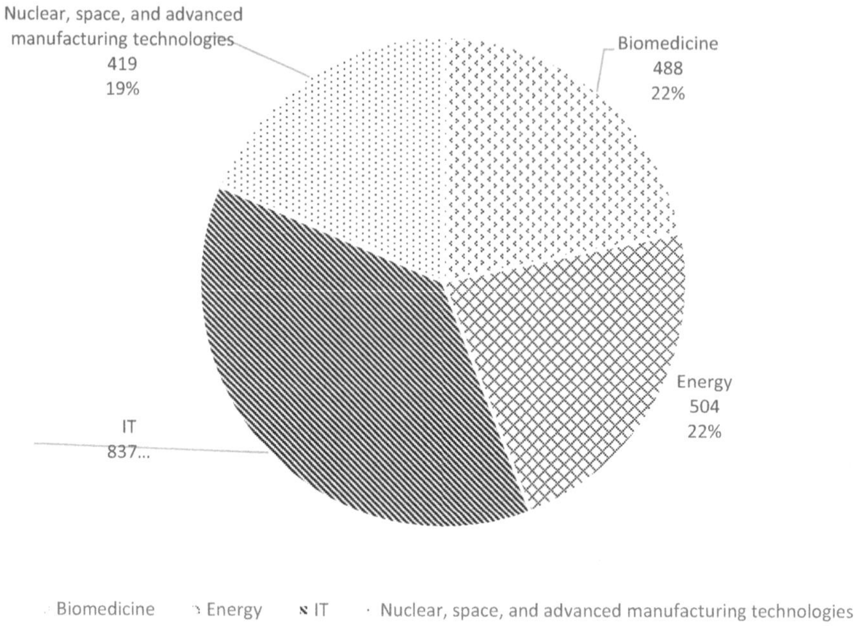

Figure 6.2 Numbers of start-ups participating in Skolkovo as of 2020, by cluster

Source: Skolkovo Annual Report (2020: 10–28)

Furthermore, media reports also stated that by the end of 2015, more firms might lose their status of Skolkovo participant if they refuse to relocate at least some of their firm to the territory of Skolkovo, in accordance with the Federal Law on Skolkovo which mandated this from 1 January 2016. Some firms that currently get a grant from Skolkovo are unhappy about such a forced move, citing above-market-rate rents for offices in Skolkovo compared to in Moscow city, and the fact that Skolkovo is about 20 km west of the centre of Moscow city (Romanova, 2015).

As of late October 2015, 81 "resident" firms (about 5% of the 1,432 "residents" as of end 2015) were physically located in the temporary buildings housing the Skolkovo technopark; 74 of these 81 "residents" had received a grant, while the remaining seven were large Russian or international partner companies of Skolkovo. These large firms are not necessarily physically present on site.

If we include the large companies, then by the end of 2015 Skolkovo had almost 1,500 companies participating. The 40 large Russian companies participating currently include Lukoil (oil), TNK-BP (oil), Sistema (large multi-industry conglomerate), Sberbank (banking), Rosatom (nuclear energy), and Renova (strategic investment).

Another source states that in Skolkovo's first four years, it awarded 150 grants to resident companies. The total amount of money disbursed in these grants equalled 9.9 billion roubles. However, it seems that the distribution of funding between the

150 grant winners is not uniform: 3.7 billion roubles went to just seven projects (Table 6.6). Most of these "mega-grants" went to the biomed cluster. This skewed distribution of the grants may simply reflect the way science funding happens globally or it may reflect the particularities of post-Soviet Russian politics and science. Many of these recipients had links – through their owners or managers – with influential political decision makers in the Kremlin, state corporations, or Skolkovo. This gives support to the hypothesis that in Russia particularly (as well as in many other countries) your chances of success are most affected by who you know. This confirms the arguments about the importance of *sistema* and informal connections to Russia's political economy (Ledeneva, 2013).

Organised events

Skolkovo has hosted and organised a variety of events since it launched. These events range from residential "retreats" for start-ups (the so-called "start-up villages") to hosting Russia's flagship, international, and annual "Open Innovations" forum, run for the seventh time in October 2018.

Skolkovo hosted and organised three annual events for start-ups between 2013 and 2015 that it called "start-up villages" (to emphasise the international spirit of the events, the word "village" is not translated into Russian). Such events bring together potential innovators, investors, industrialists, and government officials in an informal, outdoor environment. Around 2,000 start-ups participated in the events between 2013 and 2015.

This is how Skolkovo described the 2015 start-up village:

> Startup Village is the only event of its kind in Russia and was held for the third time in 2015. The most important goal of the event is to enable communication between startup founders and successful entrepreneurs, large industrialists, investors, bureaucrats, and between the startup people themselves! We are the only startup conference held in the outdoors and on the site of the future town of Skolkovo. Hence, every participant can see with their own eyes how the first innovation centre in Russia is being built.[28]

A major incentive for participating in a competition of this sort is presumably the extent of the prizes on offer. In 2013, there were 96 participants of whom the following were awarded prizes:

- Twenty finalists each received 150,000 roubles.
- Three winners were chosen from the finalists and awarded 300,000 roubles (third place), 600,000 roubles (second place), and 900,000 roubles (first place).[29]

How were the winners selected? The criteria encompass five dimensions, incorporating the quality of the product or process proposed, business and financial aspects, human capital (in the form of the project team), the feasibility, and the level of technological innovation (innovative globally/in Russia/nowhere).

Table 6.6 Biggest recipients of Skolkovo grants, 2011–2014

No.	*Name of project*	*Organisation/company receiving grant*	*Owner/ senior management links*	*Sum awarded (million RUB)*	*Associated Skolkovo cluster*
1	Creation of research centres of quantum optics and quantum technologies	International research centre of quantum optics and quantum technologies	**Vladislav Surkov** was initiator of this international research centre	893.4	Own cluster
2	Development of medicine for treating auto-immune illnesses, prevention of anxiety disorders, reducing alcohol dependency, and preventing Alzheimer's disease	Pharma Bio company	Main owner: **Prof. V. Deygin**	653.9	Biomed
3	Development of medicine for treating cancer and auto-immune diseases and slowing the ageing the process down	Holding company "Bioprocess Capital Partners"	Businessman **Mikhail Mogutov** (owns 53.6% stake); **Vneshekonombank** (25.1% stake); deputy director for innovation at Kurchatov Institute, **Mikhail Rychev** (21.3%).	557.6	Biomed
4	Development of a Compreno technology system for understanding and translation of natural language texts	"ABBY Info Poisk," the R&D branch of the Russian company ABBYY (www.abbyy.com)	Main owner: the entrepreneur **David Yan**	473.4	IT
5	Creation of photo biological, microbial, and combustive elements to convert liquid waste from alcohol production into electricity	British company M Power World	The director of M Power World between September 2009 and September 2010 was **Prof. Igor Goryanin**, who was later (when grant was approved) the head of Skolkovo biotech cluster. He now holds the Chair of Systems Biology in the School of Informatics, University of Edinburgh, United Kingdom.	395.7	Biomed/ Energy

6	Research to increase the quality of thin-film solar modules for the Russian solar firm Hevel Solar (a joint venture of the Renova Group and Rosnano)	Scientific technological centre of thin-film technologies in energy, The Ioffe Institute for research in physics and technology under the Russian Academy of Sciences	Owners: Victor Vekselberg's large Russian conglomerate, Renova Group (51%); and Rosnano state corporation (49%).	383	Energy efficiency
7	Development of a drug to treat flu, "Triazavirin" (entered Russian market in the autumn of 2014 priced at 600–900 RUB)[27]	Urals Centre of Bio-pharmacological Technologies	Urals Centre controlled by the family of the Russian State Duma deputy, Alexander Petrov.	369.7	Biomed

Source: translated from Reyter and Golunov (2015: 13)

It is difficult to evaluate these events in terms of concrete results because of a lack of data on total prize money distributed, expenditures, revenues, survival rates of winning projects, and partnership or investment agreements brokered because of the events. Nevertheless, the fact that Skolkovo has organised annual events such as the start-up villages over successive years undoubtedly raises its public profile as a place bringing together dynamic and engaged individuals. They contribute to a critical mass of emerging dynamism. There is nevertheless a risk that such activity is disjointed and just becomes one-off annual gatherings, which would hinder the development of interactions in a system of innovation.

Performance of Skolkovo, 2009–2013

In terms of progress in developing the ecosystem elements between 2009 and 2013, Skolkovo had less evident success compared to the mission-oriented elements. Nevertheless, there are some striking developments to note. In the initial phase, the Skolkovo Foundation succeeded in welcoming a higher than planned share of independent members of the investment (grant-giving) and tender committees, as well as of the budget commission. Moreover, in this phase, 12 large partner companies signed agreements about opening R&D centres in Skolkovo and five leading international universities signed cooperation agreements – although signing such agreements is just a first step and does not commit its signatories to very much. In addition, interactions with legislative and executive bodies is a part of building an ecosystem: Skolkovo demonstrated such interactions by submitting amendments to the Federal Law on Skolkovo and signing ten agreements with bodies of executive power (Table 6.7).

Table 6.7 Planned and actual indicators of ecosystem-oriented activities of Skolkovo: end 2009 to end 2011 (initial phase)

Key performance indicator	*Target*	*Achieved*
Share of independent members of the investment (grant-giving) and tender committees, as well as of the budget commission, %	50	58
Number of large partner companies that have signed agreements with Skolkovo about opening R&D centres, units	10–15	12
Number of leading international university partners that have signed agreements with Skolkovo	4	5
Interactions with bodies of legislative power of the Russian Federation	Na	Necessary amendments to Federal Law 244 submitted to federal lower house of parliament
Agreements with bodies of executive power of the Russian Federation	Na	10

Source: Efimov (2014: 26)

Table 6.8 Planned and actual indicators of ecosystem-oriented activities of Skolkovo: end 2011 to mid-2012 (rapid growth phase)

Key performance indicator	*Target*	*Achieved*
Total number of participants of Skolkovo innovation centre, people	500	793

Source: Efimov (2014: 27)

Table 6.9 Planned and actual indicators of ecosystem-oriented activities of Skolkovo: mid-2012 to mid-2013 (rethinking the mission of Skolkovo phase)

Key performance indicator	*Target*	*Achieved*
Number of collective use centres located across Russia and accredited to Skolkovo, units	14	14
Number of jobs created in R&D centres of key partners created according to agreements with Skolkovo, units	500	4,126
Volume of *external* co-financing for construction of innovation centre, billion RUB (USD)*	34 (approximately USD 1 billion)	39.7 (approximately USD 1.25 billion)
Share of new members of online community (measured by ratio of registered accounts to total number of unique web visitors)	1.5	2.0

Source: Efimov (2014: 28–29). *Historical exchange rate as of 15.06.2013 1 USD = 31.7 RUB from www.xe.com/currencytables/?from=RUB&date=2013-06-15#table-section

In its period of rapid growth (2011–2012), the only indicator of ecosystem-building that is apparent is a rapid increase (63%) in the number of participants of the Skolkovo innovation centre (Table 6.8).

From 2012 to 2013, Skolkovo was more successful in developing ecosystem elements (Table 6.9). First, 14 collective use (shared services) centres were accredited to Skolkovo, located all across Russia. These are run by commercial companies and are a means for them to offer their services on the private market. In September 2015, Skolkovo hosted a forum of all collective use centres from across Russia – hence acting as a catalyst for networking among these R&D centres together. Second, the key corporate partners of Skolkovo hugely over-achieved in terms of creating over 4,000 jobs in their R&D centres. Third, Skolkovo did well to attract nearly 40 billion roubles in external (i.e. private) co-financing for the construction of the innovation centre in this period. Finally, Skolkovo developed its online community as measured by the number of registered users on its website per unique web visits.

Summarising Skolkovo's experience with Stage 2 of the growth model, Skolkovo has not yet fared well in building up critical mass. This is primarily due to the ongoing construction of the main site just outside Moscow city. Once construction is completed in the late 2019 or 2020, the pace of building critical mass among participating start-ups, as well as the process of creating linkages with other actors in innovation processes elsewhere in Russia, needs to accelerate. While Skolkovo has supported and organised a wide range of innovation events since 2010 (e.g. Start-up Village, Open University events, launch of the Skolkovo EdTech Hub in July 2021), there has been little by way of strategic approach behind these events.

Stage 3 – global linkages

As stated at the start of this chapter, the Skolkovo innovation centre encapsulates the latest, most visibly international stage in Russia's STI policy. Since its beginning, international linkages have been strongly emphasised in its strategic focus, resources, and key actors.

Strategic focus

From its beginning, the Skolkovo Foundation spread the message widely that one of the innovation centre's aims was to integrate Russian science and technology into the global economy.

Skolkovo has the potential to become a hub of international networking. Its location on the edge of Moscow city helps through proximity to international airports, Russia's leading universities, and the capital's concentration of skilled human capital. Thus, the innovation centre can deepen international R&D networking and sourcing, as well as potentially help establish linkages in knowledge-based activities between foreign firms and domestic firms.

The international dimension was ingrained in the project from the very start, in its policy motivation. After Medvedev's presidential speech in December 2009 in which he first raised the idea of creating a new modern technological centre analogous to Silicon Valley and other foreign centres, a working group was formed. This group was chaired by Vladislav Surkov (then First Deputy Chief of Staff to the President) and consisted of Arkady Dvorkovich (then Assistant to the President of the Russian Federation); Anatoly Chubais (chair of Rusnano); German Gref (former minister for economic development and trade, then CEO and chairman of the executive board of Russia's largest bank, Sberbank); Boris Gromov (the governor of Moscow region); representatives of key ministries; and three foreign experts. These foreigners were Esther Dyson, a famous American angel investor; Sven-Thore Holm, one of the founders of the now successful Swedish Ideon Science Park; and Dominique Fache, one of the founders of Sophia Antipolis Science Park in France. In the end, the working group never met but the fact that they invited three leading foreign experts in venture capital and innovation infrastructure is indicative of the top-level desire to learn from international experiences and make Skolkovo international (Rashidov, 2012).

Resources

In reality, Skolkovo has so far fulfilled its pledges to cooperate with international companies. By the end of 2011, 11 multinationals had signed cooperation agreements with Skolkovo (Rashidov, 2012). By January 2013, this figure had increased to 19 multinationals. These include Siemens (German origin), Nokia (Finnish origin), Boeing, IBM, Johnson & Johnson (all of American origin), and Tata (Indian origin). Siemens, for example, had just over 200 employees engaged in R&D based in Skolkovo by early 2013.

Yet, a cooperation agreement is not the same as actual investment. By the end of 2011, Nokia, Siemens, Ericsson, IBM, Dow Chemical, EADS, and General Electric had allocated a total of 135 million EUROS for building their laboratories in Skolkovo and for researchers' salaries (Rashidov, 2012).

According to the author's survey of STPs (see Chapter 5), there were no big foreign firms listed as residents in Skolkovo's technopark. This suggests that the multinational companies that have signed agreements with Skolkovo are classified as partners, not anchor-tenants in the innovation centre.

Effect of international sanctions

Have the sanctions imposed on Russia by Western countries had any negative effects in terms of driving away multinationals or reducing Russia's integration into global technology markets?

Western sanctions on Russia were first imposed in March/April 2014 in response to events in Ukraine in February 2014. Data on the technology balance of payments compiled by the OECD suggest that sanctions had no adverse effect on money paid to Russia for intangible knowledge (e.g. patents and licences) in 2014 or 2015. Indeed, the technology balance of payments (receipts at current prices and exchange rates) increased from 2011 to 2015, meaning that Russia received more money in 2015 than in 2014 for technology (Table 6.10). As a share of Russia's GDP, this payment was very low at just 14.7% in 2015 in terms of GDP (compared to 44% in United Kingdom and 54.6% in Germany in the same year, see Table 6.11), which indicates the strong inward orientation of the Russian

Table 6.10 Russia's technology balance of payments: receipts (at current prices and exchange rates) in million USD, 2005–2015

	2005	*2010*	*2011*	*2012*	*2013*	*2014*	*2015*
Russian Federation (million USD)	391.6	627.8	592.6	688.8	773.7	1279.2	1654.7

Source: OECD (2018) Main Science and Technology Indicators.

Table 6.11 Technology balance of payments: payments as a % of GDP in 2015

Country	*%*
Russian Federation	14.7
United Kingdom	44.0
Germany	54.6

Source: OECD (2018) Main Science and Technology Indicators.

economy. These statistics could be because of the delayed effect of sanctions or the targeted nature of the sanctions to a select number of firms in the defence, finance, and energy sectors.

Turning to Skolkovo and how it may have been affected by international sanctions, as of mid-2016, 26 multinationals were listed as partners of Skolkovo compared to 40 large Russian companies (Skolkovo Foundation, 2016b). Hence, between 2013 and 2016, a period of tense geopolitical relations between Russia and Western countries, Skolkovo nevertheless managed to sign cooperation agreements with seven more multinationals.

Cooperation with multinationals is not the only element of Skolkovo's drive to internationalise. We also see the involvement of foreigners in SkolTech (principally, in terms of the pivotal role played by MIT in setting up SkolTech) and as senior staff of Skolkovo Foundation. First, SkolTech was modelled on the MIT in the United States and MIT professors and staff were paid to advise the new SkolTech on strategic and operational issues. Second, the Founding President of SkolTech from 2011 to 2016 was an American Professor of Aeronautics and Astronautics and of Engineering Systems at MIT, Edward Crawley. Crawley remains a professor in the space centre of SkolTech. A worrying sign of a possible reversal in Skolkovo's internationalisation efforts to date is that Crawley's successor as SkolTech president is a Russian scholar, Alexander Kuleshov. However, it is premature to evaluate the future development of SkolTech based only on the nationality of its second president. At the senior management level within the Skolkovo Foundation, we similarly see a trend of declining foreign nationals as Skolkovo has developed. For example, the initial Vice President for International Partnership Development in Skolkovo was an Irish national and former politician; his contract, however, was not renewed beyond 2014.

The Open University of Skolkovo (OUS) has cooperated with six countries to date, mainly former CIS countries. Students and young researchers and entrepreneurs from these countries have participated in OUS events. OUS cooperates most actively with Belarus (especially for the winter and summer schools OUS organises). Up to 2015, all events run by OUS have been in the Russian language but in July 2016, it held its first event in English.[30] The OUS also has ambitious plans to increase cooperation with other BRICS countries. For example, in the field of agriculture, the OUS sees scope for greater international cooperation because Russia and the other BRICS countries are among the world's biggest producers and buyers of agricultural goods (interview with a deputy executive director of OUS, May 2016).

The OUS has also had success in cooperating with multinationals in life sciences. It has organised an annual "pharma school" for three years in a row from 2014, partnering with the global market leaders: Pfizer, Bayer, BioMarin Pharmaceutical Inc., and Sanofi. The "pharma school" provides additional training for students and young researchers about the development and commercialisation of new medical drugs. The seminars, lectures, and masterclasses are taught by leading researchers, developers, and engineers from the corporate world over a period of two months and are held on two evenings per week.

Skolkovo seems to be continuing its international, outward-looking position in 2018. In 2017, Skolkovo's technology park earned the international standard "ISO9001 accreditation," considered the "Oscars of management quality." Western sanctions seem to have made Skolkovo officials look increasingly to other, non-Western countries for cooperation. At the large-scale St. Petersburg International Economic Forum in May 2018, India's Bhaum Telecom Ventures Private Limited agreed to work with Skolkovo to support and promote innovative projects in Russia and India.[31] Moreover, cooperation with Israel and China continues. In 2018, Israeli firms are collaborating to help set up Skolkovo's new medical cluster (started in 2015). Moreover, a Russian-Chinese fund is investing in Israeli companies that do business in Russia. Officials in Skolkovo are hopeful that talks to create a free trade zone between Israel and the Eurasian Economic Union will conclude in 2018.[32] However, as of June 2019 negotiations were continuing. The Eurasian Economic Commission's trade minister, Veronika Nikishina, told media that they were on track to sign free trade zone agreements in 2020 with Israel and Egypt.[33]

How institutional context affects Skolkovo

The predatory nature of the Russian state, with its multiple groups of elites who compete for resources and power, may be a possible threat to Skolkovo's potential as a source of economic growth. An alternative explanation is that Skolkovo may also help the Russian state and its *sistema* sustain itself because it remains a high priority state-supported project, even if there is evidence of inter-elite conflict and disagreement over it. The literature discussed in Chapter 2 on the ambivalence of technology and in the motivations behind the development of new technologies (Ledeneva, 2018: vol. 1: 14) is relevant here because we may see ambivalence in Skolkovo, which through operating from within the system ultimately may help to sustain the broad political system and *sistema* which created it. The concept of *sistema* (see Chapter 2) describes the distribution of power in Putin's Russia and the prominent role of informal networks to maintain this power. *Sistema* helps political and economic elites regulate access to rents from natural resources and appoint people loyal to President Putin; part and parcel of how *sistema* works is competing groups of elites.

Skolkovo faced threats of closure by rival groups of political and economic elites in 2013 with a wave of corruption allegations that saw key Skolkovo officials arrested and budgetary funds withheld. Corruption allegations do not necessarily mean that actual corruption has taken place: "practically any Russian public official who made decisions on allocation of funds could be accused of violation of some regulations" (Yakovlev, 2014: 17). Russia launched its high-level "fight against corruption" in the mid-2000s, using strict administrative oversight as a tool in this fight (Yakovlev, 2014: 17). Unfortunately, the lack of transparency and high level of arbitrariness in Russia's political economic system mean that almost any official with a grudge can use some administrative mechanisms to accuse their rival(s) of corrupt activities. The anti-corruption campaign has not led to a decline in actual corruption; it has, however, given security and law enforcement agencies more influence and power (Yakovlev, 2014).

The "grabbing hand" of bureaucrats and other officials, as well as corruption and public accusations of corrupt activities threaten the development of Skolkovo as an innovation ecosystem.[34] Gel'man argues that Skolkovo is following a similar trajectory as other success stories in Russia (e.g. the Soviet space programme) and other countries and is already a failed project because of changed policy priorities and a change of political leaders (when Putin became president again in 2012). This trajectory is one of initial success driven by (i) initial support from senior political leaders, then (ii) rapid results visible due to a high concentration of resources and symbolic returns but followed by (iii) limited multiplicative effects; (iv) a change in political leadership then meant that (v) the project lost its high-profile status and became a failed project (Gel'man, 2018). While Gel'man may be premature in his negative conclusion on Skolkovo's performance to date, Skolkovo is undoubtedly challenged by political economy factors which undermine Skolkovo's openness and transparency. Openness and transparency are central to the innovation city becoming a functional ecosystem. First, officials (often those in the lower levels of Russia's vast bureaucracy) stand to benefit from big personal gains at the expense of the large sums of public funds transferred to Skolkovo. Second, employees of the various organisations that are part of the Skolkovo project may have incentives to siphon off some funds for personal gain.

Throughout 2013, various English and Russian language media outlets reported on allegations of corruption at Skolkovo which surfaced as part of an audit by Russia's Investigative Committee and a later inquiry by the Prosecutor General's Office. For example, in mid-February 2013, two managers in the Skolkovo project (Kirill Lugovtsev, former director of the finance department of the "Skolkovo Foundation for New Technologies Development and Commercialization Centre," and Vladimir Khokhlov, general director of the customs-finance company "Skolkovo") were accused of embezzlement of funds equal to nearly USD 800,000 or 23.8 m roubles (Radio Free Europe Radio Liberty, 2013). They were arrested. Other examples surfaced between 28 February 2013 and 1 March 2013. Four leading Russian daily broadsheets (*RBK Daily*, *Izvestia*, *Vedomosti*, *Kommersant*) published reports about alleged corruption at Skolkovo in that period. These allegations were:

1. Alleged money laundering concerning the transfer of federal funds totalling 3.5 billion roubles – intended for Skolkovo – from the state budget to a private bank. Investigations centred on the fact that this money appeared to sit in an account of the bank for a long time and that the ultimate owner of this bank (Metkombank) is Viktor Vekselberg, who is also the president of Skolkovo Foundation. Skolkovo publicly denied any wrongdoings, saying these financial transfers to Metkombank were returned last year, and a vice president in Skolkovo Foundation said that the transfer was made in 2010 because Skolkovo is a non-state foundation and cannot receive state funds

directly (Grigoryev, 2013; Khairuk and Petrov, 2013; Sergeyev and Trifonov, 2013; Nikolsky and Pismennaya, 2013).
2. Alleged transfer of a grant worth 400 million roubles from Skolkovo to an organisation that is not legally allowed to receive such grants given that these are aimed at firms resident in Skolkovo (a vice-president of Skolkovo Foundation later said that the recipient of this grant was SkolTech university and so this transfer was in accordance with the 2010 federal law on Skolkovo) (Grigoryev, 2013; Khairuk and Petrov, 2013; Sergeyev and Trifonov, 2013; Nikolsky and Pismennaya, 2013).
3. Alleged transfer by a daughter organisation of Skolkovo (the Foundation for New Technologies Development and Commercialization Centre) of more than 37 million roubles in 2011 to subcontractor organisations for work done without contracts (Grigoryev, 2013; Khairuk and Petrov, 2013; Sergeyev and Trifonov, 2013; Nikolsky and Pismennaya, 2013).
4. The Investigative Committee also initiated a criminal case against a then senior vice-president of Skolkovo Foundation, Alexei Bel'tyoukov, who was accused of illegally transferring USD 750,000 to the bank account of the parliamentarian, Ilya Ponomarev, over a 12-month period from February 2011 to February 2012. Bel'tyoukov and Ponomarev denied this wrongdoing, stating at the time that the latter had an official contract to deliver a series of lectures across Russia and carry out some research work for Skolkovo. A spokesperson for the Investigative Committee commented that this case was sparked by a communication from the right-wing opposition parliamentarian, Vladimir Zhirinovsky, about a possible crime committed by Ponomarev (Rossiskaya Gazeta, 2013). This indicates that this is a case of political in-fighting between two rival politicians.

Later accusations emerged in the media based on the inquiry by the Prosecutor General's Office. In October 2013, the prosecutors claimed that the Skolkovo management had overpaid for some services, such as promotional videos (paid 54 million roubles, while the real cost stated by prosecutors was 5 million roubles or less) and consulting services (for which Skolkovo paid 600 million roubles, whereas the alleged real cost was 200 million roubles). In addition, the prosecutors claimed that Skolkovo gave grants through "shadow schemes" which issued funds to "allegedly fictitious" companies or firms affiliated with Skolkovo, some of which were located in offshore zones (Kravtsova, 2013).

More recently, in July 2016, the Auditing Chamber together with the Federal Security Service of the Russian Federation published their findings from the monitoring exercise of the use of federal funds by Skolkovo from 2013 to 2015. On the positive side, this monitoring found that Skolkovo Foundation had created all the necessary legislative framework for Skolkovo innovation centre and had passed 2,735 local normative acts concerning its activity. Moreover, the monitoring found that at the end of 2015, there were nearly 1,500 companies registered as participants (including grant recipients and non-grant recipient participants). Some of the target indicators were found to have been significantly over-achieved, notably those concerning intellectual property applications between 2013 and 2015. On the negative side, in contrast, the investigation concluded that a third of the grant allocating committee of Skolkovo Foundation (5 of 15 members) was either a founder or a head of a company that applied for grants or for participant status between 2013 and 2015 (Audit Chamber, 2016). The same day as the Audit Chamber released its report, a statement from the Skolkovo Foundation's press service said that the Foundation had carried out its own internal monitoring; consequently, it had removed the status of participant from 305 legal entities (Skolkovo Foundation, 2016a).

Of course, it could be that these allegations are unfounded and simply part of an attempt by different branches of the state to undermine Skolkovo. The state is not a homogenous entity, as the concept of Sistema implies. Skolkovo is funded directly by the powerful Ministry of Finance and enjoys the support and patronage of several high-ranking political officials (including Prime Minister Medvedev, Surkov, Dvorkovich, and to a limited extent President Putin). Gel'man (2018) argues that Skolkovo is primarily Medvedev's pet project and that Putin is at best ambivalent to its fate, and at worst hostile to it. At the same time, some government officials or bureaucrats could be jealous of Skolkovo's generous state support and wish to sabotage its success. For example, in its article published on 1 March 2013, Vedomosti quoted the first deputy chair of the Duma Committee for science and technology, Dmitry Novikov (member of Russia's Communist Party), as saying that "Skolkovo has been a mistaken project from the beginning, the resources . . . should have gone to existing science centres instead" (Nikolsky and Pismennaya, 2013: 1). Some observers have commented that "these investigations are part of an ongoing feud" between the law enforcement agencies, known to be anti-liberal and hardliners, and the more liberal officials led by Medvedev (Kravtsova, 2013).

It is beyond the scope of this chapter to fully understand whether these allegations are true or not. Yet, the fact that these allegations of corruption and irregularities have surfaced in the media indicates that an ambitious project such as Skolkovo cannot be insulated from the informal practices prevalent in Russia, even if it functions as an enclave. Indeed, understanding the political economy aspects of contemporary Russia (in other words, issues of control, funding, and political fighting between different branches of the state) is imperative to gain a realistic assessment of the performance of Skolkovo innovation centre so far. Such informal practices influence how Skolkovo develops.

Conclusions and further work

The conclusions section of this chapter aims to interpret Skolkovo using the three-stage model outlined in Chapter 2. As shown in this chapter, Skolkovo was created by senior state officials as a new kind of innovation hub to try to support first movers in five industrial sectors of strategic importance to Russia (Stage 1 of the three-stage growth model; see Chapter 2). At the same time, Skolkovo has aimed from the outset to build international links (Stage 3 of the growth model). These international links encompass creating partnerships with multinational enterprises and educational links (e.g. between MIT in the United States and Skoltech). It encapsulates the latest, most visibly international stage in Russia's STI policy, yet the extent of international linkages remains, thus far, quite limited.

Up to now, Skolkovo has fared less well in resolving collective action problems and building critical mass. Construction was scheduled to finish in 2019 and the pace of building critical mass among start-ups participating in Skolkovo as well as the process of creating linkages with other actors in innovation processes elsewhere in Russia may accelerate. This chapter argued that while Skolkovo has supported and organised a wide range of innovation events since 2010 (e.g. Start-up Village, Open University events), there has been little by way of strategic approach behind these events.

Skolkovo's internationalisation efforts were particularly noticeable in its first few years. We saw this in its strategic cooperation with MIT to build a graduate-level institute of technology from scratch, its recruitment of foreigners into senior management positions in Skolkovo Foundation, and its signing of partnership agreements with several multinational enterprises. The sanctions imposed on Russia in 2014 after Russia annexed Crimea from Ukraine have not seemed to disrupt Skolkovo much, with seven more multinationals signing agreements with Skolkovo between 2013 and 2016. However, these agreements with multinational companies have not yet been translated into much R&D cooperation or investment. Moreover, there have been fewer foreign nationals in senior management positions in Skolkovo since 2015, something which perhaps indicates that Skolkovo is turning its focus inwards, or that foreigners see Russia as a less attractive place in which to do business and to live than in the earlier part of the 2000s (Stage 3).

Neo-Schumpeterian approaches to economic growth and the innovation systems and innovation policy literature (as discussed in Chapter 2) highlight the importance of interactions between different actors on R&D and innovation processes. This suggests that Skolkovo's impressive scale of state investment in R&D and innovation cannot be sufficient for growth without indirect linkages. Interactions with the rest of the Russian innovation system and economy are crucial for Skolkovo to have economic impact. International linkages ensure world excellence and a flow of new ideas and fruitful interaction with national R&D. Skolkovo's NTBFs should be one of several inputs into technology-based economic growth of Russia and should operate as specialised suppliers of new technologies. The formation of NTBFs is important as one way that modernisation projects such as Skolkovo can contribute to technological modernisation and economic growth. However, stimulating NTBFs should not be the primary objective of Skolkovo. In fact, the primary objective of Skolkovo should be "to become the basis for a vast ecosystem that spans all of Russia" (The Economist, 2012, no page number). The rich experience of the science and technology cluster that developed in Cambridge, United Kingdom, from the late 1970s shows that R&D firms often contribute to the regional economy not by making new products, but rather by providing knowledge-intensive business services, especially R&D contract services (Probert et al., 2013). So, instead of expecting Skolkovo firms to extract value from their research through direct commercialisation of their S&T, their major contribution could be R&D services. In that respect, Skolkovo's aims are multifaceted and include the diverse possible impacts of R&D on the economy and national innovation system.

Russia lies behind the technological frontier. Skolkovo should, therefore, not focus exclusively on nurturing world-leading innovation. Hence, a possible role of Skolkovo is to help bring in world-leading technologies from abroad that can be imitated or improved on by Russian firms. Yet, technology transfer from other countries relies on a favourable wider institutional context, which, with the current climate of sanctions and geopolitical tensions between Russia and Western countries, is under threat.

Notes

1 See in particular the work of Mariana Mazzucato, Professor in the Economics of Innovation and Public Value at University College London: https://marianamazzucato.com/books
2 In his speech at a national forum on nanotechnology in October 2009, President Medvedev emphasized that Russia must reduce its national economic dependence on oil exports and reorient towards technology-based growth.
3 This section is based on a co-authored working paper (Radošević and Wade, 2014) although it has since been updated.
4 SkolTech plans to launch undergraduate degrees too although as of July 2021, these plans are still forthcoming.
5 www.skoltech.ru/research/en [last accessed 6 April 2021].
6 Website of Open University Skolkovo (OUS): https://opus.sk.ru/about [last accessed 28 July 2021].
7 Website of Edtech Sk: https://edtech.sk.ru/#about [last accessed 28 July 2021].
8 According to online map tool offered by the Russian language search engine yandex, http://maps.yandex.ru [last accessed 20 September 2012].
9 Skolkovo website, http://sk.ru/foundation/team/p/foundationboard.aspx [last accessed 25 June 2019].
10 "Skolkovo – eto ne kakoy-to 'mezhdusobouchik'; eto publichny proekt. Prichem proekt, vokrug kotorovo, v konechnom schete, dolzhno razvivatsya vse nashe modernizatsionnoe napravleniye. Poetomu nashi grazhdane dolzhny byt' polnostyou v kurse tovo, chto delaetsya, a takzhe v kurse tovo, kakim obrazom finansiryoutsya eti programme. Informatsiya dolzhna byt' absolutno otkrytoy i publichnoy: chto uzhe sdelano, chto budet sdelano v dalneishim" (Skolkovo Foundation, 2011). Reported in The Moscow Times (2011), April 25. Available at: https://www.themoscowtimes.com/2011/04/25/medvedev-hopes-to-teach-at-skolkovo-one-day-a6571 [last accessed 20 March 2022].
11 Skolkovo is located about 20 km west of the centre of Moscow city. Administratively, it is part of Mozhaysky District of Moscow city, which has the status of federal city.
12 In April 2017, Skolkovo Foundation merged the space and telecommunications cluster with the nuclear and new industrial technologies cluster (Izvestia, 23 March 2017. Available at: https://iz.ru/news/673010 [last accessed 27 April 2018].
13 While ICT is a relatively new industrial sector in Russia, it builds on quite strong capabilities in the late Soviet period in computer science. Akademgorodok and Tomsk in Siberia were pockets of excellence for Soviet computer science, although Russia still lagged behind Western countries in terms of computer science publications in the *Web of Science* database (Indukaev, 2018; Tatarchenko, 2013).

14 This section is based on Radošević and Wade (2014) although it has since been updated.
15 Historical rates for currency exchange used here is the rate on 31 December 2010. Xe, an online currency converter tool showing historical rates. Available at: www.x-rates.com/historical/?from=USD&amount=1&date=2010-12-31 [last accessed 1 July 2016].
16 Based on GDP figures from World Bank's World Development Indicators, Russia's GDP (current USD) was 1.9 trillion USD (1,858,000,000,000 USD) in 2011 (World Bank, 2011).
17 For more information on the corruption allegations concerning Skolkovo, see the next section "How institutional context affects Skolkovo."
18 A later source states that Skolkovo received a total of 58.1 billion RUB between 2013 and 2015 in federal subsidies (Audit Chamber, 2016). This is not inconsistent with the figures quoted above for the years 2010–2014. Conversions to US dollars as per historical exchange rate on 31 December 2014. Available at: www.x-rates.com/historical/?from=USD&amount=1&date=2014-12-31.
19 The following information on the construction progress of the various elements of Skolkovo "city" is from the Russian language section of the official website of Skolkovo, under the heading "khod stroitelstva." Available at: http://sk.ru/city/p/main_objects.aspx [last accessed 27 October 2015].
20 https://sk.ru/city/gymnasium/p/about.aspx, last accessed 28 October 2015; and Skolkovo website for up-to-date information.
21 This paragraph is extracted from a co-authored working paper (Radošević and Wade, 2014).
22 This paragraph is extracted from a co-authored working paper (Radošević and Wade, 2014).
23 The number of innovative start-ups has increased rapidly from 368 in February 2012 to 941 in August 2013 and the majority of start-ups (approx. 33%) are in the IT cluster (Skolkovo official website [last accessed 22 March 2013] (Kouzbit, 2013). As of late 2018, the number of start-ups participating in Skolkovo in some way was 1809 (http://sk.ru/foundation/results/annual_reports_ru [last accessed 22 January 2019]).
24 Last two paragraphs here based on a co-authored working paper (Radošević and Wade, 2014).
25 This subsection is adapted from a co-authored working paper (Radošević and Wade, 2014).
26 Between 2015 and 2020, the space and nuclear clusters amalgamated to form one cluster together with advanced manufacturing technologies.
27 A brief history of the development of Triazavirin drug can be found online at: www.influenza.spb.ru/institute_for_population/preparat_triazavirin. Website of the Research Institute of Influenza (RII), which was established in 1967 as a lead institution under the Ministry of Public Health of the USSR. Website in Russian [last accessed 8 May 2015].
28 Website of Startup Village, https://startupvillage.ru/main/ru [last accessed 16 September 2015].
29 Source: Skolkovo Foundation (2013) Regulation on holding the closed competition for investor attractive research projects during the Startup Village conference. 27 May 2013, No. 127. Available at: http://2013.startupvillage.ru/pages/startups.do [last accessed 13 May 2015].
30 Summer school on high technologies for agriculture called "Smart Agro," 3–8 July 2016.
31 Skolkovo news (2018). Available at: http://sk.ru/news/b/news/archive/2018/05/24/skolkovo-i-indiyskiy-venchurnyy-fond-zaklyuchili-soglashenie-na-pmef.aspx [last accessed 29 May 2018].
32 Skolkovo news (2018). Available at: http://sk.ru/news/b/news/archive/2018/05/25/a-dvorkovich-vidit-bolshoy-potencial-sotrudnichestva-s-izrailem.aspx [last accessed 29 May 2018].

33 "EAEU May Sign Free Trade Zone Deals With Israel, Egypt In 2020 – Economic Commission," *Fahad Shabbir*, 26 June 2019, UrduPoint News/Sputnik. Available at: www.urdupoint.com/en/business/eaeu-may-sign-free-trade-zone-deals-with-isra-654405.html [last accessed 27 June 2019].

34 This section on the corruption allegations concerning Skolkovo is from a co-authored working paper (Radošević and Wade, 2014). It has been modified and updated in places.

References

Adelaja, T. (2012) 'Putinomics 2.0: Putin's Economic Reforms Will Be Merely Cosmetic'. *Russia Profile Special Report: the State of the State*. [Online] 2, IX, pp. 26–28. Available from: http://russiaprofile.org/politics/57098.html [last accessed 26 September 2014].

Amsden, A. H. (1989) *Asia's Next Giant: South Korea and Late Industrialization*. New York; Oxford: Oxford University Press.

Åslund, A. (2007) *Russia's Capitalist Revolution: Why Market Reform Succeeded and Democracy Failed*. Washington, DC: Peterson Institute for International Economics.

Åslund, A., Guriev, S. and Kuchins, A. (2010) *Russia after the Global Economic Crisis*. Washington, DC: Peterson Institute for International Economics.

Audit Chamber of the Russian Federation (2016) *Skolkovo Foundation Has Achieved the Majority of Its Target Indicators for 2013–2015 of Its Sub-Programme "Creation and Development of the Skolkovo Innovation Centre"* [*'Fond "Skolkovo" v 2013–2015 gg dostig bolshinstva tselevykh pokazateley podprogrammy Sozdaniye i razvitiye innovatsionnovo tsentra "Skolkovo"*, 14 July. Available at: https://vc.ru/n/audit-skolkovo [last accessed 19 July 2016].

BBC4 (2014) 'Cosmonauts: How Russia Won the Space Race'. A documentary first shown on BBC4 on October 13 2014 (director Michael Lachmann). Further Information Available in the UK at: https://www.bbc.co.uk/programmes/b04lcxms [last accessed 20 March 2022].

Connolly, R. (2011) 'Financial Constraints on the Modernization of the Russian Economy', *Eurasian Geography and Economics*, 52:3, pp. 428–459. Available at: 10.2747/1539-7216.52.3.428

Dezhina, I. (2013) 'Technology Platforms in Russia: A Catalyst for Cluster Development?', Paper Presented at Triple Helix 11th International Conference, London, 8–10 July 2013 (unpublished).

The Economist (2012) 'Can Russia Create a New Silicon Valley?' *The Economist*, 14 July. Available at: www.economist.com/node/21558602 [last accessed 31 July 2016].

Efimov, A. (2014) 'Evolution of a System of Performance Indicators for the State Support of Innovation Based on the Case of the Skolkovo INNOVATION CENtre' ['Evolyoutsiya sistemy pokazatelei rezultativnosti mer gosudarstvennoy podderzhki innovatsii na primere innovatsionnovo tsentra "Skolkovo" '], *Innovatsii I investitsii* [*Innovation and Investments*] 32/269 (pp. 22–34).

EBRD – European Bank for Reconstruction and Development (2012) *Diversifying Russia: Harnessing Regional Diversity*. London: EBRD. Available online at: https://www.ebrd.com/news/publications/special-reports/diversifying-russia.html [last accessed 21 March 2022].

Ergas, H. (1987) 'Does Technology Policy Matter?', in Guile, B. and Brooks, H. (eds.) *Technology and Global Industry*. Washington, DC: National Academy Press.

Gel'man, V. (2018) 'Exceptions and Rules: Success Stories and Bad Governance in Russia', Paper for presentation at the 50th Annual Convention of the Association of Slavic, East European, and Eurasian Studies, Boston, December (pp. 1–26) [unpublished paper].

Government of the Russian Federation (2008) *Long-term Socio-Economic Development Strategy of the Russian Federation to 2020 No. 1662, November* [Ministerstvo Ekonomicheskogo Razvitiya Rossiyskoy Federatsii, Kontseptsiya Dolgosrochnogo Sotsialnogo Ekonomicheskogo Razvitiya Rossiyskoy Federatsii, 2020, № 1662]. Available at: http://www.economy.gov.ru/wps/portal/e-russia [last accessed 23 February 2011].

Government of the Russian Federation (2010b) *Federal Law No. 244, September 28. On the innovation centre of Skolkovo* (pp. 1–17). Available to download in English from: http://community.sk.ru/cfs-file.ashx/__key/telligent-evolution-components-attachments/13-372-00-00-00-00-42-01/2010_5F00_09_5F00_22-Federal-Law-no.244_5F00_En.pdf [last accessed 26 September 2014].

Government of the Russian Federation (2010a) *Decree of the Government of the Russian Federation of 26 July 2010, No. 565* [Postanovlenie pravitelstva Rossisskoy Federatsii, 26 July 2010, No. 565] Moscow. Published on 4 August 2010 in *Rossiskaya Gazeta*. Available at: http://www.rg.ru/2010/08/04/skolkovo-dok.html [last accessed 31 July 2016].

Grigoryev, A. (2013) 'SKR proveryaet aferu na 3.5 milliard rublyei, vydelennykh "Skolkovo"' [transl. 'Investigative Committee of Russia investigates fraud worth 3.5 billion roubles allocated to "Skolkovo"], *Izvestia*, 28 February. Available at: http://izvestia.ru/news/545861 [last accessed 20 March 2022].

Indukaev, A. (2018) 'Re-Valuing Research in Modern Russia (2000–2018): From Innovation Policy to Scientific Entrepreneurship? [original in French: 'Revaloriser la recherche en Russie moderne (2000–2018). De la politique de l'innovation à l'entrepreneuriat scientifique?']', Thesis submitted for the degree of PhD in sociology, anthropology, and demography at the University of Paris-Saclay, Paris, France.

Karo, E. and Kattel, R. (2015) 'Innovation Bureaucracy: Does the Organization of Government Matter When Promoting Innovation?', Paper provided by Lund University, CIRCLE – Center for Innovation, Research and Competences in the Learning Economy in its series Papers in Innovation Studies with number 2015/38. Available at: https://ideas.repec.org/p/hhs/lucirc/2015_038.html [last accessed 30 December 2019].

Kravtsova, Y. (2013) 'Skolkovo Warned Over Potential $4Bln in Misspending', *The Moscow Times*, 30 October, issue 5246. Available at: https://www.themoscowtimes.com/2013/10/30/skolkovo-warned-over-potential-4bln-in-misspending-a29120 [last accessed 20 March 2022].

Khairuk, S. and Petrov, I. (2013) 'Proverka dlya Vekselberga' [transl. 'Checks for Vekselberg'], *RBK Daily*, 1 March. Available at: https://www.rbc.ru/newspaper/2013/03/01/56c1bb4a9a7947ac7f7abebf [last accessed 20 March 2022].

Kinossian, N. and Morgan, K. (2014) 'Development by Decree: The Limits of "Authoritarian Modernization" in the Russian Federation', *International Journal of Urban and Regional* Research 38/5 (pp. 1678–1696). Available at: https://doi.org/10.1111/1468-2427.12159.

Kommersant (2010) 'State to invest 54 billion roubles in Skolkovo' [Gosudarstvo vlozhit v tsentr "Skolkovo" 54 milliard rubley], *Kommersant*, 5 August 2010. Available from: http://www.kommersant.ru/doc/1482479 [last accessed 31 July 2016].

Kouzbit, O. (2013) 'Skolkovo Secures $4 Billion State Funding Until 2020', *East-West Digital News*, 8 August 2013. Available at: http://www.ewdn.com/2013/08/08/skolkovo-secures-4-billion-state-funding-until-2020. [last accessed 31 July 2016].

Ledeneva, A. (2013) *Can Russia Modernise? Sistema, Power Networks and Informal Governance*. Cambridge: Cambridge University Press.

Ledeneva, A. (ed.). 2018. *The Global Encyclopaedia of Informality: Understanding Social and Cultural Complexity*, Volume 1. London: UCL Press. Available at: https://doi.org/10.14324/111.9781911307907.

Lenihan, C. (2012) 'Russia's Skolkovo in Comparative and Historical Perspective', Presentation at workshop on Russia's Skolkovo in Comparative and Historical Perspective, UCL SSEES, London, 13 June.
Leydesdorff, L. and Meyer M. (2006) 'Triple Helix Indicators of Knowledge-Based Innovation Systems', (Report) *Research Policy* 35/10 (pp. 1441–1449).
Nikolsky, A. and Pismennaya, A. (2013) 'SKR provyerayet novye danniye o vozmozhnykh pravonarusheniyakh v "Skolkovo"' (trans. 'Investigative Committee of Russia checks new information about possible violations in "Skolkovo"'), *Vedomosti*, 35, March 1. Available at: https://www.vedomosti.ru/politics/articles/2013/03/01/skolkovo_pod_lupoj and http://dlib.eastview.com/browse/doc/28734295 [last accessed 26 March 2022].
OECD (1998) *The OECD Jobs Strategy: Technology, Productivity and Job Creation Best Policy Practices*. Paris: OECD.
OECD (2018) *Main Science and Technology Indicators (MSTI)*. Paris: OECD Publishing. Available at: https://doi.org/10.1787/msti-v2018-1-en [last accessed 30 November 2019].
Probert, J., Connell, D. and Mina, A. (2013) 'R&D Service Firms: The Hidden Engine of the High-Tech Economy?', *Research Policy* 42/6–7 (pp. 1274–1285). Available at: https://doi.org/10.1016/j.respol.2013.03.004.
Radio Free Europe Radio Liberty (2013) *Russian Skolkovo Foundation Managers Under Financial Investigation*, February 12. Available at: http://www.rferl.org/content/russia-skolkovo-foundation-managers-under-investigation/24900092.html [last accessed 26 September 2014].
Radošević, S. (2003) 'Patterns of Preservation, Restructuring and Survival: Science and Technology Policy in Russia in the Post-Soviet Era', *Research Policy* 32/6 (pp. 1105–1124).
Radošević, S. and Wade, I. (2014) 'Modernization Through Large S&T Projects: Assessing Russia's Drive for Innovation-Led Development via Skolkovo Innovation Centre, Economics and Business', Working Papers 131, Centre for Comparative Economics (CCE), UCL SSEES, London. Open access mode via UCL Discovery. Available at: http://discovery.ucl.ac.uk/1454656 [last accessed 31 June 2021].
Rashidov, O. (2012) *Skolkovo: prinuzhdeniye ko chudu* [transl. *Skolkovo: A compulsion to a miracle*] Moscow: Mann, Ivanov, and Ferber.
Reyter, S. and Golunov, I. (2015) 'RBC Investigation: What's Happened With "Skolkovo"' ['Rassledovaniye RBK: chto sluchilos' so "Skolkovo"'], RBC Online and Published in No. 4, 23 March 2015. Available at: http://www.rbc.ru/special/business/23/03/2015/550 9710a9a7947327e5f3a18 [last accessed 30 June 2016].
RIA Novosti (2013) 'News Bulletin From RIA Novosti on 18 October 2013' ['Soobscheniya informatsionnykh agentstv. 18 oktyabrya 2013 goda, 18:30, Moskva'], *RIA Novosti*, 18 October 2013. Available at: minfin.ru/common/upload/library/2013/10/main/18.10.13.pdf [last accessed 25 June 2016].
Rice-Oxley, M. (2015) 'Inside Skolkovo, Moscow's self-styled Silicon Valley', *The Guardian*, 12 June. Available at: https://www.theguardian.com/cities/2015/jun/12/inside-skolkovo-moscows-self-styled-silicon-valley [last accessed 20 March 2022].
Romanova, S. (2015) 'Fond "Skolkovo" teryaet rezidentov: kakiye prichiny podtalkivayout ikh k ukhodu' [transl. 'Skolkovo Foundation is Losing Residents: What Reasons Are Pushing Them to Leave'], *Vedomosti*, 5 June. Available at: http://www.vedomosti.ru/management/articles/2015/06/05/595343-fond-skolkovo-teryaet-rezidentov [last accessed 28 March 2022].
Rossiskaya Gazeta (2013) 'O Skolkovo bez nauki: Sledstvenny komitet Rossiskoy Federatsii' [transl. 'About Skolkovo without science: Investigative Committee of the Russian

Federation'], *Rossiskaya Gazeta,* 22 April. Available at: http://sledcom.ru/press/smi/item/508544 [last accessed 20 March 2022].

Ruchnov, K. M. and Zaytseva, Y. G. (2011) 'Krizis naukogradov Rossii' [transl. 'Crisis of naukograds of Russia'], Published on the Official Website of The Free Economic Society of Russia as an entry for the competition 'Future of the Economy 2011'. Available at: http://www.mosveo.ru/images/stories/00008.doc [in Russian] [last accessed 20 March 2022].

Sakwa, R. (2010) 'The Dual State in Russia', *Post-Soviet Affairs* 26/3 (pp. 185–206). Available at: https://doi.org/10.2747/1060-586X.26.3.185.

Salter, A. J. and Martin, B. R. (2001) 'The Economic Benefits of Publicly Funded Basic Research: A Critical Review', *Research Policy* 30/3 (pp. 509–532).

Sergeyev, N. and Trifonov, V. (2013) 'S dyengami "Skolkovo" ne sdelali nichevo novogo' [transl. 'In "Skolkovo" they haven't made anything new with the money'], *Kommersant,* 1 March. Available at: http://www.kommersant.ru/doc/2138358 [last accessed 20 March 2022].

Skolkovo Foundation (2013) 'Regulation on Holding the Closed Competition for Investor Attractive Research Projects During the Startup Village conference'. 27 May 2013, No. 127. Available at: http://2013.startupvillage.ru/pages/startups.do [last accessed 13 May 2015].

Skolkovo Foundation (2016a). 'Fond "Skolkovo" zayavil, chto viyavil narusheniya s grantama do otcheta schetnoy palata', 14 July. Available at: https://rns.online/it-and-media/Skolkovo-zayavil-chto-fond-viyavil-narusheniya-s-grantami-do-proverki-Schetnoi-palati-2016-07-14 [last accessed 19 July 2016].

Skolkovo Foundation (2016b) Available at: http://sk.ru/net/partners/p/skpartnerslist.aspx [last accessed 21 July 2016].

Skolkovo Foundation (2016c) *Annual Report for 2015.* Available at: http://sk.ru/foundation/results/annual_reports_ru [last accessed 31 July 2016].

Skolkovo Foundation (2020) *Annual Report for 2020.* In Russian. Available at: https://old.sk.ru/foundation/results/annual_reports_ru/ [last accessed 22 November 2021].

Skolkovo Annual Report (2018) Available at: www.sk.ru [last accessed 31 December 2018].

Sturgeon, T. J. (2000) 'How Silicon Valley Came to Be', Chapter One in: *Understanding Silicon Valley: Anatomy of an Entrepreneurial Region.* Kenney, M., (ed.) Redwood city, California: Stanford University Press.

Tatarchenko, K. (2013) ' "A House with the Window to the West": The Akademgorodok Computer Center (1958–1993)', PhD Dissertation, Princeton University, November (unpublished).

The Times (2008) *Russia's lessons in capitalism,* November 16 [Online] Available from: http://business.timesonline.co.uk/tol/business/management/mba/article4962457.ece [last accessed 26 September 2014].

World Bank (2011) *World Development Indicators 2011.* Available at: http://data.worldbank.org/country/russian-federation [last accessed 25 July 2016].

Yakovlev, A. (2014) 'Russian Modernization: Between the Need for New Players and the Fear of Losing Control of Rent Sources', *Journal of Eurasian Studies* 5/1 (pp. 10–20). Available at: https://doi.org/10.1016/j.euras.2013.09.004.

Yegorov, I. and Koretsky, A. (2013) 'Triple Helix Concept and Problems of Innovation Development in Russia and Ukraine', Paper Presented at Triple Helix 11'h International Conference, London, 8–10 July 2013 (unpublished).

7 Conclusions

Summary

This book has attempted to understand why Russia is performing comparatively poorly in innovation outcomes. It took a multidisciplinary approach to examine why Russia is not doing as well in economic catch-up and innovation as, for example, China. Following Taylor's (2016) emphasis on the political economy of science, technology, and innovation (STI) policies, it suggested that a country's political economy model (the nature of rents, distribution of power in an authoritarian regime, and the approach used for industrial and innovation policy) is an important driver of innovation performance.

Through an analysis of the case of Russia, this book has examined how authoritarian regimes deploy infrastructurally based policies, creating science towns and science and technology parks (STPs) to ignite modernisation and innovation. The book sees the policy initiatives of science towns and STPs as part of the evolutionary path of STI policy in the Soviet Union and Russia. In terms of control and funding, these policies are mainly top-down from the federal centre and predominantly led by domestic political and economic elites. They are inspired by, and to some extent are copies of, foreign institutions and policies. Some foreign actors have been involved, along with local organisations in implementing science towns and STPs, most notably in the case of Skolkovo (Chapter 6) in its first few years.

The empirical material presented in the book (Chapters 4–6) is interpreted by drawing on a model of economic growth rooted in the literature on ECG, evolutionary theory, and systems of innovation. This model sees growth processes as occurring in three stages, starting from the micro or most local level where the role of first movers (firms or organisations such as a STP) is critical. The second stage takes places at the meso level, at which a critical mass of firms and state agencies is built up and institutions such as firm associations, public agencies, or design bureaus are formed to assist with inter-organisational cooperation and firm learning. The third stage is when firms and other organisations form global linkages and become globally competitive.

This conceptual framework is helpful to understand the issues involved in accelerating – or initiating – technological modernisation. Initiating sources of growth ("growth poles" as first defined by Perroux, 1949[1]) that are not based

DOI: 10.4324/9781003256205-7

on natural resources is a policy challenge that Russia has set for itself since the early 2000s, relying on government intervention. Innovation and technology are public goods, hence the need for public action. Yet, the risk of government failure in this endeavour is extremely high because of the difficulties in designing and implementing innovation policies effectively.

The main empirical findings were laid out in Chapters 4–6. These chapters constitute one of the first historical accounts of the Soviet Union's and Russia's pursuit of the evolutionary path of STI policy from a political economic perspective (although of course, there are many excellent works by economists and science policy specialists on various aspects of the Soviet R&D system since the "sputnik" shock of 1957: see the landmark Organisation for Economic Co-operation and Development (OECD) report on science policy in the USSR, Zaleski et al., 1969; Berliner, 1976; Amann and Cooper, 1982; Yaremenko, 1981; Cooper, 2008; Rowland, 1996 on Soviet closed cities or ZATOs).

Chapter 4 gave a historical account of the creation of two science towns in the Soviet Union and tracked their evolution over time up to the present day. These two towns – Obninsk in Western Russia, about 80 km from Moscow and Akademgorodok in the large Siberian city of Novosibirsk – were built in the late 1950s. While their creators envisioned linking the places up to regional and national industry, they functioned as quite isolated enclaves, albeit with international collaboration to a limited extent (such as scientist visits for joint projects or conferences). In the Soviet period, these towns never managed to nurture any first movers (scientists) at the micro level although the two places were home to a handful of pioneering research institutes; neither Obninsk nor Akademgorodok was able to generate outcomes (e.g. setting up firms) at a micro or local level because of the lack of any "market" in the Western sense in the Communist planned economy. In their strategic orientation on science, they formed part of the Soviet Union's state-led, top-down missions for nuclear energy (in the case of Obninsk) and basic Research and Development (R&D; Akademgorodok). The two towns flourished in the 1960s in terms of receiving substantial state resources and carrying out R&D. However, they later faced a time of stagnation from the mid-1970s that lasted up until the mid-1990s, exacerbated by the crisis period following the collapse of the Soviet Union. Obninsk and Akademgorodok lost their scientific purpose, and local and regional political and economic elites realised the towns had to adapt to the realities of the new market economy or perish. They chose the path of adaptation. Obninsk and Akademgorodok pursued more explicit internationalisation strategies from the 1990s compared to the more hesitant internationalisation activities in the Soviet era. As a result, each place has some global linkages (which have been developed and maintained over several decades), but their linkages remained marginal vis-à-vis the overall scale of the towns' activities.

In general, these towns are not at the technology frontier, yet each contains one or two organisations which are at the forefront in their respective disciplines. In terms of performance in fundamental R&D, Akademgorodok – and to a lesser extent, Obninsk – has been quite successful in producing fundamental research (as seen in publications data). Between 1991 and 2016, Akademgorodok Novosibirsk produced a much greater volume of scientific publications (and more citations per publication between 2005 and 2013) than Obninsk. Akademgorodok's superior publication record is consistent with its founding mission of being a centre of research excellence.

However, neither Akademgorodok nor Obninsk has had much success in building on their knowledge and R&D capabilities through commercialisation. With some notable exceptions, these two science towns have not yet forged national and inter-regional linkages through, for example bringing about an increase in the number of new production or service-providing firms created, using patents to bring new products to market, or developing global linkages through value chains. Obninsk's experience in building industrial clusters since 2010 has had some success in creating new jobs and attracting in large Russian firms (e.g. Russian pharma companies) – thus apparently building a critical mass of commercial interactions, primarily within the domestic economy. Akademgorodok's technology park is one of the most successful parks in Russia if we look at a range of "conspicuous statistics." For example, it has helped create and nurture many new technology-based firms and train school pupils and university students to international levels.

Chapter 5 analysed Russia's experience with implementing STPs since the early 1990s, based on a purposive survey of 17 such parks. Several different economic and political actors (federal and regional state, private, and public–private actors) in Russia have enthusiastically initiated a wave of STPs since the early 1990s. Since 2000, they have received greatly increased strategic support from the state. There are now 125 officially recognised STPs geographically spread across Russia (as of 2017) and funded by the federal or regional state, private enterprises, or a combination of public and private resources. Although outcomes are varied, in several regions of Russia many new, innovative and hi-tech firms are being set up within STPs. In seeking to find opportunities for growth as well as ways to overcome or lessen binding constraints or obstacles to innovative entrepreneurship, some STPs are even acting as entrepreneurs themselves. The first movers in this context are the specialised management companies organising and operating STPs in Russia, along with some of the firms residing in these STPs. This means that there are strong possibilities of creating varied outcomes at the micro level. The diversity of founders of STPs is associated with increased chances of varying outcomes or positive variations of performance. Regional variation in the organisation and impacts of STPs in Russia is also evidence of the institutional hierarchy concept (Chapter 2) whereby while the national level of institutions and rules remains fairly constant, on a regional and local level, there is more dynamism as actors experiment with different policy approaches and are able to flexibly interpret the rules set out by institutions.

The key national level institutional framework for STPs was Russia's economic modernisation agenda that began in the early 2000s (as described in Chapter 2, section "Historical overview of technological modernisations in Russia: from the 18th century to the 21st century") and more specifically, the 2006 Russian

Government's programme called "Creation of technoparks in the sphere of high technologies in the Russian Federation." The policy framework focused on the construction phase of STPs, neglecting the later stages of creation of linkages with external organisations. Thus, Russian STPs were not necessarily intended to become economically relevant entities for their local or regional economies but were initiated as self-contained developer projects (or real estate projects) to provide new facilities to reportedly support the creation of new firms and support R&D and technological development. Some of the STPs profiled in Chapter 5 have expanded to become locally or regionally relevant. They are not only nurturing new innovative firms but also building linkages with local universities and local populations through skills training courses.

However, few of the post-2000 generation of STPs in Russia have strong linkages with globally leading universities, and this limits the scope for knowledge transfer. Moreover, the evidence presented in Chapter 5 showed that managers of 11 of the 17 STPs surveyed felt that their park's resident firms completely lack ready-for-market technologies, which was perceived as a key barrier for firm development in Russian science or technology parks. Those STPs are therefore not responding to an economic demand for new technologies (or creating the demand) and have some ways to go before they are a significant contributor to their local and/or regional economy.

Russian parks have generally not managed to forge global linkages. The exception is the sharp rise seen in 2015 in Russian STPs' membership of an international STP industry association, the International Association of Science Parks and Areas of Innovation (IASP). While membership of this association gives the STPs more exposure globally, it gives limited opportunities for international production links.

Chapter 6 brings the story up to date as the focus on Skolkovo encapsulates the latest, most visibly international stage in Russia's STI policy. Yet, the extent of international linkages produced and sustained by Skolkovo remains, so far, quite limited. The innovation hub of Skolkovo, established in 2010, aimed to create and nurture first mover firms in five industrial sectors that reflect the Russian state's national priority industries: ICT, biomedical science, energy-efficiency, space, and nuclear technologies. It has given out substantial financial resources in the form of grants to new or young firms; as of 2020, there were 2,248 participating firms or projects in Skolkovo. Russia lies behind the technological frontier; hence, Skolkovo's potential may not come from exclusively nurturing world-leading innovation, but rather from bringing in world-leading technologies from abroad that can be imitated or improved on by Russian firms. Yet, technology transfer from other countries relies on a favourable wider institutional context to facilitate cross-border trade and knowledge sharing, which, given the current sanctions and geopolitical tensions between Russia and Western countries, is under threat.

Skolkovo has not yet fared well in building up critical mass. Once construction is completed, the pace of building critical mass among participating start-ups, as well as the process of creating linkages with other actors in innovation processes elsewhere in Russia, needs to accelerate. While Skolkovo has supported and organised a wide range of innovation events since 2010 (e.g. Start-up Village, Open University events), there has been little by way of strategic approach behind these events.

Skolkovo's internationalisation efforts were particularly noticeable in its first few years and have declined over the last few years. At the beginning, Skolkovo's internationalisation activities included a strategic cooperation with MIT in the United States to build a graduate-level institute of technology from scratch, recruitment of foreigners into senior management positions in Skolkovo Foundation, and the signing of partnership agreements with several multinational enterprises. The sanctions imposed on Russia in 2014 after Russia annexed Crimea from Ukraine have not seemed to disrupt Skolkovo much, with seven more multinationals signing agreements with Skolkovo between 2013 and 2016. However, these agreements with multinational companies have not yet been translated into much R&D cooperation or investment. Moreover, there have been fewer foreign nationals in senior management positions in Skolkovo since 2015. This indicates either that Skolkovo is turning its focus inwards or that foreigners see Russia as a less attractive place to do business and live than in the earlier part of the 2000s.

Russia as an illustration of the evolutionary model of economic growth

This book has analysed the empirical cases of science towns, STPs, and Skolkovo as a hybrid between a science town and a technology park. It did this by using a conceptual framework that breaks economic growth and innovation down into three stages, starting from the most local (micro) level and ending at the global (building global linkages) level. Tables 7.1–7.3 take each stage in turn and give a summary of how the empirical cases have been interpreted using the framework. For each case, three dimensions were examined at each stage: (i) policy focus, (ii) resources, and (iii) institutions.

Why has neither Obninsk nor Akademgorodok generated significant economic impact from their R&D and innovation? And why are the two places not more globally connected? It is argued that the reasons lie in the institutional context in Russia, in particular, the political actors with power, the ruling institutions, and the laws. The institutional context captures the different facets of decision-making: the governance structure whereby decisions are implemented, the identity of decision-making actors (public or private), and the potential benefits to those actors which incentivise their decisions. The conceptual perspectives that this book draws on to understand the empirical material all incorporate the institutional context, that is modernisation policy agenda, the idea of rents or who benefits from modernisation processes, innovation systems, and theories that help us understand the political economy of authoritarian political regimes, including the concept of *sistema* to explain Russia's authoritarian system under Putin. These issues shape how the three-stage model of growth plays out in reality.

The model of economic growth rooted in the literature on evolutionary economic geography, evolutionary theory, and systems of innovation does not

Table 7.1 Summary of empirical cases: Stage 1

	Obninsk	*Akademgorodok in Novosibirsk*	*Science and technology parks (STPs)*	*Skolkovo*
Stage 1	**Policy focus:** Strong mission in nuclear R&D until late 1970s > decline in 1980s-1990s > renewed policy focus on STI in 2000s (pioneer of federal state naukograd programme)	**Policy focus:** Range of R&D priorities (emphasis on basic R&D) supported by top level of state > survival mode from late 1970s to 1990s in the absence of state policy interest > renewed policy focus on knowledge generation (publications) in STI in 2000s	**Policy focus:** Weak governance for STPs until 2006; Diversity of types of organisations founding STPs associated with greater chances of "positive variations of performance"); Post-2007 generation of STPs focused on construction – few incentives for creating linkages with external organisations	**Policy focus:** Clear mission to develop state-directed strategic technologies in five key sectors; continued support from senior political elites, including but not only Putin > after 2012, more political conflicts over Skolkovo between elite groups noticeable.
	Resources: *Significant state resources in USSR > very little in 1990s > some increase in 2000s.*	***Resources:*** *Significant state financial and labour resources until late 1970s > decline until 2000s > some increase in state financial resources in 2000s but labour shortage and ageing workforce in R&D*	***Resources:*** *Very limited resources in 1990s and until 2005; Quite significant (but less than Skolkovo's budget) – approximately USD 379 million of federal state funds between 2007 and 2014 (plus co-financing from regional budgets)*	***Resources:*** *Significant state resources from beginning in 2010 (approximately USD 3.9 billion total state financing between 2013 and 2020); Good performance of external co-financing of participants' projects up to 2013, but secured less than target for private investment in 2013*
	Institutions: Only state institutions > more diversity of state and private, for example small enterprises in 1990s > more stratification since 2000, some private firms still; a couple of sector-leading institutes/firms	**Institutions:** Only state institutions in USSR > emergence of small enterprises created by scientists in 1980s–1990s as survival mechanism > in 2000s, state + SMEs (e.g. experiment with technology parks); a couple of sector-leading institutes/firms	**Institutions:** Quite diverse types of first movers setting up STPs (federal and regional state actors, universities, big research institutes, private, and public–private)	**Institutions:** Predominantly state institutions but part of mission is to engage start-ups and bigger private (and state) firms in its ecosystem.

Source: Author.

Table 7.2 Summary of empirical cases: Stage 2

	Obninsk	*Akademgorodok in Novosibirsk*	*Science and technology parks*	*Skolkovo*
Stage 2	**Policy focus:** Diversity of research institutes in USSR > regional policy to support industrial clusters important for building critical mass of firms but limited implementation to date.	**Policy focus:** Emphasis on collective efforts in small local area + policy from late 1960s of "a belt of introduction" (*poyas vnedreniya*) to stimulate research industry linkages via design bureaus and research institutes – limited effectiveness in practice > economic crisis prohibited forming of critical mass in 1990s – early 2000s > similar to Soviet "belt of introduction" policy (technology park) introduced > policy of "Akademgorodok 2.0" since 2017 aims to increase critical mass of research and innovation regionally but too early to evaluate	**Policy focus:** Governance of post-2007 STPs lacked strategic incentives for parks to form linkages with external organisations; Some STPs have become locally or regionally important; Post-2007 STPs lack close ties with a university, limiting scope for new knowledge transfer and absorption	**Policy focus:** Aim to build up critical mass, more limited implementation so far (construction delays have been a barrier to forming a physical community/ecosystem).
	Resources: *Limited since creation of town.*	***Resources:*** *Significant resources until late 1960s > decline until early 2000s > resources mainly through technology park since 2010 (state–private initiative with 0.25 billion USD total initial investment)*	***Resources:*** *Limited since 1990s*	***Resources:*** *Key part of Skolkovo is its grant-giving mechanism to start-ups and teams of researchers to develop innovative ideas.*

Institutions: Institutions for scientists to, for example, socialise and network, branches of all Soviet institutes in USSR > not in 1990s > branches of federal organisations, Council of Directors, AIRKO institution and RTTN in 2000s.	**Institutions:** Institutions for scientists to, for example, **socialise and network** but not many other institutions for critical mass formation in USSR > critical mass of rapidly growing **ICT firms** achieved locally by 2000 > strengthened university-research institutes' linkages, and in 2000s > second **technology park "Akadempark"** has had some success in building research industry linkages and hence in building critical mass; a key role of **two local business associations** that have emerged since 2000 in supporting local economic development and critical mass formation of high-tech industry.	**Institutions:** Few large firms (Russian/foreign) in Russian STPs; Weak ties with finance providers (banks, start-up funds, venture capital, etc.)	**Institutions:** State corporations, large Russian (but no foreign) private firms, start-ups, medium-sized firms, teams of researchers/scientists from universities and research institutes to work on specific projects, graduate students. Limited interactions within Skolkovo "ecosystem" to date.

Source: Author.

Table 7.3 Summary of empirical cases: Stage 3

	Obninsk	*Akademgorodok in Novosibirsk*	*Science and technology parks*	*Skolkovo*
Stage 3	**Policy focus:** Limited and tightly controlled international cooperation in R&D (not really in production) in USSR > some policies for international policy learning in R&D in 1990s > in 2000s, regional policy to attract multinational companies (MNCs) and be a nationally important region for industrial clusters ***Resources:*** *Little resources for internationalisation activities in USSR or 1990s > small increase in 2000s; some MNCs' investment in 2000s (pharma, automobiles, food processing sectors) and some MNCs built factories and R&D facilities; in one of Russia's regions (Kaluga) with highest levels of inward foreign investment.*	**Policy focus:** Internationalisation aims in theory were constrained by political, economic, and ideological context in USSR > some policy interest in international learning on R&D and entrepreneurship in 1990s and 2000s, as well as in university; US patenting quite high up to 2016 ***Resources:*** *Limited resources for internationalisation activities in USSR (mainly knowledge exchange) or 1990s (policy and industry learning, for example study tour in 2000 for business leaders funded by US Trade Department) > a small increase in 2000s but constrained by political and economic context of federal state.*	**Policy focus:** Limited but was federal state push for many Russian STPs to join International Association of Science Parks and Areas of Innovation in 2015. ***Resources:*** *Limited resources for internationalisation activities in 1990s; more such resources in 2000s but not for production links.*	**Policy focus:** Initially, significant state policy to help Skolkovo develop international linkages (MIT collaboration, policy motivation, for example three international members of strategic working group). Since 2015, less international linkages visible. ***Resources:*** *Predominantly federal state funding (from Kremlin).* *19 MNCs signed cooperation agreements with Skolkovo by January 2013 (26 MNCs in mid-2016) but limited actual foreign investment/engagement on the ground in Skolkovo by these companies (e.g. no foreign companies in Skolkovo technopark).*

	Institutions: Not in Soviet period; limited international patenting since late 1970s > 1990s emergence of RTTN as catalyst for international networking (but limited in work in Obninsk, more national/ international in scope, just based in Obninsk).	**Institutions:** Some sector-leading research institutes have international linkages in USSR, 1990S, and 2000s > only 1 MNC with R&D facilities located in Akadempark technology park as of May 2015.	**Institutions:** Russian STPs have few if any international linkages	**Institutions:** Few MNCs or foreign organisations (e.g. MIT) actively involved in Skolkovo, especially since 2015. Foreign firms and partner organisations continue to cooperate in limited capacity with Skolkovo (tokenism, to show their regime loyalty?)

Source: Author.

consider the political and institutional context. This section shows how the model operates in practice and how the outcome has been shaped by the political and economic context in the case of Russia.

The first contextual element omitted from the evolutionary model of growth relates to how Russia's economic modernisation policy agenda is formed. This agenda began in the early 2000s. It has focused too much on kickstarting initiatives for growth and has given insufficient attention to how to foster linkages between firms, research institutes, finance-providing organisations, and state institutions that are important for innovation according to the interactive model of innovation.

The second, politico-economic contextual element omitted from the evolutionary model hinges on the concepts of rent and economic incentives from innovation. Innovation often confers rent through patents, albeit limited in duration. One way of interpreting state support for innovation in authoritarian systems is as a way of creating alternative sources of rent to natural resources, even while producing economic benefits in the form of output and jobs.

How do economic and political rents affect the different stages of the three-stage growth model? Public subsidies given in the different stages vary by nature and the risks of corruption (meaning capture and abuse of rents) also change at each stage. Because in Russia, formal rules and informal practices overlap substantially (Barsukova and Ledeneva, 2018), it is hard to assess this.

At the first stage – the micro or most local level – the role of first movers (firms or organisations such as a STP) is critical. Rents here could come from setting up a science town or STP (via the federal or regional state subsidies available to help create them), or from the grants available to new or young firms if they take up residence in one of these places. The first mover could also get rents at this stage if it can protect the rents via patenting or other means.

The second stage takes place at the meso level, at which a critical mass of firms and state agencies to support RDI funding, assistance with marketing and sales, etc. is built up, and institutions such as firm associations, public agencies, or design bureaus are formed to assist with interorganisational cooperation and firm learning. A critical mass is important for the creation of viable industrial sectors and for an interactive national innovation system. This book has analysed (Chapters 4–6) some examples of incentives at regional level to set up these kinds of institutions (e.g. business associations, council of research institute and factory directors, and local government administration), but the political incentives are quite limited.

The third stage is when firms and other organisations form global linkages and become globally competitive. The incentive in forming such linkages is the ability to buy and sell on the global market, which is obviously bigger than any regional or national market. However, Russian firms and research organisations faces numerous obstacles here, including institutional rules on exporting, customs regime, and international standards, testing, and certification practices governing the sale of products and processes globally.

Table 7.4 applies Khan's typology of rents (2017) to post-Soviet Russia.[2] In the 1990s, political rents had negative consequences for growth as the loans for shares

Table 7.4 Rents in Russia: a typology and the main beneficiaries, 1990–2016

Type of rents	*Sub-periods*			
	1990s	*2000–2004*	*2004–2008*	*2008–2016*
Political	Negative-loans for shares scheme made a select few oligarchs very wealthy.	Big business main beneficiaries of these rents (though increasing state gains in oil and gas)	State officials the principal beneficiaries of rents.	State officials the principal beneficiaries of rents.
Natural resources	Negative – narrow distribution of rents to oligarchs and some state officials (privatisation process).	Rents reallocated to government bureaucrats and *siloviki* actors.	State officials the principal beneficiaries of rents.	State officials the principal beneficiaries of rents.
Schumpeterian (Innovation)	Very limited. "1st generation" of technology parks generated small rents because of limited state investment (and virtually no private investment)	Very limited.	Emergence of more rents from innovation. Blocked by strong resistance to change from the elites from security agencies (*siloviki*) and from extensive capital outflows out of Russia.	Emergence of more rents from innovation (creation of R&D funding institutions such as Rosnano and Skolkovo).

Source: Based on Khan (2017), applied to Russia by the author of this book.

scheme made a small number of individuals, called oligarchs, very wealthy. In the natural resources sector, rents were also narrowly distributed. Rents from innovation were very limited: for example, the first generation of technology parks generated low rents because of limited state investment, virtually no private investment, and poor performance in terms of revenue generation or new jobs created. In the period from 2000 to 2004, big businesses were the main beneficiaries of political rents while government bureaucrats and members of the security agencies (*siloviki*) benefited most from natural resources rents. From 2004, state officials took greater control of the economy and so became the principal beneficiaries of both political and natural resources rents. Rents from innovation began to emerge from 2004 to 2008 but encountered obstacles from elites in the security agencies and from capital outflows beyond Russia (Yakovlev, 2014). Since 2008, potential rents from innovation grew with the creation of R&D funding bodies such as Rosnano and Skolkovo which received substantial state investment.

The third contextual element omitted from the evolutionary model of growth relates to the nature of Russia's innovation system. This system is predominantly a public R&D system not an enterprise-based one, which means that the first stage has been easier to achieve to some extent than the second or third stages. State supported policies, such as science towns or STPs, may have the advantage of substantial investment; however, this is insufficient to create first movers in a particular industry. The weaknesses of enterprises in Russia's innovation system means that the likelihood of firms becoming first movers (Stage 1 of the three-stage growth model) or forming a critical mass (Stage 2 of the same model) is low.

The fourth contextual element omitted from the evolutionary model of growth relates to how the concept of *sistema* affects each of the stages in the growth model. Ledeneva (2013) emphasises that the Russian state's formal priorities are undermined by the power of informal networks' priorities. This concept can be seen in the sphere of economic modernisation and innovation policy making. In Stage 1, the *sistema* determines whether infrastructurally based policies creating science towns and STPs get approved or not. This may explain, for example, why the number of STPs supported under the 2006 government programme for hi-tech parks changed quickly from 7 to 9 and then 12 (see Chapter 6). In Stage 2, *sistema* affects who gets the economic and political rents and who cooperates with which branches of the state. In Stage 3, *sistema* influences the creation or not of global linkages: informal power networks may permit global linkages to be formed.

Contributions of the book

A key theoretical contribution of the book is in demonstrating how authoritarian regimes implement STPs and science towns as instruments of modernisation and innovation policy. An authoritarian regime chooses these models as key modes of support (see Chapter 3 for an overview of other instruments implemented in Russia) because they are relatively easy to control on the one hand, and because on the other hand, they are a popular policy option globally and so seen as a "desirable" tool for catching up with nations that are at the technology frontier.

The book draws on and adds to three strands of literature. First, it engages with and complements **the social science literature on modernisation and the state**. What is meant by modernisation? Is it more realistic to talk about a plurality of modernities and modernisation paths? The literature on modernisation policy in non-Western contexts supports the idea of multiple paths of modernisation and outcomes (democracy, authoritarian regime, etc.). Russia has pursued technological modernisation by borrowing and reproducing certain institutional forms and mechanisms from a Western context and creating new structures and processes that display strong Soviet legacies because of path dependency and the slow nature of institutional and regime transformation. The case studies of two Russian science towns and a sample of Russian STPs analysed in the present book (Chapters 4–6) offer novel empirical evidence that sheds light on how an authoritarian country has experimented with diverse policies to ignite technological modernisation.

Russia's economic modernisation of the early 21st century is also predominantly directed in a top-down manner by political elites and controlled by domestic actors, although local (municipal and regional) initiatives do exist (e.g. the *naukograds'* strategy of survival through development in the 1990s; see Chapter 4, section "The 1990s: a period of deep economic crisis and a search for solutions"). Thus, the book contributes to a political economy model of modernisation that considers foreign and domestic aspects of modernisation, as well as the issue of who controls actual modernisation policies (state, non-state, or other). It also emphasises the heterogenous nature of the state by showing the role of local, regional, and national political and economic elites.

Second, the book contributes to **the literature on the political economy of innovation systems and STPs, science towns, and clusters**. This is connected to, and furthers, the growing literature on developmental states, innovation, firm and industry upgrading, and institutional transformation. This present research expands the literature on industrial policy and innovation in East Asian countries, many of which have had authoritarian regimes leading successful industrial policies (e.g. under General Park Chung-hee's repressive authoritarian rule from 1963 to 1979, South Korea pursued a policy of export-oriented industrialisation which boosted the country's economy). The research presented in this book also offers empirical evidence from an authoritarian country that helps us understand how firms and organisations can transform from being in an isolated enclave to being globally connected, pointing out the obstacles faced along the way which are related to the institutional context. Russia's science towns and STPs have not yet managed to form many global linkages.

Third, the book contributes to **the literature on governing science and technology in authoritarian regimes**. It explores the tensions between authoritarian control and the networked character of a competitive, innovative economy. As discussed in Chapter 6, Skolkovo may also help the Russian state and its *sistema* sustain itself because it remains a high-priority state-supported project, even if there is evidence of inter-elite conflict and disagreement over it. The literature (see Chapter 2) on the ambivalence of technology and in the motivations behind the development of new technologies (Ledeneva, 2018: vol. 1) brings relevant insights as Skolkovo operates from within the system, thereby ultimately helping to sustain the broad political system and *sistema* which created it. The extent to which this hypothesis applies to science towns and STPs would merit further investigation. The wider significance of the book is that it examines how authoritarian states with weak institutions – as exemplified by the case of Russia – govern STI as tools of modernisation policy.

Finally, the book contributes to the narrative in Western social science that can be summed up as Russia is not just about Putin. In other words, to understand Russia it is not enough to confine academic and policy studies to the President of Russia – the role of the presidency and the leadership role of Vladimir Putin in designing and acting a core player in the political and economic system.

Scope for further research

The first empirical chapter (Chapter 4) analysed just two contrasting science towns: Akademgorodok in the Siberian city of Novosibirsk and Obninsk in Kaluga region, in the Western part of Russia. To better understand the evolution and contribution to R&D and innovation of these Soviet-era science towns, studying more science towns both across Russia and in other post-Soviet countries would be interesting.

The original survey of Russian STPs' management covered only 13% of the 125 technology parks that existed in 2017 (Chapter 5). The sampled parks are in 12 regions of Russia out of 44 regions with a technology park, meaning that less than a third of regions with a technology park as of 2017 were included. While this sample is regionally representative, it was not sectorally representative of all STPs, nor was it random within Russia. Hence, a second suggestion for further research is to expand the STP survey to be representative of all technological/industrial sectors in which Russian STPs are active.

Third, innovative clusters represent a policy that the Government of Russia has supported since 2012. Innovative clusters are now dynamically developing alongside the science towns, STPs, and Skolkovo analysed in this book and hence would merit further research of their performance in international comparison and relative to the other innovation projects pursued by Russia.[3]

Notes

1 Francois Perroux was a French economist who first defined the concept of a growth pole in 1950 as a focus of economic development in an abstract economic space. Later scholars (in particular Jacques Boudeville) introduced differing definitions of the term and it evolved to mean a focus of development in a geographic space: 'the concentration of highly innovative and technically advanced industries that stimulate economic development in linked businesses and industries.' ('Geography name', http://geography.name/growth-pole, last accessed (15 June 2019))

2 Chapter 2 introduced this stream of literature on rents; here that literature is applied to the Russian case.

3 The Russian Cluster Observatory, or Rossiiskaya klasternaya observatoriya, RKO (established in 2012 as part of the Institute for Statistical Studies and Economics of Knowledge (ISSEK) of the National Research University Higher School of Economics, Moscow) is doing important analytical, methodological, and networking activities in this field. See https://cluster.hse.ru/ [last accessed 30 December 2019].

References

Amann, R. and Cooper, J. M. (1982) *Industrial Innovation in the Soviet Union*. New Haven, CT and London: Yale University Press.

Barsukova, S. and Ledeneva, A. (2018) 'Concluding Remarks to Volume 2: Are Some Countries More Informal Than Others? The Case of Russia', in Bailey, A., Barron, S., Curro, C. and Teague, E. (eds.) *Global Encyclopaedia of Informality, Volume 2: Understanding Social and Cultural Complexity*, Bailey, A., Barron, S., Curro, C. and Teague, E. London: UCL Press (pp. 487–492). Available at: https://doi.org/10.2307/j.ctt20krxgs.14

Berliner, J. S. (1976) *The Innovation Decision in Soviet Industry*. Cambridge, MA: MIT Press.

Cooper, J. (2008) 'Soviet and Russian Research, Development and Innovation', in Durlauf, S. N. and Blume, L. E. (eds.) *The New Palgrave Dictionary of Economics*, 2nd edition. Basingstoke, Hampshire: Palgrave Macmillan (pp. 1–5). Available at: https://doi.org/10.1057/978-1-349-95121-5_2289–1 [last accessed 30 December 2019].

Khan, M. H. (2017) 'Introduction: Political Settlements and the Analysis of Institutions', *African Affairs* (pp. 1–20). Available at: https://doi.org/10.1093/afraf/adx044

Ledeneva, A. (2013) *Can Russia Modernise? Sistema, Power Networks and Informal Governance*. Cambridge: Cambridge University Press.

Ledeneva, A. (ed.) (2018) *The Global Encyclopaedia of Informality: Understanding Social and Cultural Complexity*, Volume 1. London: UCL Press. Available at: https://doi.org/10.14324/111.9781911307907.

Perroux, F. (1949) 'Les Macrodécisions et La Théorie Des Choix', *Zeitschrift Für Nationalökonomie/Journal of Economics* 12/2–4 (pp. 198–206). Available at: http://www.jstor.org/stable/41803657.

Rowland, R. H. (1996) 'Russia's Secret Cities', *Post-Soviet Geography and Economics* 37/7 (pp. 426–462). Available at: https://doi.org/10.1080/10889388.1996.10641026 [last accessed 30 December 2019].

Taylor, M. Z. (2016) *The Politics of Innovation: Why Some Countries Are Better Than Others at Science & Technology*. Oxford: Oxford University Press.

Yakovlev, A. (2014) 'Russian Modernization: Between the Need for New Players and the Fear of Losing Control of Rent Sources', *Journal of Eurasian Studies* 5/1 (pp. 10–20). Available at: https://doi.org/10.1016/j.euras.2013.09.004 [last accessed 31 July 2021].

Yaremenko, Y. V. (1981) *Strukturnye izmeneniya v sotsialisticheskoi ekonomike* [transl.: *Structural Changes in a Socialist Economy*]. Moscow: Mysl'.

Zaleski, E., Kozlowski, J. P., Wienert, H., Davies, R. W., Berry, M. J. and Amann, R. (1969) *Science Policy in the USSR*. Paris: OECD Publishing.

Appendices

Appendix 1: Chronology of modernisation in post-Soviet Russia

The table here sets out the key milestones (systemic changes) in Russia's broad modernisation drive from the early 1990s to the present, including in the field of R&D policies but also in economic and fiscal arenas and institution building of relevance to R&D and innovation.

Year	*Policy/institution/initiative*	*Broad economic policy periods & global context*[1]
1990	5-year 'Technoparks of Russia' federal programme started, under which 42 parks were created by 1995.	
1992	Programme of mass privatization of enterprises started (including 'voucher auctions' which handed control to insiders i.e. managers and controlling shareholders; and from 1995, privatization auctions).[2]	
1992	Russian Foundation for Basic Research (RFBR) established	
1994	Russian Foundation for the Humanities (RFH) established	
1995	Start of 'loans-for-shares' auctions of large companies, which let a few well-connected 'kleptocrats' buy Russia's most strategically important companies at bargain prices.[3]	
1997	New Criminal Code introduced on 1 January, which permits criminal sanctions for violations of intellectual property rights (IPRs). Implementation of the law remained weak.[4]	
1999	Federal law No. 70 on the status of *naukograds* in Russia (amended in 2015)	
1999A	Vladimir Putin appointed Prime Minister of Russia in August	
1999B	Vladimir Putin nominated as Acting President of Russia (according to the Russian Constitution) on 31 December after Yeltsin resigned. Putin became President after winning 53% of the popular vote in elections held on 26 March 2000, and was inaugurated on 7 May 2000.	**1999–2003: 'Reform years'** of President Putin's first term
2000	Official creation of 'science town' with legal status	

Year	*Policy/institution/initiative*	*Broad economic policy periods & global context*[1]
2001A	Presidential Council for Science and High Technologies created to provide strategic leadership and guidance for Science &Technology	
2001B	Patent Law amendment to intellectual property (IP) regulations – commercialized intellectual property rights to some extent	
2001C	Start of a 2-year 'debureaucratisation campaign' led by the Russian Ministry for Economic Development to reduce administrative barriers for entrepreneurs, which had some successes but lacked the full support of the rest of the Government of Russia.[5]	
2002A	First Federal Target Programme (2002–2006); 'Science and Technology Development Guidelines until 2010 and beyond' – most important federal programme for funding applied research	
2002B	Creation of the Russian Technology Transfer Network (2002–2006)	
2002C	Russian *Code of Corporate Conduct* introduced (modelled on corresponding EU documents) but not legally binding.	
2003	Main Guidelines of Public Policy in Science and Technology	
2004	Restructuring plan of R&D public organisations (2004–08)	**2004–1st half of 2008: "Statist" years** of President Putin's second term
2005	Federal Law on Special Economic Zones (SEZs) to support R&D entities with R&D that is almost ready for market launch.	
2006A	Federal programme No. 328 for Technoparks in the sphere of high technologies	
2006B	Creation of Russian Venture Company and 19 Regional Venture Funds	
2006C	Creation of open joint-stock company SEZ to develop Special Economic Zones	
2006D	Strategy for Development of Science and Innovation in Russia up to 2015 – aims to improve government funding programmes and foster science and industry linkages	
2007A	2nd Federal Target Programme (2007–12): innovation initiatives in higher education	
2007B	Creation of state corporations in high tech sectors (Rosnano for nanotechnologies; Rostekhnologii for defence and high-tech industries; Rosatom for nuclear technologies)	
2008A	New Russian Civil Code introduced on 1 January, which incorporates revised copyright law of 2006 allowing for prison sentences of up to 5 years for violating copyright laws. Implementation of the law remained weak.[6]	
2008B	Long-Term Economic Development Plan ('Strategy 2020') published	
2008C	Restructuring of IPR legislation, tax treatment of R&D and patenting activities	
2008D	Creation of the status of National Research Centre	

(*Continued*)

Year	*Policy/institution/initiative*	*Broad economic policy periods & global context*[1]
2009A	Presidential Commission for Modernisation and Technological Development	**2nd half of 2008–2013: World economic crisis and recovery**
2009B	Regional Universities (7 universities granted) and National Research Universities (14 universities granted) created	
2009C	Restructuring of financing of Russian Academy of Sciences	
2009D	Launch of high-tech division of MICEX (Russia Stock Market)	
2010A	15 new universities given status of National Research University	
2010B	Creation of Technology Platforms	
2010C	Launch of Skolkovo innovation centre near Moscow	
2010D	Restructuring of Government Commission on High Technology and Innovation	
2010E	Creation of Russian Defence Innovative Projects Agency	
2010F	Innovative Mega Projects	
2011A	Fully-fledged S&T Foresight 2030 study initiated by the Russian Ministry of Education and Science to identify national S&T priorities	
2011B	Programme for development of innovation in machine-building sector	
2011C	Government Development Scenario for the Russian Economy up to 2030 published	
2011D	Government Strategy for the Development of Innovation in Russia up to 2020 published	
2012A	Government long-term Programme for Shipbuilding industry	
2012B	Government approval of environmental programme up to 2020	
2012C	May (inaugural) presidential decrees, which were key directives on the development of the economy, science, technology, education, and other industries in the social sphere. Contained both qualitative guidelines and target quantitative indicators to be achieved by 2018.	
2012D	Russia joined the World Trade Organisation (WTO) on 22 August.	
2013A	Reform of Russian Academy of Sciences (RAS) – very unpopular among scientists and researchers; brought RAS under more direct control of government; transferred management of RAS property to the control of a new state agency, the Federal Agency of Scientific Organisations (FANO)	
2013B	Project 5–100 programme aimed to make a select group of leading Russian universities more competitive in the global research and education market	
2014	Federal Law No. 488 'On Industrial Policy in the Russian Federation' gives first official definition of concept of 'industrial cluster' in Russia	**2014–present:** war in Ukraine, Russia's growing

Year	*Policy/institution/initiative*	*Broad economic policy periods & global context*[1]
2015	Eurasian Economic Union (EAEU) came into effect on 1 January as an economic union of states in Eastern Europe and central and northern Asia. Current members of the union are Armenia, Belarus, Kazakhstan, the Kyrgyz Republic, and Russia.	isolation from the global economy, and stagnation
2017	Project to create "Akademgorodok 2.0" (would integrate Akademgorodok with nearby biotechnology-focused Koltsovo *naukograd* and the agriculture-specialised centre of Nizhniy Yeltsovka) first discussed in Novosibirsk region; supported by SB RAS, Novosibirsk State University, and regional administration	

Source: Vercueil (2014) based on Bofit (2011–2012), OECD (2011) and Government of the Russian Federation (2011); additions to Vercueil (2014) by the author of this book; Sokolov and Chulok (2016), Black et al. (1999), Dyker (2012), Guriev (2019).

Appendix 2: List of interviews

This table lists all the interviews carried out by the author for this research. After careful consideration, the author decided to anonymise interviewees so just their job title and organisation, city location, and the month and year in which the interview took place are listed here.

No. of respondent	*Position & Organisation*	*Location*	*Date of interview (month, year)*
1	A deputy head of city administration for economic development	Obninsk	November 2011, April 2013
2	Director, Obninsk Centre of Science and Technology	Obninsk	November 2011, June 2012
3	Director, Agency of Innovation Development-Centre of Cluster Development of Kaluga oblast	Obninsk	November 2011, June 2012
4	Scientist in Dept. for Computer-Aided Control Systems, National Research Nuclear University "MEPhI" Obninsk Institute for Nuclear Power Engineering	Obninsk	June 2012, October 2012
5	Co-founder, Russian Technology Transfer Network (RTTN)	Obninsk	November 2011, June 2012
6	Chief editor of a local newspaper	Obninsk	June 2012
7	Official in Rosnano	Moscow	November 2011
8	An advisor to a vice-president, Skolkovo Foundation	Moscow	June 2012, April 2013, November 2015

(*Continued*)

No. of respondent	*Position & Organisation*	*Location*	*Date of interview (month, year)*
9	A director, Department of Legal Policy and Social Development, Skolkovo Foundation	Moscow	April 2013
10	A deputy director, Department of Legal Policy and Social Development, Skolkovo Foundation	Moscow	April 2013
11	A director of development for IT-projects	Moscow	April 2013
12	Two foreign-born professors, Moscow School of Management Skolkovo	Moscow	April 2013
13	Lead expert on cooperation with development institutions, Akadempark	Akademgorodok Novosibirsk	November 2012, September 2013
14	Two senior researchers, Institute of philosophy and Law, SB RAS	Akademgorodok Novosibirsk	November 2012
15	Senior academic, Programme Expertise and Monitoring Unit, Presidium of the SB RAS and the Institute of Petroleum Geology and Geophysics	Akademgorodok Novosibirsk	November 2012
16	Head, Centre for Public Affairs, SB RAS	Akademgorodok Novosibirsk	November 2012, September 2013
17	Chair of Board of Directors, Institute of Chromatography "EcoNova", Ltd.	Akademgorodok Novosibirsk	November 2012,
18	Director of association 'SibAcademInnovatsiya', and director of ZAO 'Mediko-biologicheski Soyuz'	Akademgorodok Novosibirsk	September 2013
19	Chair of SibAcademSoft regional association of IT companies & General Director of SoftLab company	Akademgorodok Novosibirsk	September 2014
20	Lead specialist on international partners, Akadempark	Akademgorodok Novosibirsk	September 2013
21	Lead specialist on residents' cooperation, managing company of park	Akademgorodok Novosibirsk	September 2013
22	Head of Department for Residents' relations, SEZ	Tomsk	September 2013
23	Deputy head academic secretary of Presidium of RAS	Moscow	June 2012
24	Senior researcher, Institute of Economics and Organisation of Industrial Production SB RAS	Akademgorodok Novosibirsk	September 2013
25	Two employees of department for science and innovation policy, Administration of Tomsk region	Tomsk	September 2013

No. of respondent	*Position & Organisation*	*Location*	*Date of interview (month, year)*
26	Angel investor (as well as lecturer at Tomsk State University & general director of an innovation management company)	Tomsk	September 2013
27	Administrator, instrumentation incubator	Akademgorodok Novosibirsk	September 2014
28	Deputy executive director of Open University of Skolkovo	Skolkovo, Moscow	May 2016

Appendix 3: Interview guide

This is the question guide that the author used for conducting semi-structured interviews. Some questions varied depending on the interviewee. The interviews were held in Russian or English depending on the preference of the interviewee. Most of the interviews conducted by the author for this research were in Russian.

1) About the creation of the entity (science town/STP/research institute).
2) About the number of current residents (firms, research and other organisations in the science town/STP).
3) About the number of residents (firms, research and other organisations in the science town/STP) who have moved away from the area in the last one year, and the reasons why.
4) About the number of patents the entity has applied for/been issued with.
5) Question for residents of science towns/STPs/research institutes on the benefits to them of being in the science town/STP/research institute.
6) About interactions between science town/STP/research institute and other entities in the same city/region and between firms and organisations in the science town/STP.

Appendix 4: Science/technology/innovation park surveys of managers and firm residents

Science/technology/innovation park survey – managers (English version)

This short questionnaire is part of a research project conducted by Imogen Sophie Kristin Wade for her PhD dissertation at the School of Slavonic and East European Studies, University College London (UCL), United Kingdom.

Imogen Sophie Kristin Wade's PhD dissertation has benefited from the financial support of Imogen Sophie Kristin Wade, the School of Slavonic and East European Studies, and University College London (UCL) in the UK.

You can contact me by email at: imogen.wade.10@ucl.ac.uk

Please return the completed form electronically to me by pressing 'submit' at the end.

I will send you a summary of responses to this questionnaire when the study is complete in 2015, as well as a copy of my final book.

*Required

1. The name of your science/technology/innovation park *
2. What kind of science/technology/innovation park do you work in?
   The type of ownership of the park
   Mark only one oval.

   - University
   - Business
   - Government (public)
   - Private
   - Other

3. If you selected 'Other' in the previous question, please specify the ownership of the park

   ____

4. Your contact email *

   ____

5. Your current job title

   ____

6. Your first name

   ____

7. Your surname

   ____

8. Approximately how many firms are located in the science/technology/innovation park?

   ____

   Reasons for being in science/technology/innovation park

9. Why do firms move to your science/technology/innovation park?
   (up to 3 answers)
   Tick all that apply.

   - Cheaper rents
   - Tax discounts
   - Infrastructure (equipment, laboratories, etc.)
   - Attractive image

- Access to finance
- Opportunities to closely cooperate with other firms in the park
- Opportunities in training, consulting, conferences, seminars, etc.
- Proximity to innovative firms
- Proximity to scientific community

Other: ____

****

Science/technology/innovation park survey – managers (Russian version)

‘Анкета для руководителей технопарков’

Уважаемый респондент! Приглашаем Вас принять участие в опросе на тему: “Инновационная инфраструктура в субъектах Российской Федерации”.

Данный опрос проводится в рамках диссертационного исследования Имоджен Уэйд, аспирантки Школы Славянских и Восточно-Европейских Исследований при университете Лондона в Великобритании. Имоджен Уэйд также является научным сотрудником Института статистических исследований и экономики знаний, НИУ ВШЭ (Москва).

Финансирование исследования осуществляется за счет следующих организаций:

- ВШЭ (Москва) – http://issek.hse.ru
- Центр гуманитарных исследований при РАНХиГС при Президенте РФ (Москва) – www.ranepa.ru
- The Centre for East European Language-Based Area Studies (CEELBAS) – www.ceelbas.ac.uk
- School of Slavonic & East European Studies (SSEES) – www.ucl.ac.uk/ssees
- University College London (UCL) – www.ucl.ac.uk

Результаты этого опроса о технопарках будут направлены международным ассоциациям технопарков и бизнес-инкубаторам, таким как например, национальная ассоциация бизнес инкубаторов США (NBIA, www.nbia.org) и международной ассоциации технопарков (www.iasp.ws/en_GB). Я надеюсь, что это будет способствовать продвижению информации о российских технопарках и высокотехнологичных компаниях на международной арене.

Я буду крайне благодарна Вам за участие в этом опросе. Заполнение анкеты займет не более 20 минут Вашего времени.

Если у Вас есть желание, то я могу выслать Вам результаты анализа данных опроса по завершении исследования. Подробная информация об исследовании находится на сайте: www.ucl.ac.uk/ssees/people/economics-and-business-research-students-folder/imogen-wade

Также Вы можете ознакомиться с моей недавней статьей о Сколково на сайте: http://discovery.ucl.ac.uk/1454656

При возникновении вопросов, Вы можете связаться со мной по электронной почте (iwade@hse.ru и/или imogen.wade.10@ucl.ac.uk)

В конце анкеты, нажмите, пожалуйста, на кнопку “ввод” (submit).

*Required

Укажите, пожалуйста, название технопарка, в котором Вы работаете. *

Укажите, пожалуйста, конкретную отрасль технопарка (фармацевтика и т.д.)

Дайте один ответ

Информационные технологии

Фармацевтика

Несколько специализации

Без специализации

Other:

Укажите, пожалуйста, название города, в котором технопарк расположен

Где находится технопарк?

Дайте один ответ

В вузе

В университете

На базе промышленного предприятия

На территории города

На территории вне города

Other:

Из каких источников финансировалось создание технопарка?

Здесь речь об основных ДВУХ источника

Частный

Государственный (субсидирования от федерального уровня власти)

Региональная власть

Муниципальные власти

Other:

Укажите, пожалуйста, профиль технопарка
Разрешен один ответ
Универсальный
Заточенный под конкретные отрасли (ИТ, биомедицина, т.д.)
Многопрофильный
Other:

Существует ли в технопарке экспертный совет?
Choose
Если в технопарке есть экспертный совет, то опишете, пожалуйста, его роль здесь
Укажите, пожалуйста, Вашу действующую должность в технопарке
Укажите, пожалуйста, примерное количество фирм-резидентов вашего технопарка на настоящий момент
Сколько примерно фирм-резидентов было в вашем технопарке ОДИН ГОД НАЗАД?
Цели пребывания в технопарке
Назовите, пожалуйста, основные причины, по которым фирмы переезжают на территорию технопарка?
дайте не более ТРЕХ ответов
Низкая арендная плата
Пакет льгот для резидентов (например, налоговые льготы, таможенные преференции)
Инфраструктура
Специальное оборудование (лаборатории и т.д.)
Повышение имиджа фирмы
Доступ к финансированию (венчурный капитал, гранты, займы и т.д.)
Возможность взаимодействовать с другими фирмами в технопарке
Возможность участвовать в тренингах, конференциях, семинарах, получать консалтинговые услуги
Близость к научному сообществу
Other:

История создания технопарка
В каком году был создан технопарк, в котором Вы работаете?
Назовите, пожалуйста, основные причины создания технопарка, в котором вы работаете
дайте не более ТРЕХ ответов

Поддержка выпуска/создания продуктов/процессов или организационных/маркетинговых методов

Поиск рынков сбыта для резидентов

Организация и проведение мероприятий для фирм

Поддержка создания и развития новых предприятий

Получение прибыли от аренды или продажи земли

Поддержка НИОКР и технологического развития

Возможность оказывать услуги фирмам – резидентам технопарка

Развитие взаимодействия между промышленностью и университетами

Поддержка новых фирм, которые занимаются производством/разработкой новых технологий

Организационная поддержка экспорта продуктов компаний, которые занимаются производством/разработкой новых технологий

Содействие трансферту технологий

Other:

Развитие фирм в парке

Назовите, пожалуйста, тип фирмы, которая наиболее успешно развивается в вашем технопарке

Тип фирмы может касаться либо размера фирмы (большая или маленькая), либо сферы деятельности фирмы. Напишите, пожалуйста, Ваш ответ внизу

Назовите, пожалуйста, тип фирмы, которая наименее успешно развилась в вашем технопарке

Тип фирмы может касаться либо размера фирмы (большая или маленькая), либо сферы деятельности фирмы. Напишите, пожалуйста, Ваш ответ внизу

Барьеры развития

Назовите основные барьеры для развития фирмы в технопарке

дайте не более ТРЕХ ответов

Отсутствие инфраструктуры

Отсутствие финансирования

Отсутствие консалтинговых услуг

Действующее законодательство на федеральном/региональном/местном уровне

Деятельность или бездействие органов местного самоуправления

Деятельность или бездействие органов государственной власти (региональной власти)

Деятельность или бездействие органов государственной власти (федеральной власти)

Отсутствие опыта работа на рынке продаж у владельцев фирм

Технологии, произведенные фирмами, не готовы к выходу на рынок
Отсутствие квалифицированных работников
Отсутствие научных работников
Other:

Фирмы-резиденты технопарка
Укажите число производственных компаний в вашем технопарке
Укажите число сервисных компаний в вашем технопарке
Укажите число крупных зарубежных компаний в вашем технопарке
Укажите число крупных российских компаний в вашем технопарке
Если в вашем технопарке присутствуют другие компании, укажите, пожалуйста, их категорию и количество
Экономическая политика и ваш технопарк
В этом разделе, нас интересует ваше мнение о ВЛИЯНИИ РАЗЛИЧНЫХ МЕР НА РЕЗУЛЬТАТИВНОСТЬ работы резидентов технопарка.
1 =:(негативное влияние
2 = никакое влияние/не знаю
3 =:) позитивное влияние
Оцените влияние НАЛОГОВЫХ ЛЬГОТ . . .
:(
1
2
3
:)
Оцените влияние СУБСИДИРОВАНИЯ ПРОЦЕНТНЫХ СТАВОК по кредитам, предоставляемым субъектам научно-технической и инновационной деятельности
:(
1
2
3
:)
Оцените влияние деятельности ИНСТИТУТОВ РАЗВИТИЯ (ОАО Роснано, Российский фонд технологического развития, ОАО “Российская венчурная компания” и ее дочерние венчурные фонды и др.) . . .
:(
1
2
3
:)

Оцените влияние создания ТЕХНОЛОГИЧЕСКИХ ПЛАТФОРМ . . .

:(

1

2

3

:)

Оцените влияние развития ИННОВАЦИОННОЙ ИНФРАСТРУКТУРЫ . . .

:(

1

2

3

:)

Оцените влияние ПОДДЕРЖКИ ТЕРРИТОРИАЛЬНЫХ КЛАСТЕРОВ . . .

:(

1

2

3

:)

Оцените влияние ДРУГИХ МЕР . . .

:(

1

2

3

:)

Если Вы оценили другие меры в последнем вопросе, то укажите какую меру

Международный опыт

В этом разделе нас интересует международный опыт

Приходилось ли Вам когда-либо ездить в заграничные командировки в рамках вашей работы в технопарке?

Выбирайте, пожалуйста, да или нет

Да

Нет

КОНТАКТНЫЕ ДАННЫЕ

Укажите, пожалуйста, ваш электронный адрес *

ФИО

БЛАГОДАРЮ ВАС ЗА УЧАСТИЕ В ОПРОСЕ! СПАСИБО ВАМ ОГРОМНОЕ!

SUBMIT

Never submit passwords through Google Forms.

Bottom of Form

This content is neither created nor endorsed by Google. – Terms of Service

Forms

Survey of firms in technology parks (English version)

Survey questionnaire for firms resident in technology parks in Russia (Author's English translation of Russian version which was used for the data collection). Version of July 2015.

****

Dear Respondent,

I would like to ask you to complete this questionnaire about innovation infrastructure in Russian regions.

This questionnaire is part of a PhD project carried out by Imogen Sophie Kristin Wade at the School of Slavonic and East European Studies in University College London (UCL) in the United Kingdom. Imogen Sophie Kristin Wade is also a research fellow at the Institute for Statistical Studies and Economics of Knowledge, Higher School of Economics (ISSEK-HSE) in Moscow.

Funding for this research project comes from the following organisations:

- Higher School of Economics (Moscow), website: http://issek.hse.ru
- Centre for Humanitarian Studies under The Russian Presidential Academy of National Economy and Public Administration, website: www.ranepa.ru
- The Centre for East European Language-Based Area Studies (CEELBAS), website: www.ceelbas.ac.uk
- School of Slavonic and East European Studies (SSEES), website: www.ucl.ac.uk/ssees
- University College London (UCL), website: www.ucl.ac.uk

The findings from this survey will be disseminated to international associations of technology parks and business incubators such as, for example, the National Business Incubator Association (NBIA) of the USA (NBIA, www.nbia.org) and the International Association of Technology Parks (www.iasp.ws/en_GB). I hope that this will help to raise awareness of the work of Russian technology parks and high tech companies internationally.

I would be very grateful if you could complete this questionnaire. It should take no longer than 20 minutes of your time.

If you are interested, I will be happy to send you the results of my survey analysis on completion of my PhD. Further information about my research project can be found on my university webpage: www.ucl.ac.uk/ssees/people/economics-and-business-research-students-folder/imogen-wade

You may also read a recent article I wrote about the Skolkovo innovation centre by clicking on the following link: http://discovery.ucl.ac.uk/1454656

If you have any questions, please contact me by email on (iwade@hse.ru and/or imogen.wade.10@ucl.ac.uk)

At the end of the questionnaire, please click on the 'submit' form.

1. Please indicate the name of your firm: ______________________
2. What is your firm's main area of business?
   Please select one option from below

   - Information and communications technologies
   - Consultancy services
   - Biomedical science and biotechnology
   - Space
   - New materials and nanotechnology
   - Energy efficiency
   - Instrumentation
   - Nuclear
   - Other: ______________________

3. Approximately when was your firm founded?
   Please select one of the following options
   Mark only one oval.

   - Less than 1 year ago
   - 1–3 years ago
   - 3–5 years ago
   - More than 5 years ago

4. Approximately how many employees did your firm have one year ago?
   Please write the number in the box below ____________
5. Approximately how many employees does your firm have now?
   Please write the number in the box below ____________
6. How long your firm been in the science/technology/innovation park?
   Please write the number of years or months in the box below ____________
7. Please describe the application process for becoming a resident of the park.
   Please write how the process was for your firm.

   ____

8. Why did your firm move to the science/technology/innovation park?
   (up to 3 answers you feel are most important for your firm)
   Tick all that apply.

   - Cheaper rents
   - Tax discounts
   - Infrastructure (equipment, laboratories, etc.)
   - Attractive image
   - Access to finance
   - Opportunities to closely cooperate with other firms in the park
   - Opportunities in training, consulting, conferences, seminars, etc.
   - Proximity to innovative firms

- Proximity to scientific community
- Other: ____________________

9. Which phase(s) is your firm involved in now?
   Please select the relevant options from the list below
   Tick all that apply.

   - R&D
   - Prototyping
   - Sales
   - Other: ______________________

10. Do you have products or services for sale (local/regional/national/international markets)?
    Please select yes or no
    Mark only one oval.

    - yes
    - no

11. If you have products or services for sale, please state below approximately what percentage of your company's sales is on the following markets:

    - Local (municipal) market

    write approximate %

    - Regional market

    write approximate %

    - National market

    write approximate %

    - International markets

    write approximate %

    - Other market(s)

    Please specify which, and write approximate % of your sales
12. Does your firm cooperate (e.g. joint contracts, internships etc.) with other firms or other organisations?
    Tick all that apply

    - None
    - Universities
    - Research institutes
    - other firms NOT in the science park
    - other firms IN the science park

- Municipalities
- Regional government bodies
- Federal government bodies
- Russian non-commercial organisations
- Foreign organisations or companies
- Other: ____________________

13. Who are your main competitor firms?
    Please select the option(s) that corresponds to your company (multiple options possible)
    Tick all that apply.

- Domestic firms in my city or region
- Domestic firms in the rest of Russia
- Other firms in former Soviet countries
- Competitors on foreign market(s)
- No competitors
- Not applicable
- Other: ____________________

14. What are the key barriers to growth for your firms?
    Please select a maximum of 3 reasons you feel are the most important for YOUR firm

- Lack of infrastructure
- Lack of finance
- Lack of business services
- Existing regulation at federal/regional/local level
- Activity/lack of activity of local authorities
- Activity/lack of activity of Regional authorities
- Activity/lack of activity of Federal authorities
- Lack of market experience of firm owners
- Technologies that we produce are far from ready for market
- Lack of skilled workforce (marketing, technical, management skills, etc.)
- Lack of scientific workers
- Other: ____________________

CONTACT DETAILS
Please write your email address here: ____________ *
Full name: ____________________
Please indicate your current job title in the firm resident in the science/technology/innovation park: ____________
Has your firm used any services offered by the science/technology/innovation park?
(If yes, please indicate which ones. If not, please indicate why not)
THANK YOU VERY MUCH FOR ANSWERING THESE QUESTIONS!

****

Survey of firms in technology parks (Russian version)

'Анкета для фирм-резидентов технопарков'

Уважаемый респондент! Приглашаем Вас принять участие в опросе на тему: "Инновационная инфраструктура в субъектах Российской Федерации".

Данный опрос проводится в рамках диссертационного исследования Имоджен Уэйд, аспирантки Школы Славянских и Восточно-Европейских Исследований при университете Лондона в Великобритании. Имоджен Уэйд также является научным сотрудником Института статистических исследований и экономики знаний, НИУ ВШЭ (Москва).

Финансирование исследования осуществляется за счет следующих организаций:

- ВШЭ (Москва) – http://issek.hse.ru
- Центр гуманитарных исследований при РАНХиГС при Президенте РФ (Москва) – www.ranepa.ru
- The Centre for East European Language-Based Area Studies (CEELBAS) – www.ceelbas.ac.uk
- School of Slavonic & East European Studies (SSEES) – www.ucl.ac.uk/ssees
- University College London (UCL) – www.ucl.ac.uk

Результаты этого опроса о технопарках будут направлены международным ассоциациям технопарков и бизнес-инкубаторам, таким как например, национальная ассоциация бизнес инкубаторов США (NBIA, www.nbia.org) и международной ассоциации технопарков (www.iasp.ws/en_GB). Я надеюсь, что это будет способствовать продвижению информации о российских технопарках и высокотехнологичных компаниях на международной арене.

Я буду крайне благодарна Вам за участие в этом опросе. Заполнение анкеты займет не более 20 минут Вашего времени.

Если у Вас есть желание, то я могу выслать Вам результаты анализа данных опроса по завершении исследования. Подробная информация об исследовании находится на сайте: www.ucl.ac.uk/ssees/people/economics-and-business-research-students-folder/imogen-wade

Также Вы можете ознакомиться с моей недавней статьей о Сколково на сайте: http://discovery.ucl.ac.uk/1454656

При возникновении вопросов, Вы можете связаться со мной по электронной почте (iwade@hse.ru и/или imogen.wade.10@ucl.ac.uk)

В конце анкеты, нажмите, пожалуйста, на кнопку "ввод" (submit).

*Required

Укажите, пожалуйста, название Вашей фирмы
Укажите, пожалуйста, основную деятельность Вашей фирмы
Дайте один ответ
Информационные технологии
Консалтинговые услуги

Биомедицина и биотехнология
Космос
Новые материалы и нанотехнологии
Энергоэффективность
Приборостроение
Ядерная энергетика
Other:

Укажите, пожалуйста, когда примерно была создана Ваша фирма
дайте один ответ
Choose
Сколько примерно сотрудников работало в Вашей фирме ОДИН ГОД НАЗАД?
Напишите, пожалуйста, сколько здесь
Сколько примерно сотрудников работает в Вашей фирме СЕЙЧАС?
Напишите, пожалуйста, сколько здесь
Сколько времени Ваша фирма является резидентом технопарка?
Напишите, пожалуйста, сколько лет или сколько месяцев в указанном месте внизу
Опишите, пожалуйста, процесс приема в качестве резидента технопарка
Для Вашей фирмы
Цели пребывания в технопарке
Назовите, пожалуйста, основные причины почему Ваша фирма переехала на территорию технопарка?
дайте не более ТРЕХ ответов
Низкая арендная плата
Пакет льгот для резидентов (например, налоговые льготы, таможенные преференции, субсидии)
Инфраструктура
Специальное оборудование (лаборатории и т.д.)
Повышение имиджа фирмы
Доступ к финансированию (венчурный капитал, гранты, займы и т.д.)
Возможность взаимодействовать с другими фирмами в технопарке
Возможность участвовать в тренингах, конференциях, семинарах, получать консалтинговые услуги
Близость к научному сообществу
Other:

Укажите, пожалуйста, в какой фазе (или в каких фазах) работы Ваша фирма сейчас находится?

Выбираете, пожалуйста, все ответы, касающие Вашей фирмы
занимаемся НИОКР
занимаемся прототипами
занимаемся продажей
Other:

Есть ли у Вашей фирмы продукты или услуги готовые к продаже (на местном/региональном/федеральном/международном рынках)?
Выбираете да или нет
Choose
Если у Вашей фирмы есть продукты или услуги готовые к продаже, то укажите пожалуйста, какая доля из всей продажи приходит из следующих рынков?
Местный (муниципальный) рынок
Напишите приблизительно в %
Региональный рынок
Напишите приблизительно в %
на федеральном рынке
Напишите приблизительно в %
на международном рынках
Напишите приблизительно в %
Другие рынки
Укажите какой именно рынок и напишите приблизительно доля продажи в %
Сотрудничает ли Ваша фирма (например, совместные контракты, стажировки т.д./ с другимим фирмами или организациями?
Ни с кем
с университетами, вузами
с НИИ
с другими фирмами НЕ в технопарке
с другими фирмами В технопарке
с муниципалитетами
с региональными властями
с федеральными властями
с российскими НКО
с иностранными организациями или компаниями
Other:

Кто ваши основные конкуренты?

Выберите, пожалуйста, тот ответ (или те ответа) которые соответствуют Вашей фирме (несколько ответов возможно)

Отечественные фирмы в моем городу или регионе

Отечественные фирмы по России

Другие фирмы в странах бывшего СССР или СНГ

Конкуренты на иностранных рынках

Конкурентов нет

Этот вопрос не касается нас

Other:

Назовите, пожалуйста, основные барьеры для развития Вашей фирмы

Дайте не более ТРЕХ ответов

Отсутствие инфраструктуры

Отсутствие финансирования

Отсутствие консалтинговых услуг

Действующее законодательство на федеральном/региональном/местном уровне

Деятельность или бездействие органов местного самоуправления

Деятельность или бездействие органов государственной власти (региональной власти)

Деятельность или бездействие органов государственной власти (федеральной власти)

Отсутствие опыта работа на рынке продаж у владельцев фирм

Технологии, произведенные нами, не готовы к выходу на рынок

Отсутствие квалифицированных работников

Отсутствие научных работников

Other:

КОНТАКТНЫЕ ДАННЫЕ

Укажите, пожалуйста, ваш электронный адрес *

ФИО

Укажите, пожалуйста, Вашу действующую должность в фирме

Пользовалась ли Ваша фирма какими-либо услугами, предоставляемыми технопарками?

(Если да, укажите, какими. Если нет, по каким причинам?)

БЛАГОДАРЮ ВАС ЗА УЧАСТИЕ В ОПРОСЕ! СПАСИБО ВАМ ОГРОМНОЕ!

SUBMIT

Never submit passwords through Google Forms.

Appendix 5: Transliteration of Russian words and names

The Library of Congress system of transliteration, as outlined below, is used in this book.

Vernacular	*Romanization*	*Vernacular*	*Romanization*
Upper case letters	*Upper case letters*	*Lower case letters*	*Lower case letters*
А	A	а	a
Б	B	б	b
В	V	в	v
Г	G	г	g
Д	D	д	d
Е	E	е	e
Ё	Ë, Yo	ё	ë, yo
Ж	Zh	ж	zh
З	Z	з	z
И	I	и	i
Й	Ĭ	й	ĭ
К	K	к	k
Л	L	л	l
М	M	м	m
Н	N	н	n
О	O	о	o
П	P	п	p
Р	R	р	r
С	S	с	s
Т	T	т	t
У	U	у	u
Ф	F	ф	f
Х	Kh	х	kh
Ц	TS	ц	ts
Ч	Ch	ч	ch
Ш	Sh	ш	sh
Щ	Shch	щ	shch
Ъ	″ (hard sign)	ъ	″ (hard sign)
Ы	Y	ы	Y
Ь	′ (soft sign)	ь	′ (soft sign)
Э	Ė	э	ė
Ю	You	ю	You
Я	Ya	я	Ya

Source: www.loc.gov/catdir/cpso/romanization/russian.pdf [last accessed 30 May 2019].

Note: The letters I, Ѣ, Ѳ and V were eliminated in the orthographic reform of 1918 and thus have not been included in the table.

Cyrillic letters have been transliterated into Latin in accordance with the aforementioned scheme. The author aimed to reflect the original Russian pronunciation as much as possible, thus the Russian letter ‘e’ is transliterated sometimes as *e* and sometimes as *ye* depending on stress. The Russian letter 'ё' is usually transliterated as *yo* (in accordance with its pronunciation, which is always stressed), with the exception of the ending of surnames where it is traditionally transliterated as *e* (e.g. Gorbachev, Ligachev). Where transliteration occurs in an original source (e.g. an author's name or title of a source), the original transliteration has been retained, and therefore may differ from the aforementioned scheme. Other exceptions have been made where an individual has a Latinised version of their name that they use in the public domain, e.g. Daria Khaltourina, Sergei Bobylev.

Notes

1 These four distinct periods of economic policy are from Guriev (2019).
2 See Black et al. (1999) for a comprehensive overview of Russia's mass privatization in the early 1990s.
3 See Black et al. (1999)
4 See Dyker (2012: 154).
5 See Dyker (2012: 158–161).
6 See Dyker (2012: 154).

References

Black, B., Kraakman, R. and Tarassova, A. (1999) *Russian Privatization and Corporate Governance: What Went Wrong?* Stanford Law School John M. Olin Program in Law and Economics Working Paper No. 178, and William Davidson Institute at University of Michigan Business School Working Paper No. 269, September 1999. Available at: http://papers.ssrn.com/paper.taf?abstract_id=181348 [last accessed 20 October 2019].

Guriev, S. (2019) '20 Years of Vladimir Putin: The Transformation of the Economy. EBRD Chief Economist Sergey Guriev on the two decade achievements and challenges of Putin's economy', *The Moscow Times*, 16 August. Available at: https://www.themoscowtimes.com/2019/08/16/20-years-of-vladimir-putin-the-transformation-of-the-economy-a66854 [last accessed 22 March 2022].

Index

Note: Page numbers in **bold** indicate a table on the corresponding page.

For Product Safety Concerns and Information please contact our EU representative GPSR@taylorandfrancis.com Taylor & Francis Verlag GmbH, Kaufingerstraße 24, 80331 München, Germany